Jeremy McMullen is a barrister. He wrote **Rights at Work** while Legal Officer of the General and Municipal Workers' Union. He is now a full-time official of the union. He has written a number of trade union pamphlets including *Law at Work*, *Health and Safety at Work*, *A Guide to the Quarries Legislation* and *The Going Rate* and contributed to many shop stewards' training courses.

Rights at Work is one of a series of Workers' Handbooks for trade unionists. The series includes Patrick Kinnersly's **The Hazards of Work: How to Fight Them** on health and safety; Christopher Hird's **Your Employer's Profits** on company accounts. Handbooks in preparation cover women workers; workers' participation; negotiating with management; young workers; fringe benefits; payment systems.

Workers' Handbooks

Jeremy McMullen

Rights at Work

A workers' guide to employment law

Pluto Press

First published 1978 by Pluto Press Limited
Unit 10 Spencer Court, 7 Chalcot Road, London NW1 8LH

Designed by Tom Sullivan
Diagrams designed by John Finn
Cover designed by Colin Bailey

Printed in Great Britain by Hazell Watson & Viney Ltd,
Aylesbury, Bucks

Contents

Abbreviations

ACAS	Advisory, Conciliation and Arbitration Service
CA	Court of Appeal
CAC	Central Arbitration Committee
CE Act	Contracts of Employment Act 1972
CRE	Commission for Racial Equality
DE	Department of Employment
DHSS	Department of Health and Social Security
EAT	Employment Appeal Tribunal
EOC	Equal Opportunities Commission
EMAS	Employment Medical Advisory Service
EP Act	Employment Protection Act 1975
FWR	Fair Wages Resolution 1946
HC	High Court
HL	House of Lords
HSW Act	Health and Safety at Work Act 1974
ILO	International Labour Organisation
IR Act	Industrial Relations Act 1971
IT	Industrial Tribunal
JIC	Joint Industrial Council
RO Act	Rehabilitation of Offenders Act 1974
RP Act	Redundancy Payments Act 1965
RR Act	Race Relations Act 1976
RRB	Race Relations Board (1965–1977)
SB Act	Supplementary Benefits Act 1976
SD Act	Sex Discrimination Act 1975
SI	Statutory Instrument
SS Act	Social Security Act 1975
TULR Act	Trade Union and Labour Relations Acts 1974 and 1976

Note on the Law in Scotland and Northern Ireland

The law described in this handbook applies in England, Wales and Scotland, although the terminology of Scots law sometimes differs slightly from the English equivalent.

Northern Ireland has substantially the same laws but they are enacted in special Northern Ireland Acts and Orders. The only major difference is that the Race Relations Act does not apply to Northern Ireland. However, the Fair Employment Act outlaws religious discrimination there.

Workers' Rights Checklist

Rights	Chapter	Continuous Employment Required	Time Limit for Claim
Race discrimination	8	—	3 months from act; 6 months if Commission sues. 5 years after non-discrimination notice
Sex discrimination	8	—	As above
Spent convictions	3	—	No specific remedy
Victimisation for TU activity	13	—	3 months from act
Dismissal for TU activity	10, 13	—	3 months from termination
Equal pay	9	—	Up to 6 months from termination
Time off for union duties (lay officials)	13	—	3 months
Time off for union activities (members)	13	—	3 months
Time off for public duties	3	—	3 months
Illegal deductions (Truck Acts)	3	—	6 years
Wages Council minimum conditions	17	—	6 years
Consultation over redundancies and protective award	20	None, but some workers excluded	3 months
Payment if employer is insolvent	11	—	—

Rights	Chapter	Continuous Employment Required	Time Limit for Claim
Itemised pay statement	3	First pay day	3 months
Minimum notice	3, 10	4 weeks	6 years (but may be reduced)
Guarantee pay	5	4 weeks	3 months
Medical suspension pay	4	4 weeks	3 months
Dismissal connected with medical suspension	4	4 weeks	3 months
Written particulars of contract	3	13 weeks	Up to 3 months from termination
Unfair dismissal	10	26 weeks	3 months
Written statement of reasons for dismissal	10	26 weeks	3 months
Redundancy pay	11	2 years	6 months
Written statement of redundancy pay calculation	11	2 years	—
Time off before redundancy	11	2 years	3 months
Maternity pay	7	2 years by 11th week before confinement	3 months
Return to work after pregnancy	7	As above	3 months (6 months if redundant)

Note: for continuous employment you normally need to have worked 16 hours a week but there are exceptions – see chapter 21.

Preface

This is not a law book. It's a book which aims to show workers how to use the law, and how to use legal argument when negotiating legal rights. At every stage I have stressed the importance of collective rather than legal action as the most effective way of enforcing workers' rights. Union organisation, collective bargaining and industrial action are the preconditions for individual rights. Putting it simply: **don't sue – organise**.

So crucial is this principle that I originally wrote this book with union rights coming before individual rights. Unfortunately, that's not the way the law is, so I am driven to arrange the chapters in a way that fits the law rather than industrial reality. Well-organised workers will necessarily turn to Part Three before Part Two, but for everyone else the order of chapters makes sense.

I have covered what I think are the major aspects of employment law, but I have not dealt with industrial democracy, pensions or health and safety, all of which are specialised subjects requiring only a partly legal approach. I have added a chapter on social security rights connected with employment and unemployment, but I don't pretend to give more than a general outline.

This book appears as most of the important changes in legislation introduced by the 1974 Labour government have taken effect. Employment law constantly changes, though, and amending legislation has been proposed on trade-union recognition, picketing and mass sackings during strikes. There will certainly be legislation on industrial democracy and company law reform which will require detailed discussion at all levels of the trade-union movement. A Bill first introduced in 1977 may be revived to consolidate in one Act the individual rights scattered through many. I have said what I think is the law based on material available to me on 9 April, 1978 but I have been able to refer briefly to several cases reported before 10 May, 1978.

I have tried to cut down heavy legal language wherever possible but by doing so the legal meaning may change slightly. For example, I say 'reasonable' instead of 'not unreasonable', 'worker' instead of 'employee', 'industrial dispute' instead of 'trade dispute'. I talk of suspending a guarantee payment, and regard redundancy as rather different from being sacked, simply because most workers do. But I have used the proper legal terms for ideas which will become more familiar with use – 'frustration of contract', 'insolvency' and 'medical suspension' for example. I have given references to all cases and statutes quoted so they can be followed up if necessary.

Contributions to the making of this book have come in many forms – analysis, criticism, technical scrutiny and practical wisdom.

I have to thank countless shop stewards of the General and Municipal Workers' Union for the ideas and practical knowledge they have given me over the years, much of which finds its way into this book. I first used some of the diagrams in *Law at Work* and I thank the GMWU for permission to reproduce them here.

I would particularly like to thank Dr Brian Bercusson, Bill Brady, Christopher Hird, Michael Kidron, Patrick Kinnersly, David Lewis, Dr Paul O'Higgins, Harry Shutt and Tom Sullivan for all they did.

They, however, can't be blamed for any aberrations of style or legal accuracy, which are all down to me. I am grateful also to Janice Dodson and Jean Phillips who skilfully deciphered and typed my manuscripts with great speed and determination.

Finally, I was able to write this book only because my wife, Debbie McMullen, was prepared for two years to share unequally the responsibilities of parent, worker and activist. I owe most to her.

Jeremy McMullen
March 1978

Part One: Using the Law

1.

Introduction–The Limits of Law

Workers and their families have always distrusted the law, and rightly so. It is not an instrument geared to our needs, and the people who administer it are unrepresentative, out of touch and antagonistic to our demands. Nevertheless, through political and industrial action workers have secured a set of legal rights which can be exploited.

Use the law only when industrial activity fails. Be aware of any possible legal remedies when submitting a claim and during negotiations, but keep a healthy distance from them. Going to law is always a risky business – it takes time, it exposes individual workers to publicity and harassment, it hardens attitudes, and workers rarely win outright. Most important, you should not regard the law as a final step in a procedure. A legal claim is quite separate from the established channels of collective bargaining – it marks the complete breakdown of the industrial machinery. You should only use the law when all prospects of solving an industrial problem through negotiation, conciliation or industrial action have vanished.

When you take legal action you hand over your most effective power to enforce your rights – industrial action. In some circumstances the laws are useful, but they should *never* be regarded as a substitute for organisation, or as an easy solution to a grievance.

This book aims to give you a basic understanding of the law at work, and to show what is achievable by law on the one hand and by organisation and industrial action on the other. Crucial to any discussion of law as a tool for working people is an appreciation of the *limits of law*. These are:

1. The law is concerned only with individual rights.
2. Parliament refuses to guarantee basic rights.
3. The law is stacked against women.
4. Employment law is constantly changing.

The law is concerned with individual rights

Labour law almost completely ignores the fact that workers organise themselves in unions. In areas where the collective aspects should be most important, the law takes no notice of the basic truth that industrial relations is about employers and *groups* of workers, not single individuals. As we shall see, the reference point for all employment law, as far as the judges are concerned, is always an individual worker's contract of employment.

This approach requires collective bargaining, trade-union organisation and collective action to be reduced to fit in with laws that recognise only individuals.

It is hopelessly unrealistic. However, in the present legal framework you cannot understand collective legal rights until you know about the individual contract of employment. This doesn't mean that your collective rights are secondary to your individual rights. You can't effectively enforce your rights except by collective action. But your rights are determined by the law and the way the courts interpret it. This handbook has to describe the law and how to use it, so reluctantly we have to take the legal non-industrial approach that is forced on us by the law. At every stage, though, the message for workers is: **your individual rights can best be enforced by collective action.**

In employment law, the importance given to the individual contract of employment means that all issues are seen as individual rather than collective problems. Judges usually treat contracts of employment in the same way as any other contract. *In theory* two parties of equal bargaining power agree on mutually acceptable terms. A free market in which a purchaser makes a deal with a seller after haggling over the price is assumed to be the background to most contracts. This view of the employment relationship· is grotesquely out of touch. Industrial reality shows a clear disparity in bargaining power between an individual worker – or if the workplace is organised, his or her union – and the corporation. A manual or clerical worker applying for a job does not have the luxury of negotiating a price for his or her labour.

If (s)he isn't prepared to work at the advertised rate (s)he won't get the job. If rates are set by collective bargaining the individual applicant has the consolation of knowing that the wages offered have been considered by members of a trade union but the applicant's ability to bargain for more is nil. Nevertheless, the courts treat the contract as a fair deal agreed by individual parties.

This means that the union has no place as of right in any litigation; of course it may provide representation. So in a factory where a hundred women get paid less than men for similar work, the *union* can't bring a tribunal claim against the employer. An individual has to come forward and bring *her* claim based on *her* contract. There is not even any formal procedure for calling it a test case, on behalf of all the other workers. Again, if a trade-union activist or shop steward is sacked, the claim must be made by that worker for what that worker has lost. No mention is made of the harm done to the other workers by losing one of their activists, or by the attack on their right to union organisation. No claim can be made by the *group* of workers as such.

Even on issues where the collective rights are obvious, organisations of workers can't exercise them. When workers want their boss to recognise their union, or demand disclosure of information, or claim terms and conditions recognised in their industry, the final step is a legal claim made by *one* individual that according to his or her contract, (s)he is being underpaid.

This is no surprise. Look at other parts of the law where there might also be collective action by working people. A tenants' association can't claim against a landlord who has failed to carry out repairs in all its members' flats. A women's group can't sue under the Sex Discrimination Act on behalf of its members. A community group can't take joint action against a factory owner who pumps noxious fumes into the atmosphere, or against a local authority which fails to provide services. Consumer organisations can't claim against manufacturers of faulty products or café owners who cause food poisoning. In all these situations an individual must prove something happened to him or her. The case is treated as a one-off problem, rather than as an advertisement of the failure of the system.

So there are substantial obstacles to taking legal action. More important, this shows that even in the courtroom, which the ruling classes totally control, they still can't countenance the organisation of working people. It is precisely because workers, women, tenants, minority groups and consumers achieve strength through organisation that facilities are denied and their collective demands are turned into individual grievances. Positive proscription such as the Industrial Relations Act, the Prevention of Terrorism Act and the offences of conspiracy and unlawful assembly are also used to prevent organisation. Conspiracy actions are aimed at the perceived evil of people getting organised or reaching agreements or holding meetings, since all of these represent a threat even if no action is ever taken.

It is entirely consistent with this attack on working-class organisation that the establishment can conduct *itself* as a united body. Owners of capital form limited companies which shelter the individuals from all legal action. Any attacks by creditors, or by workers who have been injured or dismissed, must be made against the corporate body. There is no ban on this type of conspiracy, nor has there been since this formula for avoiding liability was facilitated in the 1850s.

Government departments, local authorities, and nationalised industries all present a united front to workers who must fight as single individuals. Claims for unemployment benefit are contested by an insurance officer who is laughingly referred to as independent, but who is employed by the government department you are suing. If you contest your supplementary benefit you face the Supplementary Benefits Commission. Disagree with your income tax assessment and it's the Inland Revenue Commission; have trouble with immigration or working papers, the Home Office; complain about police action against you and it's the police themselves!

So the failure to recognise the rights of workers' *organisations* is merely an example of the operation of the wider legal and political structure. Divide and rule. The individual worker is singled out and must stand alone, usually without Legal Aid, subject to victimisation and harassment, and facing a complex corporate body.

Parliament refuses to guarantee basic rights

The United Kingdom now has an advanced set of individual rights, and procedures for obtaining collective security. The progress made since 1963 has been rapid in vast areas of labour law.

In 1963 minimum periods of notice were laid down, and you got the right to written details of your contract. Since 1965, your employer has had to pay you if he makes you redundant. In 1968 racial discrimination in employment was outlawed. From 1972 your boss can't sack you unless he gives a specific reason and justifies his decision.

By 1978, you had specific rights in limited circumstances to: equal pay and equal opportunities, maternity pay and leave, pay during certain lay-offs, payment of money owed if your employer goes bust, and a trial period in a new job if you are made redundant.

Organised workers have rights too – protection against victimisation for being a trade unionist, recognition of your union, time off with pay for lay officials, disclosure of information and recognised terms and conditions. This is an impressive list of rights but there are lots of rights that are *essential* for all working people but which are *not* guaranteed by law. Also, as we shall see in every part of this book, **having a right is not the same as getting it enforced.**

You have no right: to strike or to persuade others to, to black products, to demonstrate, to picket, to be treated equally, to organise a union or to work. Parliament's failure to guarantee these basic rights means that all the individual rights it has provided are strictly limited. If you can't get your rights by collective action, their value is diminished.

Nothing illustrates so comprehensively the limits of the law as the *Grunwick* dispute. This case is mentioned frequently in the following chapters simply because it contains all the lessons the trade-union movement must learn about law and industrial action.

Grunwick process films in two North London factories. In 1973 the TGWU failed to get recognition and strikers were sacked. In August 1976 some workers walked out in protest against the sacking of a colleague for refusing compulsory overtime. Pay was very low – 77p. an hour – conditions were bad, compulsory overtime of up to 30 hours a week was common, discipline was summary and sackings were frequent. Staff turnover in the mainly

Asian female workforce was 100 per cent a year. The workers joined the clerical union APEX, which made the strike official.

The company sacked 137 strikers, APEX asked the Union of Postal Workers and other unions for support, and made a legal claim to the Advisory, Conciliation and Arbitration Service (ACAS) for recognition. Management consistently refused to deal with APEX or ACAS. Supported by the National Association for Freedom and right-wing Tory MPs, Grunwick sought an injunction against the UPW. ACAS conducted a ballot but as the company refused to give the names and addresses of employees, ACAS could ballot only the strikers. It recommended recognition but the company didn't budge. By June 1977 the strikers got support for mass picketing from rank and file trade unionists. Hundreds of pickets were arrested and many convicted. But APEX and the TUC refused to campaign for further mass picketing, the cutting off of essential services or sympathetic action. A court of inquiry recommended reinstatement of the strikers, or compensation, and said recognition of APEX would be 'helpful'. Grunwick ignored the report and sued ACAS over the way the ballot was conducted. The House of Lords decided that it was lawful to ballot the strikers, but the non-strikers should also have been allowed to vote. So the ballot was invalid and APEX had to start all over again in 1978. *Grunwick v ACAS* 1977 (HL)

The effects of the Grunwick dispute on the labour movement are devastating. Quite simply, it shows that some degree of management consent is required before workers can enforce their rights in the courts. Management is expected to be willing to meet a union, to conciliate, to respond to ministerial requests, to compromise and to accept non-binding decisions of influential bodies.

George Ward, the managing director, exploded this convention, and showed that the existing laws are useless against an obdurate employer with right-wing support.

Look what happened to the rights workers thought they had until Grunwick:

1. You have the right to join a union – but Grunwick members of APEX and TGWU were sacked without compensation when they did so.

2. You have the right to withdraw your labour – but if all strikers are sacked, none can claim unfair dismissal.

3. You can ask ACAS to recommend recognition – but ACAS has no power to demand co-operation by an employer.

4. ACAS can recommend recognition – but this isn't legally binding on employers.

5. You have the right to picket – but this doesn't

override police powers to arrest you for obstruction and other minor offences, or allow you to stop vehicles.

6. Selective action in support of strikers is not illegal – unless you are a postal worker.

On the other hand, **direct action was effective**. Mass picketing *did* stop vehicles entering the factories. The pickets massively outnumbered the police, so selective arrests were impossible. The boycott of mail *did* starve Grunwick of incoming orders. The strike *did* lead to wage increases of 25 per cent during the 1976–77 5 per cent pay policy (although only the scabs got the increase). If the TUC had given physical support for continuation of these pressures, and treated the strike as the fundamental matter of principle that the 1977 Congress recognised, the Grunwick workers' action would have succeeded.

Despite Parliament's refusal to guarantee basic rights, the *judges* have developed a 'right to work', although no trade unionist asked to devise a definition, would have come up with theirs. Lord Denning says you have a right to work if your union expels you for 'unreasonable or capricious reasons', and you lose your job. If a union refuses to accept you in an industry where workers have successfully organised themselves, you can exercise your right to work, and sue the union.

Lord Denning, however, says nothing about other aspects of such a right. It's OK for working people to attack each other in the courts but they can't attack employers or the government. For example, if you are blacklisted for being a union activist and can't get a job, you can't enforce your right to work.

Nor can you sue the government if its policies are responsible for your being out of work.

If you are unfairly dismissed or made redundant, tribunals cannot enforce an order that your employer should take you back. During a dispute, if you are all sacked or locked out, you have no right to go back to work.

As long as you are paid wages, you can't usually demand the right to do the job you are employed to do.

So, while you have rights to certain specific benefits, you don't have some fundamental rights. In the long run, your entitlement to most workplace rights depends on your ability to organise, to strike, to picket and to remain in work. Without these basics, the other benefits are restricted to monetary compensation, adding nothing to job security or improved conditions at work.

The law is stacked against women

It did not become illegal to discriminate on the grounds of sex until the end of 1975. The figures for earnings given on page 120 show the huge gap between men and women at work. In law, women have comparatively recently achieved a measure of independence from their husbands. Only six weeks before the Sex Discrimination Act came into effect a High Court judge (Mr Justice Caulfield) in a case involving a negligent solicitor, was saying:

> Even in present times, when there is a movement by women for equality with men, a sensible wife, certainly in a united home, does not generally make the major decisions. A solicitor should not take instruction from a wife when a husband is available. (*Morris v Duke-Cohan & Co*)

The absence of women judges and tribunal members contributes to the prevalence of this blatant sexism. In 1977 women made up 2 per cent of High Court judges, 3 per cent of tribunal chairmen and only 22 per cent of lay members.

Most employers are male, so in this handbook your boss is always 'he'.

Most tribunal cases cited involve men, and they are often supervisors or middle management. Manual working-class men and women feature proportionately less in tribunals because they are likely to be in unions and able to fight a sacking by industrial methods. But it is clear that the manager stands a better chance at a tribunal because he is from the same salaried, middle-class, male environment as the legal chairman and the nominee from the employers' organisations.

Many of the legal advances won in courts and tribunals are made by middle-class men. Rank-and-file workers naturally benefit from these – that's why so many middle-class cases are quoted in this handbook – but they do so by a sidewind not by design.

Employment law is constantly changing

The limits of law can alter very quickly. Employment law is dynamic. It changes according to political, economic and industrial pressures. Its fluctuations record events in labour history and bourgeois responses to them.

The Conspiracy and Protection of Property Act 1875

was passed after London gasworkers had been prosecuted for conspiring to break their contracts. The Act gave workers some protection against conspiracy charges. (It also made prosecutions easy for other offences, though.) The Trade Disputes Act 1906 protected you if you persuaded others to strike; it also prevented unions from being sued. The Act was passed by a Liberal government after pressure from new Labour MPs following a successful legal action by the Taff Vale railway company against the railworkers' union, which cost the union £35,000 in costs and compensation.

The Trade Disputes Act 1927 outlawed political or anti-government strikes and attempted to wreck unions' political fund-raising. It was pushed through by the Tories after the collapse of the General Strike and the defeat of the miners the previous year.

The Industrial Relations Act 1971 followed the Labour government's attempts in 1969 (*In Place of Strife*) to curtail industrial militancy. Both were defeated by united working-class opposition. Heath's statutory incomes policy of 1972–74 and his government were killed by a national miners' strike, supported by other unions. Labour's pay policies of 1975–78 were responses to the economic threats of inflation, unemployment and the international bankers' pressure on the pound. The employment legislation of 1974–76 was the government's answer to pressure from industrial and political organisations for a floor of rights in employment; and as part of the social contract, it was exchanged for voluntary wage restraint.

So throughout the last hundred years employment law has been bent according to political, economic and industrial forces. It has also been bent in a very marked way by the judges who, through malicious ingenuity especially during the 1960s, managed to tear down the protections that workers thought they had had for sixty years. Parliament has been able to undo only some of the harmful effects of this judicial joy-riding. The marks made by the now defunct National Industrial Relations Court and judges in other courts are still visible and still restrict workers' activity. If industrial action provides the dynamic for change the judges will continue to provide the dynamic for reaction within any new labour legislation.

Provided you are aware of the limits of law, you can use your legal rights to advantage. There are situations where direct action is not on – for example, some workers may decide not to support you to resolve what they see as a purely individual grievance. Or the law may provide better rights than anything you could hope to obtain by collective action. For example, there were only a handful of women workers in 1976 covered by collective agreements which gave them rights as good as the right to return to work for up to 29 weeks after childbirth. The Employment Protection Act guarantees this.

You might take legal action to improve your terms and conditions in a period of wage restraint, when increases given under the Employment Protection Act or the Fair Wages Resolution are exempt. Or you could clarify the legal terms of your contract by making a claim to a tribunal, and so make direct action unnecessary.

In all of these situations the following guidelines are essential.

1. Organisation, negotiation and action are more effective than legal action.

2. While pursuing collective action, don't ignore the possibility of legal action at any stage.

3. Often the *threat* of legal action can be a tactical advantage in negotiations.

4. Use the cases in this handbook to *prevent* your boss taking unilateral action which tribunals and courts have said is unfair.

2.

The Legal Framework

Access to the law and lawyers / what the law consists of / Acts, Regulations, the Common Market, Codes of Practice, cases / the framework of your rights / who enforces the law / the courts, tribunals, Central Arbitration Committee, Certification Officer, Registrar of Companies and the Advisory, Conciliation and Arbitration Service.

This chapter gives you the background to the rights described in this handbook. It is important to understand how the legal system deals with your rights when you try and enforce them, and how your rights fit into the legal system.

Access to the law

'Ignorance of the law is no excuse' say the judges. But knowing what the law is is not simple. Traditionally lawyers have not specialised in subjects as lacking in profit as the enforcement of workers' rights, and they have not been taught them at law schools. The laws relating to land, property, companies, shipping, insurance, banking, business transactions, tax, patents and (since state Legal Aid) crime all involve big money. Where there is money there are lawyers. Only in the 1970s did lawyers begin to turn their attention to employment matters, mainly to advise their client companies how to minimise the effect of workers' new rights. So expertise in the field has been difficult to find.

Nor do lawyers tend to live or practise in areas where industrial workers can easily reach them. If you find a solicitor who deals with workers' claims in industrial tribunals, you then have to cut through the mystery of the profession – the language, the procedures, the restrictive practices and the un-

certainty. All of these may make you apprehensive about even
seeking advice.

Then there is the cost. **Legal Aid** (see page 354) is available for *advice* on tribunals but doesn't run to providing free
representation. So solicitors may require a substantial down
payment before taking up your case.

Naturally, the first thought of an organised worker
needing information or help is the union. Law Centres,
Citizens' Advice Bureaux and the Advisory, Conciliation and
Arbitration Service (ACAS) (addresses on page 399) also give
advice. You can even try your public library. All large libraries
take at least one series of law reports and have copies of the
Acts, Regulations and some textbooks. Most specialist law
libraries are owned by the legal professions or universities.
There is no reason why you should not be allowed to read in
your local polytechnic or university.

But first you need to know what the law consists of.

What is the law?

Acts of Parliament

Law is made up from a number of different sources. The
most important is Parliament. A **Bill** introduced in Parliament,
passed by both the House of Commons and the House of
Lords, and given the royal assent by the Queen, becomes an
Act, a **statute**. This is law from the moment it receives the
royal assent, although its implementation might be delayed to
a specified date or brought in in stages. The Employment
Protection Act (EP Act) was like this.

The main provisions of an Act are set out in numbered
sections with fine details and amendments and repeals of
earlier Acts left to schedules at the back. There are usually
sections giving definitions of the words used ('interpretation'),
and when it is to become effective ('commencement'). There
is no index, only a contents ('arrangement of sections') at the
front. There are sub-divisions of the Act, and most sections
have a brief note in the margin giving the gist.

Statutory Instruments

Sometimes an Act will give power to ministers or to the
'Queen in Council' (that is, with ministers) to make laws on
detailed aspects of the Act or on administrative changes. For
example, there is a limit of £100 on the weekly earnings you can

count for claiming redundancy pay. The Employment Secretary must each year consider whether to increase this figure. If an increase is made, it will be in a **Statutory Instrument**. This method of allowing for a minister to amend Acts is known as delegated legislation. In the employment field delegated legislation is subject to Parliamentary approval.

Statutory Instruments are cited by name, year and number, for example, Industrial Tribunals (Labour Relations) Regulations SI 1974 No. 1386. Because they are more numerous and detailed than the Acts, they are often difficult to find in libraries. But they are just as important.

Common Market Laws

Since the UK joined the Common Market (EEC) in 1973, binding regulations can be made without being passed by Parliament. The EEC Treaty set up the institutions of the EEC, and it is binding on the states which signed it. There are certain parts of it that give rights to individual citizens. These are 'directly applicable' without the need for the UK Parliament to pass any legislation. Article 119 on equal pay is directly enforceable in the UK.

Regulations of the EEC are binding. For instance, Regulation 1612/68 gives workers the right to look for and take up work in member states.

Directives are binding but member states can decide how to put them into practice. The Directive on equal treatment for men and women (No. 76/207/EEC) is put into practice by the Sex Discrimination Act. Some unconditional Directives, though, are 'directly applicable' and you can enforce them in the UK courts (*Van Duyn v Home Office* 1974 European Court).

Decisions usually relate to specific industries or states and are binding on the organisation concerned, for instance, that a particular course of action is contrary to the Treaty.

Case Law

What distinguishes the English legal system, and those based on it as in the USA and most Commonwealth countries, from other systems is the extent to which decisions of judges create binding precedents. This is known as the **common law.** In dealing with cases, tribunals and judges are bound by decisions of judges in higher courts, unless the facts of the cases can be 'distinguished'. This means that the judge doesn't follow the earlier case because he says the facts differ in kind from the present case. If you quote a case which involved the same sort of facts as your own, the principle of the earlier decision must be followed.

The judges are employed merely to interpret the law as laid down by Parliament or as interpreted in other cases, and to apply it to the facts of the case before them. In practice, as we shall see, they create law too.

If the law is obscure, it can, with rare exceptions, only be cleared up by bringing a case. The courts will not hear hypothetical cases or questions.

Codes of Practice

The Health and Safety at Work Act (HSW Act) and the Employment Protection Act give scope for the Health and Safety Commission and ACAS to publish Codes of Practice. These are most important in setting standards for industrial practice and negotiations. There are Codes on discipline, disclosure of information and time off. They are written in more understandable language than statutes. You cannot take your boss to a tribunal if he breaks a Code of Practice in the same way as you can if he breaks an Act, but tribunals and courts *must* consider any relevant codes in any case that you do bring. So the Code on discipline must be considered if you claim unfair dismissal, and the Code on disclosure if your boss rejects your union's demand for information. In organised workplaces the rules set by codes are often more significant for everyday industrial relations than Acts of Parliament.

International Law

Laws of other countries have no effect in the UK. The UK has signed a number of international agreements which, while not legally binding, are regarded as such by the government, for example, conventions of the International Labour Organisation (ILO) and the Council of Europe.

Who enforces the law?

The legal framework in which your rights and duties as a worker are enforced is illustrated by diagram 1 on page 17. The way you exercise your rights and the remedies available if you are prevented from doing so vary. Diagram 1 shows the operation of your rights.

Diagram 1 Legal Action

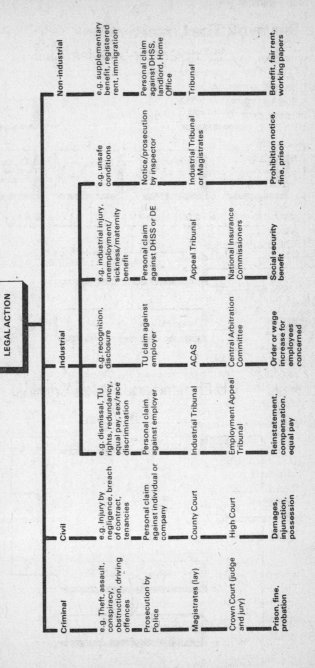

LEGAL ACTION

Criminal	Civil	Industrial				Non-industrial
e.g. Theft, assault, conspiracy, obstruction, driving offences	e.g. Injury by negligence, breach of contract, tenancies	e.g. dismissal, TU rights, redundancy, equal pay, sex/race discrimination	e.g. recognition, disclosure	e.g. industrial injury, unemployment/sickness/maternity benefit	e.g. unsafe conditions	e.g. supplementary benefit, registered rent, immigration
Prosecution by Police	Personal claim against individual or company	Personal claim against employer	TU claim against employer	Personal claim against DHSS or DE	Notice/prosecution by inspector	Personal claim against DHSS, landlord, Home Office
Magistrates (lay)	County Court	Industrial Tribunal	ACAS	Appeal Tribunal	Industrial Tribunal or Magistrates	Tribunal
Crown Court (judge and jury)	High Court	Employment Appeal Tribunal	Central Arbitration Committee	National Insurance Commissioners		
Prison, fine, probation	**Damages, injunction, possession**	**Reinstatement, compensation, equal pay**	**Order or wage increase for employees concerned**	**Social security benefit**	**Prohibition notice, fine, prison**	**Benefit, fair rent, working papers**

Diagram 2 **The Legal System**

a: England and Wales/Civil

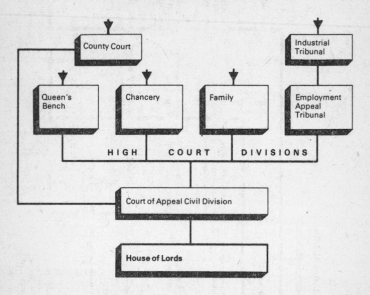

b: England and Wales/Criminal

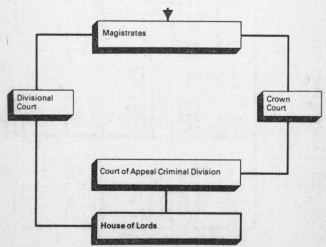

Diagram 2 **The Legal System**

c: Scotland

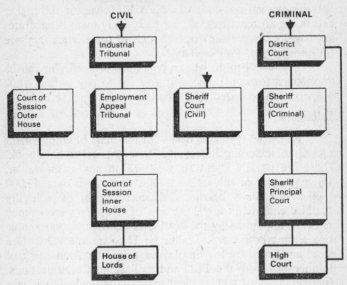

d: Northern Ireland/Civil and Criminal

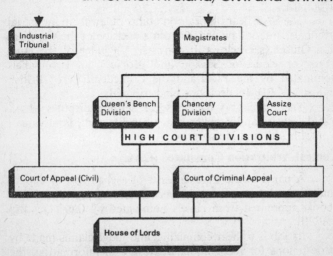

The Courts

Diagram 2 on pages 18-19 illustrates the relationship between the various courts in the UK. Judges of the higher courts are all barristers, almost exclusively men. Magistrates are usually lay part-timers, although in some cities they are full-time lawyers ('stipendiary').

If you fail to do what a court has ordered you can be imprisoned for contempt or, if you fail to pay a debt, your property can be seized by the bailiffs.

Tribunals

Industrial tribunals deal with the mass of employment legislation, including almost all of the rights in this handbook. There are usually about sixty sitting on any given day in different parts of the UK. In 1976 there were over 46,000 applications for a hearing. Tribunals consist of a legally qualified chairman (only 3 per cent of chairmen were women in 1977), appointed by the Lord Chancellor, and two people representing both sides of industry. They are selected from a panel appointed by the Employment Secretary consisting of nominations from the TUC and management organisations. There are about 2,400 lay members of whom only 22 per cent are women. The appointments are reviewed every three years. They are bound by decisions of the High Court and the Employment Appeal Tribunal (EAT), but not of other tribunals.

The EAT hears appeals on points of law from industrial tribunals, and on law or fact from a decision of the Certification Officer (see below). It consists of a judge of the High Court or Court of Session and people from two panels nominated by the TUC and the Confederation of British Industry (CBI). Its decisions bind tribunals.

There are also tribunals for settling disputes about social security and supplementary benefits, rent, land values, mental health and immigration.

Central Arbitration Committee (CAC)

A panel of the CAC consists of a chairman or deputy chairman who may be a lawyer or an academic, and two people appointed from panels nominated by the TUC and the CBI.

Its job is to hear complaints and judge claims made by trade unions for recognition, disclosure of information, the going rate and some aspects of equal pay. It can make an award which specifies terms and conditions. These take effect as part of the contract of employment of every worker covered by the award. There is no appeal, unless the CAC goes outside its terms of reference, in which case you go to the High Court.

Certification Officer

The Certification Officer is required to judge claims for independent status by trade unions. It is a precondition for the exercise of all the union rights in this handbook that the union is certified as independent. The right of appeal to the EAT on law (or *fact*, an unusual right) is given to unions refused a certificate of independence. He also oversees the accounts, and to some extent the rules, of trade unions.

Registrar of Companies

All companies are required to register at Companies House in England and Wales, Scotland or Northern Ireland – addresses page 400.

The Registrar, in theory at least, is supposed to check annual accounts filed there and take action, which can include starting criminal proceedings, against defaulting companies and their officers.

Advisory, Conciliation and Arbitration Service

ACAS was established as an independent body by Parliament in the EP Act. It is administered by a Council which consists of TUC, CBI and academic advisers.

Its functions are:

■ Advice: to employers, unions and individuals on industrial relations and legal problems.

■ Conciliation: at the request of either party in a dispute. ACAS automatically receives copies of all individual legal claims to tribunals and will attempt to conciliate with the parties' advisers.

■ Voluntary arbitration: at the request of *both* sides.

■ Enforcement of the EP Act: ACAS also has a role in the first stage of procedures for enforcement of various legal rights under the EP Act including recognition, disclosure of information and the going rate.

Part Two: Individual Rights

3.

Your Contract of Employment

What is a contract / why it's important / where to find the law / who has a contract of employment / before you make a contract / what's in the written part / written particulars, pay statement, collective agreements, Wages Council orders, works rules / what's unwritten / custom and practice, employers' and workers' general obligations / ending the contract / how to claim for breach of contract / collective action / and a summary

What is a contract?

You make contracts every day. Some look more formal than others, such as an agreement to buy a house or an insurance policy, but they are basically the same as agreements to buy bread or travel on a bus. The essential feature is a binding agreement in which an offer by one person is accepted by someone else. It involves a benefit to one of them or a detriment to the other, or an exchange of benefits. **It is a promise that can be enforced in the courts.**

Not all promises can. You wouldn't think your wife should be able to sue you if you promise to do the dishes provided she cooks dinner, and you go back on your word. Neither of you intended that a *legal* obligation should arise. If you promise to make a donation to a charity it cannot sue you if you later refuse, unless the promise is in writing and witnessed formally. This is because the charity has not, in exchange for your promise, given you any benefit or acted to its detriment on your behalf. Your promise is a gift, and is entirely one way. So without a written 'deed' it is unenforceable in the courts.

Contracts need not be written or signed. If you buy a second-hand car there is usually no paperwork except the insurance and registration book. You may get a receipt saying how much you paid but the agreement is unwritten. It is no less binding in law because of it. But **proving** there was an agreement, or what was intended at the time of sale, is a lot easier if you have drawn up a list of the main points – such as, is there a guarantee, how many miles has it done, is it in good running order, and who is going to pay for the dent in the wing?

How important is your contract of employment?

The contract of employment is the starting point for many aspects of your working life. You can't discuss the effect of strikes, of refusing to accept instructions, discipline, sacking, lay-offs or equal pay without the lawyers forcing you back against your contract, examining what it says and, equally importantly, telling you what is unwritten. Even union rights that are won through organisation are enforced by reference to individual contracts of employment.

Although the contract is so important, the amount of information that is written, or even discussed, at the time you take up employment is often very limited. Only in 1963 did it become obligatory to put into writing certain details of contracts of employment. If you are not in a union, and not subject to any collective agreement, this is the only piece of written data you get. Yet there are enough **unwritten** rules for the judges to tell you exactly where you stand.

Despite the obvious and continuing inequality of bargaining power between a worker and an employer, the courts treat your contract as if every item is suggested, discussed, negotiated, compromised and agreed. The very essence of all the rules that follow in this chapter is that there is an **agreement** made by willing equal parties. It may not make sense to treat an employment contract like a contract to buy a used car, but the courts do.

Where to find the law

Much of the law on contracts of employment is made by judges. The Contracts of Employment Act 1972 (CE Act) sections 1–4 deals with some rights (written particulars and notice), The Employment Protection Act 1975 (EP Act) gives others: section 59 (time off for public duties); section 81 (itemised pay statements). The Truck Acts 1831 and 1896 and the Payment of Wages Act 1960 apply to some groups of workers.

Who has a contract of employment?

Workers and employees

There is a difference between a worker and an employee. The difference is generally ignored in this book because almost all workers are employees, most of the individual rights apply only to employees, and worker and employee are used interchangeably by most people. All employees have contracts of employment. Some people work for themselves or are in partnership; some are directors of companies; some are neither workers nor employees – policemen, for instance, who 'hold office'. The main group of non-employee workers consists of self-employed '**independent contractors**'. It is important to recognise the difference because being an employee has a number of consequences:

■ You are entitled to most of the statutory rights in this book – time off, redundancy pay, protection against unfair dismissal, etc.

■ You and your boss are subject to the unwritten general obligations of a contract of employment.

■ You are both liable to pay social security contributions.

■ Your boss deducts tax from your pay.

■ Your boss must be insured against claims by you for personal injury.

■ Your boss is subject to levies, for example, for industrial training, and must notify the Department of Employment (DE) of certain impending redundancies.

The difference between an employee and an independent contractor is easier to see than to define. For example, a taxi driver and a full-time company chauffeur do the same work but the taxi driver is often self-employed. There is a similar distinction between a freelance writer and a newspaper reporter, or a casual window-cleaner and a permanent care-taker, or a jobbing electrician and an electrical fitter in a big factory.

The courts have not laid down a clear rule about how to tell whether a person is employed or self-employed. The key question is: are you in business on your own account? If you are, you are self-employed and work under a **contract for services**. If not, you are an employee and work under a **contract of service**.

In deciding this question you must look at the realities of the relationship, not simply what the worker and the employer say or write.

> Michael Ferguson was hired as a labourer on a building site. He agreed to a labour-only sub-contract (Lump). He was injured and successfully claimed £30,000 in damages. The Court of Appeal (CA) said that the reality of the situation was employer–employee, so his employers were liable as they did not provide a guardrail where he was working. The employers told Mr Ferguson where to work, provided him with tools, told him what work was to be done and paid him wages. This in reality meant he was an employee not a self-employed contractor.
> *Ferguson v Dawson* 1976 (CA)

Section 30 of the Trade Union and Labour Relations Acts 1974 and 1976 (TULR Act) defines an **employee** as some-one who has entered into, works under or has worked under a contract of employment. This includes apprentices. The definition of a **worker** is wider. It includes employees, potential employees, self-employed people (except self-employed mem-bers of the 'professions') and government workers. Excluded are the police and the armed services.

Self-employment in the building industry

The 'Lump' is the name given to labour-only sub-contracting in the building and civil engineering industries. Typically, it takes the form of a group of workers, each self-employed, who agree with a sub-contractor that the sub-contractor will find work for them with a main contractor. There are other forms. In all cases the main feature is that the worker is paid a lump sum, and (s)he is supposed to pay income tax and social security contributions out of that sum.

The Lump has advantages for workers and employers. It enables both of them to evade the legal liabilities imposed on them.

It undermines union organisation in a badly organised industry, and contributes to its appalling safety record. Despite union pressure over many years no effective measures had been taken to crush the Lump. In 1977 a new system of certification was introduced. Limited companies and self-employed workers in the building industry must carry new certificates with photographs. Tax must be deducted by employers from every payment made unless a valid certificate is produced. Weekly tax returns must be made by sub-contractors.

So, almost five years after a national building strike against the Lump, and the imprisonment of the Shrewsbury building workers (see page 311), the government took some steps to control self-employment. But the lack of union organisation and the haphazard nature of building work means that abuses continue.

Before you make a contract of employment

Legal consequences can arise even before you enter into your contract.

1. Discrimination on the grounds of race, sex and being married is outlawed. Employees, potential employees and independent contractors have equal rights.

2. Under the Disabled Persons (Employment) Acts 1944 and 1958, employers with more than 20 regular workers must employ a quota of registered disabled workers (usually 3 per cent), and if they are employing less than their quota, they cannot fill a vacancy with a non-disabled person unless exempt. The penalty is a fine of £500, but prosecutions are extremely rare.

3. Women and workers under the age of 18 are prevented by the Factories Act and the Mines and Quarries Act from working certain hours and in certain occupations.

4. Under the Rehabilitation of Offenders Act 1974 (RO Act) you are entitled to forget some 'spent' convictions. When applying for most jobs you can forget about convictions for various crimes for which you got less than two-and-a-half years in prison, which occurred some time ago, and since which you have gone straight. The length of the period of rehabilitation varies according to the sentence and your age on conviction.

For example:

Imprisonment for between 6 and 30 months	10 years' rehabilitation
Imprisonment for less than 6 months	7 years' rehabilitation
Fine	5 years' rehabilitation
Conditional discharge, probation, binding-over	1 year or date on which order expires (whichever is longer)

There are numerous exceptions (see SI 1975 No. 1023) which mean that you have to disclose your convictions if you are applying for a job as: a doctor, lawyer, accountant, dentist, vet, nurse, midwife, optician, chemist, law clerk, constable, traffic warden, probation officer, teacher, health or social worker; or if you need a licence to carry on your trade. In all other cases you are entitled to say you have no record.

See also *Hendry v Scottish Liberal Club* (page 173).

Making the contract

Once you accept an offer of a job, the contract is made. The details are known as **terms and conditions**. You may have talked about the basic elements of the work – the pay and the hours – but many other details are often included because of collective agreements or legislation, such as pension rights, training, union rights and sickness.

There are also many obligations that you and your boss are required to adhere to because they are automatically considered to be part of every contract of employment unless they are expressly excluded. These are **implied terms** under the **common law**. In this chapter they occur as custom and practice, and general obligations imposed on employers and employees. Common law implied terms include your boss's duty to pay you and provide a safe system of working. For your part, you must work and co-operate, obey reasonable instructions within the scope of your contract and be trustworthy.

The time to object to any aspect of the deal is at the time you are offered the job. This may be relevant advice for managers and senior staff, but for most workers the chances of objecting individually to bits of a contract are virtually nil. After you accept the job, it is too late to start demanding different terms, unless you are organised and can apply sanctions.

Your contract may be made up of:

1. Terms expressly agreed – your Contracts of Employment Act statement is often evidence of what these are.

2. Terms included from collective agreements.

3. Terms included because of a Wages Council Order, or an award of the Central Arbitration Committee, for example, for the going rate (see chapter 7).

4. Works rules.

5. Terms implied by custom and practice in your trade.

6. Terms implied by the common law which impose general obligations on employers.

7. Terms implied by the common law which impose general obligations on employees.

All of these are dealt with in the following sections.

The written part of your contract

1. Contracts of Employment Act statement

The CE Act 1972 (section 1) lays down minimum periods of notice that every worker is entitled to. (See page 147.) Section 4 requires employers to give employees a list of the main terms of the contract of employment. The rationale of this part of the Act is that workers should be told exactly how they stand on the main points of their contracts, so it is easier in a dispute to prove what the terms are.

Section 1 of the Act applies to all employees except: part-timers who work less than 16 hours a week (plus exceptions – see page 341); registered dockers; seamen; overseas workers; Crown and some National Health Service workers; and employees whose *entire* contract is written (very rarely found).

Within 13 weeks of starting work your boss must give you your own copy of a written statement setting out the following particulars.

1. Identity of the employer (such as the company name, or what it trades as) and employee.

2. Date employment began, whether any previous service counts as continuous and if so when it began. There are clear rules about strikes, illness, lay-off and transfer, but a note that previous service counts will prevent employers subsequently denying that this is true.

3. Job title. This is not a conclusive description of what you actually do. In considering, for example, suitable altern- ative work if you are redundant or pregnant it is what you actually do that is important, not what it's called. The Act does not require a job description.

4. Rate of remuneration, or method of calculating it. Remuneration includes *all* forms of pay. This is crucial as redundancy and other payments depend on contractual en- titlement to pay. Overtime rates should be specified.

5. Whether paid weekly, monthly, or at some other interval, and whether you work a week or month in hand.

6. Hours of work, and normal working hours.

7. Annual, public and other holidays, rights to holiday pay and to accrued holiday pay on termination.

8. Provision for sickness and injury – for example, when a doctor's note must be given, and sick pay.

9. Pension rights (unless you belong to a scheme established by statute, as do government, National Health Service and local authority workers).

10. Amount of notice you must give, and are entitled to receive. Even if this is the same as the minimum under the CE Act the periods must be spelt out.

11. Disciplinary rules that apply to you.

12. The name or description of a person you can apply to if you are dissatisfied with *any* disciplinary decision against you, or if you want to bring up a grievance, and how to apply.

13. The procedure following such an application.

14. Whether or not a contracting-out certificate under the Social Security Pensions Act is in force.

15. If the contract is for a fixed period, the date it expires.

Points to note about the statement

a. Instead of specifying the information in paragraphs 1–11 and 13, the statement can refer you to a document which you have a reasonable opportunity to read while at work. So you may see a reference to a collective agreement, or to the works rules, or to the EP Act (for minimum notice periods) provided it is accessible to you at work, or to the pension scheme deeds.

b. If there are no details to be given in paragraphs 1–10, the written statement must say so. If you don't get sick pay, for instance, this must be recorded. But you must be told about the information required in paragraphs 11–15.

c. Paragraphs 11–13 do not apply to rules, procedures and decisions relating to health and safety. So there is no obligation to give you details about disciplinary action that might be taken against you if you break safety rules. This sort of thing must be covered by your boss's policy statement under the Health and Safety at Work Act 1974 (HSW Act). (See Kinnersly, *The Hazards of Work*, London, Pluto, 1978.)

d. It must be stressed that the statement is *not* your contract or even *conclusive evidence* of what its main points are. It is important to realise the difference. As we shall see, there is far more to a contract than the matters contained in the list above. Although the chances of saying that the written statement does not correspond to what you agreed are slim, it is still possible to overturn the statement by evidence from custom and practice or of what was said. The statement is of *written particulars* of your contract, and other facts can be brought up to show that something else was intended.

How to get a written statement

If you do not get a written statement within 13 weeks of starting work, or if you dispute the accuracy of it, you can apply to an industrial tribunal for an order that your boss should supply one. See page 357 for the procedure. You can apply while you are employed, or up to **three months** after you have left the job.

Signing the statement

There is nothing in the CE Act that requires you to sign the written statement, although in practice you are often asked to sign one copy and keep the other yourself. You do not benefit from signing the statement or signing that you have received it. In fact, it could be to your disadvantage. The Court of Appeal told John Mercer, a gas conversion fitter who claimed redundancy pay based on a 54-hour week, that by signing a written statement fixing a 40-hour week he had formed a written contract that could not be varied. (See page

255.) This was probably incorrect, but as the law now stands it shows that you can be prejudiced by signing.

If you refuse to sign and are sacked you can claim unfair dismissal, as D. Turner, a barman at Yate's Wine Lodge in Blackpool, did. He consulted his union and refused to sign a statement foisted on to him after seven months' service. He was sacked, not uncoincidentally, after he started organising for USDAW.

If you sign, make sure your boss signs too.

Changing the statement

No change in your contract can be made unless you agree, or agree to changes being made automatically following collective agreement with your union. But once changes have been agreed the EP Act requires your boss to notify you formally within one month. He must give you a written note. But he need do no more than show it to you and keep it in a place that is reasonably accessible to you. **Demand your own copy.**

If your original statement says that changes will be recorded automatically in some specific way – for example, following a Joint Industrial Council (JIC) agreement – it is not obligatory to inform you, although you are still entitled to see all the changes made. You should insist on your union giving you the information.

Itemised pay statement

Most workers have the right to get an itemised pay statement. Merchant seamen, share fishermen and people who work less than 16 hours a week (plus exceptions – see page 341) are excluded. It is not explained why such workers should not have an equal right to know where their money goes.

Section 81 of the EP Act says you must get an itemised pay statement every time you are paid. The statement must set out:

■ gross wages
■ fixed deductions
■ variable deductions
■ net wages
■ method and amounts of payment if it is not all paid in the same way.

If you have several **fixed deductions**, such as union contributions, rent, or payments under an attachment-of-earnings court order, your boss need not specify each separate

amount. He must state the **total amount** of all your fixed
deductions each payday *and* he must give you a standing
written statement once a year specifying the amount of *each*
fixed deduction, the intervals at which it occurs and its
purpose.

How to get a pay statement

If you do not get a statement, or think the statement is
inaccurate, you can apply to an industrial tribunal **within
three months** to get a declaration of what particulars should
be given.

If your boss makes any deduction without giving you a
pay statement, even if he has not broken your contract, the
tribunal can order him to repay any amount deducted in the
13 weeks prior to your claim. A threat of legal action could
therefore be useful in getting a pay statement.

2. Collective agreements

As we shall see (page 253), bits of a collective agreement
can be sucked into your own contract if you have agreed to
this. This generally happens with wages, hours, holidays and
other **substantive terms**. It does not usually apply to purely
procedural terms of the collective agreement specifying, for
example, a health and safety grievance procedure, or the procedure for avoiding disputes. Consequently, it would be
difficult to say you broke your contract if you did not carry out
procedure. But the law is unclear on this point and the courts
could conceivably decide against you.

3. Wages Councils, arbitration awards and incomes policy

Wages Councils and Statutory JICs can make orders
for minimum rates that must be observed. These are automatically incorporated into your contract if you are in an
appropriate industry. See chapter 17.

Terms and conditions awarded by the Central Arbitration Committee (CAC) take effect as part of every affected
worker's contract. The CAC awards terms and conditions in
claims for equal pay, the going rate, recognition and disclosure
of information.

The government's incomes policy can also affect your
contract of employment. Under the incomes policies of 1972–
74 and 1975–78 employers were protected from some actions
for breach of contract. While the Labour government's policy
is described as voluntary, the Remuneration, Charges and

Grants Act 1975 is distinctly obligatory. If your boss has promised you a rise of £8 a week, and then refuses to pay because of the voluntary pay policy or the 10 per cent guidelines on wage increases, you cannot sue him for breach of contract. If he does pay you, he may be prevented from passing on the increased wage-cost in a price rise.

4. Works rules

The law on works rules is a mess. Sometimes they form part of your contract, sometimes they don't. Because they are so varied it is impossible to give anything but general guidelines.

The rules are likely to be in your contract if you sign them, or if they are posted in notices in your workplace. They can also be **implied terms** of your contract if they are so well-known in the trade in your area that both you and your boss are assumed to know they will form part of your contract. If you do not abide by contractual works rules you are breaking your contract.

If you don't sign the rules, or if you register your objection to, say, some of the disciplinary offences, you may prevent them forming part of your contract. Even if you do sign the rules, they don't always become contractual. In the railmen's work-to-rule in 1972 (see page 291) the courts considered the British Rail rules. The Court of Appeal said that although the rules were signed by every worker they were not contractual. **But they were instructions about how the railmen should do their job.** Provided they were lawful and reasonable they had to be obeyed.

The differences between a contractual rule and a lawful instruction are:

1. A contractual rule can be altered only with your consent. Instructions can be changed without consultation or agreement.

2. By sticking to a contractual rule, you are merely *carrying out* your contract. If you disobey instructions which are lawful and reasonable you are *breaking* your contract.

3. If you interpret instructions in a way which is so unreasonable that it creates chaos, or frustrates the commercial purpose for which you are employed (whatever that means), you are breaking your contract – for instance, the railmen's work-to-rule.

Since you are likely to be bound by works rules either because they are contractual, or because they are reasonable and lawful instructions, it is often advisable for your union to negotiate with your boss over them. You can in this way also negotiate rules which are binding on management – to test machinery, supply safety equipment, and guarantee rest periods, for instance.

5. Custom and practice

In many industries custom and practice governs workplace relations as effectively as written agreements. A custom may be so well known that it is not worth putting in writing, or it may suit management and unions to keep the arrangements relatively loose. In law, a custom can be binding if it meets three conditions.

1. It must be 'notorious' so that it is almost universally observed and everyone involved knows about it;

2. It must be reasonable (although the courts have often taken the employers' view of this); and

3. It must be so certain that you know exactly what effect the custom has on you.

The major areas in which custom and practice are relevant are dealt with as they arise elsewhere in this book, so a brief look here at some examples is sufficient.

On **discipline**, lower wages were paid to Lancashire weavers for bad work. This practice was even supported by the weaving unions which obtained a special exemption from the Truck Acts which would make these deductions illegal (see page 71). In 1931 Thomas Sagar challenged the practice but the Court of Appeal said he had gone to work fully knowing of it, as did every weaver in the trade in Lancashire. The practice was reasonable and its application was clear. So the bosses were able to refuse to pay full wages for work *they* considered sub-standard.

On **notice**, the old cases show that workers in some trades and domestic service are entitled to a month's notice, to be given on the first day of the month. This custom overrides the right to minimum notice under the EP Act if it provides longer notice.

On a custom of **negotiating** rates, Charles Wallace showed that there was a custom for negotiations over rates to precede any pipe-bending work he did and successfully claimed unfair dismissal when his boss refused to negotiate. (See page 165.)

A custom of **providing work** was acknowledged by the courts in 1906. Mr Devonald, a steelworker on piece-work, was laid off for two weeks during slack trading, and then given four weeks' notice, as required by agreement. His boss tried to show that by custom and practice he had a right to lay off workers whenever he felt trade was bad. But the Court of Appeal conceded that 'the workman has to live', and should be given the opportunity of piece-working during his notice – *Devonald v Rosser* 1906 (CA).

6. Employers' general obligations

There are general obligations under the common law that are *implied* in every contract of employment, even though nothing is written or even mentioned. These include the duty:

- to pay wages and salaries
- not to make unauthorised deductions
- (in some cases) to provide work
- to provide a safe system of work
- to obey the law
- to allow time off

There is no duty to provide holidays or references.

Wages and salaries

If you have done the work, you are entitled to be paid. If you are hired and then not taken on, or given only a few days' work, you are entitled to be paid the amount you would have received had your boss not broken his contract – at least up to the value of your notice-money.

The way in which 'a week's pay' is calculated for assessing your entitlement to many of the rights in this book is explained in chapter 21.

Deductions

Deductions from wages must be made for PAYE income tax, social security contributions and attachment-of-earnings court orders (to pay fines and maintenance).

Deductions from your pay may be outlawed by the Truck Acts. Dating from 1831, these prevent employers paying in kind (truck) for work done, and allow deductions to be made only for certain specified purposes. Payment in tickets exchangeable only at the company store – the old butty shop – is illegal. The Acts today give rise to a number of problems: 1. who is covered, 2. how payment is made, 3. exceptions and 4. enforcement.

1. The Acts apply only to 'artificers' and 'workmen engaged in manual labour'. It is often difficult to draw the

line if you do manual and non-manual work but a (rather unhelpful) rule has been laid down that you are covered if the manual work you do is your 'real and substantial' employment, but **not** if it is merely incidental or accessory to it. In other words, is the manual part more important than the mental? So the courts have applied the Acts to sewing machinists, bus drivers who do some repair work, and TV repairmen, but not to bus conductors, typists, hairdressers, railway guards and shop assistants, although some parts dealing with deductions and fines *do* apply to shop assistants.

2. The 1831 Act says how wages are to be paid:

> The entire amount of the wages earned by or payable to any artificer . . . in respect of any labour done by him . . . shall be actually paid to such artificer in the current coin of this realm, and not otherwise.

It can be paid in notes, but payment by cheque, postal order or money order or into a bank account is forbidden unless you request it **in writing** and your boss agrees. And an Act of 1883, expressing the worst of Victorian fears, says: 'No wages shall be paid to any workman at or within any public-house, beershop or place for the sale of any spirits, wine, cyder or other spirituous . . . liquor.' Bar staff are exempt.

3. There are many exceptions. You can agree to a deduction if the amount is forwarded direct to someone you appoint – your union, or a charity, or Christmas club, for instance. Your boss is entitled to make deductions for medicine, fuel, tools, materials, rent, food, and hay for your horse! But the sums must be agreed **in writing**, reflect the true value of the goods and, for tools, be audited every year. Wages Councils can specify maximum lodging allowance deductions. Deductions for fines and damaged goods are subject to stricter controls – see page 71. No deduction can be made for supplying equipment needed under safety legislation (HSW Act section 9).

4. The Acts are enforced (if that is the right word) by the Wages Inspectors of the DE. On conviction in the magistrates court your boss can be fined £10, or £100 for three or more offences. But this doesn't give *you* any money. You have to sue in the county court for your proper wages. The fact that you may have agreed to deductions being made does not prevent you suing. Such agreements are illegal.

Similar laws to the Truck Acts apply to seamen and textile workers.

If you are not protected by any statute you can sue in a county court for any improper deductions, but your boss is not guilty of a criminal offence. So all white-collar and many blue-collar workers are at risk. Your rights to written particulars of your contract, and itemised pay statements, are no substitute for a clear and well-policed Act preventing deductions from every worker's wages. The Truck Acts are a shambles and should be replaced by an Act applying to all workers enforceable in tribunals and criminal courts.

Providing work

There is no right to work. Mr Justice Asquith said in 1940:

> Provided I pay my cook her wages regularly she cannot complain if I choose to take all or any of my meals out. (*Collier v Sunday Referee*)

There are, though, three groups of workers who are legally entitled to complain if they are not provided with work, even when they are being paid:

1. Workers whose earnings vary according to their performance and attendance: Anyone paid by results or commission, or on variable shift premiums or given the opportunity to work overtime needs the physical opportunity to work. They work for basic wages **and** for the chance to earn extra. (See *Devonald v Rosser* above.)

2. Skilled workers: When Joseph Langston resigned from the AUEW at Chryslers in 1972, and was suspended on full pay for almost two years, he succeeded in his claim for a right to work. He was held to be in category **1.** above, but Lord Denning in the Court of Appeal said that it was arguable that:

> in these days an employer, when employing a skilled man, is bound to provide him with work. By which I mean that the man should be given the opportunity of doing his work when it is available and he is ready and willing to do it. *Langston v AUEW* 1974

3. Performers and writers: An actor or singer promised a leading part and then prevented from performing, and an editor not allowed to write, both lose the opportunity to gain publicity and enhance their reputation. They work for that as much as for the money in some cases.

Providing a safe system of work

Your boss is required to take reasonable care for your safety. This means providing:
- a safely operating system of work
- safe tools, plant and materials
- adequate supervision
- trained, efficient personnel

Your boss must take care not to expose you to risks that could be foreseen by a reasonable person. He will be liable for all the reasonably foreseeable consequences (such as injuries and loss of earnings) of any failure to take this care. He is also responsible for defective equipment that he has bought from some other firm if you are injured and can show that the defect was due to someone's fault elsewhere, even if you do not know whose – Employer's Liability (Defective Equipment) Act 1969.

If you are injured by the negligence of a fellow-worker you can **also** claim against your *employer* provided the act occurred in the course of employment. Since the Employer's Liability (Compulsory Insurance) Act 1969, all employers have to be insured against claims by injured workers.

Protecting your property

You are not covered if your property is stolen or damaged while you are working, unless your boss has failed to act following a number of similar incidents. If you want to protect your property against theft or breakages, and your employer's own insurance doesn't cover it, you could ask him to take out a separate policy, or force him to give you an undertaking to reimburse you.

A works rule or a notice on the wall or in the car park saying your boss is not responsible for loss or damage to your property is not always binding on you. He can escape liability for *negligence* only if it is 'reasonable' for the notice to apply, and this depends on your relative bargaining position, your awareness and what happens in practice – Unfair Contract Terms Act 1977.

All employers have a general duty to provide welfare arrangements that are, so far as is reasonably practicable, safe (HSW Act section 2).

If you work in a factory, office or shop your boss must provide 'adequate and suitable accommodation' for non-working clothes (Factories Act 1961 section 59; Offices, Shops and Railway Premises Act 1963 section 12). This does not guarantee safety, but frequent thefts and damage would make the lockers 'inadequate'. You can sue and your employer can be prosecuted by the health and safety inspectors, or ordered to improve the arrangements.

Obeying the law

Your boss must obey the law. He is also under a personal obligation to *you* which requires him to observe statutes.

> Thomas Hill collided with a motor-cyclist while driving his boss's lorry. He didn't know his boss had not insured the lorry. When the motor-cyclist was awarded damages, the court said Thomas's *boss* had to pay because he was legally obliged to comply with the law requiring compulsory insurance, and to indemnify his employees against losses. *Gregory v Ford* 1951 (HC)

The judge in this case said:

> There must be an implied term in the contract of service that the servant shall not be required to do an unlawful act ... [and] that the employer will comply with the provisions of the statute.

This implied obligation can be very useful in situations where enforcement of the law by the authorities is minimal. If for example, your boss is legally bound to you not to break the Health and Safety at Work Act, he is breaking your contract if he doesn't comply with it.

Time off

Lay representatives and members of recognised independent unions have the right to time off for union activities (see page 232). A legal right to time off is given in two other situations. Redundant workers can look for new work, or retrain (see page 201). And you can have time off for certain public duties.

Section 59 of the EP Act says employers must give you time off so that you can carry out your duties if you are a member of a

- magistrates' bench
- local authority
- tribunal
- health authority
- governing body for any maintained school

Duties include attending meetings of committees, subcommittees and other approved functions. No mention is made of time off for training for these duties, but you could argue that training is a necessary activity.

The amount of time you can get is that which is 'reasonable in all the circumstances', bearing in mind:

1. the amount of time required generally to carry out the duties, and any particular duty on any given day;

2. the amount of time off you have already had for union duties and activities; and

3. the effect of your absence on your employer's business.

Employers may use this catch-all phrase to try to stop working people taking up public positions. You could ensure fair treatment if you put these rights into collective agreements. British Nuclear Fuels, for example, agree to 24 *paid* days off a year for councillors and JPs.

The Act says nothing about pay for the days off you take. In most cases you receive payment from the body you attend. **But again you should use collective agreements to guarantee average earnings.**

How to claim time off for public duties

If you don't get time off you can apply to a tribunal **within three months**. See page 357 for the procedure. The tribunal can award compensation which relates to your loss and to your boss's 'default'. Payment of compensation in this case is penal since you are not likely to have suffered a financial loss by being refused time off.

Holidays

Wages Councils, Agricultural Boards and Statutory JICs fix holidays. In other industries in Britain there is no statutory right to *any* holidays, with or without pay, not even to bank holidays. Some Acts (such as the Factories Act) do require women and young people to be given days off, but nothing is said of payment, and anyway other days can be substituted. Holidays and holiday pay depend entirely on collective bargaining and management benevolence.

There is one exception. If you are given minimum notice which covers your holiday period, you can get holiday pay. (CE Act schedule 2 para 2.)

References

You have no legal right to a reference. If your boss writes a false reference, you may not be able to sue him for libel because this type of correspondence is often protected. He could, however, be prosecuted under the Characters of Servants Act 1792. If he tells the truth, there is nothing you can do.

You do have a right to a **written statement** giving particulars of the reasons for your dismissal if you are sacked – see page 182.

7. Workers' general obligations

To work and co-operate

Your primary obligation is to turn up for work and personally do what you have agreed to do. You are not obliged to do more than your contract requires, so you do not have to work cheerfully, or with goodwill, or do overtime if you are not required by your contract to do so.

Section 7 of the Health and Safety at Work Act says, in relation to any legal duty of your employer, that you must 'co-operate with him so far as is necessary to enable that duty to be . . . complied with'. This section has been desperately overplayed by employers. **Co-operation applies only to legal duties that are laid down in some Act or regulation.** Nevertheless, threats of legal action by employers against workers and safety representatives who refuse to submit to, say, new machinery or new working practices have occurred. Employers say they are fulfilling their *general* duty to take reasonable care by introducing new, safer equipment. **But you should not allow them to override custom and practice without agreement.** Section 7 does not require you to co-operate in this way.

To obey orders

The courts say you must obey any lawful and reasonable instructions your boss gives you. You are **not** required: **1.** to obey orders that are unlawful in that they involve you in some criminal or civil wrong, or **2.** to work on unsafe machinery, or **3.** to go outside the strict boundaries of your contract – working voluntary overtime, for instance.

Sackings following refusal to obey orders are a major source of unfair dismissal complaints. See pages 163–6 for examples.

To take reasonable care

You must take reasonable care in the way you go about your work. If you do damage or cause injury because of your carelessness, and your employer loses money, you can be ordered to pay him back. You are most unlikely to be sued for such losses but it has happened.

> One day in 1949, Martin Lister, a Romford lorry driver, was reversing in a yard. He backed into his father, Martin Lister senior. People said he was negligent. Martin senior claimed against his employer on the grounds that he was responsible for the negligent acts of his employees. Knowing that the company was insured, he expected to be paid. The company refused to pay so Martin senior went to court. The judge found that Martin junior had been careless, and that the company was responsible for his acts while in the course of his employment. He awarded £2,400 and costs, but said that Martin senior was himself partly to blame so he cut down the damages by a third to £1,600. The company then claimed off their insurance, which paid up. But then the *insurance company* forced the employers to sue Martin junior for the £1,600. He had an **obligation to take reasonable care** and to reimburse his employers if they lost money due to his lack of care. A majority of the House of Lords said OK. Martin junior was forced to pay his employers the amount *they had paid to his father*. *Lister v Romford Ice* 1957 (HL)

The practical impact of this case on industrial injuries is now minimal since most insurance companies have agreed not to force legal actions like this. It is bad for public relations. But as a principle it remains operative, and as an illustration of the judges' inhumanity it is a classic.

In *Dennis v Campbell* 1976 (HC) a betting-shop manager broke his obligation to take care when he gave credit to a punter, contrary to instructions and trade practice. The court ordered him to make good his boss's £1000 loss when the punter defaulted.

To be trustworthy

If you give away secret information about your boss's business you are breaking your contract which requires 'faithful service'. Union organisation can be weakened by this obligation. At least one union official has been prevented from asking pub workers about wages, expenses and takings.

Information given to lay or full-time officials for the purposes of negotiations (see chapter 6) is not subject to this restriction. But disclosure of secret information by individual workers may involve a breach of contract.

In the railmen's case (page 292), Lord Denning found that workers are under an implied obligation 'not wilfully to disrupt' their employer's business. This is probably wrong because it is so wide and subjective ('wilfulness'). But it is a possible weapon for employers in a dispute.

If you are considered to be untrustworthy, **your employer and his security staff are not entitled to search you unless you have agreed,** either generally in your contract, or on the occasion in question. You can resist with reasonable force. Only the police have the (limited) right to search.

Patents, copyright, inventions and your own work

You must work only for your employer during working hours. Your own time belongs to you, but this can be bought out if you agree that you won't work for anyone else while being employed by one employer. You can even agree to restrictions on your freedom to work once you leave. It is one of the many contradictions of capitalism that although the free market is paramount, workers who pick up experience, skill and ideas can be prevented from working for employers or from setting up on their own. Only if a written stipulation in your contract has the effect of starving you out will the courts say the restriction is an unjustifiable 'restraint of trade'.

> In 1977 the English and international cricket authorities changed their rules and banned from Test and county cricket any player who signed for Kerry Packer's cricket circus. Three players and Packer challenged these rulings. The High Court said that the bans were in restraint of trade. They prevented players from earning a living during the winter months even though the cricket authorities guaranteed them no employment. The unlimited bans could not be justified in the interests of the players and the cricket authorities, or in the public interest. *Greig v Insole* 1977 (HC)

Many scientists, research workers, writers and teachers create new material, and there is often a clause in their contracts saying who owns what. If there is no such stipulation, the general rule for **written material** is contained in the Copyright Act 1956. This says the boss has copyright over everything you write in the course of your employment. Newspaper writers, though, retain their own copyright.

For **inventions** and **patents**, your boss gets the benefit, but *only* if you are employed on your normal duties, or duties specifically given to you, and it is expected that an invention might occur, or if you have a *special obligation* to further your boss's interest (Patents Act 1977). If the invention is of outstanding benefit to your boss you have the right to claim a *fair share* of the profits. If the invention is just a minor part of your work, you own it even though you created it while at work for your employer.

Ending the contract

A very serious breach of contract, which goes to the root of the contract or shows that one side does not intend to be bound any longer by one or more of its essential terms, ends the contract. This is **repudiation**, or if your boss does it it is often called **constructive dismissal**. The contract can end if it is **frustrated** by an unforeseen event. It can end by **termination**, with or without notice, by either party. All of these are dealt with in chapter 10. If it is for a fixed period or for a specific task, the contract ends when this is completed.

Even though your contract is brought to an end according to the common law, that is by your boss giving you proper notice, you may still be entitled to claim a **statutory** right – discrimination, unfair dismissal, redundancy pay. See chapters 8, 10, 11.

Claims for breach of contract

For organised workers, the response to your boss's breach of contract should be negotiations or direct action. If you want to bring a legal claim you must sue in the county court or the High Court. You may get Legal Aid for advice and representation.

Since tribunals deal with statutory rights, **common law** claims by workers are rare. The courts have the power to order your boss to pay damages for losses you suffer for breach of contract.

Very rarely, the courts have given remedies to workers which have had the effect of continuing contracts of employment. In one case, a worker's contract was ordered to continue because the relationship of 'mutual trust' had not been broken – *Hill v Parsons* 1971 (CA). People who are 'office-holders', like policemen and some trade union officials, have also got the courts to give them the right to continue in office, instead of merely getting damages. But section 16 of the

TULR Act prevents courts from making orders to compel people to work, and in practice courts don't order employers to keep workers on. Tribunals have power to order reinstatement, (see page 180) but if your employer refuses to comply he can't be forced to take you back.

The Lord Chancellor and the Scottish Secretary have power to extend the jurisdiction of tribunals to cover some breach of contract claims. These are claims when you are also claiming some other right – for example, written particulars of your contract; or if you quit or are sacked – for example, arrears of wages. (EP Act section 109).

Some breaches of contract are also **criminal** offences – orders to work with unsafe machinery, illegal deductions, underpayment in Wages Council industries. In these cases, inform the Health and Safety Inspector, or the Wages Inspector, and your union.

Your boss can sue you if you break the contract. In practice this rarely happens. The Coal Board did it in 1956 following a ban on Saturday working, and other employers have got injunctions in disputes (see page 301).

Collective action

The law of contract is concerned only with individuals. *In fact*, employment contracts depend heavily on collective agreements and custom and practice established by organised workers. **Your only hope of getting any movement towards equality of bargaining power in contracts of employment is by collective action.** The courts treat all aspects of your contract as though they have been **agreed**. By union organisation you can ensure that all aspects *are* negotiated and agreed.

Summary

1. Every employee has a contract of employment, even though there may be nothing written or signed.

2. You have rights before you make a contract of employment – rights connected with disablement, discrimination and 'spent' convictions.

3. Your contract may include some written terms – set out in a statement, collective agreement, Wages Council order, arbitration award or works rules.

4. Unwritten terms of contract can be implied from custom and practice in your industry.

5. Every contract of employment contains, unless specifically excluded, unwritten general obligations on employers – to pay wages, not to make deductions, to provide safe conditions.

6. Employees have general obligations too – to work, co-operate, obey reasonable instructions, take care and be trustworthy.

7. A contract can end by resignation, dismissal (with or without notice), very serious breach of contract, or by a totally unforeseen event which makes the contract impossible to carry out.

8. You can claim damages in the courts for breach of contract, but the courts rarely give you the right to be reinstated if you are sacked.

9. As an individual worker, the law of contract is stacked against you. Realistic steps towards control over your contractual conditions can only be made through collective action.

4.

Sick Pay and Medical Suspension

Your right to be paid when sick / sick pay and social security / sickness while you are under notice / suspension on health and safety grounds / your right to be paid / offers of alternative work away from hazards / how to claim your pay / collective action / and a summary.

Medical reasons may prevent you working in several ways. You may be incapable of work, or be advised by your doctor not to work, or you may decide that conditions are so unsafe that you refuse to work. Or you may be suspended by your boss for health and safety reasons.

If you are sacked or in danger of getting the sack because of your ill-health or incapacity you may be able to claim unfair dismissal. **By using the arguments and cases set out on pages 159–163, you may be able to protect your job.**

If you are off work for medical reasons you have the right to payment in some of the following ways:

1. as wages from your employer according to your contract of employment

2. as pay from your employer according to your EP Act rights during suspension on medical grounds

3. as maternity pay from your employer (see chapter 7)

4. as social security benefits (see chapter 12)

This chapter deals with 1. and 2.

Where to find the law

Contractual rights to sick pay are based on common law. The Contracts of Employment Act (CE Act) requires written particulars of sick pay (section 4). Pay while suspended on medical grounds is provided for by the Employment Protection Act (EP Act) sections 29–33.

Sick pay

Contractual rights

There is no general **statutory** right to sick pay. The idea that sickness is a problem for the worker and not for the employer is still common. Collective bargaining has achieved some basic entitlement to sick pay for about 70 per cent of all workers. The rest must rely on common law or the 'charity' of their employers.

The contractual position is that **if sick pay is provided for by your contract – whether it is specified in writing, orally agreed, implied from custom and practice or incorporated from a collective agreement – the courts will uphold your legal right to sick pay.**

We have seen (page 29) that your boss must give you written particulars of any terms and conditions relating to sickness and injury. If there are no such terms, the statement must say that. If you don't get a written statement, or disagree with one you do get, you can complain to a tribunal.

Collective agreements vary considerably in the rights they give. If better sick pay is given by other employers in your industry, you could improve yours by claiming under Schedule 11 of the EP Act for the going rate (see chapter 17). If you have no right to sick pay, a claim under Schedule 11 based on the general level of conditions would be likely to succeed, in view of the widespread acceptance of sick pay schemes throughout the country.

If you can't get sick pay through collective bargaining, or by drawing attention to the fact by demanding written particulars, or by a Schedule 11 claim, the courts can use their power to decide that you are covered. When the Lord Chancellor gives tribunals the jurisdiction to hear breach of contract claims, tribunals will decide this. (EP Act Section 109.)

Courts and tribunals firstly ask about what was discussed at the time you were hired, and then look at custom and practice in the industry. If that fails to show whether or not sick pay is provided, courts and tribunals *may* say there is a 'presumption' that pay should continue as usual during sickness. One judge said that a production manager in a skirt factory was entitled to be paid his basic rate **and** his bonus while he was off sick for two months. The judge said:

> Where the written terms of the contract of service are silent as to what is to happen in regard to the employee's rights to be paid whilst he is absent from work due to sickness, the employer remains liable to continue paying so long as the contract is not [terminated] by proper notice, except where a condition to the contrary can properly be inferred from all the facts and the evidence in the case. If the employer – and, of course, it will always be the employer – seeks to establish an implied condition that no wages are payable, it is for him to [prove it].
> *Orman v Saville Sportswear* 1960 (HC)

So in the absence of any definite evidence about what is to happen during sickness, you are entitled to the benefit of the doubt. This advantage is limited since you must be told about sick pay in your written particulars under the Contracts of Employment Act (CE Act). If these say you get nothing while sick, they probably (but not necessarily) override the presumption.

Sick pay and social security benefits

Courts have held that social security benefit for sickness is **additional to**, not **instead of**, any contractual rights. The DHSS can't reduce your benefit if you get sick pay. Many employers, however, insist on deducting social security benefit from sick pay, despite the fact that you have paid for your social security benefit with your contributions. You should therefore fight any attempt by your boss to offset social security benefit against sick pay.

Sickness while under notice

The only time that your boss is under a **statutory** obligation to pay you during sickness is when

■ you are entitled to the minimum notice under the CE Act, or up to one week extra

■ you are given notice and

■ you go sick while serving your notice (CE Act schedule 2)

Example: You have been employed for four-and-a-half years. You are entitled to a minimum of four weeks notice under the Act. If your contract gives you five

weeks or less, you can get paid for all those weeks, even
if you are sick and even if your contract gives no right
to sick pay. But if your contract gives you a right to six
or more weeks notice (that is, more than one week above
the minimum) you don't have a right to sick pay.

Suspension on health and safety grounds

Suspension or dismissal?

What if your boss tells you not to come to work for the
sake of your own or other people's health? You can claim
reinstatement or compensation for unfair dismissal (see page
180). If you are sacked following a doctor's examination under
regulations listed in the EP Act schedule 2 dealing with lead,
paint, asbestos, rubber, tin, chemicals, pottery dust and radio-
active substances, or **approved codes**, you can claim unfair
dismissal, provided you have **four weeks' service** (not 26 weeks
as usually needed for unfair dismissal). These regulations
generally require employers to remove workers from exposure
to certain substances following examination by a medical
adviser from the Employment Medical Advisory Service
(EMAS).

For example, in the case of ionising radiation, workers
must be taken off their normal job if their film-badges show
that certain limits have been exceeded. An EMAS doctor
must tell your employer if your health would be endangered
by continued exposure to lead or other chemicals.

Dismissal following a doctor's recommendation under
one of the regulations or codes may be unfair since suspension
will be the more reasonable solution. If the plant is closed
down as a result of many of you being suspended, you may
get **redundancy money** and **medical suspension pay**.

The rules on suspension are just the same as those
applying to suspension for discipline and shortage of work.
**Employers have no right to suspend without pay unless your
contract allows this.** See page 55. If it does and you are
suspended, you may be entitled to medical suspension pay
under the EP Act.

Who can claim medical suspension pay?

Section 29 of the EP Act entitles you to be paid if you
are suspended from work, or from work you normally do, by

an employer who is acting in accordance with a doctor's report made under one of the regulations or codes described above. Contracts for 12 or less weeks are excluded.

It is important to realise that this right is extremely limited. It does not come into operation if you are suspended for medical reasons not falling under one of the specific regulations. It may not apply to suspension following a prohibition or improvement notice issued by a Health and Safety Inspector, or situations where workers demand closure of part of a plant for safety reasons. You may have to negotiate ad hoc terms in these circumstances but if you are suspended you can **argue** as follows:

1. You have a contractual right to be paid unless your contract says otherwise. Failure to pay is breach of contract **and** it may be grounds for claiming constructive unfair dismissal (page 55).

2. If you refuse to work in conditions which violate a code of practice under Schedule 2 of the EP Act, you can treat yourself as suspended.

3. If your boss forces you to work in unsafe conditions contrary to the HSW Act or any regulation, he is breaking your contract and you can claim as in **1.** above and report him to the Health and Safety Inspector.

You can claim medical suspension pay if you have been employed for four weeks or more. If you are actually **incapable** of work you are excluded. In other words, the right applies only if you are suspended because further exposure may be dangerous, and does not apply if things have got so bad that physically you cannot work. You have to claim sick pay under your contract and social security benefits. These may be worth less than medical suspension pay.

Alternative work

You won't get paid if your boss offers you suitable alternative work, whether or not it is work within your contract, and you unreasonably turn this down (section 30). Guidance on what this means can be found in the cases on redundancy (page 196). A general rule is that you are not obliged to take a cut in wages. But tribunals may say it is unreasonable to refuse a lower paid job on a *temporary* basis.

You may also lose your right to pay if you do not fall in with reasonable requirements your employer imposes for making sure you are available. Clearly, there is a danger here that established working arrangements could be disturbed under the threat of withdrawal of medical suspension pay, but the key word is 'reasonable'. For example, your boss may insist you don't go on holiday, or that you report regularly to your workplace. These might be reasonable requirements.

How much can you get?

You can get 'a week's pay' (see page 344) every week for up to 26 weeks. Your boss can offset this by any money he is bound to give you under your contract. Ex gratia payments can't be offset. If you are still not authorised to go back to your normal job, your EP Act right runs out. It might be advisable to insert a clause in your collective agreement providing for pay during suspension on health and safety grounds. Payments under an agreement like this would be offset against your right under the Act, but they could last beyond the 26-week period.

Temporary replacements

If your job is taken over by another worker hired specifically for this purpose, (s)he can be sacked when you return, provided (s)he was informed **in writing** at the time (s)he was taken on that (s)he would be sacked on your return. But your boss must still show he acted reasonably in actually carrying out the sacking – he must look for alternative vacancies etc. However, if the replacement has not worked for more than 26 weeks (s)he can't claim unfair dismissal.

How to claim

If you are refused pay you can make a claim to a tribunal **within three months**. See page 357 for the procedure. If you succeed, the tribunal **must** order your boss to pay you.

Collective action

The rights provided by the common law are not judge-proof and the statutory rights are puny. You can take sick pay **out of** the area of employer benevolence and **into** the area of workers' rights if you are organised. Only by union action can you guarantee your rights.

Summary

1. At common law, courts have held that pay must continue during sickness.

2. Your CE Act statement must say what rights you have during sickness.

3. Sick pay can't be deducted from social security benefit. Benefit can be deducted from sick pay only if your contract provides for this.

4. You have a right to be paid for 26 weeks if your boss suspends you from your normal work following a doctor's report made under certain health and safety laws.

5.

Lay-Off and Short-Time

Your right to pay during a lay-off / where to find the law / contractual rights / guarantee payments / when you can claim them / who can claim / how much you get / suspending the guarantee / industrial disputes / collective agreements / how to claim a guarantee payment / the effect on social security benefits / trade union demands / lay-offs leading to redundancy / collective action / and a summary.

Many industries are covered by collective agreements which guarantee wages during temporary periods when work is not available. In fact, these agreements define the occasions when employers can *escape* paying wages. They apply mainly to manual workers.

The Employment Protection Act (EP Act) gives all workers the right to a minimum payment if they are laid off in certain circumstances. Longer term lay-off gives you the option of claiming redundancy pay.

Whether you negotiate collective agreements, or make ad hoc arrangements, or use your legal rights, your argument is the same. **Loss of production and disruption is a business risk assumed by employers. Workers should not suffer from lay-offs or wage cuts** when employers refuse to accept the consequences of the risk they have voluntarily undertaken in the name of profit.

Agreements or legal rights guaranteeing income security stand or fall according to three tests:

1. do they provide adequate levels of remuneration while employment lasts?

2. can they be suspended? and
3. in what circumstances and with what warning can they be suspended?

Where to find the law

The Employment Protection Act 1975 deals with rights to guaranteed wages (sections 22, 28). See Redundancy Payments Act 1965 for redundancy pay following lay-off or short-time (sections 5–7).

Contractual rights

Your employer has no right to suspend you from work, to cut your minimum rate, to put you on short-time working or to lay you off unless this is provided for in your contract. Without your agreement, your boss's action is a breach of contract, and in some cases you can treat this as grounds for claiming unfair dismissal and redundancy pay.

> G. Smith, a foreman, was told by his boss on 8 February 1974 that he was being suspended for two or three weeks and it might be the beginning of April before he would be back at work. On 20 February 1974, Mr Smith got work elsewhere. On 25 February 1974 he asked for and received his cards. He claimed redundancy pay. Lord McDonald said his contract didn't allow his boss to suspend him, he hadn't agreed to it, and it amounted to a sacking. *An employer is not entitled unilaterally to suspend his employee unless there is some provision express or implied in the contract of employment permitting him to do so* said the judge. G. Smith got his redundancy pay. *McKenzie v Smith* 1976 (Scottish Court of Session)

You can claim unfair dismissal and redundancy pay, or, if you go back to work, you have the right to be *paid* for the days you were suspended. If you agree to the suspension, or if your contract is governed by a collective agreement which gives your boss the right to suspend, his action is *not* illegal.

> The engineering national agreement gives employers the right to suspend workers in certain circumstances. Burroughs Machines left the EEF. During a strike in one part of the company, workers were laid off in another. They claimed that as they were no longer covered by the national agreement, the company had no right to suspend them and that this amounted to dismissal. The court decided that the men's contracts still depended on the EEF as it was in force when they had been hired. So the em-

ployer could legally suspend them. *Burroughs Machines v Timmoney* 1977 (Scottish Court of Session, Inner House)

In contracts where employers do have the right to suspend workers or put them on short-time you have the right to claim a **guarantee payment** under the EP Act.

Guarantee payments

You can claim a guarantee payment from your boss under section 22 of the EP Act 1975 in two situations

■ your employer's need for the kind of work you do (or can be required to do) is lessened,

■ an 'occurrence' affects normal working in relation to your job.

These situations include a fall in orders, bankruptcy of a customer, lack of raw materials and sudden temporary setbacks such as power failures, floods, fires, bad weather and some industrial disputes. But they don't seem to cover redundancy occurring as a result of your employer *ceasing* to carry on business. Here you would claim redundancy pay (see chapter 11) and it may be worth claiming a guarantee payment as well. If redundancy follows a lay-off, claim both.

If, as a result of one of the above events, you are not given work, you are entitled to payment. You must be deprived of work for a whole working day because the Act talks of 'workless days'. **This gives employers the chance to avoid payments.** All they have to do is call you in and give you work for a short period of time. This means you are not deprived of work throughout a normal working day so no payment is due, even though your earnings for the time you work are minimal. Refuse to leave the site, and claim your contractual right not to have your earnings reduced.

Payments are made for workless days, each day leading to a separate payment. This is sometimes going to be more beneficial than arrangements providing for a guaranteed **weekly** earnings level, because you could be laid off for two days and yet receive more for three days' work than you would under the weekly guarantee in your collective agreement. Under a **daily** assessment each day is treated as entitling you to the statutory payment. A day means from midnight to midnight, but if your working day would normally spread over midnight there are special rules. If you would normally work more hours before midnight than after, for instance on a 6 p.m. to 2 a.m. shift, the first day is regarded as the workless day. If you would normally work 8 p.m. to 4 a.m., or work more hours after midnight than before, the second day counts instead.

If the lay-off or short-time working continues you should bear in mind the circumstances in which this can itself constitute redundancy – see page 64.

Who can claim?

Share-fishermen, dockers, and people who mainly work outside Great Britain or for their spouses can't claim. Some *groups* of workers are also deprived of the right to claim. These are:

1. workers who have less than four weeks' continuous employment;

2. part-time workers (that is, less than 16 hours a week with exceptions – see page 341);

3. workers hired on fixed-term contracts of 12 weeks or less;

4. workers who are hired for a particular job which is not expected to last more than 12 weeks.

If you actually work more than 12 weeks you *can* claim whatever your contract says or you previously were told by your boss. If you have no normal working hours on the day in question, such as a school cleaner during the school holidays, you are also excluded.

Why are all these workers excluded from the right to guarantee pay? The loss of a normal day's pay is no less serious just because you are on a short contract or have recently started a job, and indeed it is *more* serious since you may have been unemployed for some time previously.

The *practical* effect of these exclusions is that industries which are notoriously prone to insecurity and a high labour turnover such as building, civil engineering, ship-repair and catering remain uncovered by the law. Without union opposition, short-term contracts and early dismissals may actually increase as employers try to escape the obligation to make payments. So remember:

1. A series of short-term contracts counts as continuous employment.

2. If you work 26 weeks you can claim unfair dismissal. You will win if you can show your boss intended by short-term contracts to avoid his obligations – see *Terry v Sussex C.C.* (page 156).

How much is guaranteed?

Payments are not based on earnings but on a day's pay using the formula for 'a week's pay' (see page 344). The method is different for different workers.

1. If you work a regular number of hours each week. Take your basic rate and any bonus, commission and conditioned (that is, guaranteed) overtime and divide that figure by the number of hours you are required to work. This gives you your 'guaranteed hourly rate'. Your guarantee payment for any workless day, subject to the government maximum, is that rate multiplied by the number of hours you would normally have worked on that day.

Example: You get £1.20 an hour for a basic 40 hour week. This comes to £48+10 per cent bonus (£4.80)+ 5 hours conditioned overtime at £1.60 an hour (£8). You work 9 hours a day, 5 days a week. Your guaranteed hourly rate is

$$\frac{£48 + £4.80 + £8}{45} = £1.35$$

Your guarantee payment for a day should be £1.35×9, or £12.15.

But this is subject to the maximum figure in force (£6.60 in 1978).

So you get only £6.60.

2. If your hours vary from day to day. Many office workers work flexitime or nine-day fortnights. They can work any hours (usually during the day, between say 8 a.m. and 8 p.m.) provided they do the stated number of hours each week, or fortnight or month. If you are laid off and your employer disputes the number of hours you would have worked you have to prove your entitlement.

3. If you are on shift, or regularly work different numbers of hours each week. Find your guaranteed hourly rate as in **1.** above, but instead of taking one week as the starting point, you look back over the 12-week period that ended the week before you were laid off. Calculate the average hourly rate. If you have recently started and therefore do not have 12 weeks' service you can look at the average hours you could have *expected* to work, and the hours done by comparable fellow-employees of your employer. If you have been absent through sickness, holidays or lay-off in the 12-week period you can look further back to make up 12 full weeks.

If you work nights, and you do more hours before midnight than after, you are deemed to be laid off on the day when you would have worked the longer hours.

Example: if you are laid off from 10 p.m. on Thursday to 8 a.m. on Friday the 'workless day' is Friday. This may operate against some workers, especially in engineering, who work four long nights and one short. You can't claim if you are laid off on your (short) Friday night as you have already claimed for the night before.

Altering normal hours

Sometimes contracts are altered temporarily during a lay-off by agreement between management and unions. If this has happened, and you have to calculate your guarantee payment, all references are to the old contract, not the new one. So your right is based on working hours in normal conditions.

Limits on guaranteed pay

Your rights are subject to the strict financial limitations imposed by EP Act.

1. The maximum you could get in 1978 in any day was £6.60, so if your calculations show that you would have got more than this you are prevented from claiming the surplus over £6.60 (see example on page 58).

2. You can only claim a maximum of five days in any three-month period. The period begins on the first of February, May, August and November in each year. If you normally work less than five days a week, for example, if you work four days at 10 hours a day, you can claim a guarantee for only four days a quarter. If your week varies you take the average number of days worked over each of the previous 12 weeks.

These limits on money and days can be increased by the Employment Secretary each year. He has to take account of the economic situation and average earnings in the country.

When these levels are compared with arrangements already existing in organised workplaces they look fairly insignificant – see page 63.

3. You are not entitled to the full guarantee payment if you receive any *contractual* payment for the days in question. This must be offset and you cannot claim your full contractual entitlement if you have been paid the guaranteed amount.

Example A: you are covered by an agreement providing guaranteed weekly earnings or minimum time rates of £30. You normally earn £50 a week. You are laid off after earning £30 in three days. The agreement does not come into operation – you have already earned your £30. But for the two idle days you can claim under the EP Act.

Example B: on the other hand, if you earn less than the agreement guarantees you – say only £20 for the three days worked – you are contractually entitled under your agreement to a further £10. When you claim your guarantee under the Act for the two idle days, your boss can say: I have already paid you £10 according to the agreement and this works out at £5 for each of the idle days. So I can offset this against my statutory obligation. You can claim only the difference between £5 and the amount of the statutory guarantee.

To get the most money in this situation DON'T claim your statutory rights. You can claim for only five days in the three-month period. Better not to waste one of these days in claiming less than the statutory maximum. Instead claim only if you have already earned more than your agreement guarantees (as in Example A above) or where for some reason the agreement is suspended. (See below.)

Suspending the guarantee

Suspension of the right to a guarantee payment is the term used in many collective agreements to show when employers can avoid payments. Under the Act your right is suspended in three broad situations:

1. if you don't take alternative work;
2. if you don't comply with reasonable requirements; and
3. if there is an industrial dispute involving your employer or an associated firm. These are dealt with separately.

Alternative work

Section 23 of the EP Act says that the guarantee is not payable if an employer has offered to provide alternative work 'which is suitable in all the circumstances, whether or not work which the employee is under his contract employed to perform, and the employee has unreasonably refused that offer'.

This is similar to the rule used in redundancy cases. It means you consider both the *objective* nature of the work itself and the *personal* reasons you may have for refusing to do it. There is no requirement that you *must* work on different jobs at lower wages. If your boss threatens to suspend the guarantee if you refuse to take the new work, threaten legal action.

Section 23 may give your employer scope unilaterally to change custom and practice and working arrangements. He may say that rules of demarcation don't apply, and he may threaten to suspend the guarantee if you don't accept new working rules, or even if you refuse them pending negotiations. Section 23 might be taken by tribunals to mean that 'in all the circumstances' of a temporary recession it is unreasonable to refuse to do alternative work even though this cuts right across existing practices and agreed procedures. Tribunals may look sympathetically on a worker who is faced with an ultimatum of either **permanently** changing his job within the same company, or losing his redundancy payment. They may be less sympathetic to workers who refuse to help their employer in a difficult period by accepting alternative work for a few days. **So use your industrial strength to counter any threat by your boss to suspend the guarantee.**

Reasonable requirements

The guarantee can be suspended if a worker does not 'comply with reasonable **requirements imposed by his employer** with a view to ensuring that his services are available', (section 23, emphasis added). This may mean that you can be required to be available at different locations or to clock in every day. We have seen that if you do some work you lose your right to a guarantee payment, since it is only available for 'workless' days. In this case, you should refuse to work or argue that your contract gives you the right to be paid in full. If the requirement is unreasonable, threaten legal action to get the guarantee.

Industrial disputes

Your employer can suspend the guarantee if you are laid off due to a dispute involving any employee of his, or of any associated employer.

This exclusion strengthens the hand of employers engaged in a dispute. It attempts to ensure that no pressure is brought to bear on them by other employers complaining that, as a result of the dispute, they have to make guarantee payments to their workers. More to the point, it has the effect of dividing workers from each other at a time when they should be closing ranks. Consequential lay-offs due to industrial disputes in the motor industry, and the media's treatment of them, frequently turn laid off workers against those in dispute.

During some disputes you lose the right to a guarantee payment but you can still claim social security benefit, for example if you are not participating in or directly interested in a dispute at your place of work (see page 212).

Collective agreements

All the parties to a collective agreement or Wages Council can apply to the Employment Secretary to have their agreement override the EP Act guarantees. The only requirement is that the agreement must allow for reference to an industrial tribunal or an independent arbitrator if any worker claims a disputed payment. Since there is no requirement that the agreement be more favourable than the EP Act, and since you can take advantage of whichever of the guarantees (that is, in the Act or in the agreement) suits you better, there is no point in closing the door to this choice by seeking exemption from the Act. The TUC has advised unions not to apply but by 1978 exemptions were granted in the following industries: civil engineering, demolition, building (England and Wales), refractories, fibreboard, footwear, multiwall sack and carton manufacture, together with several individual company exemptions.

How to claim a guarantee payment

If you have not been paid your guarantee in accordance with the EP Act you can apply to a tribunal. See page 357 for the procedure. The claim must be filed **within three months** of the day for which you are claiming.

If a tribunal hears the claim and agrees with you, it must order your employer to pay you the full amount under the EP Act. If he cannot pay because he has gone bust you can apply to the Department of Employment. (See page 206.)

Lay-offs and social security

You can't claim social security benefits for a day when you receive a guarantee payment. Careful timing by agreement on short-time working and lay-offs can give you the maximum combination of guarantee and social security payments. See chapter 12 for rules on social security.

Lay-offs and continuity

A temporary cessation of work does not break your continuity of employment. In fact, the time when you are laid off counts as part of your continuous employment. See page 339.

Trade union demands

Many workers are already covered by collective agreements which provide better protection than the EP Act. The statutory right to a guarantee arises in many more circumstances than in most agreements. For example, in chemicals and electrical cable making the guarantee is suspended if there are circumstances 'beyond the employer's control'. While many agreements provide for suspension, this can only be done with **notice** (e.g. two weeks in chemicals) or by **agreement** (for example, engineering). The EP Act guarantees are automatically suspended without the need for notice or agreement.

Most existing agreements require you to be available for work and exclude you from payment if you are sick, on holiday, or are not ready and willing to work. The National Working Rules for the building industry, for example, require you to be available for work in your own or 'any other suitable building industry occupation, or at any other site where work is available', a very onerous stipulation.

Exemptions during disputes are found in almost every collective agreement. In some the guarantee is suspended whenever there is a dispute *anywhere*, or in any firm which is covered by the agreement – as in engineering, shipbuilding and repairing, and building. Perhaps the best is the British Steel agreement which disqualifies workers only if there is a dispute at the same *plant*.

The value of the statutory guarantee is small when compared with arrangements already existing in organised workplaces. In engineering you are guaranteed 40 hours at the minimum time rate, and there is no maximum duration. At Fords you get 80 per cent of your personal hourly rate for up to 15 days during any one lay-off. In the building industry you get your standard weekly rate for your normal hours (but after one entirely workless week this can be suspended). The rubber industry agreement provides payments for a year.

By juggling social security payments and collective agreements you can usually do better than the EP Act. **Payments under the Act are taxable.**

If you are negotiating a guaranteed pay agreement you should demand the following:

1. No suspension except by agreement or after long notice

2. Pay should be given in a dispute to all workers not involved

3. The EP Act should not be taken as a guide on the amount or duration of payments.

Redundancy through lay-off/short-time

You can claim redundancy pay in some periods of lay-off or short-time working (LOST). If your boss has no right in the contract of employment to lay you off, you can claim unfair dismissal and redundancy pay. If there is a right to lay-off, claim a payment. You can claim redundancy pay while your contract is still alive.

This section applies **only to employees who are entitled by length of service etc. to claim redundancy pay**. For details see pages 155, 186. The usual definition of redundancy does not apply to LOST situations. Instead, section 5 of the RP Act says you can activate the complex procedure if you have been laid off or put on short-time (or a combination of both) for

 ■ four consecutive weeks, or
 ■ six weeks in any 13-week period

The definitions are important: lay-off means you receive no pay at all. Short-time means you receive half of a 'week's pay' (see page 344) or less.

You can start the ball rolling on a claim for redundancy pay following this timetable:

1. LOST continues for the appropriate period, that is four or six weeks.

2. Not later than four weeks after this period you tell

your boss in writing that you intend to claim redundancy pay.

3. Within seven days your employer must give you written counter-notice that you can resume work. It must state that, within the next four weeks, work will be resumed for a minimum of 13 continuous weeks without any LOST.

4. Whether or not your employer gives notice, if there is no resumption within four weeks of your notice, you must claim redundancy from your boss and give notice of termination according to your contract.

5. If your employer does not give you redundancy pay, you apply to a tribunal for it. See page 357 for the procedure.

There are many pitfalls in this technical procedure, and you should consider the consequences of giving notice to terminate. It may be a useful tactic for you to give notice of your claim, but giving notice to terminate is very risky.

Collective action

The statutory rights are no substitute for direct action to attack unilateral changes in job security. Rearrangement of hours of work, and loss of earnings, **can** be stopped by union action.

Summary

1. Unless your contract allows it, your boss can't suspend you or lay you off without your agreement.

2. If he does you can claim for breach of contract, unfair dismissal and redundancy pay.

3. If he does have the right to lay you off, you can claim a guarantee payment under the EP Act.

4. The right to pay can be suspended if you aren't available for work, don't comply with reasonable instructions, or if there is an industrial dispute involving your employer or an associated employer.

5. Many collective agreements provide better protection. You can claim the best of both rights if you have an agreement.

6. You can claim social security benefit during some lay-offs.

7. You can claim redundancy pay after lay-off or short-time working over a specified period.

6.

Discipline

Management's view of discipline at work /
your protection against action for taking part
in union activities / discipline which is
discriminatory on the grounds of race or sex /
protection against being prejudiced for having
a conviction / your contractual rights on
discipline / rules and procedures / the Code
of Practice / the forms of discipline –
warnings, reprimands, fines, deductions,
suspension, demotion and transfer / the
special rules for police, armed forces, merchant
seamen, apprentices, and the professions /
whether you should negotiate disciplinary
rules / what to include in your agreements /
disciplinary action against management? / and
a summary.

The extent to which your employer is able to take
disciplinary action against you is directly related to your
organisation and bargaining strength. Shopfloor discipline is
one of the areas of labour law *least* affected by statutory
rights and *most* affected by workers' resistance. In well-
organised workplaces no disciplinary action is carried out if
there is organised dissent.

The Tories have long recognised this. In 1968 they put
forward a plan to regulate discipline and to stop strikes
(*Fair Deal at Work*), in which they said (on page 42):

about two-fifths of all stoppages and about one-fifth of
days lost through strikes stem from disputes about 'the
employment or discharge of workers and other working
arrangements, rules and discipline'.

Number two on the Tories' list of 'main causes' of disputes, after pay claims, was 'dismissal or disciplining of fellow-workers'.

Disputes over discipline are a more serious threat to management than disputes over wages. Employers expect workers to want more money than they are prepared to pay; and bargaining, coupled with industrial action, are essential features of industrial relations. A dispute over disciplinary action taken against a worker has, though, two dangerous implications for employers. It shows an outright resistance to management prerogative, and it demonstrates the extent of workers' solidarity over what management sees as purely an individual matter.

Successive governments have tried recently to mould discipline into a manageable form. They have done this by encouraging agreed disciplinary procedures rather than by direct legal intervention. Whether or not unionised workers should get involved in agreements relating to disciplinary procedures or disciplinary rules is discussed at the end of this chapter.

Disciplinary action is taken to be management's response to an individual's fault, either as a punishment or as an attempt to correct it. Such statutory rights as there are – the law of contract and the Code – all treat discipline in this personal way. **Discipline should, however, be regarded as a single example of an action that could be taken against all other workers. For this reason collective support is as important as it is in enforcing every other right.**

The scope of this chapter is disciplinary action **short of dismissal**. For dismissals, see chapter 10.

Where to find the law

The Contracts of Employment Act 1972 (CE Act) section 4 requires written particulars of rules; the Advisory, Conciliation and Arbitration Service (ACAS) Code of Practice on Disciplinary Practice and Procedures ('the Code') gives the framework. The Truck Acts 1831–96 deal with fines and deductions. The Sex Discrimination Act 1975 (SD Act) section 4, Race Relations Act 1976 (RR Act) section 2, Employment Protection Act (EP Act) section 53 and the Rehabilitation of Offenders Act 1974 (RO Act) outlaw discrimination.

Trade union activity

As we shall see (page 224), you have the right under section 53 of the EP Act not to have action taken against you by your employer if the purpose is to prevent or deter you from being a member of an independent trade union, or joining in its activities at an appropriate time. Penalising you in any way, or subjecting you to disciplinary action, would entitle you to claim at a tribunal an unlimited amount of compensation.

It doesn't matter what form the deterrence or penalisation takes. If you are denied a Christmas bonus because you took part in union activities (which might include industrial action in pursuit of your union's objectives) you can complain, even though the bonus was a non-contractual gift from the boss which you could not demand as of right. Your boss must show why he took action against you, and that it wasn't anything to do with your union rights.

Union representatives also have the right under the Code (see below) not to be disciplined until their full-time official or senior representative has been involved.

Racial and sex discrimination

Discrimination is dealt with in chapter 8 but it should be noted here that victimisation because you brought a claim, or intended to, or gave evidence at a hearing, is specifically outlawed (SD Act section 4 and RR Act section 2).

Living down a conviction

We have seen (page 26) that you are under no obligation to disclose spent convictions when answering questions. If your boss discovers that you have a record which you are entitled to regard as spent, any disciplinary action taken against you is unlawful, **even if your contract permits it** (for example, suspension). Section 4 of the RO Act makes it unlawful for an employer to 'prejudice [a worker] in any way in any occupation or employment'.

How do you exercise this right? Parliament drafted this legislation without *specifically* providing either a remedy for you or a punishment for your employer. This means that you can challenge 'prejudicial' action (short of dismissal) only by alleging breach of contract or suing for defamation. Collective action, therefore, is the only effective method.

Your contractual rights

Your boss can take action short of dismissal only if it is provided for in your contract or if it does not affect your contractual rights. In your hands, theoretically at least, is the extent to which you let disciplinary action happen. If you do not concede the right, there is none. If you allow your boss to write works rules establishing penalties for breach of them, or if a collective agreement deals with them, you are liable to be disciplined. You can't stop action that doesn't strictly affect your contractual rights. If a non-contractual benefit is withheld, for example, you have no legal cause for complaint, unless it is victimisation for union activity.

The general advice, therefore, is: **don't agree to disciplinary penalties in a contract or agreement.** Operating against you if you take this line is the fact that the CE Act requires a written statement of rules.

Written rules and procedures

The CE Act requires employers to give written particulars to most workers. These must spell out 'any disciplinary rules applicable . . . or refer to a document which is reasonably accessible . . . and which specifies such rules'. The purpose of this section is to introduce clear rules which would cut down the number of disputes over discipline, and would restore to management its right to discipline. It also has the effect of encouraging employers to introduce a contractual duty on workers to submit to discipline. In fact, the Act does not allow employers to make *new* rules – it simply says that if they exist, they must be set down.

If you don't have clear rules and management's power to discipline is regulated by your collective resistance, there is often no point in accepting a written statement of the rules. If rules actually exist and are operating to your satisfaction, there is no harm in having them in writing. But if they are only periodically enforced, or do not exist, **you should not accept a codification in a written statement as this will usually become contractual.** Many employers have tried to introduce *new* rules since this requirement came in in 1976, on the pretext that the law required new rules to be formulated.

The CE Act says you must be told of the disciplinary procedure and that you have a right of appeal from *any* disciplinary decision (although there must presumably be a limit on this) to a specifically designated person. The form and content of agreed procedures are not laid down in the Act, and are dealt with below.

The Code of Practice

The Code of Practice encourages negotiated procedures for dealing with discipline. The Code lists 'essential features' for any agreement. It should: be speedy; be written; state the range of disciplinary actions and who they apply to; say who has authority to discipline; provide for notice of any complaint, and for a right to state a case and be accompanied by a representative; require management to investigate the case carefully and to give the reasons for any penalty; ensure that no dismissal occurs for a first breach of discipline except for gross misconduct; and give a right of appeal to a level not previously involved.

The Code recommends (paragraph 12) that the following steps should be taken in all cases except those for which the rules allow instant dismissal:

1. formal oral warning, or, for 'more serious issues'

2. written warning, setting out the nature of the offence and the likely consequences of further offences

3. final written warning saying further misconduct will lead to suspension, or dismissal, or some other penalty

4. transfer or suspension (if allowed by contract) or dismissal.

Details should be given in writing to the worker, who should be told of his/her right of appeal. Records should be kept, but breach of discipline should be removed from records after an 'appropriate period of satisfactory conduct'.

Special provisions should be made for **people working nights,** or working in **isolated places** who don't have access to someone in authority. **Union representatives** should not be disciplined beyond a possible oral warning until the case has been discussed with a full-time official or senior representative. Workers accused of **criminal offences** outside employment should not be sacked if a charge is pending or if they are in custody awaiting trial. Conviction should not be an automatic reason for sacking – see pages 169–173 for general rules.

What kind of disciplinary action?

Warnings

Warnings, either oral or written, can be given even if there is no mention of them in your contract. This is because they do not detract from your basic contractual rights. Cumulatively they may do, in that they can lead to dismissal, but since they are not contrary to any of your rights under your contract, your boss can give them out.

The steps laid down in the Code should be followed. Warnings should be unambiguous and clearly specify the offence, and the consequences of further offences.

Reprimand

Unless some penalty infringing your contractual rights is attached, a reprimand is within the scope of every employer's prerogative.

Fines and deductions: all workers

It follows from the law of contract that your boss cannot fine you or make a deduction from your wages unless there is a very clear rule or custom allowing this. If such a rule exists, your boss in fining you does not go outside the contract and you have no legal right to object, except when the fine is larger than that permitted, or made in inappropriate circumstances. Otherwise, failure to pay wages due to you amounts to a breach of contract. You have a choice of *legal* remedies: 1. you can stay at work and sue for the money due to you as a result of this breach; or 2. you can claim that this breach is so serious that it shows your boss is not prepared to carry on with the contract, and leave. You can then claim that this amounted to constructive unfair dismissal.

Fines and deductions: manual workers and shop assistants

We know (page 36) that **workers covered by the Truck Acts** must be paid the whole of the wages they have earned in 'current coin of the realm'. Only specified exceptions are allowed. Disciplinary fines or deductions therefore constitute offences. The 1896 Truck Act, however, introduced a relaxation which gives any employer the power to levy fines, and to make deductions for 'bad or negligent work or injury to the materials or other property of the employer'. The power is fairly tightly regulated by the Act and the following conditions must be met:

1. You have signed a written contract, or you have access to a notice in a prominent place showing the terms of your contract, which provides for fines or deductions

2. Any fine or deduction made is in accordance with this contract

3. Written particulars of the 'offence' and the amount of the fine or deduction are given to you on each occasion.

In addition to these conditions, a **fine** can be imposed only if:

a. your contract specifies events that can lead to a fine and the amount

b. the particular event causes or is likely to cause loss or hindrance to your employer

c. the amount is reasonable; and

d. your boss keeps a register of all fines

and a **deduction** can be made only if:

a. it does not exceed the loss caused to your boss by you or workers you are responsible for; and

b. the amount is reasonable

Deductions for bad work are still common in the textile trades. Disciplinary fines, for example for bad time-keeping, are common in many industries. Some of these are expressly excluded from the requirements of the 1896 Act. Despite this legal control on employers' powers – and these all ultimately derive from an agreement in your contract to accept them – the courts have allowed employers to abuse the law.

In one case it was decided that a worker was paid to do *good* work, and if he did *bad* work he got a lesser price. In other words there was one wage for bad work and one for good work, rather than a deduction from the normal wages:

> Thomas Sagar, a Lancashire weaver, produced cloth by the piece. One week he received 1s. less because of carelessly produced work. When he claimed under the Truck Act the Court of Appeal said that there had been no deduction. His work had not been up to scratch so he got paid only what the defective goods were worth. He had not actually earned the full amount he would have got if the work had been good, so there could be no deduction from it. *Sagar v Ridehalgh* 1930 (CA)

This pedantic distinction applies not only to piece-workers. If you are entitled to a good timekeeping bonus, it can't be 'deducted' until you have achieved full attendance. So you can't claim under the Truck Act until the bonus becomes due and is withheld.

Suspension with pay

Your boss can suspend you on full pay. If you are in one of those rare groups of workers who have a right to be provided with work – piece-workers, skilled workers, performers and artists – your boss can't suspend you. See page 37.

Suspension without full pay

Suspension on anything less than full pay is unlawful unless you have agreed to this in your contract, or by custom. See page 55. If you turn up for work and are locked out or if you are disciplined by means of temporary suspension, you are entitled to claim for the wages due to you or even to resign and claim you have been unfairly dismissed. **Don't accept a right to suspend for disciplinary reasons in your contract or agreements** unless you feel that it is useful to have a middle road between warnings and a sacking. Without such a right, suspension is a breach of the contract to provide wages to a worker who is ready and willing to work.

> Mr Hanley took a day off work so his boss suspended him without pay for a day. He claimed 6s. 2d. The High Court said his employers could have sacked him, or claimed damages from him. Instead, they did neither. They treated the contract as still alive, and 'took upon themselves to suspend him for one day; in other words to deprive the workman of his wages for one day, thereby assessing their own damages for the servant's misconduct. . . . They have no possible right to do that'. *Hanley v Pease & Partners* 1915 (HC)

You can claim your wages, but it would be most unlikely that a court would force your boss to take you back to work (TULR Act section 16). You might think that suspension without full pay is also an offence under the Truck Acts, as a fine or deduction. But the courts have applied the law to protect employers of piece-workers from this suggestion. They say you are entitled to all the wages you have earned. If you don't work because your boss has suspended you in accordance with your contract, you are not entitled to wages, so there can be no deduction from them. If there is no deduction, your boss does not infringe the Truck Act. **But**, if you have not conceded the right to suspend, and you are not on straight piece-work, suspension *will* be an offence under the Truck Act.

Demotion and transfer

Demotion, or transfer to a job not covered by your contract, is a breach of contract. It will often be a breach so serious that your boss is really showing that he is tearing up the contract. You can claim unfair dismissal if you quit after refusing a move not authorised by your contract. That is constructive dismissal.

This does not apply if you have accepted a flexibility or mobility agreement. A disciplinary transfer may not be a breach of contract if you are covered by this kind of agreement. **Be wary of negotiating flexibility agreements**.

Workers subject to special discipline

The Police and Armed Forces

The services are covered by stringent disciplinary rules. These rules are archaic, unnecessarily strict, and undemocratic. The right to go before a civil court with a jury, and be represented by a lawyer, are excluded. The powers given to the authorities go far beyond the powers of any employer and include corporal punishment, imprisonment and physical labour. The police are subject to internal disciplinary bodies and, for senior officers, local watch committees.

Merchant seamen

Seamen are subject to the Merchant Shipping Act 1970, which made reforms in ship discipline. Most of a master's power to discipline can be taken over by ship disciplinary committees. In fact, experiments with such committees proved unsuccessful. Men didn't want to serve on them, and others preferred to be disciplined by their skipper. A master still retains the right to arrest and to fine. A Bill was introduced in 1977 to provide new rules on ship discipline.

Apprentices

Ancient rules allowing masters to 'chastise' apprentices are now obsolete. Apprentices are more protected than other workers against disciplinary action, particularly dismissal.

The professions

There are special disciplinary bodies in all the professions. They have various powers including disqualification. Teachers, doctors, dentists, lawyers, nurses, opticians and architects all have their own rules, enforced by a disciplinary authority.

Should you negotiate disciplinary agreements?

The Code positively encourages joint regulation of both rules and procedures. It also envisages the possibility of joint adjudication. There are pros and cons in this approach. On balance you are better off not negotiating **rules**, while at the same time agreeing **procedures**.

In a well-organised workplace, you are giving up your control over discipline if you put the **rules** in writing. If the views of your workmates are usually accepted in disciplinary matters, so that no disciplinary action or sacking takes place unless it is deserved, you gain nothing by agreeing to written rules. In less organised sectors, the codification of rules can be detrimental when it comes to challenging disciplinary action or making a claim for unfair dismissal. This is because flexibility in treatment is reduced, and employers can easily show to a tribunal an offence specifically covered by an agreed rule. Furthermore, the **absence** of agreed rules (and procedures) will make it harder for employers to show they acted reasonably.

If you choose to have a set of rules, the advantages are that you always know where you stand, and if they are followed there is no scope for favouritism or victimisation. Workers may be more inclined to observe them if they are arrived at through negotiation rather than by management decree.

Procedures are different. It is usually in your interest to be guaranteed a right to warnings, an appeal and representation. There is no ideological bar to trade unionists negotiating a procedure, but there may be if you jointly fix rules and penalties. The only time it may benefit you *not* to have an agreed procedure is when you are claiming unfair dismissal. Tribunals don't like employers who neither have procedures nor follow the Code.

If you already have a fairly long procedure which is better than that in the Code it is still advisable to put it in writing. Otherwise your boss may convince a tribunal that he has followed procedure if he merely takes the (minimum) number of steps set out in the Code, but fails to exhaust the *agreed* procedure.

On **adjudication**, many trade unionists feel that it is better to have disciplinary matters decided by a body which includes workers. This is probably right, but there are few procedures which leave decisions to an appeal body with a **majority of workers** on it. For the most part, workers are involved only to give credibility to a decision.

Improving on the Code

The Code sets out to give practical advice. It is extremely influential, whether or not a procedure is agreed, in setting standards against which disciplinary action can be judged.

It has many shortcomings, though. If you are going to negotiate rules and procedures, you can aim a lot higher. The Code represents a minimum, not an optimum, or even a norm. The following are realistic bargaining objectives:

1. Steps in the procedure. These should be increased to include more warnings. Suspension should only be accepted as a penalty if you think it is the only way of avoiding a dismissal. A suspended worker should be given the right to return to work to interview witnesses and collect evidence.

2. Instant dismissal. This should be regarded in organised workplaces as obsolete. All potential dismissals should go into procedure. If the offence is bad enough, you are less likely to win a claim for unfair dismissal if your boss sacks you on the spot, and this right is written into a procedure.

3. Records. These should be destroyed if you have had no similar offences for six months.

4. Special workers. The procedure should apply to all. Probationary workers and new starters are particularly vulnerable as they may not know the ropes, and they should have all the protection of the procedure.

5. Rules. It often reduces flexibility if you specify rules and offences.

Disciplinary action against management?

In some circumstances you could take action against management. If they infringe the Truck Acts or the Health and Safety at Work Act, or fail to take action on hazards quickly enough, you could 'warn', or take direct action, or inform the authorities. Your boss has a contractual obligation to you to observe the statutes – see *Gregory v Ford* (page 39). Why not take disciplinary action against your boss if he breaks your contract?

Summary

1. Disciplinary action is illegal if it shows discrimination on the grounds of sex, race, trade union activity or spent convictions.

2. Disciplinary action must be authorised by your contract. It is illegal if it affects your contractual rights.

3. Workers covered by the Truck Acts can agree to disciplinary deductions and fines. If you don't agree, or if they aren't customary, they are illegal. Strict rules regulate deductions and fines.

4. The Code of Practice lays down minimum guidelines that should be followed, including warnings, appeals, representation and the form of procedures that should be negotiated.

5. The CE Act says your boss must give you written particulars of disciplinary rules, and who you can appeal to.

6. Disciplinary action against one worker, if it is unchallenged, can become a threat to others. It is essential for organised workers to establish rights of representation and appeal, and to take collective action in support of colleagues unfairly disciplined.

7.

Maternity

The need for maternity rights for working women / the law and collective bargaining / summary of your rights / table showing legal protections / dismissal connected with pregnancy / the right to alternative work / how to claim unfair dismissal / maternity pay under the Employment Protection Act / social security maternity allowance / payment / how to claim pay / maternity leave / refusal to take you back / how to claim the right to return / temps / pitfalls / specimen letter to your employer / recommended timetable for claiming your rights / collective action.

Men can't have babies. This overworked statement of fact has been the reason for unequal treatment of men and women, and for the lack of job and income security of pregnant workers. Before 1976 protection for women workers was provided, if at all, only by collective and individual agreements. Social security benefits are available to those women who have paid the necessary number of contributions, but these don't guarantee job security. Parliament has been slow to give legal rights, but this is related to the lack of interest shown in the past by industry. Well-organised workers have a lot to answer for. The national agreement for the engineering industry, for example, covering probably 400,000 women workers, says nothing about maternity leave or pay.

This inadequacy of collective bargaining will be remedied only when the campaign for maternity rights ceases to be regarded as a woman's issue and becomes a demand affecting the whole of the working class. During an economic recession, a woman's income and job security are crucial to many families – even more so if she is a single parent. So while maternity rights can be exercised only by women, they are in fact rights won for all workers. Collective bargaining must now improve on the legal rights and make good the defects noted below.

1. There are no rights on paternity in the UK. Other countries recognise paternity rights, such as Sweden, where seven months' leave can be taken, by either the mother or the father or alternately.

2. The law excludes large numbers of working women from the right to maternity pay and to return to work. You need to have worked continuously for over two years in the same job. Since many women of child-bearing age will have entered employment quite recently, or will have changed employers within that period of time, the rights are restricted.

The reason for excluding so many women is purely financial. As with the original unfair dismissal laws, which also required two years' service before they could be activated, the main object is to satisfy the demands of the labour movement by conceding the principle of maternity rights, while making sure that the financial effect of this concession on employers and government is minimal.

3. It could be said that **the social security system has imposed a rigidity** on agreements and now on the maternity rights in the Employment Protection Act (EP Act). Payments can be claimed only during the 11 weeks before and seven weeks after confinement. This is quite inconsistent with a woman's need to choose when to begin and end her leave.

Where to find the law

The Employment Protection Act 1975 (EP Act) deals with dismissal (section 34), maternity pay (section 35–47), the right to return (section 48–52), alternative work (section 34).

Summary of rights

The table on page 80 shows what rights you have. **If you have been working for the same employer for 26 weeks at 16 or more hours a week** (plus the usual exceptions – see page 341) you have:

1. the right not to be dismissed simply because you are,

Maternity Rights

Right	Who can claim	When does protection begin	When does protection end	Extension
Social Security maternity rights	Women with sufficient contribution record	11th week before expected week of confinement	18 weeks later	None
Maternity pay	Women with 2 years' service at 11th week before confinement	11th week before expected week of confinement	6 weeks later	The 6 weeks can be taken any time after 11th week before confinement
Right to return to work and to claim unfair dismissal if refused	Women with 2 years' service at 11th week before confinement	11th week before expected week of confinement	29th week after week of confinement	See Notes 1 and 2 below
Right to claim redundancy pay if refused right to return due to redundancy	Women with 2 years' service at 11th week before confinement	11th week before expected week of confinement	29th week after week of confinement	See Notes 1 and 2 below
Right not to be dismissed for reasons connected with pregnancy	Women with 26 weeks' service at date of dismissal	On pregnancy	Indefinite	—
Right to be offered suitable available vacancy if incapable of normal work	Women with 26 weeks' service at date of dismissal	On pregnancy	Indefinite	—

Note 1: Employer can extend once for 4 weeks on giving specific reasons. Employee can extend once for 4 weeks on giving medical certificate.

Note 2: Employee can extend if it is unreasonable to expect her to return e.g. because of industrial action. Must return within 14 days of action ending.

or have been, pregnant or for any reason connected with this

2. the right to be given suitable alternative work if you become incapable of doing your normal work, and a vacancy exists

3. if your contract is suspended while you take maternity leave, the right to claim unfair dismissal if you are sacked while on leave

If you have been working for the same employer for two years by the 11th week before your expected week of confinement you have:

4. the right to take maternity leave starting any time after the 11th week before confinement

5. the right to maternity pay for the first six weeks of absence whether or not you intend to return to work

6. the right to return to work at any time within 29 weeks of the week of confinement

7. if redundancy arises while on leave, the right to be offered any suitable alternative work which exists when you return to work

8. the right to claim unfair dismissal if you are not allowed to return to your old job after your absence

If your own contract or collective agreement deals with maternity:

9. the right to take advantage of any term that may be better than the EP Act

If you have made sufficient social security contributions:

10. the right to maternity allowance, with earnings related supplement if appropriate. You can get the flat-rate maternity grant if you *or your husband* has made the necessary contributions.

Dismissal connected with pregnancy

Who can claim?

Provided you have **26 weeks' continuous employment** and fulfil the usual conditions for protection against unfair dismissal (see page 155) you can complain to a tribunal if you are sacked while you are pregnant. Your boss must give a reason for sacking you and justify it in the normal way. However, because you may have difficulty in doing some jobs, and will want time off for hospital visits, and because you are going to cost money and demand the right to maternity leave, you are likely to be extremely vulnerable to dismissal at this time. Some **additional protection** is given by the EP Act whether or not you qualify for **maternity pay** or **maternity leave**.

If you are sacked you can challenge it:

1. if you are sacked because you are pregnant

2. if you are sacked for any reason connected with pregnancy and your boss doesn't offer you alternative work

Sacking because of pregnancy

If you are sacked because of pregnancy, even though you are quite capable of carrying on at work, you are automatically considered as unfairly dismissed. Your boss must give his reason for dismissing you (if you request it – EP Act section 70). He must prove some reason other than pregnancy. If he can't, you are unfairly dismissed. He may even be quite open about it – pregnant models, air stewardesses or sales representatives do not conform to the image put over by sexist employers. Protection against being dismissed for other reasons, such as having a child (rather than being pregnant) is given by the general law on unfair dismissal:

> Genevieve Pillet, an unmarried marketing assistant, was sacked while pregnant. She wasn't entitled to statutory maternity leave and was refused even three months' leave. Her boss said she wouldn't be able to do her job properly if she had a child. Ms Pillet got £2,023 compensation.
> *Pillet v Land Settlement Association* 1977 (IT)

Sacking for reasons connected with pregnancy

Your boss might try to sack you for reasons *connected with* your pregnancy. He might object, for example, to your having sick leave or time off to attend hospital or classes, or because you have psychological problems which may affect your work (concentration, for example), or because you need to take time out to nurse the baby, or because you can't work long hours, or stand, or do heavy work, or adjust to shift-working. You can claim unfair dismissal in these and similar situations, but your boss can use the defence given in section 34 of the EP Act.

Section 34 says that your boss *can* sack you for a reason connected with pregnancy if:

■ you can't adequately do the work you are employed to do; **or**

■ you can't carry on doing that work without breaking the law.

But, if a suitable vacancy exists, he must offer it to you.

This means:

1. Your boss must prove that you are incapable. Incapacity justifying dismissal is assessed in terms of skill, aptitude, health and mental and physical qualities (Trade Union and Labour Relations Act schedule 1), and may include incapacity due to repeated absences. But because pregnancy involves only a **short-term** incapacity, dismissal on those grounds might be unreasonable.

2. If you can do the job to some extent, your boss may be unreasonable in sacking you, because it is only reasonable to sack you if you can't *adequately* do the job. You will have to challenge any attempt to redefine performance levels at your workplace.

3. In any event, your boss must prove he acted reasonably in all the circumstances in sacking you.

4. Your boss *must* offer you a suitable alternative job if a vacancy exists. If he doesn't, he must *prove* that no suitable vacancy exists.

Suitable vacancy means that it must be suitable for you to do and appropriate in the circumstances. If you are given a new contract, the terms and conditions must be 'not substantially less favourable' than in the previous one, particularly those affecting the capacity and location in which you worked. If you are offered less money or different hours, you will have to weigh up whether it is substantially less favourable. Your boss must prove a job was offered and it was suitable.

Vacancies with associated employers don't count. The obligation to offer work applies only if there is a vacancy with the employer you work for (or a successor if the firm is taken over). So although workers who are affected by an industrial dispute involving employees of an associated employer cannot claim guarantee payments (see page 61), there is no corresponding *obligation* on employers to offer women work with associated employers. Employers are required to behave reasonably though, so you might succeed in showing that it was reasonable to expect your boss to look for vacancies among associated employers in the same group – see *Vokes v Bear* page 178.

Since you may not have access to the files on whether vacancies exist or are likely to arise even in your own firm, constant exchange of information between workmates is essential. You could also try a claim for disclosure of information under the EP Act (see chapter 16).

The situations in which a **law** prevents an employer from keeping on a worker who is, or has been, pregnant are few. Section 34 applies only where an Act of Parliament or a specific regulation forbids employment. It does *not* apply to your employer's own rules or custom and practice. The fact that in your firm women workers habitually quit, or are required by an agreement to quit, in the 11th week before confinement does not mean your employer is complying with a *law*. The kind of regulation envisaged is section 75 of the Factories Act which requires employers to take women off the job if a medical adviser of the Employment Medical Advisory Service (EMAS) says they are exposed to lead, or radioactivity, or under other regulations. But in these situations workers who are not given alternative work and are temporarily laid off are entitled to 26 weeks' pay for **medical suspension** (see chapter 4). Faced with this alternative, employers may be acting unreasonably in sacking a woman worker when suspension is all that is needed to comply with the doctor's order.

When must the offer be made?

Finally, the offer of new work must be made before you are sacked, and the work must start immediately after the old work finished.

How to claim unfair dismissal

Claim unfair dismissal **within three months**. See page 357 for the procedure. If you would have been entitled to maternity pay and maternity leave had you not been sacked, tell your boss (in writing is best) before you leave, or as soon as is reasonably practicable, that you intend to claim the right to return to work with him.

Remedies for dismissal

If you are unfairly dismissed you preserve your rights to maternity pay and to return to work. If you are fairly dismissed because, for example, you are incapable of adequately doing your job and no vacancy exists, your rights are also preserved. **But** in both these cases the rights are preserved **only if** you would have had two years' continuous service by the 11th week before the week you expect your baby. If that is not the case, you may get compensation or even reinstatement according to the normal powers of tribunals when dealing with unfair dismissal (see page 180).

Maternity pay

Who can claim?

In order to qualify for maternity pay under section 35 of the EP Act you must fulfil certain conditions.

The starting point is the week you are expecting your baby to be born. That week is known as the 'expected week of confinement'. The previous week, ending on the Saturday night, is the first week before the expected week of confinement. (Confinement means the birth of a living child, or a still-birth after 28 weeks' pregnancy). **Your rights depend on your status at the beginning of the 11th week before the expected week of confinement.** In order to claim maternity pay and the right to return to work you must:

1. have had two years' continuous employment by the beginning of the 11th week

2. still be 'employed' (even if you are not actually working) at the end of the previous week. You are 'employed' even if you are fairly or unfairly dismissed (see above) before this date.

3. normally work at least 16 hours a week (plus the usual exceptions – see page 341)

4. inform your boss that you intend to be absent because of pregnancy. He can request that you put it in writing, and anyway it is advisable to do this. You should notify him as soon as possible. If you give less than three weeks' notice of your intention, you *may* lose your rights.

5. **if he requests** provide him with a doctor's or midwife's certificate showing the expected week of confinement.

Conditions **1.** to **3.** are compulsory. If you don't comply with **4.** because it was not reasonably practicable – you might be off sick or your baby might be unexpectedly early – you must provide the information as soon as possible. If you fail to provide it or to give a certificate when requested, your employer can withhold payment until you do – but then it must be backdated. **You can get maternity pay whether or not you return or intend to return to work after the birth.**

How much is due?

The EP Act aims to give you six weeks at 90 per cent of your 'week's pay' (see page 344). Your boss must make up the difference between social security maternity allowance and 90 per cent of a week's pay. **You get the same amount from your boss whether or not you are entitled to social security maternity allowance.** If you are entitled to earnings related supplement on your maternity allowance this will bring you up to or above 100 per cent. **Maternity pay is taxable if your contract continues but is tax-free if it is terminated. Maternity allowance isn't taxable.** So you may be taking home more in the first six weeks of your maternity leave than you were while working.

Example: assuming the following

Your weekly earnings are £52

Your 'week's pay' is £50

Maternity allowance is £14.70, and you have made sufficient social security contributions (see page 210).

Your 'reckonable' weekly earnings in tax year 1976/77 are £44

So your earnings related supplement (ERS) on this is £7.91

You get:

A. From your boss: $£50 \times \dfrac{90}{100} = £45$

Less maternity allowance $-$ £14.70

Total £30.30

B. From social security:

Maternity allowance £14.70

Plus ERS (after two weeks) £7.91

So you receive in total:

For first two weeks: £30.30+£14.70 = £45

For next four weeks: £30.30+£14.70+£7.91 = £52.91

For next 12 weeks: £14.70+£7.91 = £22.61

Plus £25 maternity grant

N.B. Maternity allowance is £15.75 from November 1978.

Your week's pay is worked out on the basis of the arrangements in force **just before** your absence. If, because of your condition, you have been forced to accept alternative work with the same employer but at a lower rate, it is the lower rate that applies for working out maternity pay. This is completely unjustified in that you may have worked, say, for five years on one set of rates and been on reduced rates for only four weeks. It is also inconsistent with guarantee payments (page 59), where your rights are not prejudiced if you accept lower rates for a while during a recession.

Contractual rights

If he is already making payments to you in accordance with your contract or a collective agreement which covers you, your boss is entitled to offset this amount against maternity pay during the first six weeks. Only *strictly contractual* or collectively-agreed payments count. An ex gratia payment or an annual bonus that isn't guaranteed by your contract does not affect your statutory right to maternity pay.

If your own arrangements are better than those in the EP Act you can claim on them. If they are not as good you can go for the better terms. And if some terms are better, some worse, you can be choosey and get both the full EP Act rights and any better terms under the agreement. Local authorities, for instance, provide four weeks at full pay and 14 at half pay. So you could get four weeks at full pay, then two weeks at 90 per cent under the Act, and 10 weeks at half pay.

How is it paid?

The right is to payment for the **first six weeks** of absence due to pregnancy or confinement. They can be taken any time after the 11th week, and they need not be taken consecutively, but if you do not quit at the 11th week you will lose some state maternity allowance (see page 213).

The Act does not say how the maternity pay is to be paid. It could be paid weekly or monthly or as a lump sum. The DE says 'the intention of maternity pay is to maintain earnings during the weeks of absence. The payment of a lump sum at the end of six weeks would be contrary to this intention' (EP Act Leaflet 4 Supplement). Ideally you want your money at the beginning of your absence.

The Maternity Pay Fund is financed by an additional 0.05 per cent on employers' social security contributions. The load is spread evenly across all employers and they cannot object to hiring women on the grounds that it will expose them to claims of maternity pay. Your employer makes the payment and then claims **a full rebate from the fund**. If he pays you according to your own contract or collective agreement, he can recoup the amount of the statutory rebate, provided that you would be entitled to claim under the EP Act.

How to claim

You should write to your employer as soon as possible saying you intend to be absent because of pregnancy. You must tell him **three weeks** before you are absent or as soon as is reasonably practicable. See specimen letter on page 92. If he refuses to pay, you can claim to a tribunal **within three months** of the last day on which you should have been paid. See page 357 for the procedure.

If you get a tribunal award in your favour and your boss still refuses to pay up, or if he has gone bust, you can apply directly to the Employment Secretary for payment out of the Fund. The Fund pays you direct, and claims against your boss if he doesn't have a reasonable excuse for not paying you. In view of the small amounts due, it is hard to envisage what excuses could be reasonable.

Maternity leave

Many agreements provide for maternity leave. The EP Act talks instead of a 'right to return to work' (section 48). The two are not quite the same but the effect of the Act is to give a period during which you can be absent from work and be protected if you are sacked, made redundant or refused work, to the same extent as if you were not absent.

Who can claim?

To claim this right you must meet the same conditions as for maternity pay on page 85. In addition you must say you intend to exercise your right to return to work with your employer.

How long does leave last?

The EP Act gives you the right to return to work at any time during the period stretching from the 11th week before confinement to the end of the 29th week after the week of your confinement. All you have to do is let your employer know you are coming back. It is best (but not necessary) to put it in writing. You must let your boss know at least one week before you intend to return. **There is nothing in the Act**

to force you to quit work at any specified date before confinement. You will lose some social security maternity allowance, though, if you work after the 11th week.

The date of return can be postponed in three different situations.

1. You can postpone your return by up to four weeks after the date you said you would be returning – the 'notified day of return' – even if this takes you beyond 29 weeks. You can only do this if you send your employer a medical certificate saying you are incapable of work 'by reason of disease or bodily or mental disablement'. You can only do it once. So **you should make absolutely sure you are fit before you tell your boss the date you are returning**.

2. After you've notified your boss of the date you intend to return, he can postpone it by up to four weeks, even if this means extending the period of absence over the 29-week limit. He must specify his reasons for doing this when he notifies you of the postponement. But the power to fix the date of return is yours – your employer can only postpone it for a limited period.

3. You can postpone your day of return because of an interruption of work which would make it unreasonable for you to be expected to return during it. A strike, for instance, would entitle you to put back your notified day of return, or to extend it beyond the 29th week if you have not already notified your boss. Your leave is extended indefinitely, even beyond the 29th week. Once the strike or other interruption is over you have **two weeks** in which to return to work.

These are the only situations when you can postpone your return date having once notified your employer or having gone beyond the 29 weeks. So you must be quite certain your health and commitments will enable you to return on the notified day. It also means **you should resist your employer's pressure at the start of your absence to say in advance when you will be back**. If this means employers are unable to plan their personnel requirements, it is the result of the EP Act. There is no reason why women workers should be prejudiced by it.

Return to what?

The right is to return to work with your employer (or successor if he has sold out or merged) in the job in which you were employed under your original contract. According to section 48, this means that the **capacity and place** in which you

could be required to work and the **nature** of the work must be
the same as those in your regular contract. The terms and
conditions must be 'not less favourable' than you would have
had if you had not been absent. So if there has been a pay
increase while you have been away, you come back on the
new rate. For all your statutory rights, like redundancy, unfair dismissal, notice and maternity pay, you have continuity
of employment throughout your leave, so you are treated as
never having been away. For non-statutory rights that you
have negotiated, such as pensions, holidays and seniority,
section 48 is ambiguous. You can argue that you are coming
back to 'not less favourable' terms only if your absence counts
for all these purposes too.

The right is unequivocal. Your boss can't decide without your consent to put you on to other work, however
suitable it is or however difficult it is to find a place for you.
**You go back to the work that you could be required to do under
your original contract.** If you accepted alternative work before
confinement under a different contract, the right to return
applies to work under your **original** contract.

Dismissal, redundancy and refusal to reinstate

Suppose you have told your employer the date you are
coming back and he says you are redundant. As you have
been away for a while you may not know the facts and you
may not be in a position to rally support for resistance. If
you are forced to rely on your legal rights, they are these:

**1. You have a right to be offered any suitable alternative
vacancy in the firm or associated firms.** This is not the same as
the employer's *defence* in the Redundancy Payments Act by
which he can avoid payment by offering suitable alternative
work. Under the EP Act it is expressed as your right to claim
any suitable work appropriate for you to do. If there is such a
vacancy and you are not given it, this is automatically unfair
and you may get a reinstatement order or compensation.

2. If suitable alternative work is not available, you will
get a redundancy payment if you are not re-hired, with your
continuous employment being reckoned to your notified day
of return, or the date redundancy occurred.

3. If your boss simply refuses to have you back and
there is no evidence of redundancy, you can claim unfair
dismissal and you may get an order for reinstatement or
compensation.

4. Your contract may say that while on leave your

contract continues and all your rights under it still apply. So if you are declared redundant or dismissed at any time after the 11th week before confinement and before you have had a chance to give a notified day of return, you can claim. You are employed (although absent from work) up to the dismissal date and may get an order for reinstatement or compensation. These rights exist *in addition to* your maternity rights so you can claim again later on if your right to return is not observed.

How to claim

Claims for refusal to allow a return to work must be made **within three months** of the notified day of return. If you are dismissed or made redundant before you fixed a date you should claim within three months. (Six months if there is a genuine redundancy and no other work is available – better to be safe with three months). See page 357 for the procedure.

Temporary replacements

Employers can take on men or women to fill vacancies temporarily created by a woman on maternity leave. These workers are extremely vulnerable since they will often not reach the 26 weeks' service required for (legal) protection against unfair dismissal.

There are three restrictions on an employer's freedom to sack a temp:

1. The temp must have been told **in writing** at the time (s)he was hired that (s)he would be sacked when a woman returned to work.

2. The temp must in fact have been sacked in order to make it possible to give work to the returning woman.

3. The employer must show he acted reasonably in sacking the temp when the woman returns. This means that he is expected to look for work for the temp in the firm or with associated employers (*Vokes v Bear* – page 178). **It is important to protect the job security of these workers by demanding equal treatment for all.**

Points to watch out for

■ If your boss sacks you at any time, ask for the reasons in writing. He must give it if you have 26 weeks' service.

■ If he sacks you before your baby is born and you

would be entitled to return to work, tell him you intend to exercise this right.

■ Give notice in writing of your intention to claim maternity pay as soon as possible. You must give this three weeks, or as soon as reasonably practicable, before you leave. If you don't, your pay can be withheld.

■ Provide a medical certificate if requested.

■ Give notice **in writing** of your intention to be absent **and** say that you will be returning in accordance with the EP Act. If you don't say this, you lose the right. At this stage you should not say when you intend to return.

■ Notify your boss **in writing** one week before you intend to return. Make sure you will be absolutely fit by that day.

■ If you aren't fit, get a medical certificate but don't postpone the date by more than four weeks.

■ Whether or not you are entitled to the right to return, make sure you aren't forced into a phoney 'resignation'. If pressure is put on you to quit, make sure you register this as a **dismissal** or exercise your right to return to work by notifying your boss.

■ Claim social security maternity allowance between the 14th and 11th week before confinement.

■ If you are sacked or are refused pay or the right to return, claim within three months.

Specimen letter to employer

Because of all the pitfalls surrounding maternity rights it may be useful to write to your employer as follows:

6 January 1978

Dear Mr Smith,

I wish to inform you that I intend to be absent on account of pregnancy.

My expected date of confinement is in the week beginning Sunday 16 April 1978 and I intend to take advantage of my rights under the Employment Protection Act to maternity pay and to return to work. I would be glad if you could arrange for my maternity pay to be paid weekly by cheque/collected by me/paid in a lump sum on . . .

Yours sincerely,

Recommended timetable

Assuming you become pregnant in week 1 and the expected day of confinement falls during week 40.

1. **Week 18:** notify your employer in writing as per specimen letter.
2. **Week 26:** claim on Form BM4 for social security maternity grant and maternity allowance.
3. **Week 29:** this is the 11th week before the expected week of confinement. Leave work. Employer starts to pay maternity pay. Social security maternity allowance starts.
4. **Week 35:** employer's liability to pay runs out.
5. **Week 41:** baby born (late).
6. **Week 48:** maternity allowance runs out.
7. **Week 69:** last date for notifying your boss in writing that you are returning. Must give one week's notice.
8. **Week 70:** you must return to work or get a postponement on medical grounds.

Collective action

The right to return to work at any time up to 29 weeks after confinement is about the only right which collective agreements rarely match. This long period should be the target for **minimum** rights in collective agreements. **Maternity rights will only be improved if union members recognise the importance for all workers of giving job security to women at work.**

8.

Discrimination

Discrimination on the grounds of race, sex and marriage / who can claim / direct and indirect discrimination / victimisation / segregation / how this applies to jobs / recruitment, terms and conditions, transfer, promotion, training, benefits, dismissal / what are the exceptions / genuine occupational qualifications / immigration and work permits / discriminatory practices / inciting racial hatred / the Equality Commissions / enforcement / how to claim / proving discrimination / remedies / trade-union action / and a summary

Some types of racial discrimination were first outlawed by the Race Relations Act 1965. Discrimination in employment was made illegal by the Race Relations Act 1968. Yet in 1974 the research group Political and Economic Planning (PEP) found that:

a coloured unskilled worker has nearly a one in two chance of being discriminated against when (s)he applies for a job; for a coloured skilled worker the chance is one in five and for a white collar worker about one in three. PEP estimates, on the basis of its samples, that 20,000 acts of discrimination in recruitment occur each year. The PEP report confirms overwhelmingly that discrimination in employment continues on a massive scale (Quoted in Race Relations Board (RRB) Report 1974, page 8).

Something had to be done. The legislative answer was the Race Relations Act 1976 (RR Act) which came into effect in 1977 and repealed the two earlier Acts. The labour movement's answer was a campaign against racism in 1976 and 1977. The Tories' answer was given by Margaret Thatcher in America on 16 September 1975:

> The pursuit of equality is a mirage. What is more desirable and more practicable than the pursuit of equality is the pursuit of equality of opportunity. And opportunity means nothing unless it includes the right to be unequal.

It is clear that discrimination, more or less overt, continues. Laws can change behaviour but not attitudes.

Racial discrimination is not constant. It can be stirred up by offensive propaganda from organisations like the National Front and the National Party, which blame racial minorities for deteriorating living standards, unemployment and bad housing. It can also flare up in an irrational response to national events. An Irish worker engaged by a Cheshire company was prevented from starting because of feeling against the Irish following the IRA bombings of Birmingham city centre in 1974. He got only £29.50 in compensation (*RRB v Clays Commercial*).

Sex discrimination is outlawed by the Sex Discrimination Act of 1975. It attempts to lay the groundwork for equal treatment in employment, housing, education and services, Figures for earnings given on page 120 show just how much work this Act has still to do in employment matters.

Laws alone can't wipe out discrimination. Trade-union action can go a long way. This is suggested at the end of the chapter.

Where to find the law

Sex Discrimination Act 1975 (SD Act); Race Relations Act 1976 (RR Act); Public Order Act 1936 section 5 (as amended), Employment Protection Act (EP Act) section 72 (compensation for dismissal).

Statutory bodies

The Equal Opportunities Commission (EOC) deals with the SD Act. The Commission for Racial Equality (CRE) deals with the RR Act. It replaced the Race Relations Board and the Community Relations Commission in 1977. Their powers and functions are described below.

Race, sex and marriage

Discrimination is illegal in employment, education and in the provision of goods, facilities, services and housing, if it is based on:

■ race, colour, nationality, ethnic origins or national origins

■ sex

■ the fact that you are married (employment only).

Discrimination on the grounds of **nationality** is still permitted in the immigration laws (see below).

Discrimination on the grounds of **language** is not included. It is contrary to the UN International Covenant on Social and Cultural Rights, which the United Kingdom has signed, and it could lead to a charge of **indirect** discrimination. **Religious** discrimination is outside the 1976 Act but it is contrary to International Labour Organisation (ILO) Convention 111 for employment matters. This has not been ratified by the UK.

Northern Ireland's Fair Employment Act 1976 deals specifically with religious discrimination. The absence of such a clause in Great Britain had led to difficulties for Jews who have been discriminated against because of their **religion** (lawful) rather than **race** or **ethnic origins** (unlawful). Under the 1976 RR Act this might constitute indirect discrimination.

Gypsies are covered if they are discriminated against on ethnic grounds. The Race Relations Board also regarded **travellers** without clear ethnic roots as being covered, although the 1976 Act does not apply directly to them.

Discrimination against a man or woman on the grounds of sex is illegal. Marital status is included for employment matters only and applies only to **married people**.

> B. C. Parsons was a child care officer at a special school. She announced her intention to get married on 31 January and was sacked on 30 January. She claimed discrimination but the Exeter tribunal said she was not married at the date of dismissal, so had no claim. *Bick v Royal West of England Residential School for Deaf* 1976 (IT)

On the other hand, if you can claim unfair dismissal (Ms Parsons had not worked the 26 weeks necessary to use this right – see page 155) you can sue under the Trade Union and Labour Relations (TULR) Act. A London tribunal gave compensation for sex discrimination as well as unfair dismissal:

> Jeanette Johnston, a reservation clerk in a Hertfordshire travel agent's, was sacked the day before she married John McLean, the assistant manager. It was 'company policy' not to have two married people working together. She successfully claimed £117 for unfair dismissal and £200 for injury to her feelings under the SD Act. *McLean v Paris Travel Service Ltd.* 1976 (IT)

Discrimination in jobs – can you claim?

Both Acts apply to **employees,** people seeking work and those listed below:

	Sex Discrimination	Race Discrimination
Employees in small firms	Must be six or more employees with same or associated employer	Yes
Employees in private households	No	No
Job applicants	Yes	Yes
Employees alleging victimisation	Yes	Yes
Contract workers	Yes	Yes
Self-employed people	Yes	Yes
Crown and NHS workers	Yes	Yes
Holders of public office	Yes	Yes
House of Commons staff	Yes	Yes
Armed forces	No	Yes
Police and prison service officers	Yes	Yes
Midwives	No	Yes
Partners	Must be six or more in same firm	Must be six or more in same firm
Trade union members and applicants	Yes	Yes
Seamen	Yes, but usually exempt as a GOQ (see page 106)	Yes, unless recruited abroad
Clergy	No	Yes

Parliament has not outlawed discrimination against **single** people on the grounds of their marital status.

The main points to note are:
1. Most of the SD Act applies only where there are at **least six employees** in the company or group of companies. No reason is given for this. Certainly discrimination by an employer does not stop being discrimination simply because the number of workers employed falls below six.

2. If you work for someone who gets work on a **contract basis** from a third person ('the principal') you can complain of discrimination by the principal, for example, if he refuses to allow you to do the work. You don't need to show there are six contract workers employed.

3. If you get work through an **employment agency**, discrimination by the agency in not sending you for jobs, and by employers in making stipulations, is illegal. Employment agencies featured frequently in the Race Relations Board's cases. Sometimes, though, discriminatory employers have been reported *by* agencies.

What is discrimination?

There are four kinds of discrimination in the Acts:
1. direct discrimination
2. indirect discrimination
3. victimisation
4. segregation

In each situation the comparison you must make is between your case and that of someone else whose 'relevant circumstances are the same. or not materially different' (RR Act section 3; SD Act section 5).

Direct discrimination

This occurs if, on the grounds of race, sex, or marriage, a person treats you 'less favourably than he treats or would treat other persons'. So favouring a white worker to a black in hiring or promotion, when both have the same qualifications, is unlawful if the favouritism is racial. You must show evidence that the intention behind the treatment was to discriminate against blacks. You can do this by pointing out the implications of various forms of conduct. **Potential** direct discrimination is illegal so you will win if you can show that someone treats you less favourably than he **would treat** a person of a different race or sex, even though no actual better treatment of such a person has in fact occurred.

Indirect discrimination

Indirect discrimination is treatment which is equal in a formal sense, but which is discriminatory in its effect on one particular sex or racial group. Practices that have developed or been introduced might intentionally or unintentionally exclude groups of people on unlawful grounds. During the passage of the SD Act many jokes were made about employers avoiding the law by applying conditions that would exclude women – advertisements for construction workers 'who must be prepared to strip to the waist during summer' or who must be over six feet tall, for example. In fact these are illegal unless the employer can prove they are justifiable criteria for the job.

Indirect discrimination occurs when someone applies a requirement or condition that applies equally to all people but which

1. is such that the proportion of people of your race or sex who can comply with it is considerably smaller than the proportion of people **outside** that race or sex who can *and*

2. the person can't justify *and*

3. is to your detriment because you can't comply with it.

So you have to answer three questions:

1. Can considerably fewer people of your sex or race comply with the condition?

The answer to this is based not on whether you can physically comply, but whether **in practice it is harder** for you to comply.

Belinda Price, aged 36, applied for a job advertised by the Civil Service. She was told candidates must be between $17\frac{1}{2}$ and 28 years old. She claimed this was indirect discrimination on grounds of sex. Far fewer women than men could in practice comply with this condition, because many women of that age are having or raising children. It didn't matter that there are roughly equal numbers of men and women under 28. The key issue was that **in practice fewer women would be able to meet the age requirement for the job.** The Employment Appeal Tribunal (EAT) agreed it was discriminatory and referred the case back to the tribunal to see if **considerably fewer** women than men could comply. The tribunal said the age bar **was** discriminatory and told the Civil Service and the staff unions to abolish or raise the age limit. *Price v Civil Service Commission* 1977 (EAT)

It is important to have your statistics with you if you are going to win your case. Even then, you may still lose on a technicality:

> Isabella Meeks worked as a clerical assistant at the Norwich office of the Agricultural Workers' Union. She worked 23 hours a week and got 91p an hour. Workers doing 35 or more hours got 110p for similar work. She complained of indirect discrimination in that she could not meet the conditions of a 35-hour week, *and* the proportion of women who could was considerably smaller than the proportion of men. Official statistics showed 97 per cent of male workers in Britain worked full-time whereas only 68 per cent of female workers did. So discrimination was proved. Discrimination in money is dealt with only by the Equal Pay Act. But, as there was no man doing the same work as Ms Meeks, the Act did not apply and she lost her case. (See page 124 for details of this anomaly.) *Meeks v NUAAW* 1976 (IT)

2. Can your employer justify the condition?

The EAT said that in deciding whether a condition is justifiable a tribunal must consider five points:

■ that the onus of proof is on the employer

■ that the condition must be genuine and necessary, not merely convenient

■ whether there will be a discriminatory *effect* if the condition is allowed to continue

■ whether the effect of the condition is balanced by the need for it

■ whether the employer càn achieve his objective by some other non-discriminatory method.

Applying these rules in Ms Steel's case, the EAT said the Post Office had discriminated against her.

> Ms L. Steel joined the Post Office as a postwoman in 1961. Because of a Post Office rule she could not, *as a woman*, be classed as a 'permanent full-time' employee. The union made an agreement which gave women the right to this status in 1975. But prior service didn't count. Length of service is crucial when applying for new rounds so when Ms Steel applied for a new round a man with *less* service got the job. The EAT said that the number of women who could comply with the seniority rule was considerably smaller than men, and the rule was not justifiable *Steel v The Post Office* 1977 (EAT)

Sometimes a condition can be justified, even though it effectively excludes all members of a particular racial group.

> A. B. Gill, a Sikh, was sacked from a meat factory because he grew a beard and started to wear a turban. The dis-

missal was held to be fair because (a) the 1970 Food Regulations required workers to wear appropriate headgear and be clean-shaven, (b) he had turned down two transfers to less sensitive jobs, and (c) the condition in the Regulations, although indirectly discriminating against Sikhs, was justified by the employer. *Gill v Walls Meat Co* 1977 (IT)

3. Is the condition to your detriment?

You can't sue unless you personally have suffered a **detriment**. But the Commissions can stop practices which would be discriminatory if the group it is applied to were not of the same sex or race (RR Act section 28. Act section 37). The Commissions can take action, even though no detriment has actually occurred to any particular worker, see example on page 109.

Victimisation

Victimisation in the anti-discrimination laws (RR Act section 3; SD Act section 4) means that someone treats you less favourably than he treats or would treat others on the grounds that you
■ brought proceedings
■ gave evidence or information in proceedings
■ helped the CRE or EOC
■ made allegations of discrimination, unless they were false and **not made in good faith**. This means you must take care to get reasonable grounds for any allegations you make.

Segregation

Segregation of people on **racial** grounds amounts to discrimination. Provision of separate but equal facilities, the philosophy of apartheid, is illegal. Segregation by **sex** is not specifically banned.

How does this apply to jobs?

The following examples mentioned in the Acts show when discrimination in employment can occur:
1. recruitment
2. terms and conditions
3. transfer and promotion
4. training
5. benefits, facilities and services
6. dismissal
7. other detriment

Recruitment

It is illegal to give instructions to discriminate to a personnel officer. Arrangements made for dealing with application forms and interviews must be fair. You can complain to a tribunal even if you haven't applied for a job. You might, for example, be put off by the arrangements made – requiring you to travel a long distance or at night if you are a woman – or by the treatment you receive on the phone.

> Ireka Francis saw an advert for a buffet assistant at Mecca's Gay Tower Ballroom in Birmingham. (The Mecca organisation appears in many RRB reports.) She was offered an interview by the catering manager but when she asked if being coloured would make a difference he said it would and put the phone down. Her claim of discrimination was upheld, the Birmingham County Court believing her story not the manager's. She was awarded £73 compensation. *Race Relations Board v Mecca* 1976 (County Court)

'Arrangements' include formal long-term arrangements for deciding who should be offered employment, and short-term decisions taken on the interview day by people responsible for hiring. **Discriminatory arrangements are illegal even if no one gets the job advertised.** Nor can employers say they want to keep a **reasonable balance** between the sexes or racial groups. The old Race Relations Act allowed this, but it isn't in the present legislation:

> Ms M. Roadburg was interviewed with three men for a vacancy as a social work organiser in Edinburgh. In fact the interviewers had already decided to appoint a man because **there were already many women in the department** and they wanted a reasonable balance. Shortly afterwards, public spending cuts were announced and the vacancy was frozen. She complained and was awarded £40 compensation by the Edinburgh tribunal for injury to her feelings. No discrimination occurred as a result of **refusing to offer** the job because the vacancy was withdrawn for economic reasons. But the prior **arrangements** not to appoint her *were* unlawful. *Roadburg v Lothian Regional Council* 1976 (IT)

Discriminatory **advertisements** can usually only be attacked by the Commissions. If you are actually discouraged from applying, you can claim in your own right, as this constitutes an unlawful **arrangement**. **Offers** of jobs on terms different from those that are or would be offered to others, for reasons of race or sex, are unlawful. You can also complain if an employer **refuses** or **deliberately omits** to offer you a job on these grounds – RR Act section 4 (1); SD Act section 6 (1).

Terms and conditions

Discrimination between men and women in pay and in other contractual terms on which they work is covered by the Equal Pay Act. As we shall see, there is a gap between it and the SD Act. Discrimination in terms and conditions on racial grounds is covered by the RR Act (section 4 (2)).

Transfer and promotion

Your boss must give equal opportunities for transfer to more favourable shifts or sites. In selecting workers for promotion employers have scope for indirect discrimination. Take the Indian bus driver who was rejected three times for an inspector's vacancy because his accent was difficult to understand. (RRB Report 1973 Appendix VI). He complained that he never had any communication difficulties at work. Imposition of a strict language requirement might be indirect discrimination under the 1976 Act against workers born abroad.

You can effectively challenge this kind of discrimination by getting an agreement to see statistics on applications, promotions and qualifications of eligible workers.

Training

If you are denied equal opportunities for training you can complain to a tribunal.

> Some AUEW stewards complained of racial discrimination by their employers, an electrical equipment manufacturer. If no skilled workers were available, vacancies for setters were filled by upgrading operators, many of whom were black. The operators would be trained by the setters. The setters imposed a ban on all training to prevent upgrading of black workers, and then they went on strike. The Race Relations Board found that their shop steward incited management to discriminate. It ordered the company to pay compensation to two black (and one *white*) operators because they had been denied training. *RRB Report 1975–76 Appendix V Case 1*

Employers can take positive action to train minorities. This is lawful if there are no people of that sex or racial group or if the group is under-represented on a particular job during any time within the previous 12 months. Once trained, the workers must be selected on merit only. Positive discrimination in selection for the actual job is unlawful. (RR Act section 38; SD Act section 48.) Similar rules apply to training for union office.

The training agencies of the government are allowed to carry out selective training in special circumstances. These include **retraining of married women** who have been at home for a few years, and **training of minority groups** for particular kinds of work where these groups are under-represented.

Foreign workers seconded to a British firm for training in skills to be exercised abroad – Arab technicians for example – are excluded from the RR Act.

Benefits, facilities and services

Employers must give equal access to all fringe benefits – for example, loans, flexitime, insurance, medical and dental care, cars, parking, clothing allowances, staff status, luncheon vouchers, bonus, creche. British Rail's policy of giving free rail travel to wives of retired male employees was declared illegal because husbands of retired female employees did **not** get it – *Garland v British Rail* 1977 (EAT).

In a decision which threatened to wreck the whole of the SD Act, the Court of Appeal said that it is lawful for employers to discriminate in providing **benefits** if the benefit is 'an administrative arrangement in the interests of safety'.

> Automotive Products employed 4,000 manual workers – 3,530 men, 400 women and 70 disabled men. A works rule allowed the women and disabled men to leave work five minutes early to avoid the crush. Fred Peake claimed this discriminated against men, as they were denied this benefit. It amounted to two and a half days a year in total. The EAT agreed, but the industrial tribunal and the Court of Appeal said that this was justifiable. Lord Denning said it was a benefit given **in the interests of safety**. *Automotive Products v Peake* 1977 (CA)

The comments in this case, particularly Lord Denning's, are full of reactionary value-judgments. He said that the Act was not designed to set aside the 'traditional chivalry and courtesy which we expect mankind to give to womankind'. Even if it was, he said, Mr Peake's complaint was so minor it could be ignored. To describe two-and-a-half days at work every year as minimal shows the insensitivity of a salaried judge to an hourly paid manual worker. The decision is clearly wrong in law, but the EOC didn't step in to support an appeal so it is binding. The EAT and tribunals can, however, 'distinguish' (see page 15) any subsequent cases they get by saying the ruling in *Peake*'s case is confined solely to the special facts of that case.

If your employer – a bank or building society, for instance – offers you **the same services as are offered to the public** and you complain of discrimination, you take your claim to a county court under the non-employment provisions of the Act. However, if the service you get is different from that given to the public, or if you have a contractual right to the service, you can complain to a tribunal. Preferential loans from a bank, cheap housing from a housing association or cheap flights from an airline are employment matters and you can take your boss to a tribunal if they are offered discriminately.

If your boss offers benefits and training given by **other organisations**, you can claim if he discriminates against you (RR Act section 40; SD Act section 50). For example, it would be illegal to refuse to nominate you for an external training course.

Dismissal

Discriminatory sacking and selection for redundancy are outlawed in both Acts, and a dismissal on grounds of race, sex or marital status is also unfair under the TULR Act. See page 357 for the procedure.

Other detriment

Both anti-discrimination Acts have a catch-all clause making it illegal for employers to subject you to 'any other detriment' on grounds of race or sex.

> The Agricultural Wages Board increased basic rates and implemented equal pay in January 1976. The new rates were 91½p an hour and 80p an hour for people working less than 31 hours a week. Two weeks later 32 women (some with 20 years' service) employed by a firm of Kent fruit packers had their hours reduced from 40 to 30, and were renamed 'part-time casuals'. No men were treated in this way. Three members of the NUAAW brought claims under the SD Act. The Ashford tribunal rejected the company's claim that the women were not on fixed hours because they were allowed to take time off for holidays and for domestic reasons. The company had subjected the women to a **detriment** so the tribunal told them to put all the women back on 40 hours at the full-time rate and to pay arrears. *Morris v Scott and Knowles* 1976 (IT)

Such a blatant attack on the women could have amounted to a sacking in itself (constructive dismissal).

Racial discrimination is often disguised. It is particularly difficult to prove where there are *some* grounds for sacking but the circumstances in which it occurs clearly point to racism.

> A hospital employed white and Pakistani stokers in the boiler-room. One Pakistani was sacked for leaving the boiler unattended for a short time, but in similar circumstances a white worker had not been. Racial discrimination was proved and £1,100 awarded. *RRB Report 1972 Appendix VI Case 2*

What are the exceptions?

Genuine Occupational Qualification (GOQ)

It is legitimate to look for workers of a particular sex or racial group in order to fill certain clearly-defined jobs. In these cases the law says that being of that sex or race is a **genuine occupational qualification**. Before looking at these jobs it is important to point out that there are limits on the GOQ exceptions.

1. Being of a particular race or sex is a GOQ for the purpose **only of recruitment, hiring, transfer, training and promotion**. Employers can't justify discrimination in the **terms and conditions** offered to applicants, or those on which existing employees work, or for **sacking** or subjecting a worker to any other **detriment**. In other words, once you get the job, further discrimination is illegal.

2. Your boss can't claim a GOQ for a job if he already employs sufficient people of the appropriate race or sex to do the job. For example, if being a woman is, on the grounds of decency, a GOQ for a job as a sales assistant in a store selling women's clothes and there are already sufficient women to deal with the 'GOQ duties', discrimination against a man might be illegal.

3. Employers relying on a GOQ exception must prove it. **It cannot be used to justify victimisation or to justify discrimination against married people.**

When being a man or a woman is a qualification for the job

An employer is allowed to discriminate against a woman (or a man) on the grounds of sex (section 7) in any of the following circumstances:

■ The essential nature of the job calls for a man because

of his physiology – for example, a model. But greater strength and stamina can't be a justification.

■ A man is required for authenticity in entertainment – for example, an actor.

■ Decency or privacy require the job to be done by a man either because there is likely to be physical contact or because there are men around 'in a state of undress' or using 'sanitary facilities' – for example, a lavatory cleaner.

■ You are required to live-in, there are not separate sleeping and sanitary facilities *and* it is unreasonable to expect your boss to provide them – for instance, a construction site worker or a seaman.

■ The job is at a single-sex establishment where people require supervision and it is reasonable to reserve the job for a person of the same sex – for example, a prison officer.

■ You provide people with 'personal services' promoting their welfare or education or similar needs, and those services can 'most effectively' be provided by a man – for instance, a member of a social work team.

■ The job is restricted by law to one sex – for example, night work in factories where there is no certificate allowing women to work nights. But a failure by your employer to apply for exemption after you request it might count as discrimination. In fact, in 1977 only 210,000 women and girls were allowed to work nights and weekends in factories.

■ The job involves work abroad which can be done, or done effectively, only by a man – for instance in the Middle East.

■ The job is one of two which are to be held by a married couple.

When belonging to a particular race is a qualification for the job

An employer is allowed to discriminate on the grounds of race (section 5) in any of the following circumstances:

■ The job involves providing one racial group with personal welfare services which can most effectively be provided by a person in the same group.

And for reasons of authenticity:

■ In entertainment – for example, an actor.

■ In art or photography – for example, a model.

■ In a bar or restaurant with a particular setting – for example, a waiter in a Chinese restaurant.

Problems with GOQs

Although the exceptions are different, the problems of GOQs are common to sex and racial discrimination. Remember that it's the tribunals that will be the judges of 'privacy', 'decency', 'most effectively performed', 'personal services' and 'reasonable'. Few chairmen and lay members of tribunals are women (see page 10). There are even fewer members from minority groups.

The exceptions can be very broad. Workers in social services, probation and teaching are vulnerable to the 'personal services' clause. Hospital and shop workers are liable to the 'state of undress' exception. If you think the clauses are being abused, challenge your boss using the official **questionnaire** (see below).

Immigration and work permits

Discrimination permitted by some legislation continues despite the two anti-discrimination Acts. The main exception to the Acts is the law on immigration, particularly the very restrictive 1971 Immigration Act.

The RR Act does not outlaw anything contained in any other Act or done by any minister pursuant to one. Conditions applying to entry into the UK are therefore legal. These are laid down in the Immigration Rules (House of Commons Papers 1973 Nos 79–82).

Work permits are not required for Commonwealth citizens who had a parent or grandparent born in the UK. If you have lived here for five years, you don't need a permit, but you should apply for any restrictions on you to be lifted. Workers from EEC countries don't need work permits in order to enter the UK to look for work. If you find work within six months, you need a residence permit (which lasts for five years, unless 'the holder is living on public funds although capable of maintaining himself').

Other Commonwealth citizens and other foreign nationals require work permits. Application is made to the Home Office and the permit – initially limited to a maximum of 12 months – is issued by the DE. It is for a specific post with a particular employer. If it runs out, your boss can apply for extension, but there is nothing you can do to force him to apply. If he refuses, you can't complain under the RR Act. If you change jobs, you must notify the DE. Registration with the police is still required unless your stay is unlimited.

Unskilled seasonal workers – hired for holiday camps or the harvest, for example – cannot stay beyond 31 October.

Other laws

Sex discrimination contained in the social security and tax laws continues unabated. Special treatment of women in the Factories Act and in specific industries such as those involving lead and radioactivity is unaffected. The EOC is investigating these exceptions.

Pregnancy, death and retirement

It is not unlawful under the SD Act for employers to discriminate by giving special treatment to women in connection with pregnancy or childbirth, or by providing death and retirement benefits, for example, specifying different retirement ages for men and women.

Under the Social Security Pensions Act 1975 employers must, though, provide equal access to occupational pension schemes. This means that from 6 April 1978 men and women must be treated equally as regards age and length of service for admission to a scheme and in the specification of voluntary or obligatory membership.

Other unlawful acts

In addition to the main forms of direct and indirect discrimination, both Acts outlaw other actions. These are contained in sections 37–42 of the SD Act and 28–33 of the RR Act. These sections are generally enforceable only by the Commissions.

Discriminatory practices

A discriminatory practice is any indirect discrimination. A **potential** discriminatory practice occurs when all the elements of indirect discrimination are present **except a victim**.

Example: if buyers in a big store are recruited from among the sales assistants and the employer demands an English education, workers educated in the Commonwealth will suffer indirect discrimination. If the requirement proves to be such a deterrent that no one educated abroad ever applies, no case will arise. But this does not make the requirement any less offensive. It remains a potential discriminatory practice, and in this case the CRE can issue a **non-discrimination notice** (see below) to have the requirement changed, even though no one has actually complained.

Advertisements

Discriminatory advertisements are unlawful. Jobs with sexual connotations such as waiter, salesgirl, postman and stewardess are discriminatory unless it is made clear that they are open to both sexes. If the job advertised requires applicants to be of a particular racial group and this is a valid GOQ, the advertisement is still illegal.

For example, an advertisement for white nurses to work in a South African hospital would be illegal, even though the jobs are abroad and not subject to the Act (RR Act section 29). There must be no trace of racial discrimination. But employers can advertise for applicants from one *sex* or the other for jobs where discrimination is permissible.

Instructions

If your supervisor, or anyone in authority over you, or whose wishes you usually implement (such as a client), instructs you to discriminate, that itself is unlawful.

London Industrial Art had a vacancy for a clerk/typist and contacted an agency. Details of an applicant were sent and an interview arranged. When the company saw she was black they sent her away and told the agency they did not want 'anyone from Africa' because Africans were not competent. The company was found liable and ordered to pay court costs. *Race Relations Board v London Industrial Art* 1975–76

Pressure

It is unlawful to put pressure on people to make them discriminate. Pressure is defined as providing or offering benefits, or invoking or threatening a detriment. It would include a strike.

Aid

If you knowingly aid someone who is discriminating, you are both liable. You can escape liability if you had reasonable grounds for relying on an assurance that the act is lawful (for example, because they tell you there is a GOQ).

Liability of employers

If you allege discrimination by, say, a personnel officer recruiting staff for a company, you can sue both the officer and the company if the officer discriminates. Employers are liable for the acts of their employees done with or without their knowledge in the course of their employment.

It is, though, a defence for employers to show that they took all reasonably practicable steps to prevent discrimination by their staff.

Inciting racial hatred

It is an offence to do or say anything in a public place which is likely to stir up racial hatred (see page 312). Enoch Powell made a speech in January 1977 invoking images of civil war as a result of immigration. If the RR Act had been in force then, he could have been prosecuted.

The Equality Commissions

Duties

The Equal Opportunities Commission (EOC) and the Commission for Racial Equality (CRE) have similar but not identical duties and powers in the spheres in which they operate. Their duties are:
■ to try to eliminate discrimination;
■ to promote equality of opportunity between men and women and between racial groups, and to promote good race relations;
■ to review the working of the two Acts and to propose amendments.

Members of the Commissions are appointed by the Home Secretary.

Members and staff are paid by the government but operate independently. Both Commissions must publish annual reports surveying general developments.

Research and education

The Commissions can undertake or assist (financially or otherwise) research and educational activities. Grants can be given to any organisation promoting equal opportunity and good race relations. The Home Secretary and the Treasury must agree to this.

The CRE can issue codes of practice on how to stop discrimination in employment. It must publish a draft and hear representations before sending it to the Home Secretary, who must put it before Parliament.

Formal investigations

The Commissions can investigate particular industries, practices and issues and these can be referred to them by the appropriate minister. The EOC, for example, examined the implementation of equal pay in five hundred companies. The Commissions can conduct **general** inquiries, but a **formal investigation** must be carried out along specified lines. A **formal investigation has to be made before the Commissions can use any of their enforcement powers.**

In a formal investigation the Commissions:

1. must draw up terms of reference;

2. must give notice, usually by advertisements in the press, unless the investigation is confined to particular individuals. In cases of racial discrimination the CRE has to inform individuals about any allegations against them. They have the right to state their case and be represented by a lawyer or anyone the Commission does not consider 'unsuitable';

3. may require disclosure of information. If you suppress or destroy documents or if you refuse to attend to give evidence, you can be fined up to £400. For general investigations, the Commissions require the Home Secretary's authority in order to require disclosure;

4. must publish their report;

5. may make general recommendations on policies, procedures and the law and can issue **non-discrimination notices** (below). The earlier race laws were weak because there was no power to compel disclosure or to enforce the law. It is essential that workers ensure that the Commissions use their new powers and follow through their reports with systematic checks.

Legal assistance

You can get assistance from the Commissions for bringing cases in courts or tribunals – see below.

Enforcement by the Commissions

Some parts of the legislation can be enforced only by the Commissions. Usually these are where no individual has suffered as a result of the discriminatory act or where the remedy is an injunction.

Non-discrimination notices

The Commissions can issue a non-discrimination notice if, during a **formal** investigation, they find evidence of unlawful discrimination. They can do this even though no proceedings have been brought already against the discriminator (RR Act section 58; SD Act section 67).

A notice lasts for five years. The Commissions can stop further ('persistent') discrimination within these five years by getting an injunction. This is dealt with below.

A notice can be issued if someone has
■ committed direct or indirect discrimination
■ applied an actual or **potential** discriminatory practice
■ published an unlawful advertisement
■ issued unlawful instructions, or
■ put pressure on an employer to discriminate.

A non-discrimination notice requires the recipient
1. not to commit any discriminatory acts;
2. to change his practices and arrangements in order to comply with **1.**;
3. to inform the Commission that he has made the changes and what they are;
4. to take reasonable steps, as specified in the notice, to tell people concerned about the changes;
5. to provide information so that the Commission can verify that the notice has been complied with; and
6. to give the information in a specified form and by a certain date.

Before issuing a non-discrimination notice, the Commission must tell the proposed recipient of its intention, give its reasons, give him at least 28 days to make written and/or oral representations, and take these into account. If it still goes ahead, the recipient can appeal, in employment matters, to an industrial tribunal within six weeks. The tribunal can quash or vary the notice only if its requirements are **unreasonable**, or **based on incorrect facts**.

As soon as any appeal is dealt with, or the time allowed for appealing has run out, the notice becomes **final**. It is operative for five years from that date, and is entered in a register which anyone can inspect and take copies of. These registers are kept at the Commissions' offices.

The Commissions can start follow-up investigations, with all the statutory powers to compel information and witnesses, during the five-year period. **These powers are in-**

**effective unless you report any breach to the Commissions. If
you have any evidence of subsequent discrimination, report it.**

Injunctions for persistent discrimination

The Commissions can get an injunction against employers and others who discriminate or are likely to.

Breach of an injunction is enforceable as contempt of
court. Robert Relf, a former Ku Klux Klan activist, was
gaoled when he refused to comply with a Birmingham court
order to remove his racist house-for-sale sign in May 1976.

How to claim

Before you make a claim to an industrial tribunal you
may need more information about the employer's practices.
This will be particularly important if you are alleging discrimination in recruitment, because you won't know much
about the employer, can't get union support and are out of
work.

To try to meet this problem you can use a **questionnaire**
(see page 356) to obtain information. The form is not compulsory, but it will be used in evidence and tribunals can draw
adverse inferences from an employer's failure to complete it.

Provided you have been employed for 26 weeks at 16
or more hours a week (plus exceptions – see page 341) and
you have been sacked, you should claim under both the TULR
Act *and* the anti-discrimination Acts. Otherwise, your claim
is restricted to the anti-discrimination Acts.

Claim **within three months** of the event you are complaining about. See page 357 for the procedure.

**The Commissions can help you to bring a case and can
provide legal aid.** If you can't get union support, you should
write to them and request it. Addresses on page 400. Sometimes they will provide legal representation in cases involving
important questions of principle. They monitor cases, too,
and occasionally offer assistance to individuals in appeals
from industrial tribunals to the EAT.

Advertisements, instructions and pressure

If you are personally affected by one of these unlawful
practices you can complain to a tribunal. For example, you
may be interested in applying for a job which is advertised in
a way which indirectly discriminates against you; or your
boss may give instructions to your supervisor not to make

overtime available to you. But the Commissions can start proceedings whether someone is directly prejudiced or not.

Proving discrimination

This is the most difficult part. The record of the first year of sex discrimination cases shows a success rate of only 19 per cent in employment matters. The former Race Relations Board usually lost when it brought criminal proceedings in the courts.

If you allege **direct** discrimination you have to bring enough evidence to show you have been treated less favourably than a person of the opposite sex or another racial group was treated, or would have been treated. This evidence must suggest that the reason was your sex or race. The employer then has to show either

1. that you were not treated unfavourably or
2. if you *were*, it was not because of your sex or race.

If you allege **indirect** discrimination you have to go much further. **You have to bring evidence** to show the employer applied a condition or requirement which is applied to everyone but which

1. you could not comply with;
2. was to your detriment; and
3. was such that a considerably smaller proportion of people of your sex or race than others could comply with it.

Once you have got over these hurdles, the employer must then prove that the requirement was justifiable. You will need firm evidence to avoid defeat on these vague terms – 'detriment', 'considerable', 'justifiable'. So prepare your case carefully.

If you can also bring a claim for unfair dismissal under the TULR Act, the burden of proving the reason for sacking and justifying it falls on your boss (see page 157).

An employer who says that discrimination is justified because of a GOQ must prove it.

Remedies

On an individual complaint to a tribunal the following remedies are available if the tribunal considers them 'just and equitable' (RR Act section 56; SD Act section 65):

1. declaration
2. compensation

3. re-engagement or reinstatement
4. recommendation of action to be taken.

Declaration

This declares your rights and says that you were unlawfully discriminated against. It is not enforceable but may have some persuasive influence.

Compensation

You can be awarded compensation for:
■ **actual** losses, such as expenses and wages;
■ **future** losses of wages and benefits;
■ injury to your feelings.

Jeanette Johnston (page 97) was given £200 for injury to feelings. The maximum amount of compensation is £5,200. Tribunals can't reduce this on the grounds that you 'contributed' to the discrimination as they can in unfair dismissal cases.

> A West Indian was sacked during his probationary period in a nationalised industry. He was a skilled mechanic and had been in the RAF and in private sector garages. His boss said he needed close supervision and was sacked. A white worker had two warnings before this happened. The West Indian was awarded £805 compensation. *Race Relations Board Report 1975–76 Appendix V Case 1.*

You can't get compensation for indirect discrimination which your employer proves was **unintentional**. (RR Act section 50; SD Act section 66). However, if you are claiming unfair dismissal as well, you (may) get up to £13,400 in total compensation (see page 182).

Re-engagement and reinstatement

Tribunals have no specific power under the anti-discrimination laws to order re-engagement or reinstatement. They can recommend action (see below). But if you link a discrimination claim to a claim under the TULR Act, the tribunal must ask if you want to go back. If it orders this and your boss refuses, additional compensation must be awarded. (EP Act section 71–72.)

Recommended action

A tribunal can make a **recommendation** that the employer should take action 'appearing . . . to be practicable for the purpose of obviating or reducing the adverse effect on the complainant of any act of discrimination'. Of course, this might include a recommendation of reinstatement, but it is weaker than a **court order**. A recommendation could specify, for example, changes in promotion, training and recruitment policies.

Trade union action against discrimination

Determined action by trade unionists to stamp out discrimination is the only way to make the Acts effective. You can't rely on the legislation alone – the burden of proof is itself a formidable obstacle to enforcement.

The TUC has recommended that unions should negotiate collective agreements with the following equal opportunity clause:

> The Parties to this Agreement are committed to the development of positive policies to promote equal opportunity in employment regardless of workers' sex, marital status, creed, colour, race or ethnic origins.*
> This principle will apply in respect of all conditions of work including pay, hours of work, holiday entitlement, overtime and shiftwork, work allocation, guaranteed earnings, sick pay, pensions, recruitment, training, promotion and redundancy. The management undertake to draw opportunities for training and promotion to the attention of all eligible employees, and to inform all employees of this Agreement on equal opportunity.
>
> The parties agree that they will review from time to time, through their joint machinery, the operation of this equal opportunity policy.
>
> If any employee considers that he or she is suffering from unequal treatment on the grounds of sex, marital status, creed, colour, race or ethnic origins he or she may make a complaint which will be dealt with through the agreed procedure for dealing with grievances.

This clause is not enough. To be effective, you should:
■ recruit all workers into unions and encourage immigrant workers to play an active part
■ press for language training courses and point out their existence

*Nationality and national origins, although included in the RR Act, are mysteriously absent from the model clause.

■ develop links with Community Relations Officers
■ oppose racist actions and attitudes wherever they occur.

Summary

1. It is illegal for employers to discriminate against you on the grounds of sex, marriage, race, colour, nationality or ethnic or national origins.

2. Discrimination means an employer treats you less favourably than he would treat another person (direct discrimination), or he makes a requirement that applies to all workers but which it is much harder for you to comply with (indirect discrimination).

3. You can complain to a tribunal if an employer discriminates against you in recruitment, terms and conditions, transfer, promotion, training, benefits or dismissal or by subjecting you to any detriment.

4. Discrimination in pay or contractual terms between men and women doing similar work is covered by the Equal Pay Act.

5. Discrimination is permitted if employers can prove that being of a particular race or sex is a genuine occupational qualification for a particular job.

6. The Equality Commissions can take legal action against people who advertise, or give help to, or put pressure on others to discriminate. You may get legal assistance from the Commissions to bring a case yourself.

7. If you win at a tribunal it has power to award compensation and to recommend that the employer take action to prevent discrimination. If you are sacked, a tribunal can order your boss to reinstate you.

9.

Equal Pay

The problem of low pay for women / the
basic elements of the Equal Pay Act / how it
fits in with the Sex Discrimination Act /
equality with a man in the same employment /
'like work' and 'practical differences' / duties,
hours, responsibility, training, skill,
experience, legal bans / job evaluation /
'genuine material differences' / location,
grading, historical anomalies and red-circling,
length of service, market forces / how to
claim / proving it / remedies / discriminatory
agreements and pay structures / how effective
is the Act? / what reforms are needed? / and
a summary.

In 1888 the TUC decided unanimously that 'it is desirable in the interests of both men and women that in trades where women do the same work as men, they shall receive the same payment'. A government committee in 1919 and a Royal Commission in 1946 said the same thing. Parliament finally responded in 1970 by passing Labour's Equal Pay Act.

The Act became effective on 29 December 1975. Despite this unprecedented lead-in period of five-and-a-half years, women's earnings are still much lower than men's, as the figures for April 1977 show. (Since, on average, men worked five hours a week longer than women, it is more realistic to compare average hourly rather than weekly earnings.)

	1. Men	2. Women	2 as a percentage of 1
Average weekly earnings	£76.80 (42.4 hours)	£50.00 (37.3 hours)	64
Average hourly earnings	1.81	1.34	74

Source: New Earnings Survey 1977

Employers still think it is cheaper to employ women. *The Sunday Times* business news gave this advice to readers on 2 January 1977 which, although tongue-in-cheek, reflects common prejudices:

> If you have to employ people, employ women. They work harder, faster and better. They are cheaper and do not strike unless really badly treated. They are also prettier. If you cannot attract women, use non-union labour, preferably immigrants. Even better, illegal immigrants.

The Equal Pay Act can be measured in terms of how differentials between men and women have narrowed. Acting against it are traditional attitudes and legacies. In the past, women have had fewer skills, fewer opportunities, less training, more breaks in continuity of employment and less union organisation than men. Those facts necessarily perpetuate unequal pay, and **low pay** for jobs which have historically been for women only.

During the first year of the Equal Pay Act, men's average hourly earnings rose by 8.5 per cent, women's by 9.3 per cent. On the actual earnings figures given above, women will, at this rate of progress, achieve equal pay in AD 2018.

Internationally, the struggle for equal treatment has been reflected in the Universal Declaration of Human Rights, the European Social Charter, the International Covenant on Economic, Social and Cultural Rights and International Labour Organisation (ILO) Conventions and Recommendations. In the EEC, Article 119 of the Treaty of Rome requires equal pay for equal work and Directive 75/117 extends this to include by 1978 work of equal value. Equal pay for equal work has been a legal requirement since the UK joined the EEC on 1 January 1973, but no claims can be brought for arrears prior to 29 December 1975, the date the Equal Pay Act came into effect.

This chapter deals with the Act and decisions made by tribunals and courts. The Equal Pay Act **can** be used strategically to improve conditions **when negotiations and industrial action fail or are inappropriate.**

Where to find the law

Equal Pay Act 1970, as amended by the Sex Discrimination Act 1975 (SD Act). (The Equal Pay Act is reprinted in full in schedule 1 of the SD Act.) Article 119 of the Treaty of Rome.

The Act's basic elements

The Act says that *in certain circumstances* men and women are entitled to be paid the same and to receive the same terms and conditions in their contracts, collective agreements and pay structures. If you don't have parity, your contract, agreement or pay structure will be amended to include the right to equal terms.

Despite its narrow title, the Act deals with **all terms and conditions contained in either a man's or a woman's contract. It applies equally to men and women**, although all the examples given in this handbook relate to women. The right to equal pay applies in any of the following three situations:

1. You are employed on like work with a man in the same employment. This means:

    a. you do the **same work,** or

    b. you do **work of a broadly similar nature** and differences are not of **practical importance** in relation to your terms and conditions.

2. You are employed on work **rated as equivalent** with that of a man in the same employment, following a job evaluation study.

Provided that in **1.** and **2.** above, the variation in your terms is **not genuinely due to a material difference** between **your case** and his.

3. You are covered by a **pay structure** or **collective agreement** which is discriminatory.

1. and **2.** are the **individual** aspects of the Act; **3.** is the **collective** aspect. Each of the basic elements is dealt with separately below (page 125 for individual aspects, page 138

Diagram 3 Your Equal Pay Act Rights

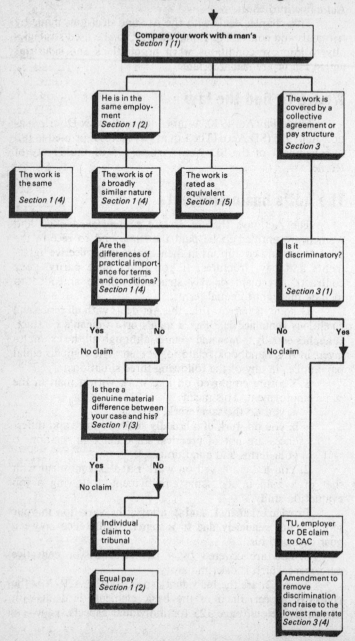

for collective aspects). Diagram 3 shows the steps you must take if you have to enforce your rights by going to law.

The Equal Pay Act deals with matters of **contract**. It says that 'equality clauses' are deemed to be incorporated into every contract. In other words, you have a contractual right to equal treatment. If there is a dispute, the tribunals can amend contracts to provide equal terms and conditions.

Conversely, anything **outside the contract** cannot be remedied by the Act. For this you have to look to the SD Act.

The right to equality under the Equal Pay Act applies if any term of your contract *is* or *becomes* less favourable than a man's. This means you can bring a claim if you are getting parity, but you think you should be getting **better** terms.

> **Example:** A job is advertised on scale 1–5. You have outstanding qualifications and six years' experience, so you enter at scale 5. A man with fewer qualifications and less experience is subsequently appointed on scale 5. You are clearly entitled to *better* terms than he is. Your right to scale 5 under your contract has therefore become relatively less favourable to you. So you can claim under the Equal Pay Act. Your contract should be amended to maintain the differential obtained through your superior qualifications and experience. (Compare *Pointon v Sussex University* page 136 below, where the tribunal decided that the woman was not in fact better qualified than the man. If she was, she might have won her case).

Sex discrimination and equal pay

There is no overlap between the SD and Equal Pay Acts. In fact there is a *gap* in the coverage which can deprive you of all protection. The Home Office *Guide* to the SD Act describes the relationship as follows (practical examples have been inserted in order to help):

> **a.** If the less favourable treatment relates to the **payment of money** which is regulated by a contract of employment, only the Equal Pay Act can apply.
> **Example:** You get 80p an hour. A male colleague gets 85p.
> **b.** If the employee is treated less favourably than an employee of the other sex who is doing the same or broadly similar work or whose work has been given an

equal value under job evaluation and the less favourable treatment relates to **something which is regulated by the contract of employment** of either of them, only the Equal Pay Act can apply.

Example: You are hourly paid. He is weekly paid and on staff status.

c. If the less favourable treatment relates to **a matter which is not included in a contract** (either expressly or by virtue of the Equal Pay Act), only the SD Act can apply.

Example: He is sent on a management training course, you aren't.

d. If the less favourable treatment relates to **a matter (other than the payment of money) in a contract, and the comparison is with workers who are not doing the same or broadly similar work** or work which has been given an equal value under job evaluation, only the SD Act can apply.

Example: Men's contracts entitle them to a cheap mortgage from the employer, yours doesn't.

e. If the complaint relates to **a matter (other than the payment of money) which is regulated by an employee's contract** of employment, but is based on an allegation that **an employee of the other sex would be treated more favourably** in similar circumstances (that is, it does not relate to the actual treatment of an existing employee of the other sex), only the SD Act can apply.

Example: You are entitled, under your contract, to a cheap mortgage, but it must be guaranteed by your husband. You know a male employee would not have to get his wife's guarantee.

Diagram 4 illustrates the relationship between the two Acts described in the above examples.

If you have followed this tortuous trail you may have noticed the gap. Isabella Meeks (page 100) fell into it. She showed that her employers **indirectly** discriminated against women by paying a higher hourly rate to people who worked 35 or more hours a week. Fewer women can work full-time than men. But since the unfavourable treatment related to *money*, only the Equal Pay Act applied. Under this Act Ms Meeks had to compare herself with a man. She could find no men doing similar work to her. So she was excluded under the SD Act and was also ineligible under the Equal Pay Act.

Diagram 4 Equal Pay and Sex Discrimination

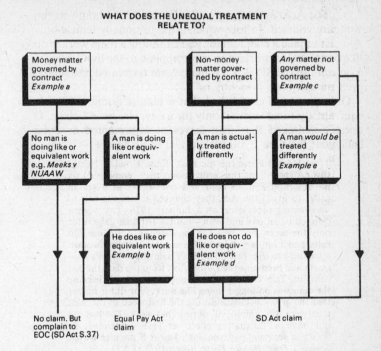

Parliament intended that the two Acts should be complementary. But the flaw occurs when no men are available for comparison, or when they are available but a tribunal rules that they are not doing similar work to you. The only straw you can grasp is to complain to the EOC. The EOC can bring proceedings under section 37 of the SD Act for the kind of 'discriminatory practice' that Isabella Meeks proved. But you can't get compensation this way (SD Act section 73).

Equal with whom?

The individual part of the Equal Pay Act depends on there being men and women in the same employment. **On the assumption that we are dealing with a women's claim** (although the same applies to men) that requirement can be broken down into two parts.

1. There must be a man

The Act requires you to find a man with whom you can compare yourself. In jobs which are traditionally female-only you can't make a claim unless you can show a male worker on like or equivalent work. You can complain to the EOC though. You *can* use the SD Act if a man *would be* treated differently, even though none presently is.

Once you have established that a man is doing similar or equivalently-rated work, if only for a day, you have a claim. It doesn't matter if that man **leaves** or **is promoted** or is **on holiday** at the time – you are entitled to his terms.

> Trust Houses Forte run the Post House Hotel at Heathrow Airport. In the grill room they employed six waitresses at 85p an hour and one waiter at 97½p. In order to avoid the Act, they changed the man's title to 'banqueting supervisor' on 5 January 1976. The women claimed equal pay and won – but the tribunal gave it for only the seven days between the date the Act came into force and 5 January. Ann Sorbie and the five other women appealed; so did THF. The EAT said the women's contracts had been amended with effect from the date the Act came in. **They could not be changed again simply because the man was no longer doing like work.** Nor did it matter that the grill was closed during the first week of the Act; they were still 'employed' during that week. The Act did not have a 'fluctuating effect' as THF contended. **So once you get equal pay, you don't lose it if the man leaves.**
> *Sorbie v Trust Houses Forte Hotels* 1977 (EAT)

What happens if you **take over from a man** but get less money than he was getting? This is usually grounds for a claim, but not always, the EAT has said. Joyce Nuttall (see below page 130) took over from a man but was paid £6.50 a week less. Her claim was dismissed because the EAT said the work she did was different. Ms Nuttall could, however, have made a claim for sex discrimination in this case because she was offered work on different terms to those that would be offered to a man.

In one case, the EAT allowed a woman to compare herself with a man who had left five months earlier, before the Equal Pay Act took effect (*McCarthys v Smith* 1978).

When you make your claim, **you** decide who you want to be compared with, **not** your employer, nor the tribunal. Once you decide, the comparison must be made with that man.

> Mary Ainsworth worked in Glass Tubes' Chesterfield factory. She re-inspected glassware after it had been inspected by a man. She got about £2 a week less and

claimed parity. The company found a male re-inspector on nights who was getting her rate and so the tribunal dismissed her claim. Supported by the GMWU she appealed. The EAT said the tribunal must consider her claim for parity with the man she had nominated. It was a short-lived success, for the tribunal later held that the work was not broadly similar. *Ainsworth v Glass Tubes and Components* 1977 (EAT)

2. In the same employment

Comparison must be with a man in **the same employment** (section 1(6)). This means you are employed by the same or an associated employer at the same establishment or at establishments in Great Britain **where common terms and conditions are observed,** either generally or for workers of your 'class'.

There is no definition of 'establishment' but factors considered under other Acts are: geographical, managerial or financial separation, separate supply and servicing arrangements. In order to claim parity across different plants of the same firm or its higher-paid subsidiaries, you would have to show a common pay scale arising out of the same negotiations with the same unions.

You can compare yourself both with employees and with self-employed workers who do work for the employer. **This could be useful if contractors are paid on a higher rate than direct labour.**

'Like work' and 'practical differences'

Section 1 (4) defines 'like work' as follows:

A woman is to be regarded as employed on like work with men if, but only if, her work and theirs is of the same or a broadly similar nature, and the differences (if any) between the things she does and the things they do are not of practical importance in relation to terms and conditions of employment; and accordingly in comparing her work with theirs regard shall be had to the frequency or otherwise with which any such differences occur in practice as well as to the nature and extent of the differences.

These questions are important in negotiating equal pay with employers. There are five major areas where employers have tried to avoid equal pay. These involve:

1. extra duties
2. different hours
3. responsibility
4. training, skill and experience
5. legal bans

Extra duties

The most frequent abuse of the Equal Pay Act involves employers weaving extra duties into men's contracts. While some of these abuses still exist, the end of the road for them was signalled in the *Electrolux* case.

> All but one of 600 women working on the fridge and freezer line of Electrolux in Luton were on grade 01. The basic rate for piecework was 4·1p. All of the 1,300 men were on grade 10, with a rate of 6·3p. The company admitted the men and women did similar work but claimed the men were obliged to accept **different duties** – to transfer to different jobs which may be less well paid or more physically demanding, to work nights and to do non-productive work. The EAT upheld the tribunal's award of equal pay. But the company later changed the women's contracts and refused to apply the ruling to any women except those who had taken their cases. There was a strike and the EOC and ACAS were called in to investigate the whole pay structure. *Electrolux v Hutchinson* 1976 (EAT)

Mr Justice Phillips said that these differences could not be regarded as important.

> For such a difference to be material . . . it must be shown that as well as being obliged to do additional, different duties the men in fact do so to some significant extent.

In other words, the key question is **what happens in practice**, not, what does the contract say? If different work *is* done by the men, the EAT says, the tribunal must then ask what is 'the nature of the work done, how often does it take place, how important is it, and so on'.

This section was interpreted in the first equal pay case to reach the EAT. The judgment was heavily critical of tribunals which take a 'too pedantic approach'.

> Barbara Lawton worked a 40-hour week cooking lunches for 10–20 directors. She was her own boss. She claimed equal pay with two assistant chefs in the works canteen who worked a 45-hour week cooking three meals a day in two sittings (that is, 350 meals). They had to prepare meals in advance and were answerable to the head chef. The EAT upheld a Nottinghamshire tribunal's award of equal pay as the difference was not of practical

importance in relation to terms and conditions. *Capper Pass Ltd v Lawton* 1976 (EAT)

Mr Justice Phillips said:

> the work need not be of the **same** nature in order to be like work. It is enough if it is of a similar nature. Indeed, it need only be broadly similar. In such cases . . . there will necessarily be differences between the work done.

He went on to say that tribunals should use a 'broad judgment' in looking at whether work is 'broadly similar', otherwise every case would fail. He said tribunals must ask the following questions.

1. Is the work of the same or a broadly similar nature? This involves a general consideration of the type of work and the skill and knowledge required to do it. It can be answered without a 'minute examination of the detail of the differences'.

2. If it is of a broadly similar nature, are the differences of practical importance in relation to terms and conditions? Disregard trivial differences 'not likely in the real world to be reflected in terms and conditions'. Once broad similarity is established it should be regarded as like work unless the differences could be **expected** to result in different terms and conditions. Then take account of the frequency, the nature and the extent of these differences. In other words, **differences are important only if, in a freely and objectively negotiated pay settlement which paid no regard to sex, they would be reflected in different rates of pay.**

Different hours

Some employers have argued that they don't have to give equal pay to workers who do similar work at different times of the day. To this, the EAT has said:

> in the context of the Equal Pay Act . . . the mere time at which the work is performed should be disregarded when considering the differences between the things which the woman does and the things which the man does . . . [In] applying section 1 (4) no attention should be paid to the fact that the men work at some different time of the day, if that is the only difference between what the women do and they do.

The facts leading to that judgment were:

> Alice Dugdale and four other women worked on quality control at Kraft's food factory in Liverpool. They worked days for £32·80 basic plus £5·80 day-shift premium. Men did similar work at night and every third Sunday morning. (Women are prevented by the Factories

Act from working at these times, unless exempt). The
men got £42·45 basic plus £11·60 night-shift premium,
that is £9·65 on basic and £5·80 on shift rate more than
the women. Supported by USDAW the women claimed
parity of basic rates. After two hearings and an EAT appeal, the tribunal said two women weren't doing similar
work. One was, and got parity of basic rates. Alice and
her colleague did similar work, but the men did slightly
more work **at night**. So the women got 90 per cent of the
men's basic rate, 10 per cent reflecting this real difference.
Dugdale v Kraft 1977 (EAT)

It is easy to see discrimination in a case where the basic
rates are different *and* where night shifts attract a higher
premium than days. If there is no premium, but the men
receive a higher basic rate, you have to apportion the rate to
take account of their availability for night. For example, if all
the men work a three-shift system and get £50 a week, and all
the women work a double day-shift for £35, the men are
effectively getting a night-shift premium of £15. It would be
difficult to show that this was 'genuinely due' to the night
work *alone*. You could argue that, say, £6 should be treated
as night-shift premium. You could then claim equality on the
new notional basic of £44.

Responsibility

Responsibility is a factor which may make a practical
difference in terms and conditions. In comparing two jobs you
must look at the circumstances in which they are done (which
would include the degree of responsibility) and not simply at
the actual work. If a mistake by the man has a more serious
effect than a mistake by the woman, he carries more responsibility. This can be a 'practical difference' under section 1 (4)
of the Equal Pay Act.

Joyce Nuttall was a production scheduler, responsible
for ordering parts and materials for the production of
fork-lift trucks. She did the same work as a man, but she
dealt with 2,400 items up to a value of £2·50, whereas he
looked after 1,200 items from £5 to £1,000. He got £6·50 a
week more. The EAT said the tribunal was wrong to
disregard *the consequences of mistakes – responsibility is a
practical difference. Eaton v Nuttall* 1977 (EAT)

The ultimate example of a difference caused by responsibility was the decision of the tribunal which found that
social worker Susan Waddington, though paid less than a man,
was not entitled to equal pay as she was *more* responsible.

Susan Waddington was a community leader paid on the national scale for social workers. She suggested opening a playground and appointed a play leader. He was paid on the youth leaders' scale and got £400 a year more, although she had overall control and was more responsible. The Nottingham tribunal said she could not claim parity. But the EAT said the tribunal had looked mainly at their job descriptions and contracts and not at the *similar nature* of the work they did. The EAT sent it back to be reheard, but the tribunal refused to alter its decision. *Waddington v Leicester Council for Voluntary Services* 1977 (EAT)

The tribunal's decision is clearly perverse. It could have said that Susan Waddington's contract had **become** less favourable than the man's (as in the example on page 123) and given her parity.

The case is also important for what was said about grading systems (see page 134 below).

Training, skill and experience

Different levels of skill and experience can make the nature of the work itself different, and so preclude equal pay under section 1 (4). (These factors might more appropriately be grounds for **personal** distinctions between a man and a woman who are employed on like work, and so be a 'material difference', within section 1 (3), which is discussed below.) The nature of the work done must be quite different when performed by someone with training, skill and experience if section 1 (4) is to be used to exclude equal pay.

For example, a machine operator with three years' experience may be doing approximately the same sort of work as a new starter. But the extra experience *may* mean that he can do it more quickly, more efficiently, with fewer stoppages and be able to recognise problems earlier and to train new starters.

Legal bans

The ban on women working in factories at nights and on Sundays (Factories Act section 93) is **not** itself a practical difference unless the work done by men in those hours is different from that done by women. As Alice Dugdale's case showed, the basic rate should be the same and a notional basic rate should be hewn out of a rate that embraces night work.

The ban on women working in certain processes, such as those involving lead and radioactivity, is probably a practical difference sufficient to defeat a claim for parity. Trade unionists should demand that the work should be made safe enough for both men and women to do it.

Work rated as equivalent

The second legal route to equal pay is through job evaluation. Before you get into any discussions on job evaluation it is advisable to be familiar with the trade-union arguments on this management technique. See, for example, *Work Study* by Jim Powell (Arrow Books). Many unions and the TUC provide training in this subject. Get time off to study if your boss proposes job evaluation.

Men and women are entitled to equality if their jobs have been given an equal value

in terms of the demand made on a worker under various headings (for instance effort, skill, decision), on a study undertaken with a view to evaluating in those terms the jobs to be done by all or any of the employees in an undertaking (section 1 (5)).

The factors listed are only a few among those that can be considered. No method of job evaluation is specified – you can use any of the accepted methods such as job ranking, paired comparisons, job classification, points assessment or factor comparison. All of these are recognised by the Advisory, Conciliation and Arbitration Service (ACAS). (ACAS is required to conciliate if you make a claim to a tribunal for equal pay).

So **like work** and **work rated as equivalent** are separate and mutually exclusive routes to equal pay. Usually a claim cannot proceed for like work if a job evaluation on the lines described in section 1 (5) has been carried out. The only exceptions to this rule are

1. if there is a fundamental error in the job evaluation, or

2. if the study is not 'valid' because it is not 'thorough in analysis and capable of impartial application'.

Two cases illustrate these points.

Job evaluation was carried out by Broxtowe Council in Nottingham. The results were not accepted in full by either the Council, the unions or the workers involved. So six women brought a claim on the basis of *like work*. The EAT said the tribunal was *wrong to disregard* the job evaluation and sent the case back for reconsideration. Only if there was a *fundamental error* could the study be disregarded and the claim proceed on the basis of *like work*. *Greene v Broxtowe District Council* 1977 (EAT)

It seems to be irrelevant that either or both sides reject the study. This means that, once made, it is difficult to ignore a job evaluation study.

In the second case, Joyce Nuttall, as we have seen, was claiming parity. During the appeal hearing the EAT found that there was a form of job evaluation and sent the case back to a fresh tribunal to consider this. She disputed the worth of the scheme because it took account of personal factors. Mr Justice Phillips said that for a job evaluation to be legally acceptable it must

> be possible, by applying the study, to arrive at the position of a particular employee at a particular point in a particular salary grade, without taking other matters into account, except those unconnected with the nature of the work. It will be in order to take into account such matters as merit or seniority etc, but any matters concerning the work (for example, responsibility) one would expect to find taken care of in the evaluation study. One which does not satisfy that test and which requires management to make a subjective judgment concerning the nature of the work before the employee can be fitted into the appropriate place in the appropriate salary grade, would seem to us not to be a valid study.

Your claim for equal pay will be in danger if a tribunal says that because there is a job evaluation, there can't be a claim on the alternative basis of **broadly similar work**. Management might conduct their own study, based on personal weightings and not on an objective analysis, and perpetuate existing discrimination. You can challenge that if there is a fundamental error or you can prove that the scheme is not 'valid' or if it isn't objective. But you can't claim you are doing broadly similar work. So management may try to block your access to equal pay by carrying out their own job evaluation study. The only way to stop this is by refusing to co-operate, or by requiring time off to learn about job evaluation, demanding trade-union representation during all stages of the job evaluation exercise, and ensuring that the study is not complete until agreement has been reached on the scheme **and** on rates of pay following it.

Genuine material differences

Once you have established that the nature of your work is broadly similar, or that it is rated as equivalent, and any differences are not of practical importance, you must then face section 1 (3). Your boss can escape equal pay if he proves that there is a **genuine material difference**, other than sex, between your case and the man's. In other words, we are now looking at you and him, not at what the jobs involve.

Factors that may defeat your claim include:
1. location
2. grading
3. historical anomalies and 'red circling'
4. length of service, age and qualifications
5. 'market forces'

Location

Tribunals have accepted that it is legal for employers to give different pay to workers in different locations.

Employees of the NAAFI in Nottingham worked a 37-hour week, whereas those in London worked 36½ hours. Robina Varley sought a reduction to 36½ hours on the grounds that men in her grade in London worked less hours for the same money. The EAT, overturning the Nottingham tribunal, said that the difference in hours was not due to sex but to the fact that *many industries work shorter hours in London. NAAFI v Varley* 1976 (EAT)

Grading system

Different grading systems can sometimes justify different rates of pay for men and women doing similar work. It seems bizarre that tribunals can abandon the factual question: 'what do the men and women do in practice?', just because there is an anomalous grading system. But this is what the EAT said in Susan Waddington's case (page 131). When you have 'nationally or widely negotiated' wage scales, and there is a disparity between a man and a woman on similar work, the EAT said that this disparity will generally be due to a **material difference other than sex.**

Clearly there is a danger here that spurious grading systems based on discrimination could defeat the Act. To some extent, limitations have been imposed on this by the EAT itself.

> When Edna Wade demanded parity with a male colleague in the same insurance office, the company claimed all employees were paid according to a fixed grading system, and this constituted a material difference. The EAT said that the company had not proved that the grading system was *not* based on sex. It was based on *personal factors*, leaving the decision to management. This kind of grading system could not provide employers with a defence under section 1 (3). *National Vulcan Engineering Insurance v Wade* 1977 (EAT)

In this case Mr Justice Phillips laid down some rules. These decide whether an existing grading scheme can be valid grounds for paying different rates for similar work. Tribunals must consider whether the scheme:

- is unisex
- is jointly negotiated
- leaves the final say to management or not
- appears to be operated fairly in relation to the men you are comparing yourself with.

A scheme which requires subjective treatment by management and which operates to grade **people** rather than **jobs** is unlikely to pass the test. A scheme negotiated nationally or throughout a large company or area usually *will* constitute a material difference. This was indicated in Susan Waddington's case (see page 131), where there was a conflict between two separate national grading schemes.

Historical anomalies and red-circling

Following job evaluation, regrading or reorganisation employees sometimes find that they are getting more than colleagues in the same grade. Naturally, unions demand that these workers shouldn't be prejudiced by the change and that they should preserve their pay. A 'red circle' is drawn round them and their wages are protected at their existing rate, even though they are in the same grade and do the same work as other workers. Red-circling *may* amount to a genuine material difference between the cases of particular men and women.

> Sylvia Snoxell and Sylvia Davies were inspectors at Vauxhall's. Though doing the same work as men they were paid less. In 1970 male inspectors were regraded into a lower paid grade. But they were red-circled and preserved their differential over the women and male new-starters. No women were red-circled as no women were on the higher (male) rate. In 1976 the women claimed parity. The EAT said the employers couldn't hide behind the red circle. *It could not be a genuine material difference if it owed its existence to past sex discrimination*, that is, the

fact that men got more than women. The two women got parity and arrears of pay to the date the Equal Pay Act took effect (14 months). *Snoxell v Vauxhall Motors* 1977 (EAT)

The EAT said the following rules apply when an employer refuses parity and says the difference is due to a red circle or historical anomaly.

1. The employer must prove that the red circle arrangement is unisex.

2. If sex discrimination in the past has in any way contributed to the variation in pay, the red circle is illegal.

3. It doesn't matter whether the discrimination occurred before or after the Equal Pay Act took effect.

4. The employer *may* succeed in proving that the red circle is not based on discrimination if men and women outside the red circle do similar work and are treated alike.

5. Once a legal red circle is established, it can continue indefinitely, but it is desirable that it should be phased out.

6. Introduction or continuation of a red circle, particularly if this is 'contrary to good industrial practice' or done without joint consultation, may make the red circle illegal. *Outlook Supplies v Parry* 1978 (EAT) (two-and-a-half years 'quite short').

7. To succeed, an employer must justify the inclusion of *every* member of the red circle. Once the red circle is established, subsequent entrants may make it illegal. *United Biscuits v Young* 1978 (EAT).

Length of service, age and qualifications

All of these can justify differences in pay provided they operate in a way that is genuinely unisex. Collective agreements or custom and practice should be examined to prove whether this is so.

Market forces

Some employers have argued that, in order to get someone to fill a vacancy, they have had to pay above the going rate paid to existing workers. The EAT has dealt with several claims where the existing workers are women and the higher paid new entrants are men. Employers have successfully claimed that **market forces** required them to pay higher rates, and proved that this was a genuine material difference.

Dr Pointon, a woman lecturer with high qualifications and long experience, was appointed on scale 5. A younger, less qualified man was subsequently appointed on the same scale. Evidence was accepted that he had more experience. He was given scale 5 because his previous job in Scotland was scale 4 and **he had to be given a rise to attract him to the new job.** Dr Pointon said her contract had become less favourable than the man's because, in effect, her differential for qualifications was eroded. The EAT said the market factor, that is, giving a higher rate to the man to attract him, was a genuine material difference. The man's previous salary was not based on sex discrimination in the past so the scale 5 rate was justifiable. *Pointon v Sussex University* 1977 (EAT)

This argument, if widely used by employers, could wreck the Equal Pay Act. It means that if women are getting such poor pay that men can't be attracted to the job, it is justifiable to pay new (male) applicants more. This happened to Karen Fletcher.

Karen Fletcher earned £35 a week. A vacancy arose. There were three external applicants, and a man got the job. He was already getting £43 in his old job, so he demanded £43 in the new job. Following job evaluation and a £6 rise, there was still a difference of £6 between them. The EAT believed that the employer would have paid the higher rate to a **man or woman** applicant earning higher wages at the date of appointment. The economic need to attract applicants was a **genuine material difference.** provided the employers would have treated a woman applicant in the same way. *Clay Cross (Quarry Services) v Fletcher* 1977 (EAT)

On the other hand, the EAT rejected similar arguments by the Coal Board, who claimed they had to give a male canteen worker on nights higher basic pay and concessionary coal because of recruitment problems (*NCB v Sherwin* 1978). This is clearly the correct approach.

Other factors

Tribunals have allowed employers to pay unequal rates for a range of other reasons. These have not yet been specifically dealt with by higher courts so the list is not authoritative. They include: legal bans (for example, on night work), greater skill, ability to do more profitable work and greater flexibility.

How to claim

Claims under section 1 dealing with individual complaints must be made to a tribunal either while you are still working for the employer you are complaining about, or within **six months** of leaving. See page 357 for the procedure.

Proving it

You have to prove:

1. you are in the same employment with a man,

2. you are doing similar work, *and*

3. in practice you will have to show that any differences are not of practical importance in setting terms and conditions. (The onus of proof in section 1 (4) isn't specified, so you have to prove what you are alleging).

Your boss must then prove:

1. you are not doing similar work, *or*

2. if you are, that **the variation** (that is the *whole* of the variation) is genuinely due to a material difference, other than sex, between your case and the man's.

Your boss must provide basic information. The EAT said in *Eaton v Nuttall*:

> it should be regarded by employers as part of their duty
> . . . to come to the hearing with the relevant information
> prepared in a comprehensive and readily assimilable form,
> including adequate details of any job evaluation system,
> or other payment method, in use.

Remedies

The tribunal has power to make a declaration that you are entitled to equal terms and conditions and to amend your contract. It can award up to two years' arrears of pay. But this can't go back earlier than 29 December 1975.

Discriminatory agreements and pay structures

Claims for equal pay usually affect groups of workers, not merely individuals. So it's right that unions should be able to present claims on behalf of *all* their members working for the same employer. Section 3 of the Equal Pay Act allows references to be made to the Central Arbitration Committee (CAC) where **agreements** or **pay structures** are discriminatory.

The basis of the claim

The wording of section 3 (4) is obscure but the DE advice contained in its booklet on the Act, and decisions of the CAC, show that a claim can be made:

1. to remove discrimination by extending to men and women any provision applying only to one sex, and

2. to raise the women to the lowest male rate.

Since the Act came into force it has become very unusual to see an explicit discriminatory reference in an agreement. That doesn't mean that discrimination has stopped. The CAC says it can look at the **practice** as well as the **form**. This is clear from the *Beckman Instruments* case:

> Beckman make electrical components in Glenrothes with a workforce of three hundred hourly-paid workers. In grade 6 there were 6 men and 7 women; in grade 7 there were, until August 1976, 214 women. Two men later joined. Grade 6 got £5·50 a week more than grade 7. The AUEW successfully claimed parity. The CAC said there was discrimination because the theoretically unisex rate for grade 7 was **unlikely to attract male wage earners** and the differential was anyway three times as wide as between any other two consecutive grades. *Beckman Instruments v AUEW* 1976 (CAC)

The procedure

A discriminatory **agreement** can be referred to the CAC by any party to it or by the Employment Secretary. **Pay structures** can be referred only by the employer (why should employers want to take their own pay structures to the CAC?) or the Employment Secretary. If your union doesn't have agreements and you can't get equal pay by direct action, get the union to ask the minister to refer the claim to the CAC.

The CAC invites a written statement and convenes a hearing for oral evidence and questions. It can then make an award which takes effect as part of every affected worker's contract. Or it can give 'advice' which is not binding.

Backdating is possible only to the date the reference was made to the CAC. Even that isn't common.

The effect

In the first year of the Equal Pay Act the CAC published 20 decisions; seven involved the GMWU, five the AUEW. All of them gave some increase, but not all of them gave equal pay in the true sense, or even the lowest male rate. References against Beechams and Imperial Tobacco ended up with a classic arbitration solution of splitting the difference between the union's and management's claims.

In some cases the CAC made an award specifying increases in money and gave **advice** for future progress.

Jentique/Metamec Ltd make clocks and furniture in Norfolk. They follow the furniture trade agreement, but graded their workforce in a different order – journeymen, sanders (semi-skilled), labourers and *women* (whom the company started to call cushion-fillers). All 313 women were on the bottom rate. All the men were on the top three rates, meaning a difference of over £4 a week. The company claimed there was no discrimination as they paid women cushion-fillers 87½ per cent of the craftsmen's rate as laid down in the national agreement. But the CAC raised the women in two stages to the labourer's rate and advised that job evaluation should lead to the semi-skilled rate. *Jentique/Metamec v GMWU* 1976 (CAC)

In the AUEW's claim against Babcock and Wilcox the company had changed 'female cleaners' to 'cleaning persons', but paid them £1 an hour as against £1.17 for (male) 'sanitary assistants'. The CAC said that discrimination could only be stopped by raising the women to £1.17 an hour. It made two clear statements of policy.

1. A mere change of title doesn't mean that discrimination has ceased. The CAC can still intervene; and

2. You don't need to establish that men and women are doing similar work in a claim under section 3. This section is 'wider in scope and does not involve the same degree of job comparison' as section 1 (individual equal pay claims).

This was illustrated in the *Jentique/Metamec* case by the fact that an individual claim under section 1 had already been turned down at a tribunal.

The value of section 3

Section 3 has proved to be useful in securing some progress towards equal pay. Its effect is limited by its accepted aim of raising female rates to that of the lowest male, and by the CAC's approach in some cases as an arbitrator rather than an interpreter of the law. Its merit is that section 3 gives unions the right to claim on behalf of their members in what is essentially a collective, rather than an individual, dispute.

How effective is the Act?

Outrageous and pedantic decisions by tribunals during 1976 got the Act off to a bad start. This, together with some celebrated equal pay **strikes**, had the beneficial effect of showing that going to law to enforce workers' rights must be regarded as a long shot.

Women workers at Trico-Folberth, for instance, got

equal pay through a strike in 1976 *in spite of* an unfavourable tribunal ruling.

> Women working at American-owned Trico in West London made windscreen wipers. Men on the same shift got higher pay. The women, members of the AUEW, came out on official strike. The *company* applied to a tribunal for a decision (section 2 of the Equal Pay Act allows employers to sue). The women, disillusioned by tribunal decisions in other cases and believing firmly in industrial action, boycotted the hearing. The tribunal said the men got a higher basic pay because they *used to* do more flexible work before their night shift was closed down. When they were transferred they did identical work but retained their higher basic rate and night-shift premium. The tribunal said this was a transitional arrangement and refused to raise the women even to the men's basic rate. The strike lasted five months until the company conceded a new pay structure giving parity. *Trico-Folberth v Groves* 1976 (IT)

Success rate

Statistics on applications made under the Equal Pay and Sex Discrimination Acts show the effect of the two Acts.

Applications	Equal Pay				Sex Discrimination			
Cleared without reference to Tribunal	1976		1977 (Jan–June)		1976		1977 (Jan–June)	
	No	%	No	%	No	%	No	%
Settled by conciliation	106	6·0	37	9·6	35	14·4	34	29·6
Withdrawn following settlement	184	10·6	56	14·5	21	8·6	8	7·0
Withdrawn, reason not known	743	42·6	135	34·9	68	28·0	41	35·6
Total	1033	59·2	228	59·0	124	51·0	83	72·2
Heard by tribunals								
Claim upheld	213	12·2	74	19·1	24	9·9	6	5·2
Claim dismissed	496	28·5	85	22·0	95	39·1	26	22·6
Total	709	40·7	159	41·1	119	49·0	32	27·8
Total – all applications	1742	100	387	100	243	100	115	100

compiled from DE Gazette

Equal pay cases present the more optimistic picture. More cases, proportionately, were settled by conciliation or withdrawn following settlement during the first half of 1977 than during 1976. Fewer applicants withdrew without giving reasons. In the **tribunals**, the success rate rose dramatically so that applicants stood almost a one in two chance of winning in 1977 as against one in three in 1976.

For sex discrimination, more cases were settled by conciliation, but still you stood a less than one in five chance of winning if your case went to a tribunal.

Against this background it is clear that **the most effective way to get equal pay and to remove discrimination is negotiation and direct action.**

Women on tribunals

Another major problem is the lack of women on tribunals. At the end of 1977, in England and Wales there were only two women out of 71 full-time chairmen and five out of 131 part-timers. And only 22 per cent of lay members were women. Trade unions must nominate *and train* more women, if tribunals are to have any credibility in enforcing equality laws.

What reforms are needed?

While the success rate may be improving and the gap between men's and women's average earnings is slowly decreasing, the major limitation on progress (apart from men) is the Equal Pay Act itself.

The TUC passed a motion in 1976 calling for equal pay for work of equal value. **This must be the objective for trade-union action.** Amendment of the Act to include this principle would advance the cause faster than any other method short of a general strike. In addition, amendments could be made to:

■ section 1 (5), to prevent tribunals implementing a job evaluation scheme if an independent union objects to it.

■ section 2 to allow an independent union to bring a claim on behalf of its members under any section of the Act.

■ section 2 (1a) to prevent employers bringing cases, as Trico did.

■ section 3 to allow backdating of awards by the CAC.

■ section 3 (6) to allow an independent union to complain about a discriminatory pay structure.

Summary

1. The Equal Pay Act applies to all terms covered by your contract of employment. It applies equally to men and women.

2. You have the right to equal treatment if you are doing work which is broadly similar to that done by a man in the same employment or which has been rated as equivalent by job evaluation.

3. Employers can avoid giving parity if they can prove that you aren't doing similar work or that the variation in pay is genuinely due to reasons other than sex, for example greater skill or red-circling.

4. Your union can challenge a collective agreement if the women get less than the lowest male rate or if it is discriminatory in practice.

5. You can claim to a tribunal and may be awarded up to two years' arrears of pay.

6. Organisation to eliminate low pay, and union action to secure equal pay for work of equal value, are the only effective ways to achieve parity.

10.

Dismissal

The steps in claiming dismissal / what does
and does not constitute dismissal / unfair and
wrongful dismissal / who can claim unfair
dismissal / what is fair and unfair / union
activity / sickness / instructions / changes in
conditions / mobility / criminal acts /
misconduct / capability / probationary
workers / unfair redundancy / legal restrictions /
how to claim / reinstatement, re-engagement,
compensation / your right to written reasons /
a checklist for fighting the sack / and a
summary.

Legal protection against unfair dismissal was created by
Parliament in 1971. Prior to its introduction, all you could
complain about if you were sacked was that you were not
given proper notice, that is, you could claim for the wages due
to you. That is **wrongful dismissal** under common law. The
right still exists but will rarely be used because claims and
remedies for **unfair dismissal** are quicker, cheaper, more informal, usually more valuable and more in tune with the
current climate of industrial relations. The situations where
wrongful dismissal is still important are illustrated on page 153.

The suggestion to provide a remedy for unfair dismissal
was made in the Donovan Report in 1968 and was taken up
in the Labour government's White Paper *In Place of Strife*.
It was the sugar on the pill of the rest of that white paper
which included registration of trade unions and agreements,
compulsory strike ballots, and compulsory cooling-off periods
before a strike. These restrictions were defeated by the trade-
union movement and Labour introduced the Industrial Relations Bill 1970. This contained rights on unfair dismissal
very similar to those in effect today.

That Bill lapsed and was replaced by the Tories' Industrial Relations Act which came into effect in 1972. Again the unfair dismissal provisions were thrown in as a sop to workers and unions to try and disguise some of the savagery that was contained in that Act. Their consultative document said:

> Both on grounds of principle and as a means of removing a significant cause of industrial disputes, the government proposes to include provisions in the Industrial Relations Bill to give statutory safeguards against unfair dismissal.

It is clear that **the most effective challenge to a sacking is industrial rather than legal action. The law can be useful as a bargaining tactic or as a threat, but the organised worker's protection against sacking has always been collective support and industrial muscle.**
Following the fall of the Conservatives in 1974 the IR Act was repealed. The parts dealing with unfair dismissal, though, were immediately re-enacted.

In 1976, 33,701 applications claiming unfair dismissal were made to tribunals. Of these, 12,530 (37 per cent) got some form of remedy through conciliation or private settlement; 8,445 (25 per cent) withdrew and 12,726 (38 per cent) went to a hearing. Of those who went to a tribunal hearing only 287 (2 per cent) got an award of reinstatement or re-engagement. Taken with the cases settled, this means that less than 3 per cent of all applicants got an order for their job back. Compensation was awarded by tribunals in 3,950 (31 per cent) of cases they heard.

In the first half of 1977 the median amount of compensation awarded was £355; 80 per cent of awards were below £1,000. Generally speaking, these figures show that if you made an application you had a better than 50–50 chance of getting **something**. If you went to a tribunal you stood a one-in-three chance of winning.

Where to find the law

You can find the law of unfair dismissal in the Trade Union and Labour Relations Act 1974 schedule 1 and the Employment Protection Act 1975 (EP Act) sections 71–80; the Code of Practice on Disciplinary Practice and Procedures; the Sex Discrimination Act 1975 (SD Act) section 6 (2); the Race Relations Act 1976 (RR Act) section 4 (2); the Re-

Diagram 5 **Claiming Dismissal**

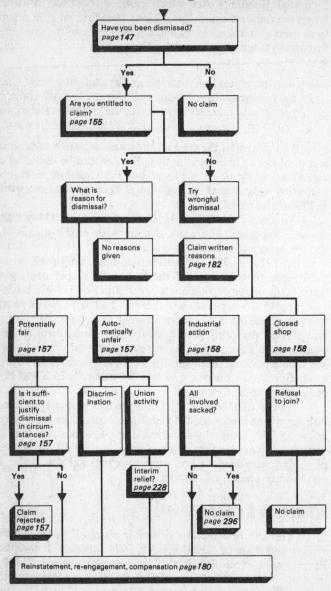

habilitation of Offenders Act 1974 (RO Act) section 4 (2). Your right to written reasons is found in the EP Act section 70.

Summary of steps

If you are considering whether to bring a claim for unfair dismissal, diagram 5 shows the steps that a tribunal must go through in dealing with your claim. Page numbers refer to pages in this chapter where the details are found.

What is dismissal?

Dismissal can take any of the following forms:

■ termination of employment by your employer with or without notice

■ refusal by your employer to renew your fixed-term contract that has expired

■ resignation if you are already under notice and want to quit before the notice expires

■ sacking due to redundancy

■ refusal to re-engage you after a strike or lock-out

■ refusal to allow you to return to work following pregnancy

■ constructive dismissal

Termination with or without notice

Proper notice means that you receive the amount of notice laid down by your contract. This must be not less than the periods given as minima in the CE Act. These are:

Less than 4 weeks continuous employment – not specified

Between 4 weeks and 2 years – 1 week

Between 2 years and 12 years – 1 week for each year of employment

12 years or more – 12 weeks

The Act requires *you* to give only one week's notice. All of these minimum periods of notice can be extended by agreement, in which case the agreed period becomes your proper period of notice. The period can be *expressly* agreed or implied by the circumstances of your relationship, or by conduct, or by custom and practice.

Sacking without notice is called summary dismissal. Even if you are given proper notice or wages in lieu you can still complain of unfair dismissal. Beware of **warnings of future dismissal**. These don't constitute notice unless a definite finishing date is specified. Once notice is given, neither side can withdraw it without the other's agreement.

You can present a claim for unfair dismissal if you are working out your notice, that is, before the dismissal takes effect – TULR Act schedule 1 para 21.

Refusal to renew a fixed-term contract

A fixed-term contract is one which cannot be terminated by either side giving notice. It is finite and both sides are bound by it for the whole of the specified period. Apprentices and some teachers are the most common examples. The only way your boss can end it is by sacking you for misconduct. If you are sacked when the contract expires, this counts as a dismissal, but the EAT has said that an employer could refuse to offer journeymen's work to his ex-apprentice, even though a union agreement required this – *N.E. Coast Shiprepairers v Employment Secretary* 1978

As we shall see (page 156), **some** workers on fixed term contracts are not protected by the unfair dismissal and redundancy pay laws **when their contracts run out**. A contract which is for a set period but which can, before the deadline, be ended by either you or your boss giving notice, is **not** a fixed-term contract as defined by the Act.

Resignation while under notice

If you are given notice by your boss, and in the meantime find other work, or decide to leave for any other reason, your resignation is treated as a **dismissal on the day you leave**. Provided you give *some* notice, however short, either orally or in writing, you can leave when you like.

> Elizabeth Walker worked in a children's home for almost 20 years. She was told at 12.30 p.m. she must leave, and was given seven weeks' notice. She was so distressed by the suddenness of the news that she finished her shift at 2.00 p.m. and walked out. Despite requests to return and complete her notice, she refused. She claimed unfair dismissal. The EAT confirmed the tribunal's finding that she had given no notice. She could not therefore claim dismissal. **Had she given some notice, her resignation would count as dismissal** and she would have been able to claim unfair dismissal. *Walker v Cotswold Chine Home School* 1977 (EAT)

So, **make sure you give some notice.**

Redundancy

We shall see (page 186) a dismissal must occur before you can claim redundancy pay. As such, redundancy is not really a separate kind of dismissal, but to many workers being made redundant is not the same as being sacked. In law it is.

Refusal to re-engage after a strike or lock-out

You have no claim for unfair dismissal if your boss sacks *all* workers engaged in industrial action, or refuses to take all of you back (page 296). If only some of you are sacked, or refused re-engagement, you can claim unfair dismissal. So with lock-outs. **If there is an element of selection,** you can claim. If there isn't, a tribunal can't even hear your claim (TULR Act schedule 1 para 7), as APEX and TGWU members sacked by Grunwicks discovered. (See page 7.)

The effects of this are far-reaching. For example, your boss might take the opportunity while you are in dispute to sack you for incompetence. *This* reason cannot be attacked on the grounds of unfairness or unreasonableness – the tribunal is precluded from hearing your case and looking at the merits.

Refusal to allow return to work following pregnancy

If you are refused re-employment on the date you have given as your return date, this counts as dismissal effective on that date. See page 82.

Constructive dismissal

This is forced resignation and occurs when your employer shows by his actions or words that **he does not intend to be bound any longer by one or more of the essential terms of the contract.** It means that your employer is doing something which strikes at the very root of your relationship and shows that he is not prepared to abide by the agreement. (*Western Excavating v Sharp* 1977 (CA).) The most obvious example is where your **pay is cut**, or your **status is reduced**:

> Mr Marriot was a foreman who had been employed for eight years. His boss told him that they were going to reduce his pay by £3 a week, and reduce his status because they were running down his department. He protested and they moved to a pay cut of only £1 a week. He worked at the new rate for three weeks under protest and then resigned, claiming redundancy. He was successful. The Court of Appeal said he was constructively dismissed. *Marriot v Oxford Co-op* 1969 (CA)

Constructive dismissal might also arise after **a change in shift pattern**, an order to **work with unsafe machinery, suspension without pay** where there is no prior agreement on this, a **'resign or be sacked'** ultimatum, an arbitrary refusal to give you a pay increase which everyone else got or **an order to move to other premises:**

> L. H. Goff and his son worked in the furniture trade in London. One day he was ordered to report on the following day to other premises two-and-a-half miles away involving an extra 15 minutes' journey each way. They both worked there for three weeks, took their two weeks' holiday, returned to work and gave one week's notice. The Industrial Court said that they had not **voluntarily agreed** to change their terms but had been dismissed, because they were faced with changed conditions. *Shields Furniture Ltd v Goff* 1973 (NIRC)

In all cases of constructive dismissal *you* must show that the following essential ingredients are present:

> the employee terminates that contract, with or without notice, in circumstances such that he is entitled to terminate it **without notice** by reason of the employer's conduct (TULR Act schedule 1 para 5) (emphasis added).

This means that the conduct must be so bad that you are entitled to quit without notice – a kind of 'gross misconduct' by your employer. In deciding whether to quit, the EAT has said that you must look *solely* at the contract and the effect on it of your boss's conduct. The surrounding circumstances may be relevant in assessing this.

> Michael Lynn was promoted to Retail Stock Controller of a large firm of clothes distributors. Soon afterwards, he got a warning letter and suffered a breakdown. He complained that he had been accused, in front of junior members of staff, of negligence, inefficiency and lack of intelligence. The company refused to meet his ASTMS official and didn't allow him a right of appeal (as required by the company's rules). He claimed this amounted to constructive dismissal as it undermined his authority. The EAT agreed that the company's conduct showed that they no longer intended to be bound by their contract with Michael Lynn. *Wetherall v Lynn* 1977 (EAT)

The EAT has also made it clear that if you are going to claim constructive dismissal **you must positively assert that you are going to exercise your right to terminate the contract.**

The rules for constructive dismissal therefore, are:

1. Your boss's conduct must be so serious that it shows he no longer intends to be bound by the contract.

2. This entitles you to quit without notice.

3. You must make it clear that you intend to regard yourself as constructively dismissed – put this in writing to be certain.

Claiming constructive dismissal is very risky. Remember it is *you* who must prove dismissal or constructive dismissal. Only then is your boss required to show reasons and prove fairness (see below). If you can't stop your boss taking action against you, try it for a while **under protest**. Claim unfair dismissal as a last resort.

What is not a dismissal?

You are not dismissed if:
- you agree to be suspended
- you resign or leave by mutual agreement
- your boss goes bust, or winds up the company, or either of you die
- the contract is 'frustrated'

Suspension

Unless suspension on less than full pay is allowed by your contract, or you consent to it, suspension is dismissal (see page 55). If you do agree to it, suspension is not dismissal, even though you take other work.

> Andrew Shute refused to pay TGWU dues while employed as a lighterman on the Thames. Union members refused to work with him. He was suspended on full pay for eight months. At the same time he was working elsewhere. He was not dismissed, but suspended. *Cory Lighterage v* TGWU 1973 (CA)

Resignation

Forced resignation is dismissal. An apparently voluntary agreement to quit can be a dismissal if the facts show your boss forced you into resigning. In the absence of pressure, you may not be able to prove dismissal. The only exception is when, in a redundancy situation, you volunteer to resign and take redundancy pay (see page 186).

Insolvency, winding-up and death

Your boss's insolvency, or the company's decision to close, count as dismissal only for redundancy purposes. You can't claim unfair dismissal if you are sacked as a result, but you *can* claim redundancy pay.

You are not sacked if a receiver is appointed to run the business till debts are paid. But if the receiver sacks you, you can claim unfair dismissal.

Your boss's death terminates your contract unless you are employed by a company. It does not entitle you to claim unfair dismissal. If your boss dies *after* you have been given notice, you can claim unfair dismissal against his personal representative. If you die, your representative or estate can still claim. With commendable realism the EP Act says that in this event 'the provisions relating to reinstatement and re-engagement shall not apply'! (Schedule 12 para 11).

Frustration of the contract

Some events automatically bring the employment relationship to an end without any need for there to be an actual dismissal or resignation. Lawyers call it **'frustration'** of the contract of employment. It occurs where some unforeseen event occurs, which is neither your nor your employer's fault. It must make carrying on the job either **impossible** or **something radically different from what was originally intended**. This rule operates in favour of employers because it is up to you to prove that you were dismissed. If you can't, and your employer argues that the contract had come to an end automatically, the tribunal has no jurisdiction even to consider whether there was any fairness or unfairness about it.

The kinds of events that are most likely to cause an automatic termination are:

- death
- serious illness or injury
- imprisonment
- legal impossibility – for example, a driving ban if you are employed only as a driver.

Genuine 'frustration' cases are rare, and the application of the rules is in many ways identical to the rules on fairness and reasonableness. For this reason, frustration due to **illness** and **imprisonment** are dealt with below with examples of sickness, misconduct and legal bans.

Although these rules often work against you it is possible to use them to *your* advantage. For example, even if you have to some extent caused the unforeseen event, it can still 'frustrate' the contract. So you won't be liable to any penalty for failing to carry it out. If a singer goes out without a coat and catches a sore throat which prevents her appearing, or if a bus driver negligently crashes his own car and because of injury is unable to carry out his duties, their employers will not be able to sue them for breach of contract. The intervening act itself (sore throat or injury) has ended (frustrated) it.

Unfair dismissal and wrongful dismissal

Protection against **unfair** dismissal is a right given by an Act of Parliament. **Wrongful** dismissal is quite different. It means, simply, dismissal without notice – 'summary dismissal' – or without the notice (or wages in lieu) that you are entitled to by virtue of your contract or the CE Act.

Since the introduction of unfair dismissal rights, claims for **wrongful dismissal** based on the **common law of contract** have become very rare. The right exists, though, and could be useful in certain circumstances. For example if you are:

■ not entitled to claim unfair dismissal (see below);

■ earning so much that the upper limit on compensation for unfair dismissal is below what you could get for wrongful dismissal. This might arise if you are sacked during a long fixed-term contract;

■ hoping to get a court order providing for your contract to be continued (see *Hill v Parsons* page 44).

Claims for wrongful dismissal have to be made in the county courts (for less than £2,000) or in the High Court. But power has been given to the Lord Chancellor and the Scottish Secretary to transfer this jurisdiction to industrial tribunals.

Legal representation paid for by the state Legal Aid Fund (see page 354 below) is available in courts but not tribunals. So if you need a lawyer, can't afford one, and are eligible for Legal Aid you might consider bringing a wrongful dismissal claim in the courts in order to get free legal representation.

Except for the right to a written statement of reasons for dismissal, the rest of this chapter is concerned only with unfair dismissals.

Who can claim?

The chart on page 155 shows the groups of employees who can make claims for unfair dismissal and redundancy pay. Something needs to be said about the exclusion of:

1. some part-timers and new starters with less than 26 weeks' continuous employment;
2. those who work abroad; and
3. those on fixed-term contracts.

Part-timers and new starters

There is no justification for Parliament to exclude these groups of workers. An unfair sacking doesn't cease to be unfair simply because the victim is a part-timer or new starter. The Act is designed to outlaw unreasonable behaviour, yet many workers are unprotected, often at the crucial time when they are learning a new job and most vulnerable. Effectively it gives your boss a free hand during your first six months. The only exception is if you are claiming you were sacked **for reasons connected with membership of an independent trade union**, or taking part in its activities.

It should be noted that **once you have worked continuously for 26 weeks, your right to claim unfair dismissal is preserved, provided you normally continue to work at least eight hours a week (see pages 338, 341).**

Employees working abroad

Employees who work abroad are also excluded. If you work abroad for only part of your time, you may still be excluded if a tribunal finds you '*ordinarily*' work outside Great Britain.

The rules that the courts have laid down are:
1. If under your contract you normally work outside Britain, and only occasionally work here, you can't claim.
2. If you normally work in Britain and on odd occasions go abroad for some special purpose you *can* claim.
3. If you work here and abroad for considerable periods of time in the normal performance of your contract, you can claim *only* if your *base* is in Britain.
4. In deciding this question, tribunals must look at the express and implied terms of your contract at the time it was agreed. So if your contract says you can be sent abroad in the normal course of your duties, a tribunal must look at the expected duration of the contract and decide, as from the start of the contract, where your base is likely to be.
5. If, using this test, your base is in Britain, it doesn't matter that *in fact* you spend more time abroad. *Wilson v Maynard Shipbuilding* 1977 (CA).

If you work in a business that requires travel – oil

Who can claim?	Unfair Dismissal	Redundancy Pay
Employees working 16 or more hours a week	Need 26 weeks service (unless alleging TU grounds)	Need 104 weeks service
Employees working 8–16 hours a week	Need 5 years service (unless alleging TU grounds)	Need 5 years service
Employees on fixed term contracts of 2 years	Yes unless specific exclusion in contract	Yes unless specific exclusion in contract
Young employees	Yes – No lower age limit	Must be 20 or over
Old employees	Must be under 65 (men) or 60 (women) or below the normal retirement age for your grade (unless alleging TU grounds)	Must be under 65 (men) or 60 (women)
Self-employed workers	No	No
Crown employees	Yes	No. Have own agreement
Health Service workers	Yes	Some. Others have own agreement
Employees ordinarily working abroad	No	No. Unless sacked while on business in Britain
Oil rig workers	Most	Most
Merchant seamen	Yes if working from British ports	No. Have own agreement
Registered dockers	Yes and have own agreement	No. Have own agreement
Share-fishermen	No	No
Employees of foreign governments	No	No
Employees of their own spouses	No	No
Domestic servants	Yes	Yes except close relative

company representative, service engineer, salesman – you can preserve your rights by getting an agreement from your boss that you won't be treated as 'ordinarily' working abroad. Such a deal can't give a tribunal jurisdiction if it finds in fact you are excluded from claiming. But the deal can give you a contractual (as opposed to a statutory) right against your employer, which you can enforce in the courts.

Fixed-term contracts

Termination of a fixed-term contract on the agreed date is classed as dismissal. You can claim if your contract is not renewed. Your boss will have to prove he acted reasonably in treating the expiry of the contract as sufficient grounds for not keeping you on.

> John Terry was employed as a physical education teacher for one year. His contract was not renewed. He claimed unfair dismissal but the tribunal held that he was sacked for a substantial reason – that is, the expiry of the contract. Mr Terry successfully appealed and the EAT sent it back to a different tribunal. It said that sometimes the expiry of a fixed-term contract *can* be a substantial reason for sacking if the worker knew he was taken on for a specific period, for example to fill a temporary gap. But in other cases where no particular purpose is served by the fixed-term, refusal to renew it will be unfair. **Workers are to be protected against being deprived of their rights through ordinary employments being dressed-up in the form of temporary fixed-term contracts,** the EAT said. *Terry v East Sussex County Council* 1976 (EAT)

If you are on a fixed-term contract you will not be able to claim unfair dismissal or redundancy pay if, **but only if**

1. the contract is for a fixed-term of **two years or more**; and *either*

    a. the contract was made before 28 February 1972 (unfair dismissal) or 1965 (redundancy pay); **or**

    b. you agreed **in writing before it expired** that you would forego your rights to claim when the contract ran out; *and*

2. the dismissal consists *only* of the expiry of the fixed term. In other words, you must agree to the exclusion of your rights and the exclusion applies only to sacking at the end of the contract. If you are sacked *before* the due date, for, say, misconduct, you *can* claim. For apprentices, see page 148.

Any other agreement not to sue, unless it is made during conciliation of a claim by ACAS, is automatically void and you can ignore it (TULR Act schedule 1 para 32).

What is fair and unfair?

Mr Justice Phillips summarised the problems any worker faces when challenging a sacking:

> The expression 'unfair dismissal' is in no sense a common sense expression capable of being understood by the man in the street. (*Devis v Atkins*)

What is fair and unfair can only be decided by the tribunal which hears your case. But you can get some idea of your chances by looking at other cases.

The legislation requires employers to prove two things. **1.** They must show that they dismissed you for one of the potentially fair reasons specified below, and **2.** They must then go on to show that it was a **sufficient reason in the circumstances**.

You have the right to require your boss to put the reasons for your dismissal in writing. See page 182 below. For it to be potentially fair the reason must:

- relate to conduct
- relate to capability: that is, skill, aptitude, health, physical or mental qualities
- relate to qualifications: that is, relevant to the position you hold
- be that you could not continue to work in the position you hold without contravening a legal duty or restriction
- be 'some other substantial reason' which *could* justify the dismissal of someone in your position
- be that you refused to join a specified union in a closed shop

These categories are ludicrously wide and no employer should have any difficulty in fitting his alleged reason for dismissal into one of them. You will normally find it difficult to attack this part of his case. But you can always attack the second part. He must go on to show that in the circumstances he acted reasonably in treating his reason as sufficient reason for dismissing *you*. **The burden of proof is on him**, so you have a slight procedural advantage during the hearing.

Automatically unfair are dismissals for union activity. Claims for unfair dismissal on the grounds of **discrimination** can be brought under the RR Act or SD Act, or, if you are in one of the groups of people entitled to claim, under the TULR Act. Tribunals have **no jurisdiction** to hear claims by workers sacked during industrial action if *all* workers involved are sacked.

Applying these rules to the cases that have occurred since 1972 it is possible to formulate a number of very broad *factual* situations covering:

■ trade union activity
■ industrial action
■ closed shop
■ sickness and injury
■ refusal to carry out instructions
■ change in conditions
■ mobility
■ criminal acts
■ misconduct
■ job performance and qualifications
■ probationary workers
■ redundancy
■ legal restrictions

What follows, therefore, is a general guide. You should always bear in mind that tribunals are free to make their own decision on any particular set of facts and are bound only by decisions of law of higher courts.

Trade union activity

Dismissal for being a member of or taking part in the activities of an independent trade union is automatically unfair. See page 224.

You can use the **interim procedure** (pages 228–9) if you are alleging you were sacked for trade union reasons.

Industrial action

Tribunals have only limited jurisdiction to hear your case if you are sacked during industrial action. (See pages 149 and 295.) If an employer sacks a worker because of pressure of industrial action, that pressure must be disregarded. In other words, the employer must bear the full responsibility and can't quote industrial pressure as a reason for his action.

Closed shop

It is not unfair for an employer to sack a worker who refuses to join a union specified in a union membership agreement. See page 259.

Sickness and injury

If you are sacked while you are sick, or because you have suffered an injury, your boss will have to prove one of two things if he is to escape liability for unfair dismissal. He must prove that the contract is **frustrated**, *or* that he **acted reasonably** in sacking you while the contract continued.

Serious or long-term incapacity

Frustration means there is no dismissal. So there is no question of it being 'unfair'. It is therefore an attractive argument for employers to make in tribunals, although it is hard to establish. The EAT said in the *Leibovici* case (below)

> There may be an event (for example, a crippling accident) so dramatic and shattering that everyone concerned will realise immediately that to all intents and purposes the contract must be regarded as at an end.

A postman who loses a leg, a lorry driver who goes blind, a labourer who has a heart attack – all of these may have their contracts frustrated. They may be given other work by their boss but they have had to abandon their original contracts.

If the event is less dramatic and certain, such as a long-term illness, it is still possible for your boss to argue that your contract is frustrated if the time comes when it can be said that **'matters had gone on so long, and the prospects for the future were so poor, that it was no longer practical to regard the contract as still subsisting'**. This is what happened in Israel Leibovici's case:

> Israel Leibovici had an accident and was off work for five-and-a-half months. He was paid for two of them. When he asked for his job back he was told it had been filled so he claimed unfair dismissal. His boss said the contract was frustrated. The London tribunal disagreed and awarded him redundancy pay. The employer appealed, successfully, to the EAT and the case was sent back for a rehearing. The EAT said the essential question is: **has the time arrived when the employer can no longer reasonably be expected to keep the absent employee's post open for him?**
> *The Egg Stores v Leibovici* 1976 (EAT)

There is no rule about the length of time that must elapse before frustration occurs – it depends on a complex set of factors that must be considered in each individual case.

In Reuben Marshall's case, his absence for 18 months didn't frustrate the contract:

> Reuben Marshall had been employed as a fitter at a London shipyard for 23 years when he went sick with angina. He received no wages and after 18 months was made redundant. He was shortly to have had an operation and would probably have been able to return after that. He was given no warning and only £50 ex gratia payment. The Industrial Court awarded him redundancy pay and rejected the employer's claim that the contract had been automatically terminated by the sickness. *Marshall v Harland & Wolff* 1972 (NIRC)

The EAT said in Leibovici's case that the following matters **must** be considered when an employer tries to avoid a claim for unfair dismissal or redundancy pay by arguing that **the contract has been frustrated**, or that **the dismissal is fair**:

1. the length of the previous employment;

2. how long it had been expected that the employment would continue;

3. the nature of the job;

4. the nature, length and effect of the illness or disabling event;

5. the need of the employer for the work to be done, and the need for a replacement to do it;

6. the risk to the employer of acquiring obligations in respect of redundancy payments or compensation for unfair dismissal to the replacement employee;

7. whether wages have continued to be paid;

8. the acts and the statements of the employer in relation to the employment, including the dismissal of, or failure to dismiss, the employee, and

9. whether in all the circumstances a reasonable employer could be expected to wait any longer.

Some of these points can be considered in detail – for example **the need for a replacement**:

> In March 1971 Eric Hebden, a sawyer with 20 years' service, stopped work to have an eye operation. He was fit to work in July 1971 but needed another operation. His employers agreed, since business was slack, that he need not work until the operation was over. He reported in every three weeks. He had the operation and was fit to work in January 1973, but his employers made him redundant. The employers said that he was a key man and so the contract between them had been frustrated. But the court said that in view of his **length of service**, the **period of incapacity**, the **conduct** of Mr Hebden and the employer during his time off **and the fact that he was not replaced**,

the contract still continued. He was therefore entitled to redundancy pay. *Hebden v Forsey* 1973 (NIRC)

If your boss gives you **sick pay,** or continues to pay your wages, it is usually evidence that the contract is not frustrated and is still alive. The courts have sometimes disregarded these factors though!

> Richard Hart was a night fitter when he went sick with industrial dermatitis in 1974. He was a key worker. Nearly two years later he was certified fit for work. His employers said he had been replaced and refused to take him back. They gave him his P45 and 6 days' holiday pay. The EAT (with the TUC member dissenting) upheld the Nottingham tribunal's decision that the contract was frustrated by the illness, **even though the employer had paid holiday money.** *Hart v A R Marshall & Sons* 1977 (EAT)

Short-term incapacity

Some tribunals have taken an unfavourable view of *short-term* illness:

> Tony Tan was a cellarman for a London wine-merchants. He had a perfect record for his first year of service, and in the second year was off sick for 16 days. During his third year he was sacked after 50 days' absence during a total of 70 working days. On almost every occasion he brought a medical certificate. The court confirmed that he had been fairly dismissed because **the employer's business requirements were such that they needed someone more reliable.** *Tan v Berry Brothers* 1974 (NIRC)

Industrial injury

If, as in Richard Hart's case, your sickness or injury is **industrial,** there are strong political and industrial arguments that you can use to insist that your contractual relationship has not been frustrated and that dismissal is doubly unfair. However, in an outrageous decision the Industrial Court decided that a painter who had suffered an industrial injury and was not able to carry out his full duties, even though he had been put on other duties for 12 years, was not entitled to either compensation or redundancy pay when he was dismissed for 'incapacity' – *Kyte v GLC* 1974 (NIRC).

Timing, consultation, alternative work and medical evidence

The principal question in all illness cases is: can your employer reasonably be expected to wait any longer for you to return?

That is not the end of the story because your boss must consider three other matters before he sacks you:

1. He must consult you and discuss the problem with you, except in the rare situation where discussion would be totally fruitless.

2. He must consider whether any alternative work is available for you. But he is under no legal obligation to *create* a new job for you to do.

3. He must take all necessary steps to ensure that he has a balanced view of the problem, and this will often include obtaining medical reports.

These rules have been laid down by the EAT in *Spencer v Paragon Wallpapers* (below), *Patterson v Bracketts* 1977 and *E. Lindsey District Council v Daubney* (below).

> Kenneth Spencer was a reeler in a paper mill. He had back trouble and was off work for two months. His doctor said he would be fit for work after another four to six weeks. His boss sacked him because the plant was very busy and he had to be replaced. The Manchester tribunal and the EAT said this was reasonable as the employer could not be expected to wait till then, there was no suitable alternative work available, and Ken Spencer was consulted. *Spencer v Paragon Wallpapers Ltd* 1976 (EAT)

This decision was very harsh but the court did make it clear that every case must be taken on its merits. The short timescale of illness, dismissal and expected recovery date in Ken Spencer's case related only to the facts of that case and can't be taken as a precedent.

When seeking **medical evidence**, employers must do so in neutral terms, being careful not to prejudge the issue. The evidence on which the decision to sack is made must be available *at the time* – facts discovered later are not relevant.

> Edward Daubney was a surveyor in a local council. He was 56 when he was sacked. The director of personnel wrote to the council's physician asking whether Edward Daubney should be retired on health grounds. The area physician examined him, and said yes. Edward was sacked without consultation. The EAT upheld the Lincoln tribunal's decision that **the council should have discussed the matter with the man** and given him time to get his own opinion, and should not have solicited a medical report in the prejudged way they did. Employers must regard the decision to dismiss as an industrial rather than a medical one. They must get all the information possible. *E. Lindsey District Council v Daubney* 1977 (EAT)

Protecting your job during incapacity

Many of the cases dealing with **long-term** sickness show a readiness by employers to treat workers as a form of commodity which, when it begins to perish, they can discard. Tribunals have modified this approach only for long serving employees. They have not attacked the general principle that employers can dismiss for 'lack of capability' workers who become sick. That employers can continue to do this, especially in cases of **industrial** injury or disease, is a classic example of the way the law is stacked against you. Clearly, it is unrealistic to rely on the law in these situations. You must use collective agreements and industrial pressure to protect the jobs of workers who are sick and therefore unable to exercise any industrial pressure themselves. Employers will always try to pick off those workers least able to defend their jobs. **So . . . if you think you are going to be sacked because of illness or disability, remember:**

1. Some events terminate your contract automatically because they make it impossible for you to carry out the original contract.

2. If the contract still continues, use the list of factors on page 160 to tell your boss he is acting unreasonably in attempting to sack you.

3. If he is thinking about sacking you, you have the right to be consulted, to discuss the problem, to get your own medical advice and to be considered for any alternative work there may be.

4. Your boss can act fairly only if he takes the decision to sack you on the fullest information available at the time.

5. Keep in touch with your boss – send medical certificates, make visits, impress on him that you are still an employee.

6. Keep in touch with your workmates so you know what jobs are available, whether redundancy is threatened, and whether your job is still open.

Refusal to carry out instructions

You are obliged to carry out all lawful and reasonable instructions that your employer or supervisor gives you. See page 41.

You are *not* required to do anything that is not in your contract (however that is put together) or which is not reasonable. Characteristically, the judges tend to take the employer's view of what is reasonable:

> It is important that the operation of the legislation in relation to unfair dismissal should not impede employers unreasonably in the efficient management of their business, which must be in the public interest. – *Dean v Eastbourne Fisherman's Club* 1977 (EAT)

They frequently overlook matters of crucial importance in workplace relationships such as long-established custom and practice, demarcation, and procedures for negotiation. Workers are often cast as bloody-minded if they fail to carry out instructions given to them by their employer. However, there are a few basic rules.

1. Criminal instructions

If you are required to do something criminal you can refuse to do it. If you are sacked it will be unfair.

> Leonard Morrish, a stores driver, was told by his manager to record in his book that he had been supplied with more petrol than he had actually taken. He was told that this was the normal way of making up deficiencies in the records, and he was told to falsify his entry. He was dismissed for failing to obey orders, and successfully claimed that he had been unfairly treated, although he was awarded only £100 compensation. *Morrish v Henlys* 1973 (NIRC)

2. Health and safety instructions

Specific instructions and sensible standards of behaviour in connection with health and safety must be observed. Failure to do so means you might be in breach of the Health and Safety at Work Act or specific regulations dealing with a particular hazard or particular premises, and you lay yourself open to a fair dismissal.

> Bowaters issued all workers with protective goggles for use while operating grinding machines. Mr Taylor refused to wear them. The company turned off his machine, because it could not be used without the operative wearing goggles (it is mandatory on employers to issue, and on workers to wear, goggles in such conditions – Protection of Eyes Regulations 1974). He was sacked. The Industrial Court upheld a tribunal's finding that Bowaters behaved fairly, because Mr Taylor had refused, and said he would continue to refuse, to comply. *Taylor v Bowater Flexible Packing* 1973 (NIRC)

If a safety instruction has not been observed for some time, or if management have known that people have not observed it *and* have taken no action, it is unfair suddenly to sack a worker for non-observance.

> John Wilcox was a gas fitter, employed on conversion to North Sea gas. It was a company safety rúle that pressures must be tested before work started. He was sacked when one day his boss found that he failed to carry out the test. He claimed that no one else did, that the company knew this and took no action, and that he should have had a warning. The High Court upheld the Middlesbrough tribunal's finding that the dismissal was *fair*. It had been proved that the employer had never 'condoned or aquiesced in that practice'. *Wilcox v Humphreys and Glasgow* 1975 (HC)

As Mr Justice Phillips said in John Wilcox's case:

> If this requirement had been ignored for ages to everybody's knowledge, it would not be right, without some kind of warning, to dismiss the first person to break it after the employers took it into their heads to enforce it.

If your boss gives you an instruction to do something contrary to a statute, he is breaking your contract, and you can refuse – compare *Gregory v Ford* (page 39 above).

3. Instructions outside the scope of your contract

You can refuse to obey instructions which are **criminally unlawful**, and also those which are **unlawful simply because they are outside the scope of your contract. If you are forced to do something which you know you are not required to do you can refuse.** Subsequent dismissal *may* be unfair.

> Charles Wallace, a sheet metal worker, occasionally did pipe-bending, but only after a special rate had been agreed on each occasion. He was asked to do this work without prior agreement on the rate. He refused and was dismissed instantly. He applied unsuccessfully to a tribunal and then appealed to the Industrial Court. There Mr Justice Brightman said 'if pipe-bending were outside his contract of employment, there could be no possible answer to his claim to have been unfairly dismissed because on any reading of the facts and evidence he would merely have been declining to carry out work which he had not contractually bound himself to perform'. The court in fact found that the job was within his contract, but the mere fact that there had been no prior negotiations according to custom and practice was sufficient to make the instruction unlawful, and he got compensation. *Wallace v Guy* 1973 (NIRC)

Because a custom or practice can become a term of a contract, if an adverse practice is developing which is not expressly agreed by yourself or your union you should take steps to stop it, or agree on a set procedure.

Remember, when refusing unlawful instructions, that employers may claim the instructions are covered by your general duty to co-operate. (See page 41).

What is the effect of an unlawful or unreasonable instruction? The alternatives are stark but you can

1. refuse to comply. Your boss would then have to take the initiative, warn you and sack you. You would claim the dismissal is unfair.

2. refuse to comply and tell your boss that you regard the instruction as so unreasonable that you are going to treat it as a sacking. You would claim constructive unfair dismissal.

3. comply under protest and take him to the county court. You would claim damages for losses you suffer as a result of the unlawful instruction (compare *Gregory v Ford* page 39 above).

4. refuse, or comply under protest, and take the matter up in formal negotiations, or industrial action.

Apart from **4**, none of these is satisfactory. As the law stands, a dispute about the scope and meaning of a contract can only be taken to a tribunal if it accompanies a complaint about a sacking or relates to the written particulars that must be given under the CE Act.

Change in conditions

A change that radically affects your conditions of work can be unreasonable, and will entitle you to claim unfair dismissal if your employer sacks you for refusing to go along with the change. In times of high unemployment and in industries with weak trade-union organisation changes may be difficult to resist. The alternative of claiming constructive dismissal is hopelessly unrealistic. Remember that **employers can't unilaterally rearrange work patterns, reduce transport facilities, introduce shift-working** or **make any other major change.**

> Mr Blakely was a foreman on day shifts in a foundry for five years. He was requested to go on nights. He refused and was sacked. He had no written contract specifying either day-shift or night-shift. The Industrial Court said that the employer had **no right unilaterally to vary the terms of his contract of employment,** even though these were not in writing. However, his claim for redundancy pay was rejected for other reasons. *Blakely v Chemetron* 1972 (NIRC)

If you don't object at once to a change in conditions your boss may argue later that this was a **variation agreed by both sides**. If you are offered alternative work in a redundancy situation, you are automatically given a right to a four-week trial period so you can see if you want to agree to the new conditions. This doesn't apply to changes made by employers where there is no redundancy. So if you want to try the changed conditions for a bit you must carry on working and specifically state that you are doing it under protest, or for a limited period.

In the *Goff* case (page 150) for example, the NIRC considered whether an order to work at another plant had been accepted by L. H. Goff and his son. The court said:

> What is an employee expected to do in these circumstances? He does not want to be out of a job. Nor, if he is a conscientious workman, does he want to let his employer down if this can be avoided. In most cases, therefore, he goes for the new job. He goes with an open mind. There is a period when he is uncommitted. During that period he makes up his mind whether he will accept the new employment, in which case he is not entitled to a redundancy payment; or whether he will leave.

In a subsequent case the court held that toolmakers who were instructed to move to another site, and worked there for two months, had not agreed with their employers that their terms and conditions were voluntarily varied. They got their redundancy pay and the court said:

> The courts have rightly been slow to find that there has been a consensual [that is, agreed] variation where an employee has been faced with the alternative of dismissal and where the variation has been adverse to his interests . . . the court has to decide the question, 'did the employee freely and voluntarily agree to vary the contract of employment?' *Sheet Metal Components v Plumridge* 1974 (NIRC)

Mobility

Many workers are forced to accept conditions in their contracts that require them to be mobile, and to accept flexible working arrangements. Employers are able to take advantage of their superior bargaining power, and introduce inducements such as travelling and subsistence allowances, in order to get the necessary agreement. If it is a part of your contract that you must be mobile, and you refuse to accept an instruction to move, you are liable to be dismissed and you may have no remedy.

Kenneth Sutcliffe, an aircraft technician stationed in Norfolk was requested to move to Scotland. His contract said that he could work at any RAF station in the UK, and he had already worked at several stations. This time, however, he objected to moving because he had bought a house and for other personal reasons. He claimed unfair dismissal and redundancy pay. The court gave him neither, saying that it was a term of his contract that he should be mobile. There was no unfairness about the order to move, and as work existed in Scotland he could not claim redundancy pay. *Sutcliffe v Hawker Siddeley* 1973 (NIRC)

Sometimes, national or local agreements or works rules may class you as a mobile worker. An exceptionally wide agreement will be struck down by the courts but this power should not be relied on too much.

An ICI works rule required workers to accept the right of management to transfer workers to another job with a higher or lower rate of pay 'whether day work, night work or shift work.' The company tried to move Mr Briggs, a process worker, to another site. They quoted the works rule. In fact, they succeeded, but the court said that if a works rule or national agreement is unreasonably wide the courts can interpret it narrowly. The court said that on the face of it the rule enabled management to transfer a man from one plant to another plant miles away and to transfer a carpenter to a plumber's job. So they said that the rule really only enabled the company to transfer a process worker to another process job. *Briggs v ICI* 1968 (HC)

If there is no specific term in your contract, and no reference to mobility or flexibility in a collective agreement, the courts may still find ways of giving your employer the right to move you around. Agreement can be *implied*, they have said, by custom and practice and by the conduct of workers and employers in the trade:

At the time he was taken on as a steel erector, Edward Stevenson agreed to accept work away from his home in Leyland. When he was asked to transfer to Blyth, Wales or Manchester he refused because the money wasn't right. He said that he was not obliged to move. There was nothing in his written contract, nor in the national agreement although this did refer to subsistence and travel allowances. The High Court said that there was an obligation for him to undertake travelling work because **all the facts surrounding his employment pointed to this conclusion.** The court approved an earlier judge's statement: 'I have come to the conclusion, though with some regret, that this appeal ought to be allowed. I say "with some regret" because . . . one cannot help feeling that in

many of these cases . . . it might have been possible to show that the employees themselves must be taken to have known at the time that when they were engaged that they were liable to be sent anywhere in the country.'
Stevenson v Tees side Bridge 1971 (HC)

Mobility is important when considering redundancy pay, because you will get your redundancy money only if there is no work available for you in *any* of the places that you are required to work. See page 194.

Criminal acts

The circumstances that constitute 'conduct' or 'some other substantial reason' sufficient to make a dismissal fair vary enormously.

The cases show four areas where problems have arisen:
1. criminal acts in the course of employment
2. criminal acts that may affect your job
3. criminal acts unconnected with your work
4. conviction prior to starting the job

Criminal acts in the course of employment

The legal basis for allowing an employer to dismiss you instantly after a criminal act in the course of employment is that you have, by your conduct, shown that you are not prepared to abide by your side of the contract of employment. It is incompatible with the fidelity and mutual trust that the courts say must exist between employers and employees for him to keep you on. In a sense it is the mirror image of a constructive dismissal. The employer's prerogative exists despite the introduction of unfair dismissal remedies.

The kinds of conduct that generally deprive you of your right to claim are theft, fraud, violence, threats, and 'industrial espionage'. There need be no criminal conviction, and there is no need for the police to be called in. Even in a situation which no one would consider heinous, instant dismissal has been upheld because the judges have accepted employers' views on the rectitude of workers' day-to-day conduct.

A betting-shop manager borrowed £15 from the till in order to place a bet. He intended to replace it the next day and did so. This was technically a crime and he was dismissed at once. The Court of Appeal said that what he did was 'incompatible and inconsistent with his duty'.
Sinclair v Neighbour 1967 (CA)

Although there is not much scope for a legal remedy against your employer if you commit crimes while at work, there are four modifications to the employers' prerogative with which you might still win an unfair dismissal claim.

Firstly, your employer must be acting on information that is available to him at the time he fires you. The Industrial Court said:

> If an employer thinks that his accountant may be taking the firm's money, but has no real grounds for so thinking and dismisses him for this reason, he acts wholly unreasonably and commits . . . unfair dismissal, notwithstanding that it is later proved that the accountant has been guilty of embezzlement. Proof of embezzlement affects the amount of compensation, but not the issue of fair or unfair dismissal. *Earl v Slater & Wheeler* 1972 (NIRC)

In other words, your boss must be acting reasonably when he deals with information that leads to a sacking. Information justifying dismissal but discovered after it can't make the dismissal fair. The microscope of reasonableness is focused on the time at which the employer makes the decision to dismiss.

> Rowland Atkins was dismissed as manager of an abattoir in 1974. His employers offered him £6,000 compensation and six weeks notice-money. Six weeks later they discovered he had been guilty of misconduct at work and withdrew the offer. He successfully claimed unfair dismissal. The company appealed to the House of Lords. They confirmed that evidence obtained after a dismissal cannot make reasonable otherwise unreasonable conduct by an employer. It might affect compensation or reinstatement, but it could not make Rowland Atkins's dismissal fair. *Devis v Atkins* 1977 (HL)

Second, he must follow a reasonable procedure and give you a chance to explain your conduct, show that you have previously been well-behaved and so on.

The court said in *Earl v Slater & Wheeler* (above) that you have to be given the opportunity to state your case, unless there could be no explanation which could possibly prevent your boss from sacking you. If you are distressed, you must be given this opportunity at a time when you are in a fit state – *Tesco v Hill* 1977 (EAT).

This firm rule was whittled down by the EAT. Warnings and an opportunity to state your case must 'as a formal practice' be given. But exceptions are permitted if following this procedure would have made **no difference at all** or if an

internal inquiry would prejudice pending criminal proceedings
– *Carr v Alexander Russell* 1976 (EAT).

The ACAS Code of Practice on Discipline (see page
70) puts the rule more firmly. Paragraph 11 says:

> Before a decision is made or a penalty imposed the
> individual should be interviewed and given the oppor-
> tunity to state his or her case and should be advised of
> any rights under the procedure, including the right to
> be accompanied.

Third, there must be no delay. If your boss takes no
action for some time it will be difficult for him to show that
what you did was so serious that it struck at the whole basis
of 'mutual trust'.

> Two oil tanker drivers were convicted of theft. It was **not
> connected** with their jobs. Their manager decided to fire
> them but kept them on till their appeal was heard 10 weeks
> later, which failed. He then fired them because there was
> a rigid policy on this and because their 'customers might
> not like it'. But the Sheffield tribunal said they were un-
> fairly dismissed, as a policy like this did not take account
> of personal qualities. If they wanted to protect themselves
> and their customers it was 'inconsistent, even if lenient' to
> keep them on. *Donson v Conoco* 1973 (IT)

A delay can also lull you into thinking the matter has been
dropped. Subsequent sacking by your boss might be unfair –
Refund Rentals v McDermott 1977 (EAT).

Fourth, sudden unannounced enforcement of a rule can
lead to unfair dismissal if an abuse has been condoned in the
past, or allowed by custom and practice to develop – see
John Wilcox's case, page 165 above.

Criminal acts that may affect your job

Some criminal acts committed outside the course of
employment may affect your job because you are actually
prevented from doing it, or because there is a **connection with
your work**. A sentence of imprisonment for 12 months might,
for example, make it impossible for you to carry out your
duties and your contract could therefore be frustrated.

> William Hare had been employed by Murphy's for 25
> years, 15 of them as a foreman. He got into a fight outside
> working hours and was sent to prison for 12 months. The
> employers said they would take him back if he was given
> any sentence other than imprisonment. He was released
> after 8 months and applied for his job again. But the
> employers refused. The Court of Appeal rejected his claim

of unfair dismissal, saying that the effect of the imprisonment was that it was impossible for him to carry out his
job. Therefore the employment had automatically
terminated (frustrated). The length of time away from his
job and his key position were major factors in deciding
this. *Hare v Murphy Brothers* 1974 (CA)

In other cases, conviction might not make it impossible
for you to work, but could **change the basis of your employment**.
A used vehicle supervisor who was disqualified from driving
for a year was held by the Dundee tribunal to be fairly dismissed. 40 per cent of his work was driving and the tribunal
said it was unreasonable to expect his boss to reorganise work
arrangements for him as a result of the ban – *Fearn v Tayford
Motor Co* 1975 (IT).

More controversially, sackings have been approved
where the conviction has been held to have little bearing on
the job. A London tribunal has said:

> it would be quite wrong as a generalisation to say that an
> employer is entitled to dismiss an employee simply
> because he has been convicted of a criminal offence. This
> dismissal can only be justified where there is some reason
> why the conviction for the particular offence makes the
> employee an unsuitable person to retain as an employee.
> *Creffield v BBC* 1975 (IT)

In that case a cameraman was sacked after he received a nine
months suspended sentence for indecent assault on a 13-year-
old girl. The BBC said he travelled abroad a lot and could not
now be relied on to uphold the BBC's reputation. And they
could not send him on filming jobs involving children. The
latter is probably a valid consideration, since the conviction
directly affected his ability to do the job. But to justify a man's
dismissal on the basis of a possible slur on a company's
reputation is wholly unacceptable, and probably would not,
as the sole reason, be accepted by tribunals.

Similarly vulnerable to the sack for crimes that might
affect their work are: teachers convicted of assault on children,
bank clerks and security guards convicted of theft, pharma-
cists convicted of unlawfully possessing hard drugs, and social
workers convicted of breaking and entering. In all these examples the apparent grounds for dismissal under the TULR
Act would be '*conduct*'. This has been defined in broad terms
by the EAT:

> Conduct does not have to be something which occurs in
> the course of the actual work, or at the actual place of
> work, or even to be connected with the work, so long as
> in some respect or other it affects the employee, or could

be thought likely to affect the employee, when he is doing his work. *Singh v London Country Bus Services* 1976 (EAT)

The facts were that Harbhajan Singh, a driver of one-man buses, was sacked following his conviction for theft and deception. It was his first offence and he was given a suspended sentence. Nevertheless, Mr Justice Phillips agreed that the bus company acted fairly, as the conviction affected Mr Singh's 'trustworthiness'.

Criminal acts unconnected with your work

Except when you are physically or legally unable to do your original job – as happened to William Hare (page 171 above) – dismissal following a conviction not connected with or affecting your work is unfair.

Convictions prior to starting your job

The Rehabilitation of Offenders Act 1974 (RO Act) gives you the right to refuse to disclose 'spent' convictions (see page 26). If you are sacked for this reason, it is unfair.

Mr and Ms Hendry managed the Scottish Liberal Club. Complaints were made and it came to light that Mr Hendry had been convicted of possessing cannabis. The conviction had become 'spent'. Both he and his wife were instantly dismissed. Both successfully claimed unfair dismissal on the grounds that the sacking infringed the RO Act. They got £576 compensation between them. *Hendry v Scottish Liberal Club* 1977 (IT)

Other convictions are not protected by the Rehabilitation Act and non-disclosure has given employers the right to sack.

G. E. Torr was sacked after working as a guard on British Rail for 15 months. On joining he had denied that he had ever had a conviction. In fact, 16 years earlier he had been given three years for larceny. This sentence is not protected by the RO Act – two-and-a-half years is the maximum. British Rail successfully prosecuted him for 'obtaining a pecuniary advantage by deception', that is getting a job, despite the fact that he actually worked for the money he received and had a good work record. BR then sacked him. The EAT upheld the tribunal's decision that this was fair. Concealment of a record affected the relationship of confidence between Mr Torr and BR, said Lord Justice Cumming-Bruce. *Torr v British Rail* 1977 (EAT)

So . . . if you have a record that is not 'spent', you run the risk of fair dismissal if you deliberately answer **no** to questions about it. Even if you work for a public body, the **spirit** of the RO Act is not observed.

Misconduct

'Gross misconduct' is one of the most frequently abused terms in industrial relations. There is no finite list of industrial offences, but if a court or tribunal does find that what you did amounted to gross misconduct it entitles your boss to dismiss you without notice, and you may not win an unfair dismissal claim.

This is only one aspect of the matter, because if there is *any* form of misconduct you may be disqualified for unemployment benefit for the first six weeks you are out of work (see page 212). You may not get wages in lieu of notice or a reference. So the term 'gross misconduct' is a very powerful and convenient weapon for employers.

It is much harder to analyse conduct which is not criminal but which may justify a sacking. Again, employers may describe as 'gross industrial misconduct' comparatively trivial things. As a broad rule of thumb you can say that if an employer wants to treat a certain act as gross misconduct he must give you formal notice of it. **Smoking in a food factory** or a **mine**, or **clocking someone else's card**, may give your employer the right to fire you instantly but only if there is a clear and well-policed rule on this (see also *Wilcox v Humphreys & Glasgow* page 165 above).

> Hugh Dalton clocked a friend's card. There were prominent notices above the clock, and also in the employees' handbook, saying that this would justify instant dismissal. Even though he had 22 years' service Hugh was fired on the spot. The Industrial Court found no dishonest motive but said it was still fair to dismiss him. The Code of Practice need not be followed in cases of gross misconduct where ample warning had already been given. In a statement reeking of the nineteenth century, the court said the company acted reasonably in view of 'the pernicious effect which laxity in enforcing these warnings may have upon practices which could develop all too quickly under factory conditions'. *Dalton v Burton's Gold Medal Biscuits* 1974. (NIRC)

The ACAS Code of Practice says that there should be an oral and a written warning before dismissal. See page 70 above. Tribunals have to take this into account, and failure to follow the recommended procedure can itself make the dismissal unfair (see *Earl v Slater & Wheeler* page 170 above).

Offensive language has occasionally been held to justify a dismissal. But tribunals, in an effort to keep in touch with industrial reality, have accepted that shopfloor relationships generate language as a matter of course which would offend middle-class ears.

> Philip Wilson was head gardener at Tolethorpe Hall, an 80-acre private estate. The owner was in the garden with his family one Sunday afternoon. He started shouting at Philip, and criticising his work, especially his failure to trim a hedge. Phil said 'if you remember it was pissing with rain on Friday. Do you expect me to get fucking wet?' After more provocation he said 'Get stuffed. Go and shit yourself'. Only the two men heard this. The judge found that Phil had a clear conscience and 'did reply somewhat robustly . . . I think he felt a certain amount of grievance . . .' He said he had not terminated his own contract by the language and had in fact been *wrongfully* dismissed.
> *Wilson v Racher* 1974 (CA)

Fighting can cause dismissals. Striking a supervisor or manager, because it affects the authority of employer over worker, will usually be found to be grounds for fair, and indeed instant, dismissal. If there is no evidence that the dispute affected the whole employment relationship, dismissal may be unfair.

> Bill McDougall, a supervisor, went for a lunch-time break to celebrate a colleague's retirement. Back at work, he reprimanded a person for bad work, who then threatened him, or possibly hit him. He hit back. He was sacked, his two internal appeals were turned down, and he claimed unfair dismissal. The NIRC confirmed that this was unfair but that he contributed to it to the extent of 30 per cent. **His action had not gone to the root of his employment relationship.** Although serious, it did not show that he had 'repudiated' his contract. He got £760 in compensation.
> *Forgings and Presswork v McDougall* 1974 (NIRC)

Evidence of aggression, provocation, self-defence and over-reaction are all factors that can affect the reasonableness of your boss's action.

Absenteeism and **lateness** are types of misconduct that depend for their gravity on their extent, and the reasons for them. For other forms of misconduct, too numerous to deal with here, the main question is: **did your boss act reasonably in all the circumstances in treating the misconduct as sufficient grounds for dismissal?**

Job performance and qualifications

Poor performance, or inadequate qualifications for doing the work you are employed to do, are reasons frequently used to disguise the real reason for a dismissal. If your employer is going to sack you on these grounds he must have given you **warning**, and an **opportunity to improve** your performance.

> Frances Wiggins ran a boutique in Southend. She was warned several times about her standards and having failed to respond, was sacked. The court found that 'the whole atmosphere was seedy and lethargic' and that the dismissal was fair because **she had had many opportunities to improve.** Management had to abide by 'general principles of fair play' and the court said they had. *Lewis Shops v Wiggins* 1973 (NIRC)

Most of the cases have concerned white-collar workers and tribunals have said that the warning need not be absolutely explicit in the case of supervisors and middle management – sometimes you can be given 'the red light' informally. So the contract manager of a shopfitting firm who did not get on with clients was held to be fairly dismissed as his attitude had been referred to on several occasions, even though no specific warning had been given – *Dunning v Jacomb* 1973 (NIRC). If you aren't given some form of indication, you are likely to win a case of unfair dismissal. T. M. Gibson, a farm manager sacked for giving an inaccurate reference on an employee, got compensation because his boss should have told him he was thinking of sacking him – *McPhail v Gibson* 1976 (EAT).

Manual workers, too, are entitled to warnings and a sacking has been held to be unfair even though it was unlikely that the employee would have improved if he'd had the chance;

> M. Bromley was a boiler service fitter. He received an oral and a written warning about his lack of enthusiasm for the job. Things came to a head when he couldn't fix the boiler, and production was lost. He got the sack and complained to a tribunal. The EAT confirmed that his boss should have pointed out his shortcomings, and given him more supervision and encouragement so he could improve. **Even though he probably wouldn't have improved, he should have been given the chance.** *Mansfield Hosiery Mills v Bromley* 1977 (EAT)

Rarely, a sacking can be fair without any prior warning if your performance is extremely bad:

> An airline pilot made **a single but very serious error of judgment** when landing his passenger plane. The plane was badly damaged. His boss, who was also on board, suspended him. Following a board of inquiry, the pilot was sacked. His claim for unfair dismissal was rejected, as his mistake was so serious as to justify dismissal. *Taylor v Alidair* 1978 (CA)

Probationary workers

Many employers, particularly local authorities, require you to work a probationary period. Once you have worked for 26 weeks you are entitled to protection against unfair dismissal. It doesn't matter what you are called – probationary, casual, temporary – provided you work the 26 weeks you are protected. But in practice tribunals often apply a double standard and say that dismissal of a probationary worker is fair in circumstances where a regular employee would be *unfairly* dismissed. Your employer may therefore find it easier to justify your dismissal on the grounds of capability in your early days. **So organised workers should resist pressure to include a special category of 'probationary worker' in collective agreements.**

Lord Justice Cumming-Bruce in the EAT laid down the following rule which tribunals should observe in considering whether an employer acted reasonably in sacking a probationary worker:

> Has the employer shown that he took reasonable steps to maintain appraisal of the probationer throughout the period of probation, giving guidance by advice or warning when such is likely to be useful or fair; and that an appropriate officer made an honest attempt to determine whether the probationer came up to the required standard, having informed himself of the appraisals made by supervisory officers and any facts recorded about the probationer? If this procedure is followed, it is only if the officer responsible for deciding upon selection of probationers then arrives at a decision which no reasonable assessment could dictate that an Industrial Tribunal should hold the dismissal to be unfair *Post Office v Murghal* 1977 (EAT)

If you are on probation, challenge any warning or criticism that you consider unfair. Don't wait till the end of your trial period, as by then an adverse dossier might have been built up, and your job may be jeopardised.

Unfair redundancy

Your employer has a complete defence to an unfair dismissal claim if he can prove you were redundant and that was sufficient reason for sacking you. But there can still be unfair dismissal in five situations:

1. You are selected for redundancy on the grounds of

your trade-union membership or activities in the union – TULR Act schedule 1, para 6 (7). See page 224. Totally disregarding this provision, and the protection against victimisation contained in section 53 of the EP Act, the EAT, by a majority, held that in selecting people for redundancy it was reasonable for a Newmarket trainer to sack five TGWU members. (*Cruickshank v Hobbs* 1977.) Having taken part in a 12-week official strike in 1975, five out of six TGWU members were not taken back. Their boss said this was due to redundancy. The EAT decision that this was fair is clearly wrong. An official strike *is* a trade-union activity, and you have the right to complain about *any* selective victimisation in consequence of it. See the *Stock* case page 297.

2. There is a procedure, or established custom and practice, for dealing with redundancies, for example, last-in-first-out, **which has not been followed** in your case – TULR Act schedule 1 para 6 (7).

3. The redundancy is announced in an unreasonable manner, or without consultation or warning.

> Redundancies were declared at an Amesbury furniture factory. There was no consultation with the union (FTATU) as required by the EP Act section 99, or prior warning as required by the IR Code of Practice para 46. The EAT said this made the dismissals unfair. *Kelly v Upholstery & Cabinet Works* 1977 (EAT)

4. Your employer fails to consider alternative work for you. He must look for alternative work for you in the same business or with associated employers before making you redundant.

> Dennis Bear, a £4,000 a year works manager, was made redundant. His company was one of 300 in the Tilling group. He got redundancy money, three months' salary, three months' use of his company house and two months' use of the company car. He was given no prior warning and no time off to look for new work. He complained that he had been shabbily treated. The court said his employer should have looked at all the circumstances and **tried to find him a job elsewhere in the group.** He received an additional £321 compensation. *Vokes v Bear* 1974 (NIRC)

Obviously the Industrial Court in that case was anxious to find in favour of a well-heeled manager, but the principle established could be used by other workers. The IR Code of Practice (para 46) says that in redundancy situations management should 'offer help to employees in finding other work'.

5. You are offered alternative work, but you are not given

enough information about it to enable you to make a 'realistic decision whether to take the new job' – *Modern Injection Moulds v Price* 1976 (EAT).

Legal restrictions

A dismissal is potentially fair if it is because 'the employee could not continue to work in the position which he held without contravention (either on his part or on that of his employer) of a duty or restriction imposed by or under an enactment'. A disqualified driver cannot continue to hold the position of driver and drive without breaking the law. Dismissal is potentially fair, although whether it is reasonable to dismiss for this reason depends on the availability of other work, and the length of the ban.

Dismissal of someone who is required to have, but does not have, a work permit is also covered by this potentially fair reason. Every case must be dealt with on the basis of reasonableness, and in one case an employer acted unreasonably when he tried to avoid breaking a legal restriction:

> Robert Pinney worked for a firm dispensing hearing aids. He didn't pass his exams within the five years required. He couldn't legally carry on working without a legal extension of his time. His boss felt he'd never pass the exams and sacked him. The EAT said that the fact that Robert's employer would have broken a statute, and been liable to prosecution, didn't necessarily mean he acted reasonably. He could have got an extension and prosecution was anyway unlikely. *Sutcliffe & Eaton v Pinney* 1977 (EAT)

The TULR Act (schedule 1 para 18) gives a government minister, or someone acting on his or her behalf, the power to block your right to claim. If the minister certifies that any action was taken 'for the purpose of safeguarding national security' that is *conclusive*. If it is alleged you were sacked on national security grounds, you can't challenge it in a tribunal.

Not only civil servants are liable to be deprived of their rights. Workers whose employers have government contracts are also particularly vulnerable – especially as they can be subjected to 'positive vetting' by the Special Branch. A certificate by or on behalf of a minister can deprive *any* worker of the right to claim unfair dismissal.

How to claim

Details of how to claim are given on page 357. The time limit is **three months** after your 'effective date of termination'. You can claim if you are under notice.

Remedies for unfair dismissal

If you win your case, the tribunal must consider **all** the remedies in the following order:
1. reinstatement
2. re-engagement
3. compensation

Reinstatement

An order for reinstatement means your boss must treat you **in all respects as if you had never been dismissed**. The tribunal must specify any benefits you should have received, arrears of pay, rights, privileges, seniority and the date by which your boss must comply with the order. You will get the benefit of any wage increase or other improvement in conditions you would have had if you hadn't been sacked. Continuity of employment for all purposes is preserved during your absence and is added to your actual service. Account is taken of any wages or ex gratia payments received from your employer in this period.

The tribunal *must* consider three factors:
1. whether you want to be reinstated
2. whether it is practicable for your boss to comply
3. whether, if you caused or contributed to your dismissal (see page 347 below), it would be 'just' to order reinstatement.

1. Your wishes

The tribunal must explain its powers and ask you what you want to do. It doesn't matter what remedy you have specified in your written application to the tribunal.

2. Practicability

The EP Act does not say what is practicable, but industrial relations, workplace harmony and personal attitudes have all been found relevant.

In only two situations can the tribunal take account of

the fact that a permanent replacement for you has been hired. The first is when your boss shows that it was **not practicable for your work to be done without hiring a permanent replacement**. The second is when your boss shows that he hired a replacement after a reasonable period of time without having heard from you that you wanted to be reinstated or re-engaged, *and* that it was no longer reasonable to have the work done except by a permanent replacement.

Because of this second defence, **it is to your advantage to include a claim for reinstatement in your tribunal application**.

3. Contributory fault

Compensation can be cut down by a tribunal which finds you contributed to your own dismissal. With the remedy of reinstatement there is no sliding scale – either it is ordered or it isn't. It would not be 'just', except following a finding of substantial contributory fault, to deny you your right to reinstatement.

Re-engagement

An order for re-engagement means you go back to work for your employer, or his successor or an associated employer. But you are not treated in every respect as though you had never been sacked. The tribunal decides what terms should apply. It must consider the same three factors as in reinstatement and it must put you back in **comparable** or **suitable** employment on terms which are, as far as is reasonably practicable, as favourable as the original terms (EP Act section 71).

The number of applicants reinstated or re-engaged following a tribunal order is very small – see page 145.

Compensation

If the tribunal does not order reinstatement or re-engagement it must assess compensation (EP Act section 73). If a reinstatement or re-engagement order is made **but not complied with**, the tribunal *must* award compensation. In other words, if your boss disobeys an order neither the tribunal nor the courts have power to enforce it. All you are guaranteed is compensation.

You can enforce an award of **compensation** by applying to the county court. If your employer doesn't comply with a county court order for compensation, the bailiffs can be sent in to seize property, or the employer's bank can be ordered to hand over funds in order to pay off the debt to you.

(the

Compensation consists of:

1. Basic award – two weeks' pay or the equivalent of your redundancy pay entitlement.

2. Compensatory award – to cover net loss of wages, future loss of wages, expenses etc.

3. Additional award – if your boss does not comply with a reinstatement or re-engagement order, between 13 and 26 weeks' pay; (between 26 and 52 weeks' pay if you were sacked on the grounds of discrimination or trade-union activity).

See page 345 for details of how to work these sums out.

Your right to written reasons

Section 70 of the EP Act gives you the right to demand from your boss a statement in writing 'giving particulars of the reasons' for your dismissal. The right is separate from the right to claim unfair dismissal and can be exercised whether or not your dismissal was fair. It is designed to give you some written proof of why you were sacked. You could use it as a reference if your boss refuses to give you one.

Who can claim?

You have a legal right to written reasons if you are in one of the groups of people entitled to bring a claim for unfair dismissal (see page 155). You must have been sacked, or be under notice, or a fixed-term contract must have expired without being renewed. Constructive dismissal is not expressly included but the interpretation given to similar rules under the old IR Act means you probably can claim.

You can ask your boss for written reasons in every case, but it is conceivable that in some situations you may not want the reasons recorded.

You can claim if you have not been given a reason, or if the written reasons are **inadequate** or **untrue**. A simple statement that your dismissal was on the grounds of 'capability' or 'conduct' is not sufficient since it does not include particulars of the reasons. The particulars requested do not need to be in a specific form. But the EAT said:

> The document must be of such a kind that the employee, or anyone to whom he may wish to show it, can know from reading the document itself why the employee has been dismissed . . . So there is no objection to its referring to other documents as well, provided that the document

which the employee receives at least contains a single
statement of the essential reasons for the dismissal.
(*Horsley Smith & Sherry v Dutton* 1977)

A reference to reasons given orally in an **interview** is not
sufficient unless the reasons are set out.

How to claim written reasons

If your boss has not responded to your request within
14 days, you can make a claim to a tribunal that he has
'unreasonably refused' to give the information. The time limit
is strict but the EAT said that an employer's inaction isn't
necessarily unreasonable. You must argue that refusal to
respond does amount to unreasonableness.

Details of how to claim are given on page 357. The
time limit is **three months** from your effective date of termination. You can make your claim at the same time as a claim for
unfair dismissal if you are pursuing both.

Remedies for failing to give written reasons

At a tribunal hearing *you* must prove you were dismissed and, if you are saying a written statement is untrue or
inadequate, you must prove that too.

The tribunal can make a declaration as to the real reason.
And it *must* award you two weeks' pay (see page 344 for
calculations). This is without prejudice to any remedies you
may get for unfair dismissal.

Fighting the sack

The first and most important rule about dismissal is:
don't take your dismissal to a tribunal. The only quick and
effective method of securing the reinstatement of a dismissed
colleague when the normal procedures are unsuccessful is
industrial action. Unfair dismissal occurs most frequently in
small firms, mainly in distribution, catering, construction and
agriculture. This suggests that the level of union organisation
is a key factor. There are fewer cases from larger firms, the
public sector and industries such as mining and shipbuilding.

This is only to say what is obvious: workers *can't*
trust the law and *can* solve their industrial disputes by solidarity and organisation. These methods carry a considerably
higher success rate, and massively more educational value,
than any number of tribunal decisions.

But . . . if you are sacked or under notice use this checklist

■ Tell the union rep and call for support from work-mates.

■ Has the proper procedure in the Code or your collective agreement been followed?

■ Have you been given proper notice? If not, demand it.

■ If you are offered wages in lieu, refuse to accept and insist on turning up for work.

■ If you think you are sacked because of union activity, contact your full-time official and claim 'interim relief' **within seven days**.

■ Demand written particulars of the reasons for your sacking.

■ Check that you are entitled to make a claim.

■ Before making a claim, get help from your union or Legal Aid. (See page 354.) Watch the three-month time limit.

■ If you are denied unemployment benefit, demand to see the employer's reply to the DHSS questionnaire. Lodge an appeal within 21 days.

Summary

1. Most workers with 26 weeks' continuous employment are protected against unfair dismissal. You can make a claim to a tribunal if you are sacked or given notice.

2. If your sacking is connected with your union membership or activities, the 26-week rule doesn't apply. You can also bring a claim under the interim relief procedure to keep your contract alive while your case is pending.

3. Most workers with 26 weeks' continuous employment can demand written particulars of the reasons for their dismissal. If this is refused, you can get two weeks' pay.

4. If you claim unfair dismissal your boss must give a reason *and* prove that he acted reasonably in all the circumstances in treating that reason as sufficient grounds for sacking you.

5. Tribunals can order your boss to reinstate or re-engage you, or pay you compensation.

6. If you don't get proper notice or wages in lieu, you can bring a claim for **wrongful** dismissal in the courts for which you may get representation under Legal Aid. (Tribunals will ultimately be given power to deal with these claims.) In practice you will get notice money if you win an **unfair** dismissal claim.

11.

Redundancy Pay and Insolvency

Who can claim redundancy pay / what
redundancy means / your employer closes
down / or is taken over / work diminishes /
reorganisation / changing conditions /
'unsuitability' / contractors / bumping /
mobility / alternative work / changes in pay,
travel, status, domestic arrangements,
security / trial periods / misconduct / strikes /
time off to look for work / how to claim /
how much is due / your rights if your boss
goes bust / guaranteed debts / a redundancy
checklist / and a summary.

The organised worker's first response to the threat of
redundancy should always be to take direct action. The purpose of this chapter is to show what is available if the fight for
jobs is lost.

Chapter 20 deals with the right of union representatives
to be consulted in advance of proposed redundancies. This
chapter looks at the individual side of redundancy, which
means payments, time off and guarantees if your employer goes
bust.

Because a financial carrot is offered for redundancy,
some workers have accepted their unemployment as a fore-
gone conclusion. In less organised and determined sectors of
industry the challenge to management's right to sack workers
has been subordinated to the task of securing enhanced
redundancy pay.

In 1975, 340,000 workers received redundancy payments.
Since the right to claim these is restricted to full-time em-

ployees with two years' service, many other redundant workers went without. The state fund, made up of levies on employers, paid out £178 million, an average of £524 to each recipient.

Where to find the law

The Redundancy Payments Act 1965 (RP Act) contains the law on redundancy pay. See also the Employment Protection Act 1975 (EP Act) section 61 for time off; sections 63–69 for rights on insolvency.

Who can claim?

The first condition in any claim for redundancy pay is that you have been dismissed. The meaning of dismissal in its various forms is dealt with on pages 147–151.

In addition, you can **volunteer** for redundancy and still be classed as dismissed. For example, in a redundancy situation management may call for volunteers before deciding finally on who must go. You can claim redundancy pay even if you are first to agree.

> Robert Peck was sick for a year. His boss suggested he take redundancy pay but wouldn't sack him while he was on the sick list. One day he turned up for work, was given none, and was sent home. He claimed his redundancy money but his boss said he had left 'by mutual agreement' and was not entitled to any. The High Court confirmed the tribunal's award of £577 saying 'the first to be made redundant are those who volunteer for it ... **The fact that the employee agreed to this redundancy is no ground for holding that it was not a dismissal** (emphasis added).
> *Burton, Allton & Johnson v Peck* 1975 (HC)

The second condition is that you must be in one of the groups of employees covered by the 1965 Act. The list on page 155 shows that many workers excluded from the unfair dismissal law are also excluded here – part-timers, the self-employed, people who work abroad, and workers over retirement age.

In addition, workers under 20 years old and workers with less than two years' service are left out, effectively excluding 80 per cent of dismissals according to National Joint Advisory Council estimates in 1967.

What is redundancy?

Redundancy is defined in section 1 of the Redundancy Payments Act 1965 (RP Act) and can be summarised as any of the following:

■ Your boss has **ceased**, or intends to cease, to carry on the business **a.** at all, or **b.** in the place where you were contracted to work.

■ The requirements of the business for employees to carry out work of a particular kind either **a.** at all, or **b.** in the place you were contracted to work, have **ceased** or **diminished,** or are expected to.

The practical situations in which redundancy arises are numerous, but they can be split up into those where:
1. the business closes
2. the business is taken over
3. a section of it decreases
4. you are asked to move
These are dealt with separately.

In all of the following situations you should bear in mind three things.

■ The closure, or shrinkage in labour, can be permanent **or temporary**. Attention is focused on the date you are sacked. If the definition fits the fact there is a redundancy situation, however transient that may turn out to be. Closure and sackings, followed in a week by re-opening and hiring of new workers, may indicate a fraud, and be grounds for other claims. But such a situation might arise quite legitimately, and if it does there is nevertheless a redundancy situation.

■ It doesn't matter for legal purposes what the *reason* for the closure or cut-back is. Typically, it may be caused by automation, lack of orders, increasing competition, unprofitability, obsolete products, asset-stripping or insolvency. The Act is concerned only with the *fact* of redundancy and not the *reason* for it.

■ Many workers sacked during the first seven years of the RP Act had their claims turned down by tribunals. They might today have a claim for **unfair dismissal**. Before 1972 there was no alternative, whereas now you should keep your eye on a possible claim for unfair dismissal if your redundancy claim is unsure.

The business closes down

This is the clearest case. It doesn't matter whether the closure is voluntary or due to insolvency. If your boss can't pay, your money is guaranteed (see page 205). If you work for a single employer who dies, and the estate does not continue the business, this too is a redundancy.

The business is taken over

Transfer of ownership of a business is dealt with in section 13 of the Act. If your boss sells out and sacks you, you get redundancy pay. If the new owner takes you on, then sacks you, you get redundancy pay from him. If he offers you work, the normal rules on **alternative work** (see below) apply. Provided the business is taken on as a **going concern** there is no break in your continuity of employment and you don't get redundancy pay. There are, though, some snags which might jeopardise your future position.

The Act applies only to changes in the **ownership of the business**. If the whole enterprise is taken over and run as before but under new management you are not redundant and you join the new management with unbroken service. But if only the **assets** of the business are taken on, and you are offered work in the same shop, there may not be a transfer of 'the business'.

> Alfred Woodhouse worked for 40 years as a machine tool setter for Crossley-Premier who made diesel engines in Derbyshire. In 1965 Crossleys moved production to Manchester and sold the plant to PB Ltd, which finished off five diesels and then made spinning machines and steam turbines. There was no transfer of trade name, customers, or goodwill, and the new product was quite different. All but one of the workers were kept on but in 1971 PB Ltd laid them off with redundancy pay based only on the six years since the sale. The Court of Appeal said that was all they were entitled to. The **business** hadn't changed hands, merely the **assets**. (He could have got redundancy pay from Crossleys in 1965 but was too late to claim in 1971.) *Woodhouse v Peter Brotherhood Ltd* 1972 (CA)

If, like Alfred Woodhouse, you are faced with a transfer you should obtain an assurance (in writing is best) from the new employers that they will treat you as having no break in your continuity of employment. The date continuous service began must be given (within 13 weeks) in your written particulars under the CE Act (see page 29). This is the easiest way to deal with the problem that you may not know precisely the details of the change in the business until it is too late. If you can't get such an assurance, claim redundancy pay from your old boss within six months of the change.

When the sale consists only of the assets, you get your pay and then start from scratch with the new boss. If there *is* a sale of 'the business' as a going concern, you won't get the money but you are regarded as continuing in employment, and your service with the old boss will count if the new boss sacks you sometime in the future.

If a proper offer of alternative work (see page 195) isn't made by the new boss before the takeover, you can get redundancy pay, *and* take the job with the new boss.

> Luigi Camelo worked for a small London company making furniture for 17 years. He was classed by the union as a journeyman but in fact worked as a labourer (at £26 a week). His boss sold out and Luigi was offered work on new terms by the new boss. There was a transfer of the whole business, but a proper offer was not made *before* the takeover. So he got redundancy money from the old boss, and started afresh on a new contract with the new boss. *Camelo v Sheerlyn Productions* 1976 (EAT)

Your kind of work diminishes

This kind of redundancy is the most fraught with legal difficulties. A typical situation is the reduction of workers employed on a particular kind of work. This can occur even if there is no reduction in *other* kinds of work – process workers can be laid off while white-collar workers are being recruited.

Claims have been made by workers subject to:
1. reorganisation
2. changes in conditions
3. employers' ideas of suitability
4. replacement by contract workers
5. bumping

Reorganisation

The courts have resolutely defended management prerogatives when reorganisation of working conditions is put forward. They have disqualified workers for redundancy pay in circumstances where their employers unilaterally changed established patterns of work. Lord Denning declared in Noreen Johnson's case (below):

> It is settled ... that an employer is entitled to reorganise
> his business so as to improve its efficiency and, in so doing,
> to propose to his staff a change in the terms and conditions
> of their employment; and to dispense with their services
> if they do not agree. Such a change does not automatically
> give the staff a right to redundancy payments. It does so
> only if the change in the terms and conditions is due to a
> redundancy situation.

The message is clear. **If you resist changes in hours, shifts and
overtime working you are not redundant unless the reason for
the change is a need to cut back in the amount of work done.**

> Noreen Johnson had worked for 20 years at a police
> station on a five-day week from 9.30 a.m. to 5.30 p.m. To
> achieve 'greater efficiency' her hours were changed to an
> alternating shift of 8 a.m. to 3 p.m., 1 p.m. to 8 p.m. on a
> six-day week. She refused, was sacked, was replaced by a
> shift-worker, and claimed redundancy pay. The Court of
> Appeal turned her down saying 'If the employers require
> the same number of employees as before – for the same
> tasks as before – **but require them at different hours, there
> is no redundancy situation**'. (emphasis added).
> *Johnson v Notts Police* 1974 (CA)

The threat of unilateral action by employers is very
serious. Indeed, the courts themselves recognise this by saying
that claims of **unfair dismissal** might arise in these circumstances
if employers artificially and unilaterally changed work
practices. Yet at the same time the NIRC and Court of Appeal
opened the door to this very threat.

Employers may use this judgment to reduce their workforce, cut overtime and **avoid payment**. The *possibility* of unfair dismissal claims is a more manageable risk than the
certainty of redundancy pay, as one company proved:

> Lesney Products, who make Matchbox Toys in London,
> had 36 setters employed on days. They reorganised the
> work pattern to require the same number of men to work
> double day shifts. The men lost overtime and faced a cut
> in wages of £14. Six men who refused to accept this
> claimed redundancy. The court rejected their claims on
> the grounds that the **amount of work and hours done had
> not decreased.** *Lesney Products v Nolan* 1977 (CA)

The Court of Appeal asserted that

> nothing should be done to impair the ability of employers
> to reorganise their workforce and their terms and con-
> ditions of work so as to improve efficiency. They may re-
> organise it so as to reduce overtime and thus to save them-
> selves money, but that does not give the man the right to
> redundancy payments.

If you are faced with this kind of ultimatum, and industrial pressure is ruled out, you should **claim unfair dismissal,** and you should investigate whether there is any reduction in your boss's need for work. If there is, then you may get redundancy pay:

> Ivan Kykot had worked as a weaver on the night-shift for seven years. His boss wanted to reorganise the work by introducing rotating day-shifts. Ivan's contract did not give his boss the right to do this. He refused to change and was sacked. Subsequently the night-shift was closed down, with only a few workers going on to days. The court said he should get redundancy pay. There was more than a simple reorganisation. The workforce had decreased and so there was a redundancy situation. *Kykot v Smith, Hartley* 1975 (HC)

Changing your conditions

The court drew a distinction in Noreen Johnson's case between an alteration in times of work, and alterations which might change the nature of the job done so that **it becomes a different task.** Changes in methods, hours, type of person employed, status, responsibility, or remuneration for example, *might* be redundancy, because the need for the *old* work has diminished.

Some changes are not clear-cut redundancies. There must be a reduction in the particular **kind of work**, not in work done **under particular conditions of employment.**

> William Chapman and nine other workers in a china clay firm in Cornwall travelled the 30 miles or so to work each day in the firm's bus. Three of the men were made redundant, so the firm said it was inefficient to provide the free bus for the others. There was no public transport so they left, and claimed redundancy pay. Seven men who lived near the works were taken on. The Court of Appeal said the men had a contractual right to transport. Withdrawal of the transport amounted to sacking the men. But the sacking was not due to redundancy because **the amount of work needed was constant.** *Chapman v Goonvean China Clay* 1973 (CA)

So, some changes constitute redundancy if the particular kind of work diminishes. If the work doesn't diminish major changes such as withdrawal of transport constitute dismissal. You could win a claim for unfair dismissal, but not redundancy pay.

You have become unsuitable

Some of the most outrageous court decisions under the RP Act have involved workers laid off because their boss feels they have become unfashionable. Since a remedy for unfair dismissal was introduced, these cases have withered away, but the ideology represented by employers treating workers like plant is still visible. The rule is that if you are sacked because you have become unsuitable, you are not redundant.

> Ms Ward worked for 18 years as a barmaid at the Star and Garter pub in Blyth. The manager decided to glamourise the pub and to employ 'young blondes and Bunny girls'. Ms Ward was sacked. She claimed redundancy pay on the grounds that *her kind of* barmaid was no longer required. The lay members on the tribunal in two hearings found in her favour. The High Court said there was still a need for barmaids in general and denied her her money.
> *Vaux Breweries v Ward* 1970 (HC)

The extent to which the judges say you are supposed to adapt to the whims of your boss, or a new boss, is illustrated by Alexander Butterwick's case.

> In 1966 the Resolution Garage in Whitby was taken over. Alexander Butterwick had risen to workshop manager after 30 years. He was dismissed because the new owners made demands of him that he couldn't achieve. Lord Chief Justice Parker and the then Mr Justice Widgery refused to give him redundancy pay. They said 'an employee who remains in the same kind of work is expected to adapt himself to new methods and techniques and cannot complain if his employer insists on higher standards of efficiency than those previously required.'
> *North Riding Garages v Butterwick* 1967 (HC)

In that case the chairman of the tribunal, and this was not disowned by the High Court judges, said, in terms of committed management bias:

> Inevitably the new management with new ideas and a natural desire for improved efficiency makes changes. Inevitably **misfits** are found **who have to be dispensed with.** No general rule can be laid down as to whether these misfits come within the scope of the redundancy payments scheme. **The slacker or scrounger who is weeded out** may well not be redundant (emphasis added).

Even if you are a skilled and conscientious worker you are still liable to become 'inefficient' or 'unsuitable', and to be sacked without redundancy pay. A Norfolk boatbuilder was sacked simply because he was 'although an excellent craftsman, such a slow and thorough worker', that his employers found his work unprofitable – *Hindle v Percival Boats* 1969 (CA).

You are replaced by contractors

What happens if your boss replaces direct labour by contract workers? It is an affront to organised and unorganised workers alike, but Parliament has encouraged the practice by classifying this as redundancy. The needs of your boss for **employees** to do the work has diminished, since it is done by **contractors**, Section 1 of the RP Act mentions employees only.

This is illustrated by a case that might have come out of Robert Tressell's *Ragged Trousered Philanthropists*.

> C. A. Evans and A. W. Ball were employed as painters by a small South Coast firm of decorators. The boss told them one day that with wages, stamps and SET going up they were 'sub-economic'. If they didn't do a fair day's work they would be sacked. They were later sacked and **replaced by lump labour.** They won redundancy pay, even though their work was still being done, because it was done by fewer 'employees'. *Bromby & Hoare v Evans* 1972 (NIRC)

In the building trades, this encouragement has contributed to the difficulty in stamping out the Lump.

Bumping

Bumping is the system by which a worker who is made redundant in one department is transferred to another, and displaces a worker with less seniority or less skill. For example, an agreement between Pilkingtons and the GMWU for the glassworks in St Helens allows dilutees to do (skilled) cutters' work in certain circumstances. If redundancy arises among the cutters, they displace the dilutees, the dilutees displace the labourers, and the labourers are sacked. Although they can see others doing their work, the labourers are still entitled to redundancy pay because their employer's *overall* requirements have diminished.

The last-in-first-out system also survives on the bumping principle. The most junior worker is entitled to redundancy pay, even though it's not his own job but a senior worker's which has become redundant.

You are asked to move

Redundancy occurs when your boss's need for a particular kind of work diminishes in the place **at which you are em-**

ployed. If your contract, either expressly or by implication or custom, requires you to work in a number of different locations you can be sacked for refusing to move. (See page 167.) If there is no such requirement you are not obliged to go. Your boss might offer you work elsewhere and this might be a **suitable alternative**. But that is a separate question and arises **only if you can't be required to move**. We are talking here only about a **contractual** obligation to be mobile.

> **Example:** you work on a building site in London, and you are a travelling operative and can be required to move. Your are told to transfer to Brighton. You are not entitled to redundancy pay. It is true that work has diminished in the place you worked, but *in law* this is defined as any place where according to your contract of employment you could be sent. As long as your boss offers you work on other sites, and you are required to be mobile, you will not get redundancy pay.

So redundancy means ... a reduction in the needs of an employer for employees to do work of a particular kind and it can occur

1. when a business closes down.

2. when it is taken over as a going concern and you aren't offered work by the new employer. If only the **assets** are taken over, you can claim redundancy pay and start afresh with the new employer.

3. when there is a reorganisation of the workforce *provided* there is less work. Rearranged hours alone are not grounds for a claim.

4. when a change in conditions means that the old job is quite different from the new.

5. when employees become 'unsuitable' to changing employment conditions.

6. when contractors are brought in, or you are displaced (bumped) by a redundant employee. In both these cases, the fact that someone is doing your job doesn't mean you are not redundant.

Offers of alternative work

In a redundancy situation, if you are offered work instead of dismissal you may lose your right to redundancy pay if you refuse the work. An offer of other work is therefore your boss's defence to your claim. The work may be on the same terms and conditions as the old or it may be a new job. This is dealt with below. First **there are four conditions which every employer offering work to a redundant worker must comply with. If any one of these conditions is not considered, you are entitled to your money.**

1. Timing

An offer must be made **before your old contract** or notice runs out. If you don't get the offer until the day after that, the offer is invalid.

The offer of renewal or re-engagement must take effect immediately or within four weeks of the old contract ending. If you finish on a Friday, you must be started by the Monday, four weeks later.

2. Who makes the offer?

Since this is an employer's defence, it is natural to look to your employer for the offer. There are two variations on this. If the company is part of a group of associated employers, an offer from any of them counts as an offer from your own boss. So does an offer from a new employer who is taking over the business.

No other offers are sufficient. **Your boss cannot offer you work with the new boss,** nor with other firms in the area even if he personally makes efforts to place you.

3. What information must be included?

The offer can be made **orally or in writing**. To be sure of what's being offered, you should insist on the details of the offer being in writing.

Whether the offer is oral or written, it must be *sufficiently* specific for you to know what is involved in the new job. If it does not differ from your old job your boss must say so. But when the employer offers a **new job,** or **different terms** he must inform you about the 'capacity and place . . . and . . . other terms and conditions of employment' – RP Act section 2(5).

You must be given enough information to enable you to reach a decision on whether to accept or reject the offer. If particulars of travel arrangements, rates of pay, duties and so on are missing, the employer hasn't made a proper offer.

4. Failure to make an offer

If there is no proper offer, your boss must pay. Even if
he makes no offer because he knows you will refuse, he must
still go through the motions.

> Ms J. Simpson worked in a small sweet shop in Reading.
> It was taken over by the Thornton's chain. Ms Simpson
> said she wouldn't work for them, would take two or three
> months' holiday, then work in a hospital or anywhere but
> a shop. So Thornton's made no offer to her. She claimed
> redundancy pay. The NIRC decided that if an employer
> wants to avoid the duty to pay, there is a strict obligation
> in the Act to make an offer, even if refusal is likely. So
> Ms Simpson got her money. *Simpson v Dickinson* 1973
> (NIRC)

Offering the same work and conditions

If a proper offer is made to you, you must consider
whether there is any change in your conditions. If there is no
change and you are offered a renewal of your old job, you can
only get your money if you *reasonably* refuse it. You might be
acting reasonably if, for example, you were given notice,
found another job, made arrangements to move and at the
last minute were offered a renewal of your old job (compare
Thomas Wragg v Wood page 198 below).

You might get an offer of work which, though strictly
within your contract, means you do different work than you
normally do. This would be an offer of work on the same
conditions. If the work is not within your existing conditions,
your case is one of 'different conditions' and the work is judged
on the grounds of suitability.

Offering different conditions

Your employer may offer you work on different terms
from your old contract. You will need to know whether you
are jeopardising your redundancy money if you refuse. It is an
invidious position to be in because you may have to choose
between accepting a poor alternative, and losing your money.

For your employer to avoid payment he must show that
there was **A. a proper offer B. of suitable work C.** which you
unreasonably turned down. In law suitability and reasonableness are separate issues. Broadly, suitability relates to the job

(objective), reasonableness to personal factors of your own (subjective). This can be illustrated by Richard Stratton's case:

> Richard Stratton was an inspector in an engineering plant. He worked four nights a week. Due to redundancy he was offered five nights, with more money and less hours. He refused and claimed his money. The offer was suitable, as it was *substantially equivalent* to his old job, but he personally objected to losing more sleep, having to travel to work once more each week, and spending less time with his family. The NIRC awarded him his redundancy pay. *Universal Fisher Engineering v Stratton* 1972 (NIRC)

In practice the two conditions get mixed up and tribunals don't always make clear the grounds on which they base their decisions. A number of rules of thumb have emerged, though, which show that offers can be safely refused for a variety of reasons. **What follows should not be regarded as an exhaustive list. In every case the test is suitability and reasonableness.**

Pay

If the money you are offered in the new job is substantially lower than in the old you can turn it down. A worker who rejected a drop of £3 8s. was held to be acting reasonably. If there were other unfavourable factors, you could reasonably refuse any drop in wages.

Travel

Two workers told to move to another London factory two-and-a-half miles away were reasonable in refusing (*Shields v Goff* page 150 above). But a Nottingham man offered work 20 miles away in Newark, with travel costs paid for nine months and on flexible shifts, was unreasonable in refusing – *Hitchcock v St Anne's Hosiery* 1971 (HC). Factors you would have to consider – and these should be made clear to you before your old job finishes – are: distance, time, expense, inconvenience, where you live.

Status

A drop in status is something you can reasonably refuse – Mr Marriott did (see page 149). So did a headmaster who was offered a job in a pool of teachers who were obliged to be mobile – *Taylor v Kent CC* 1969 (HC). Raymond Harris, a joiner and apprentice master, was reasonable in turning down work as a bench joiner without the status that went with teaching apprentices, even though his wages and staff status would have been the same – *Harris v Turner* 1973 (NIRC). But a *chargehand* shipwright unreasonably refused to move to another dock as a shipwright – *Collier v Smiths Docks* 1969 (HC).

Domestic arrangements

Refusal to take a job because it disrupts your family or social life is often a valid reason. A foundryman who turned down a suitable double day shift job because his wife was an invalid, got his redundancy money – *Allied Ironfounders v Macken* 1971 (HC).

Uncertain future

If you reject a job because it may not last very long, you run the risk of forfeiting your redundancy money. Provided the job offered is of a regular nature, even though it may not be very secure, you should take it. Joan Street turned down a clerical/typist job because it would probably last only 12–18 months (*Morganite Crucible v Street* 1972). Sir John Donaldson, in the NIRC, said she acted unreasonably and refused to award her any redundancy pay. He remarked:

> No employment (with the possible exception of judicial employment) can be said to be almost permanent.

His own judicial employment in that court proved to be no exception!

Combined with *other* factors, though, fears of job security can give reasonable grounds for refusing a job with your present employers.

> Horace Wood was given notice by the construction company he worked for. He got a job elsewhere but on his last day at work he was offered suitable alternative work. He refused to take it on the grounds that he was 56, had fears about future redundancy in the industry, had accepted a job outside and anyway the offer came unreasonably late. The EAT upheld his award of £800 saying his grounds were reasonable, when considered altogether. *Thomas Wragg v Wood* 1976 (EAT)

Trial periods

When you are offered a job on **different** terms, section 3(5) gives you the right to a **trial period** on the new job. This applies however slight the variation in terms or location or capacity of employment. It lasts for **four weeks** and gives you the chance to try the new job.

During this period you are free to quit, and claim redundancy pay calculated up to the day the old job ended. If your boss won't pay, the new job is scrutinised in the usual way, to see if it was suitable and if you were unreasonable. If you are sacked during the trial period – because, say, you are not efficient enough – you are taken to be redundant on the date the old job finished, and are entitled to payment.

If you refuse to take the trial period, your boss might refuse to pay. A tribunal will test the new job and your refusal for suitability and reasonableness. Theoretically your refusal should not affect these questions, but tribunals may be more ready to consider you unreasonable if you fail to try it out.

Extending the trial period

You can extend the trial period for the purposes of **retraining** provided you make a written agreement **before you start work** specifying the date the period is to end, and your terms and conditions when it does.

Logically there is no reason why the period should not be extended by agreement to give you a longer trial, or to let you take holidays, but section 3 (6) talks only of retraining. Your boss might be unable to recoup his rebate if he agrees to an extension for other reasons.

Alternative work – summary

1. An offer must be made by your boss, or the new boss in a takeover, before your notice expires. It must be specific about the main conditions of the new job, which must start within four weeks of the old job.

2. If your contract is renewed without changes, it will usually be unreasonable for you to refuse it.

3. If the work or conditions of the new job are different, you lose redundancy pay if it is *suitable* and you *unreasonably* refuse it.

4. Less pay, lower status, more travel, domestic arrangements and insecurity are all factors to be considered.

5. You are entitled to a four-week trial period in any new job.

Redundancy and misconduct

The Act deals specifically (sections 2 (2) and 10) with sackings for misconduct in a redundancy situation. These rules can be summarised according to whether you are sacked before or after you have been given notice of redundancy. Employers are keen to use these rules because they can use them to avoid redundancy pay. If you lose redundancy pay because of these rules it is almost certain you will also lose any unfair dismissal claim you bring.

Misconduct before notice of redundancy

Suppose a redundancy situation arises but no one has yet been given notice. Your boss discovers you have been stealing from the works. This is grounds for instant dismissal. So he picks you out for redundancy. He can sack you instantly, or with less notice than you are otherwise entitled to. If he lets you work out your notice he *must* give you a written statement that he thinks he is entitled to sack you instantly because of your misconduct but he is letting you work out your notice.

In either case, you don't get your redundancy pay.

Misconduct after notice of redundancy

If you are under notice of redundancy and your boss then sacks you for gross misconduct, you don't automatically lose your redundancy pay. You can apply to a tribunal. It has discretion to pay you all or some or none of your money, according to what it thinks is just and equitable in the circumstances. In other words, it substitutes its judgment for management's.

This right applies only to a sacking while you are working your **statutory** notice.

> **Example:** You have been employed for four years. The CE Act entitles you to a minimum of four weeks' notice. Your contract gives you six weeks. If you are sacked for gross misconduct during the first two weeks, you don't get redundancy pay. But if you are sacked in the last four weeks (that is, the statutory notice period) you do.

Redundancy and strikes

Similar rules apply during strikes in a redundancy situation. The risk of losing your rights may affect your decision to resist redundancy by industrial action, so the rules are important.

Striking during notice

The classic case arises when you are given notice of redundancy and decide to strike in protest. If this occurs during your statutory notice period under the CE Act you do not jeopardise your redundancy money (that is, if the strike does not avert the sackings). But your boss can require you to make up the days lost through the strike.

The definition of a strike (see page 290) includes a cessation of work, and a refusal to work for an employer, Accordingly a sit-in and a work-in are both covered.

Redundancies declared during a strike

Employers regularly threaten redundancies during a strike. Sometimes it is genuine, sometimes just a scare tactic. You may lose your right to redundancy pay, as W. Simmons did. (See page 296.) The EAT said Hoovers could refuse to pay because the right to pay is protected only when a strike occurs *after* notice of redundancy has been given.

Since employers are, as we have seen, entitled to sack strikers, they can avoid redundancy payments quite easily. However, the EAT in the *Simmons* case said that a strike in response to deliberate provocation or unreasonable demands by an employer will not prejudice your rights.

If a tribunal says you caused the redundancy yourself – by striking or inefficiency, for example – you are still entitled to redundancy pay. Again, this is because the law applies to the *fact* of redundancy, not the reasons for it.

Time off during notice

If you are under notice of redundancy you might want to start looking for a new job or retraining before you actually sign on as unemployed. Some collective agreements require employers to provide time off with pay, and travelling expenses, for workers under notice.

The EP Act gives you a legal right to time off. Section 61 applies if, at the date you are due to be sacked, or proper notice would have run out, you would be entitled to redundancy pay. This section applies to Crown and National Health Service workers (the other provisions on redundancy don't).

You have two rights:
1. to be given a 'reasonable' amount of time off
2. to be paid for it

The purpose of these rights is to enable you **to look for work, or to make arrangements for training** for future employment. You must show that this is how you intend to use your time off.

There is no definition of what is reasonable. This would depend on the difficulty in obtaining work, the time and travel involved, the range of jobs you are looking at, and the requirements of a training agency.

The right to unpaid time off is quite separate from the right to be paid, and is restricted only by what is 'reasonable'. But if your boss fails to give you time off, or fails to pay you, his liability is limited. This may indirectly impose a restriction on the amount of paid time off you can demand.

If your boss denies your rights you should claim to a tribunal **within three months** of the day on which you wanted time off. See page 357 for the procedure. The tribunal can order your boss to pay, but he can't be made to pay more than **two days' pay**. Any pay you get under your contract must be offset against these two days. This means that if your boss pays you while you work out your notice, but refuses to release you for job-hunting, you can't get any more money from him.

Leaving during notice

Supposing you get a job and want to start before you have worked out your notice? You can give notice to finish earlier, and this does not affect your redundancy pay *provided* you take the following steps:

1. You have been given the minimum notice you are entitled to under the CE Act. If you have been given longer you must wait until you are in the statutory minimum notice period. For example: if you are entitled to four weeks under the CE Act, but six weeks under your contract, the right to leave earlier applies only during the last four weeks.

2. You give your boss **in writing** the minimum notice required by your contract.

3. If your boss doesn't object, you can leave when your notice to him expires. Redundancy pay is calculated to this earlier date.

Your redundancy pay may be affected as follows:

4. If he does object, he must **in writing** request you to

withdraw your notice and warn you that if you don't, he will contest your right to redundancy pay.

5. If you still go ahead and leave, you don't necessarily lose your redundancy money. Tribunals have power to look at all the reasons on both sides, and award you all or part or none of the money.

Lay-off and short-time

Remember that lay-off without pay, and short-time working on half-pay or less, can constitute redundancy and unfair dismissal. See pages 64–5.

How to claim redundancy pay

You must make a claim for redundancy pay **within six months** of your dismissal. If you have worked for a trial period, the six months run from the date your trial period ended. You should make your claim either by writing to your boss (or the receiver/liquidator if he has gone bust, or personal representative if he has died), *or* by applying to a tribunal. See page 357 for the procedure.

If you have not received a written statement giving particulars about the reasons for your dismissal, you should demand this in accordance with section 70 of the EP Act (see page 182 above).

Proving it

You must show you were sacked. If your boss says you resigned, you have to show you were constructively dismissed or voluntarily accepted dismissal on the grounds of redundancy. The onus then shifts to your employer. There is a presumption that if you were sacked, it was because of redundancy. Your boss must then try to disprove this.

How much is due?

The method of calculation

Redundancy pay is calculated according to the same formula as the **basic award** in unfair dismissal cases. This is set out on page 348. Use the ready reckoner on page 349 to check the calculations.

Tax and unemployment benefit

Redundancy pay is tax-free. Additional redundancy pay made, for example, because of a collective agreement or as an ex gratia payment, is tax-free up to £5,000. Anything over that is taxed.

Redundancy pay does not affect unemployment benefit but may affect supplementary benefits. Pay in lieu of notice may be taxed, so it is advisable to have this tied up as 'severance pay', or additional redundancy pay, to avoid reductions.

Pensions

Employers can offset redundancy pay against an occupational pension scheme in limited circumstances. These are set out in leaflet RPL 1 obtained from union and DE offices. Briefly, they can't offset repayment of your own contributions, or pensions or lump sums which accrue more than 90 weeks after your dismissal. If your boss does not exercise this limited right to offset, he can claim the normal rebate from the state fund (see below).

Statement of calculation

You have the right to a written statement explaining how your boss works out the payment. If he fails to provide this he can be fined £20 for a first, and £100 for a second, offence.

Who pays?

Your employer pays you. He is entitled to claim a rebate from the state fund to which all employers contribute. The rebate is 41 per cent of the statutory amount he has paid to you. He can't reclaim higher amounts, for example, sums paid under a collective agreement.

If your employer goes bust, or otherwise refuses to pay, the whole of your statutory payment is guaranteed by the state fund – see below.

Your rights against an insolvent employer

If your boss goes bust owing you wages, holiday pay, redundancy pay and so on you will be able to recoup some of these debts from the state fund. Your rights on insolvency depend on what the debt consists of. There are four different methods of dealing with them.

1. Fully guaranteed debts

If your employer goes bust, and you are entitled to **redundancy pay**, the state fund guarantees the full statutory amount. Make a claim to your employer's liquidator/receiver and then apply to your local DE office.

All statutory **maternity pay** is refunded to employers so this is guaranteed if your employer goes bust before paying you. In addition the whole of the following debts are guaranteed:

- **basic award** of unfair dismissal compensation
- minimum notice money due to you according to the CE Act
- repayment of an apprenticeship premium.

2. Partly guaranteed debts

If your debts are accrued on a weekly basis, such as arrears of pay, the state fund will guarantee the following debts up to £100 each week:

- arrears of pay (including the **priority debts** listed below) for up to *eight* weeks
- holiday pay for up to *six* weeks.

The Employment Secretary can raise the £100 upper limit each year.

3. Priority debts

If you still have money owing to you after the state fund has met fully and partly guaranteed debts you can claim against the company as a preferential creditor. This would happen if you had **arrears of wages** in excess of eight weeks, or £100 a week, or were entitled to more than minimum notice. The most you can claim for the *whole* of these debts is £800. The limit set by the 1948 Companies Act was increased in 1976.

The debts for which you rank as preferential creditor are
- arrears of pay during the previous four months
- notice pay
- holiday pay
- guaranteed wages
- payment for medical suspension
- pay due to union representatives while carrying out duties or training
- pay while looking for work, or retraining, during notice

■ a protective award following redundancies

Sick pay is not specifically mentioned but it could be classed as arrears.

As a preferential creditor, you get paid before some shareholders and other creditors out of any money or assets the company has left. But you rank equally with the tax, Social security and rating authorities, who are also preferential. You might get a percentage of what's due to you.

4. Unsecured debts

For any other money owed you, you have to take your chance with the shareholders and all the other creditors. The kind of debts envisaged are

■ priority debts of over £200 after the state fund has met its obligation to you.

■ compensation for unfair dismissal (excluding the basic award), victimisation, sex and race discrimination.

How to claim

Claim **redundancy** pay in the way described above. For loss of **notice money** use Form IP2, and for other debts Form IP1 (see pages 379–80). Write to your employer's representative, that is, the receiver, liquidator or trustee. He should send you Forms IP1 and 2. You complete the relevant form and return to the representative, who then passes it to the DE. The DE arranges for the representative to pay you.

If you don't know who the representative is, or if you don't get paid within six months of applying, write direct to the DE.

For other preferential debts, and unsecured debts, you need a 'proof of debt' form from the receiver/liquidator handling the company's affairs. Write to the company's registered office. If there are a number of you, your union official can file a form on behalf of all of you.

Who are the losers?

The guarantees in the EP Act are a substantial advance on the slight protection afforded since 1948. They still don't cover all kinds of debts, nor the whole of those that are protected. Parliament has gone some way to recognising that money owed by employers to workers is in a different category from other debts. It should go further.

Shareholders take a conscious risk when they invest in a company which they hope will increase their capital. Companies trading with each other do so to further their own profits. If their judgment is unsound, or the company is unreliable, it is right that they accept the risk of loss. Workers, on the other hand, because they are not involved in such decisions, can't control the finances of their employer and don't have an effective free choice in seeking jobs, should not be put at risk. They should be fully compensated by the state fund for any collapse or failure to pay. Employers should be required to pay more into the fund to meet this eventuality.

The other gap in the protection is that the rights apply only if your employer is insolvent, that is, he can't pay. If he simply disappears without trace, as sometimes happens in the textile and building trades, you have no protection.

Redundancy checklist

Collective measures to fight redundancy are listed on page 334. **They are the most effective ways to prevent closures and lay-offs.** If you are made redundant you will be entitled to some or all of the following rights as an *individual*:

■ time off with pay for retraining or to seek new work
■ notice or wages in lieu
■ written statement of reason for dismissal
■ redundancy payment and statement of how it is calculated
■ a protective award (see page 331) if your employer has not consulted the union
■ unfair dismissal if a redundancy procedure has been ignored, or you have been selected unfairly, for example on trade union grounds
■ a guarantee from the government of some debts if your employer goes bust
■ tax rebate if you are out of work.

Summary

1. You are entitled to redundancy pay if your boss's need for employees to do work of a particular kind either ceases or diminishes.

2. Your boss can avoid paying you if he offers suitable alternative employment and you unreasonably refuse to take it.

3. You have a right to a trial period if you are offered work on new conditions.

4. You have a right to take time off with pay for job-hunting or training if you are given notice of redundancy.

5. If you are laid off or put on short-time you might be entitled to claim redundancy pay and unfair dismissal.

6. If your employer is insolvent, some debts owed to you are guaranteed by the government, and you get priority over shareholders for some other debts.

7. Organised workers should regard the existence of these rights as minimum standards on which to negotiate, if direct action to oppose redundancy fails.

12.

Social Security

Your rights under the social security system /
contributory and non-contributory benefits /
unemployment, maternity, sickness and
invalidity benefits / industrial injury, disease,
disablement and death / earnings related
supplement / supplementary benefit / what
to do if you are denied your rights /
collective action / and a summary.

The social security system consists of a wide range of
benefits and services. Within the system, some benefits are
entirely free to everyone, such as some health services; some
are available only to employees; some only to unemployed or
retired people; and some only to workers who have paid a
specific number of contributions. This chapter deals only with
those rights connected with employment. Of necessity, this
account is an outline only. Pensions are omitted entirely.

Although described as benefits you have a *right* to them
and can claim your rights through legal channels.

Where to find the law

Social security benefits are found in the Social Security
Act 1975 (SS Act); pensions in the Social Security Pensions
Act 1975; and supplementary benefits in the Supplementary
Benefits Act 1976 (SB Act).

Definitions

Before looking at the benefits, it is important to get
some definitions straight:

■ **Social security benefit** (as used in this handbook):
benefit paid under the SS Act 1975, including national insurance benefits.

■ **Supplementary benefit:** benefit paid under the SB Act 1976.

■ **Contribution:** payment made to the DHSS by employed or self-employed workers, employers, and people who make voluntary payments.

■ **Dependant:** wife, husband, children, adult relative.

■ **Lower earnings limit:** the weekly earnings at which you begin to be liable to pay contributions.

■ **Benefit year:** the year, starting on the first Sunday in January, in which you first claim benefit.

■ **Doctor's statement:** doctor's note advising you to stay off work until a given date ('closed' statement) or that you should not work until after a set period ('open' statement) You must get a closed statement before you go back to work.

■ **Relevant tax year:** the year ending on 5 April *before* the year in which you claim.

■ **Interruption of employment:** days when you are unemployed or incapable of work.

■ **Earnings related supplement** (ERS): payment made in addition to some benefits.

Contributions

There are four classes of contribution:

Class 1: paid mainly by employees and their employers.
Class 2: paid by self-employed 'earners'.
Class 3: paid voluntarily by employees and self-employed people in order to get benefits they wouldn't otherwise be entitled to, or to make up contributions paid.
Class 4: paid by self-employed people engaged in a trade or profession.

You can be **credited** with paying some contributions if you are unemployed, or sick, even if you don't actually pay.

In order to claim full benefits for unemployment, sickness (and invalidity) and maternity, you must have paid sufficient contributions in the relevant tax year. These must add up to 50 times the amount someone would have paid if they were on the 'lower earnings limit'. In 1977/78 this limit was £15. If contributions are payable at the rate of 5·5 per cent you need to have paid contributions equivalent to £15 × 50 × ·055 = £41·25.

You can get reduced benefits if you have paid the equivalent of 25 contributions at the lower earnings limit. You can also be **credited** with some contributions and still qualify.

What benefits?

The following list shows the main benefits that you and your dependants may be entitled to. The classes of contributions are described below.

Benefit	Contributions needed
Unemployment+ERS+dependants	Class 1
Maternity allowance+ERS+dependants	Class 1 or 2
Maternity grant	Class 1, 2 or 3
Sickness+ERS	Class 1 or 2
Invalidity	Class 1 or 2
Widows allowance+ERS+dependants	Class 1, 2 or 3
Pensions+dependants	Class 1, 2 or 3
Child special allowance	Class 1, 2 or 3
Death grant	Class 1, 2 or 3
Attendance allowance	None
Non-contributory invalidity pension	None
Industrial injury Disablement Industrial death	None, but must usually be employee
Supplementary benefit	None

Sex equality has not yet come to the social security system. Some benefits are available only to men. Others are available to women and their dependants on different terms from those applying to men. Official discrimination therefore continues.

Unemployment benefit

You have a right to unemployment benefit if you

1. have paid the appropriate value of Class 1 contributions.

2. are unemployed or laid off due to an interruption of work for at least two consecutive days in any period of six (Sundays don't count).

3. don't earn more than 75p for any day you are out of work, and

4. are available for full-time employment.

Benefit is not paid for the first three days ('waiting days') or beyond 312 days.

You may be disqualified for benefit

1. for up to six weeks if you voluntarily left your job 'without just cause'.

2. for up to six weeks if without good cause you refuse to accept or apply for suitable employment notified to you by the DE.

3. for up to six weeks if you lost your job due to your 'misconduct', that is, 'such misconduct as would lead a reasonable employer to terminate a claimant's employment'.

4. throughout an industrial dispute if you are laid off. But you *will* get benefit if you can prove you are not taking part, or directly interested, in the dispute.

You can get ERS increases for dependants and supplementary benefits in addition to unemployment benefit (see below).

Claim benefit by registering on your first day of unemployment at your local unemployment benefit office (DHSS). Take your P45 and your national insurance number.

Maternity benefits

You can get the lump sum maternity grant if you **or your husband** have paid the appropriate value of Class 1, 2 or 3 contributions.

You have a right to the weekly maternity allowance

1. if you have paid the appropriate value of Class 1 or Class 2 contributions.

2. if you are expecting, or have just had a baby,

3. if you do no work on the days for which you are claiming, and

4. even though you may be getting maternity pay from your boss.

Payment is made weekly for 18 weeks starting in the 11th week before the week your baby is due. Claim maternity benefits on form BM4 available from the DHSS and child health clinics.

You can get ERS, an increase for dependants and supplementary benefits in addition to maternity allowance.

Sickness benefit

Diagram 6 (pages 214–15) shows what rights you have if you are sick or injured. The social security system provides better benefits for injury or disease caused by employment. The benefits for industrial injuries are dealt with below.

You have a right to sickness benefit if you
1. have paid the appropriate value of Class 1 or Class 2 contributions.
2. are incapable of work for two or more consecutive days within any six (Sundays don't count).

Benefit is not paid for the first three waiting days of incapacity. It is paid for 28 weeks. After that you go onto **invalidity benefit** (see below).

You can get ERS, an increase for dependants and supplementary benefit in addition to sickness benefit. Claim to your local DHSS **within six days** of becoming unable to work, enclosing a **doctor's statement** if you can. If not, make sure you give your name, address, date of birth and national insurance number.

Invalidity benefit

You have a right to invalidity benefit if you are incapable of work after 28 weeks and during all of that time you were entitled to sickness benefit or maternity allowance. You get invalidity allowance if you are under 60 (men) or 55 (women) on the first day of incapacity. This is increased according to how *young* you were when first incapacitated. Otherwise you get invalidity pension. If you don't qualify for either of these you can get non-contributory invalidity benefit.

You can get an increase for dependants and supplementary benefits in addition to invalidity benefits. The DHSS will automatically pay invalidity benefit once sickness benefit runs out.

Diagram 6 **Social Security Benefits**
a: Industrial incapacity

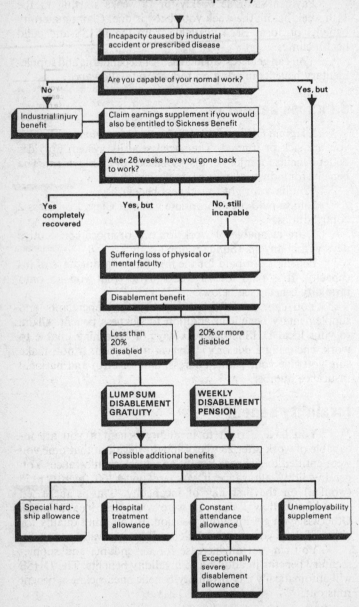

Diagram 6 **Social Security Benefits**
b: Industrial death

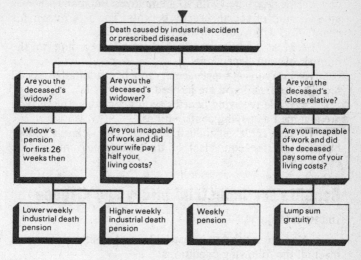

c: Non-industrial incapacity

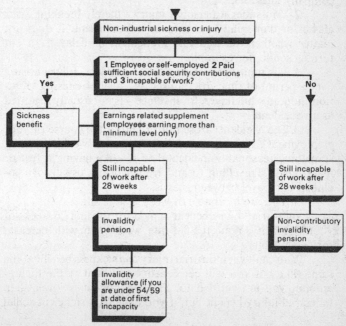

Notes to diagram 6

1. These benefits are not affected by any benefit or sick pay scheme negotiated with your employer. But many schemes take account of social security benefits. This is a matter for negotiation with your employer, not the DHSS.

2. Most benefits can be increased according to the number of your dependants.

3. You can get **supplementary benefit** in addition to social security benefits if you are in need.

4. While receiving benefits, you get credits, that is, you are regarded as paying contributions.

5. You can't get industrial injury *and* sickness benefit but you get the equivalent of the highest amount you are entitled to.

Benefits for industrial injury and disease

Industrial injury

You are entitled to **industrial injury benefit** provided you meet all the following conditions:

1. You are an employee or office holder (for example, a company director).

2. You suffer a personal injury – merely breaking your glasses or damaging your tools is not sufficient. It does not matter whether the injury is immediate or delayed – a cut turning septic, for example.

3. The injury was caused by an **accident**. Injury arising over a period of time from a **process** – drilling causing vibration-induced whitefinger, for instance – is not usually regarded as an accident.

4. The accident 'arose out of and in the course of your employment'. This means while you were at work, or doing something reasonably incidental to it – like having a rest or meal break. Travelling to and from work is usually *not* included but travel between sites is.

5. You are incapable of work as a result.

Industrial injury benefit is paid for the first 26 weeks of your incapacity. You get a flat-rate, weekly sum with increases for dependants.

You can't get industrial injury *and* sickness benefit at the same time but you will get benefit equivalent to the highest amount you are entitled to. Sickness benefit is lower than industrial injury benefit but, if you have paid sufficient social security contributions and have earnings above a set figure you are entitled to ERS in addition to sickness or industrial injury benefit. No benefit is paid for the first three waiting days of your incapacity.

You may also get supplementary benefits.

If you have any accident at work, report it to your supervisor and union rep, and see that it is recorded in the accident book.

To claim industrial injury benefit, get a **doctor's statement** from your doctor or hospital. Fill in the back and send it to your local social security office **within six days** of your incapacity (or within 21 days if it is your first ever claim). If you cannot get a doctor's statement, notify the social security office in writing anyway. You may be disqualified if your claim is late.

While you are receiving any social security benefit you will be credited with contributions for the purpose of future claims. However, for many claims, you need to have made a minimum number of actual contributions.

Industrial disease

You are entitled to **industrial injury benefit** if you meet the following conditions:

1. You contract a prescribed industrial disease. There are 50 of these recognised by the government. Pneumoconiosis and other lung diseases, and occupational deafness are also recognised for *special* benefits.

2. You are or have been employed in an occupation recognised by the government as providing a risk of this disease.

3. The disease is due to the nature of your work.

4. You are incapable of work because of it.

The procedure for claims is the same as for industrial injuries (see above).

Disablement due to industrial injury or disease

You are entitled to **disablement benefit** if your meet the following conditions:

1. You have an industrial injury or suffer from a prescribed disease.

2. You suffer a 'loss of physical or mental faculty' as a result. This means that your power to enjoy a normal life is impaired. It is assessed by reference to the condition of a normal healthy person of your age and sex.

Disablement benefit is paid as a weekly pension if, by using this reference point, it is decided that you are 20 per cent or more disabled. If you are less than 20 per cent disabled it is paid as a lump sum gratuity. Your disability can be permanent, like losing an eye, or temporary, like a broken leg.

You receive disablement benefit automatically if your 26 weeks on industrial injury benefit expires. Because disablement benefit is designed to compensate for **disability** not incapacity for work **you can claim whether or not you are off work**. So you can receive benefit if you never book time off, or when you return to work, or when your industrial injury benefit runs out after 26 weeks.

Disablement benefit can be increased as follows:

■ **Special hardship allowance** if you are unable to go back to your regular work or do work of an equivalent standard.

■ **Hospital treatment allowance** if you are in hospital.

■ **Constant attendance allowance** if you need someone to look after you during the daytime.

■ **Exceptionally severe disablement allowance** if you need permanent constant care.

■ **Unemployability supplement** if you are likely to be permanently unable to work or earn more than a limited amount.

■ **Supplementary benefit**

Industrial death

You are entitled to industrial death benefit if you are the widow or dependant child of a man who died as a result of an industrial injury or prescribed industrial disease. Certain dependants and widowers can claim if they are incapable of supporting themselves and were supported by the deceased.

The benefit is paid as a weekly pension. A higher rate is paid to widows with dependant children, and certain others.

ERS is paid if the deceased had paid sufficient social security contributions at the time of his death.

To claim, fill in the back of the (free) Registrar's death certificate and send it to your local DHSS office. They will then send you form BW1 on which you claim your rights.

Earnings related supplement

ERS is paid as an increase on unemployment, maternity, sickness and some widows' benefits provided you have paid sufficient Class 1 contributions. You can also get it on industrial injury benefits if you are *also* entitled to sickness benefit, that is, because you have paid sufficient contributions.

ERS is not paid for the first 12 days of unemployment or incapacity. It lasts for 26 weeks (that is, until 28 weeks after you first became unemployed).

If you are **suspended** and put on short-time working, you can't get ERS until you have been off for six consecutive days. You must then wait a further 12 days before you get it. For example, if you are working a three-day week, you won't be able to claim ERS.

ERS is paid automatically by the DHSS once the 12 waiting days are over.

All your benefits, dependant's increases and ERS must not amount to more than 85 per cent of your weekly earnings.

Supplementary benefits

You have a right to supplementary benefits if your 'resources are insufficient to meet your requirements' (SB Act 1976 section 1).

Your benefit can be reduced by 40 per cent for reasons corresponding to the six-week disqualification for unemployment benefit. You don't have a right to supplementary benefit if you are involved in an industrial dispute, but your dependants can get it. Anything over £1 that you get in strike pay reduces the benefit payable. You might still get a payment if you are in 'urgent need'.

You can't normally get supplementary benefit if you are in full-time employment. But you can if you have just started and, for example, have to work a week in hand, or if your earning power is reduced because of disability. Anyone can get a one-off payment to meet an 'urgent need'.

Once you are getting supplementary benefit you also get, for example, free prescriptions, dental treatment, school meals.

Claim at your local DHSS office.

If you are denied your rights

Insurance officers employed by the DHSS make decisions about your entitlement to social security benefit. You can appeal. The letter which rejects your claim, or makes a decision on your benefit, will include details of how to appeal. Appeals are heard by Local Tribunals and Medical Appeal

Tribunals. Anyone can represent you at these tribunals. Try your union. Legal Aid is available under the **green form** scheme (see page 354) for preparation but not representation.

Appeals against decisions on supplementary benefits are heard by Supplementary Benefit Appeal Tribunals. They decide essentially questions of fact, that is, needs and resources. You can appeal since January 1978 on a point of law to the High Court. Legal Aid is available there.

Collective action

Social security benefits are paid by the state but this doesn't mean that collective action is inappropriate in this area of workers' rights. If you have good collective agreements on sickness and maternity, or good safety standards so that accidents at work are prevented, or take direct action to prevent sackings, you don't need to resort to social security benefits. Collectively, you can even negotiate to manipulate social security benefits and wages, for example, in short-time working, in order to maximise your money.

Summary

1. You are entitled to the major social security benefits – unemployment, maternity, sickness, invalidity, widows allowance and pension – if you have paid sufficient social security contributions.

2. Some benefits don't depend on your having paid contributions.

3. Benefits are paid for **industrial** injury, disease, disablement and death without the need for contributions. But you must usually be an employee at the time of the accident or disease and it must arise out of and in the course of your employment.

4. Supplementary benefit is not usually paid to people in employment. It is payable to anyone whose resources are less than their requirements.

Part Three: Union Rights

13.

Trade Union Membership

The importance of the right to union membership / where to find the law / protection against dismissal and victimisation for union activity / who is protected / your basic rights / what are union activities / when is an appropriate time / rights of union reps / how to claim / proving it / remedies / time off for union activities if your union is recognised by management / your rights within the union.

Your most basic rights as a worker are the right to be a trade unionist and to organise the union at your workplace. Only through exercising these rights can you begin to reduce the scope of your employer's prerogatives, and to achieve the most elementary improvement in terms and conditions. Union organisation is the key to resisting unilateral pressure and to gaining control over your working environment. The law has been slow to recognise these basic rights and even now protection is limited. Nevertheless, collective action backed up as necessary with the threat of legal action can give you some scope in which to organise.

This chapter deals with three rights:

1. to be a union member, and to take part in its activities at an appropriate time

2. if your union is recognised, to take time off for union duties and activities

3. your rights within the union

They are expressed as 'protections' rather than as positive rights to organise, as they are in the USA and on the continent. To some extent the first two rights reduce employers' traditional freedom to manage in the way they choose.

Ironically, as we shall see when looking at union activities in *Crouch's* case (page 224) and the closed shop in *Langston's* case (page 37), the courts' desire to protect reactionary anti-unionists under the Industrial Relations Act has resulted in an *extension* of the rights of trade unionists.

Where to find the law

Unfair dismissal: Trade Union and Labour Relations Act schedule 1 and the Employment Protection Act sections 71–76 (remedies); interim procedure: section 78; victimisation: section 53; time off: section 57–58 and the Advisory, Conciliation and Arbitration Service (ACAS) Code of Practice. Rights within the union: Trade Union Act 1913, Trade Union (Amalgamations) Act 1964, and the Trade Union and Labour Relations Act (TULR Act) section 7.

Protection against dismissal and victimisation

Who is protected?

All members and people who try to become members of independent trade unions are protected if they are dismissed or victimised **for a reason connected with their membership**. Only share fishermen and workers who ordinarily work outside Great Britain are excluded. If your union is recognised by your employer you have the specific right to time off, in some cases with pay (see page 232).

One glaring omission from the rights dealing with union organisation is that they apply only to employees. So *applicants* for jobs are not protected against discrimination at the point of hire, except on racial or sexual grounds. Blacklisting of applicants is by no means uncommon, and evidence of this has been provided.

At the Old Bailey trial in 1973 of the employees of the Christopher Roberts private detective agency, on charges of conspiracy to obtain confidential information, it was revealed that the firm had been employed to check on workers' political activities. Besides being employed by banks, solicitors, insurance firms and individuals, this and other detective agencies had frequently been engaged by non-unionised companies to investigate the background of prospective employees to make sure that their labour force was not 'infiltrated' by union members.

Tony Bunyan, *The Political Police in Britain*, pages 250–1, Julian Friedmann 1976.

There are a number of trade associations and federations and specialist organisations engaged in blacklisting and surveillance of political and industrial activists. Common Cause Ltd, the Economic League, Industrial Research and Information Services, British United Industrialists Ltd, and the former Complete Security Services Ltd, a one-time subsidiary of Securicor Ltd, all collect and disseminate information on individual workers and unions. Yet the EAT has confirmed that there is no redress for a blacklisted worker denied a job because of his union activities.

> Philip Beyer, a well-known union activist, knew that he was blacklisted as a result of his activity in UCATT. In 1975, in order to get work as a bricklayer with Birmingham Council, he gave a false name. He was discovered within an hour and sacked. In 1976, using his own name, he again got a job with the Council but was again sacked the same day. The reason given was his earlier 'deceit'. The Birmingham tribunal found that he had been sacked because of his union activities and ordered his reinstatement. On appeal, the EAT said the law protected only activities **while an employee**, not **before becoming an employee**. So blacklisted workers have no right to bring a claim. *City of Birmingham District Council v Beyer* 1977 (EAT)

A simple amendment should be made to apply the protection not only to 'employees' but also to 'workers', as this includes persons **seeking** work (TULR Act section 30). Even the Industrial Relations Act (IR Act) gave this protection.

Your basic rights

You can claim reinstatement and compensation if you have been dismissed unfairly. Your employer must give

reasons for sacking you and must show he acted reasonably.
Dismissal for being a member of an independent trade union
or wanting to take part in its activities is automatically unfair.
If your employer victimises you to such an extent that you
are forced to resign, this counts as dismissal too – 'constructive'
dismissal. If you do not give in to pressure and remain at work,
you can complain of victimisation. You are therefore given
the right (TULR Act schedule 1 para 6) not to be dismissed
for:

■ being a member of an independent trade union, or
proposing to join one;

■ taking part in its activities 'at any appropriate time';

■ refusing to join a trade union that is not certified as
independent.

And you have the right to claim compensation (EP Act
section 53) if action short of a dismissal is taken against you –
in other words, if you are victimised – and can show that your
boss intended:

■ to prevent or deter you from exercising these rights;

■ to penalise you for doing so; or

■ to compel you to join a non-independent union.

These rights are fundamental and look pretty good on
paper. The problem comes in proving your case. To start with,
there is the definition of **'union activities'** and when is considered to be an **'appropriate time'** to indulge in them.

What are trade union activities?

Section 58 of the EP Act deals with union activities but
this applies only to members of independent unions **recognised**
by their employers who want to take time off for union work.
(See page 232.) They include 'any activities' of your union, and
activities in which you are **representing** your union, for example
at trades councils, or local joint committees. But if you have
been dismissed or victimised there is no definition of union
activities. Since an employer must give time off for these
activities when he recognises the union, you can argue that it
is reasonable to outlaw dismissal and victimisation for taking
part in these union activities on the premises during meal-
breaks, and after work, even when he does not recognise your
union.

Some clear rules have arisen as a result of an important
case involving the Post Office.

On the day the Industrial Relations Act came into force
in 1972, several members and officials of the Telecom-

munications Staff Association claimed the right to take
part in the activities of their union which had registered
under the Act. The PO refused as it recognised only the
Union of Post Office Workers. So Walter Crouch and
several others appealed to a tribunal and from there all
the way to the House of Lords. They won the right to
organise at telephone exchanges; a right, in effect, to
disrupt stable industrial arrangements and to undermine
the unregistered but much larger UPW. The House of
Lords recognised and upheld the right of union members
to take part in union activities on their employers'
premises, **whether or not the union is recognised.**
Post Office v UPW and Crouch 1974 (HL)

Judgments made under the IR Act are still effective, and
the right to take part in union activities is preserved in substantially the same form in subsequent legislation. The *Crouch*
judgment is the source for our definition of union activities.
Lord Reid in the House of Lords said:

> Men carrying on activities of their union on their
> employer's premises must do so in a manner which does
> not cause substantial inconvenience either to their
> employer or to fellow workers who are not members of
> their trade union – and employers must tolerate minor
> infringements of their strict legal rights which do them no
> real harm.

**So you have the right, on your employer's premises and at 'any
appropriate time', whether the union is recognised or not, to**
- recruit members
- collect subscriptions
- distribute literature
- leave literature lying about
- have a table in the canteen for union affairs
- occasionally hold meetings (provided you arrange
this with your employer)
- meet lay officials of the union who are also employees
of your firm (provided you arrange this with your employer).

This obviously falls short of what you should demand
and put in your agreements, as it omits such basic needs as
provision of a notice board, internal mail facilities, notification of new employees and the right to bring in a union
official or other adviser (for instance, on health and safety).
And the court's decision excludes the following rights:
- to be recognised and to negotiate
- to take part in any activities that require your employer's active assistance
- to take part in any union activities that involve 'sub-

stantial inconvenience' to your employer or other workers.

Still, the positive rights provided are a useful start to organising.

What is an appropriate time?

You have the right to take part in union activities in three broad situations which are:

- outside working hours
- during working hours if you have your employer's consent
- during working hours if there is an arrangement or agreement with management.

'Outside working hours' means during meal-breaks, tea-breaks and rest periods, and before and after work. Even if there is no formal meal-break, or if you are paid during meal-breaks, you are still entitled to carry on union activities. Nor does it matter that your boss has forbidden you to exercise your right. He cannot overrule the EP Act.

The EP Act does not specifically restrict the right to times when you are supposed to be on the premises, but there is a risk that if you come back to a shift on your rest day you may be a trespasser. Several judges in *Crouch's* case were very conscious of the employer's property rights, and of the threat to them of workers organising to the fullest extent, so they restricted the times during which you can organise, even though you are organising outside working hours. Lord Justice Scarman said:

> An employer may determine by the contract of employment or workshop practice, when and where a worker may lawfully be on his premises outside working hours; if a worker is there within the ambit of such permission, he may take part in trade union activities provided nothing is required of his employer other than permission to be there.

So permission is still required if you plan a recruitment drive on an unorganised shift, or on premises of your employer other than those where you are entitled to be.

If permission is given either for a specific occasion, or for union purposes in general, you are safeguarded by the EP Act. And if there is merely a loose arrangement, or custom and practice, or even acquiescence in your taking time off, you are also safeguarded. But not otherwise:

> Leonard Robb worked for a bus company. He joined the TGWU and was appointed shop steward. **During working hours** he tried to persuade others to join. His

boss moved him to other work 'in order to isolate him'. The tribunal and the EAT agreed that Leonard had been victimised because of his union activities. But as these activities took place in working hours without permission he was not protected by the law. *Robb v Leon Motors Services* 1977 (EAT)

So the appropriate time for activities in a **non-recognised** union is always subject to your employer's permission – slightly less restricted outside working hours than in, but still restricted. (See footnote, page 239). This means you must use your industrial strength rather than the law to enforce your basic workers' rights.

Rights of union officials

1. Union lay reps

Union lay officials (for example, shop stewards, collectors, branch secretaries), can probably make the definition of union activities include those of an organiser. In *Crouch's* case, Lord Denning said Crouch was entitled 'to carry on all such reasonable activities as are **normally carried on by a branch organiser**' and Lord Reid said he could in his own time **visit his members at other sites when they weren't working**. Union activities must include elections and activities of branch officials. The Code of Practice on discipline (see page 70) says **no action should be taken against a union rep until the matter has been discussed with a full-time official or senior rep.**

2. Full-time officials

Crouch was an employee. Non-employee officials and organisers have no special rights. They are not allowed to enter factories or even company car parks to give out literature or collect forms. All this must be done outside the gates. In the USA, non-employees have the right to enter premises if 'no other channels of communications' are available for getting the union message across. This applies where workers live in, such as on ships or farms, in holiday camps, hotels, company towns, and in shopping centres. Also in the USA, officials can enter any premises if the employer discriminates about the distribution of literature – giving staff associations the right to recruit but not an independent union, for instance.

So far the only step towards this kind of right in the UK is that taken in the North Sea oil industry, where access of union officials to oil rigs is now a condition in the licence granted to operators.

How to claim

If someone has been sacked or victimised for trade-union activity the best way to put it right is by direct action. In a tribunal the claim must be made in the form of an **individual** grievance, there are massive difficulties in proving it, and the remedies are weak. As in almost every other area of labour legislation it is the individual, not the union, who must complain even though the issue is a collective one.

If you decide the only way to enforce your right is by going to law you must claim (see page 357) **within three months** of the victimisation or sacking, or **within seven days** if you invoke the **interim relief procedure** (below) to stop a sacking.

Using the interim procedure

The 'interim relief procedure' applies in respect of dismissal for union membership and activities. Section 78 of the EP Act says that if you are dismissed a claim can be submitted up to seven days after the date of dismissal. If you are given notice you can claim as soon as you get it. The form must be accompanied by a letter from a union official (who has been given specific authority by the union to make these statements) saying that (s)he thinks you were dismissed for a reason connected with the union. Your boss will be given seven days' notice and a quick (interim) hearing will be held in front of a tribunal chairman. He has power to declare that wages should still be paid and that your contract should exist pending a full hearing of your case. He would do this if the employer fails to turn up or refuses to take you back, or cannot disprove your allegations.

The procedure is designed to prevent strikes. It might also stop employers buying out union activists by sacking them and willingly paying compensation. If legal action is taken quickly the job might be saved. The threat of instant legal action by a dismissed activist may sometimes be as effective as a walk-out, and to this extent the interim procedure can be very useful. But if an employer genuinely wants to be rid of a union activist there is still no legal way that this can be prevented – he may be forced to pay substantial compensation for refusing reinstatement but it may be worth it to his business.

If you are using the interim procedure there are four points to watch.

1. The application is separate from, and additional to,

the claim for unfair dismissal although you can claim both at the same time.

2. If you have asked for and been given no reason for dismissal, make a separate claim for 'refusal to give a written reason' on your form (see page 182).

3. The claim for an interim hearing must be accompanied by a statement that your union is independent, and that your official is specifically authorised to make this kind of statement – at least one early application by a full-time official in Leeds was turned down because he could not show a specific authorisation, the tribunal chairman showing no sympathy for the purpose of the procedure.

4. The procedure applies only to dismissals where your official thinks the principal reason for dismissal was your union membership or activity. One way in which employers can obscure their bias is by taking advantage of a redundancy to sack activists. If there are genuine redundancies the principal reason for your dismissal could well be redundancy, but your **selection** for dismissal might be motivated by your union activity. Strictly speaking, you cannot claim on the interim procedure unless the *main* reason for dismissal was union membership or activity. So make sure your claim is expressed in terms of the *main* reason for dismissal being union activity, and redundancy only secondarily.

How do you prove it?

1. Dismissal

Dismissal for union membership or activity is automatically unfair as it is for an 'inadmissable reason'. But proving it is very difficult. Every employer will dress up his dismissal in terms of some other reason such as redundancy, absence or bad time-keeping. He has to *prove* this reason as the basis for his dismissal, but you will have to show it was really because of your trade-union membership or activities. The burden of proof is on you (contrast victimisation below) and successful cases are extremely rare. Tribunals are rarely prepared to say that an unfair dismissal related to trade-union membership. Nevertheless, occasionally they do:

> Wages at a small toolmakers in Tamworth were paid well below the national rate. Ten workers decided to join the GMWU and their official sent a letter to the manager. As soon as he read it he entered the workshop and told them 'Piss off, cobblers to all of you. I won't have any unions in my factory'. Three hours later he gave them

their wages and a letter saying that they were being made redundant. The tribunal refused to accept any of the employer's evidence and said that all the workers had been dismissed because they had joined the union. Six of them shared compensation of over £1,000. *Asson v Brampton Toolmakers* 1975 (IT)

2. Victimisation

Proving victimisation can be even harder. At least when a dismissal occurs there is no disputing that fact, but if you have to show that some subtle pressure was brought to bear on you, and then go on to allege that the reason for it was your union membership, the problems are almost insuperable. Victimisation in the form of a failure to distribute overtime fairly can be proved, but surveillance, general harassment, exaggerated enforcement of works rules, frequent allocation of dirty jobs or strict supervision are things every worker can spot but are difficult to make stick in a tribunal. Threats can be difficult to prove, but they are illegal and cases have been won – *Brassington v Cauldon Wholesale* 1977 (EAT) (employer, during ACAS inquiry, threatened to close down rather than recognise the TGWU). Parliament has not given you the right to send written questions to your boss as a preliminary step to get his statement before bringing a claim. This is available if you allege sex or racial discrimination.

If you succeed in showing that action of a particular kind took place, the EP Act says that your boss must then show why he did it, **and must prove that his purpose in doing it was nothing to do with your union activity**. Despite the fact that this substantial burden of proof is on your employer, you will have to bring evidence about his attitude to unions, and be prepared to make your own case. There are still two problems. If the tribunal agrees you were victimised but not because of your union activity you will lose your case. But the reason for taking the action – as a punishment for example – or its consequences, may not be within your boss's power under your contract of employment. So you can challenge him on those grounds. This can't be done while you are in a tribunal – breach of contract is a common law matter for the county court (at least until the Lord Chancellor decides to give power to tribunals to deal with it).

Secondly, your employer may persuade the tribunal that he did not *intend* to be anti-union, even though the practical effect of his action could still mean that you and other workers were intimidated from joining a union. The

EP Act outlaws only action that is **intentionally** discriminatory, not action that in fact is.

Remedies

1. Dismissal

If you have been unfairly dismissed a tribunal can order your reinstatement in the same job and on the same conditions; or re-engagement in the same firm in a different job; or compensation. Reinstatement is the only effective remedy for a sacked activist because otherwise the trade-union organisation he or she built up will suffer, and other workers will be intimidated by the employer's apparent success in the sacking. Compensation is no substitute for a job in any case and it is meaningless in anti-union sackings.

Compensation up to a total of £5,200 for any losses suffered can be awarded, together with two weeks' pay or your equivalent of a redundancy payment, whichever is greater (see page 345). If an order is made for reinstatement or re-engagement, you can be awarded between 26 and 52 weeks' pay if the order is disobeyed. But nothing is available to compensate fellow workers for the loss of a union activist or of the benefits that can flow from organisation.

2. Victimisation

For victimisation, **no maximum amount of compensation is specified** and there is scope for a penal element. You can get compensation for your actual losses (denial of fair overtime, for instance) and expenses (cleaning of clothing if you constantly get the dirty jobs), and you can also get an amount to take account of the extent to which your rights have been infringed (EP Act section 56). So if you lose potential rights – if your boss threatens to close down if the union is recommended for recognition by ACAS – you can claim compensation. Amazingly, the one remedy that you would expect to be given and the one that could be most effective is omitted: an employer cannot be ordered to stop victimising a worker. So if your boss does it again you must start a whole new legal claim. While workers can be required by injunction to stop picketing or occupying a factory if the courts consider it unlawful, employers systematically carrying on victimisation cannot be ordered to stop. For an action as serious as intimidation of a trade unionist there is no reason why a tribunal should not award amounts in excess of the maximum £13,400 available for unfair dismissal in these circumstances.

Time off for activities of recognised unions

A necessary feature of collective agreements is the right of union representatives to carry out their duties without loss of pay, and to receive union training. The EP Act gives legal rights and these are clarified by the ACAS Code of Practice on time off. The Code positively supports collective bargaining and strongly urges unions and management to negotiate agreements on all aspects of time off covered by the Code.

The Health and Safety at Work Act gives safety representatives of recognised independent trade unions the right to time off, with effect from 1 October 1978. Your rights under this Act are not specifically dealt with in this book. Since many shop stewards are also safety representatives, they can take advantage of the Health and Safety at Work Act or the EP Act, whichever gives better rights. Safety representatives also fit the description of 'official' for the EP Act for many of the duties they carry out.

The EP Act gives three sets of rights. In the circumstances described below you can take time off:

1. with pay for union duties connected with industrial relations
2. with pay for training in industrial relations
3. without pay for certain union activities

The right to paid time off for union training is very important. The TUC provides material for day-release training courses throughout the country in association with local colleges and the Workers' Educational Association. Some unions have their own training colleges providing short residential courses – ASTMS, EETPU, NUR and TGWU. GMWU has two colleges. Most unions offer training in-company, or day-release, or at weekend schools. In 1977 the government gave £650,000 to the TUC to support union training.

Who gets time off?

You have the right to time off if you are an official of an independent trade union recognised by your employer. Recognition means recognised for collective bargaining (see page 241) or recommended by ACAS.

'Official' means an employee elected or appointed in

accordance with the union's rules to be a representative of employees at a particular workplace. It includes shop stewards, convenors, staff representatives, collecting stewards, chapel officers (in printing), and safety representatives. Branch secretaries are included if they represent members in the procedure at the particular workplace.

As an official your right is to time off for union **duties** and **training**.

Members have the right to time off for union **activities**.

Who pays?

Officials must be paid when carrying out union duties and training. If your pay does not vary according to the amount of work you do, your boss must pay you as if you had been working. If your pay varies – for example because you are on piece-work or bonus – you are entitled to average hourly earnings.

The Code says nothing about pay for members who take time off for union activities. In many workplaces, management have agreed to time off with pay during working hours to attend mass meetings. You will have to negotiate your own arrangements for paid time off either ad hoc or on a regular basis.

How much time off is reasonable?

You are entitled to a 'reasonable' amount of time off. There is no definition of what is reasonable in the Code, which urges unions and management to come to local agreements. Agreements normally allow as much time off as is necessary for **officials** to carry out their duties. You should ask for enough time off for *members* to take part in all union activities.

The Code does, however, give some general factors which would influence what is reasonable. Management need to ensure that the operational requirements of the enterprise are fulfilled. So services to customers and to the public, safety, the needs of continuous process industries and particular problems of small firms are all relevant factors.

You will have special requirements for time off if you work shifts or have spread hours, or work part-time or in isolated locations, or have domestic commitments. Officials have problems of communication and members have problems in attending branch meetings in all these situations.

The Code says you should try to arrange union meetings at times that are least inconvenient from management's point of view – towards the end of a shift or just before or after a meal-break. If you require time off as an official for training or to attend meetings you should give as much notice as you can, giving the reasons for needing time off and saying where the meeting is taking place and how long it will last. The Code does *not* give management the right to veto your decision if they think the meeting is unreasonable. Management have to provide cover for you when you are gone, but you should ensure that this is done by agreement.

Trade union duties

If you are an official you have the right to paid time off to carry out 'those duties which are concerned with industrial relations between your employer and any associated employers, and their employees'. The primary purpose of this definition is to restrict the right to occasions when you are carrying out a role envisaged by a jointly agreed procedure.

You must be given time off to carry out duties for such purposes as:

■ collective bargaining with management, for example, at negotiations and on joint committees

■ informing members about negotiations and consultation, for example, at mass meetings

■ meeting lay or full-time officials to discuss industrial issues connected with your employer, for example, at the trade union side of a joint negotiating committee, or prior to raising a grievance in procedure

■ interviewing members on grievances and disciplinary matters

■ appearing on behalf of members at an outside official body, for example, at an industrial tribunal

■ explaining the industrial relations structure to new employees whom you will represent, for example, at induction training or interviews with new starters

In order to carry out your duties the Code says your boss should provide basic facilities such as accommodation for meetings, a phone, a notice board and 'if justified' office facilities. These are not defined but would include a desk, filing cabinets, secretarial help, and access to a photocopier.

All union lay officials should take advantage of the above facilities if you have not already negotiated them in your agreements. Certainly the right to interview new starters and to demand basic office equipment are important extensions in the Code.

Trade union training

The Code says that officials *should* undertake training. You have the right to paid time off to attend courses which are:

1. relevant to your duties concerned with industrial relations between your employer and employees, and
2. approved by your own union or the TUC

No syllabus is laid down, but management is entitled to see the programme for any course you propose to go on. You need initial basic training in shop stewards' duties, and further training if you have special responsibilities, or if you are involved in new areas of collective bargaining. For example, you might be a trustee on your company's pension board or management might want to introduce work study or job evaluation. You will need union training in order to represent your members effectively. You can also go on training courses if your knowledge gets out of date – training in labour law, for example.

Trade union activities

You have the right as a member of a recognised independent union to reasonable *unpaid* time off to take part in any activities of your union, or in which you are representing your union. This means that during working hours you can:

■ vote in union elections
■ attend meetings
■ attend meetings of your union or branch executive committee, or annual or special conferences
■ represent your union on external official bodies e.g. Trades Councils.

The Code rightly points out that management has an interest in allowing time off for members to attend meetings during working hours. For example, a meeting may be necessary to discuss an urgent industrial issue. It is in the interests of management and union that decisions are made at representative meetings of members. In many cases, holding a meeting in working hours may not adversely affect production or services.

Industrial action

The Code deals specifically with time off in connection with industrial action. The guidelines laid down are:

1. There is no obligation to permit workers to take

time off to carry out union activities which consist of industrial action.

2. When members are directly affected by industrial action by another group of workers, they and their officials may need to hold an emergency meeting.

3. If industrial action has not occurred, management should not alter existing time off agreements.

4. If an official is taking part with members in industrial action, there is no right to time off.

5. But, if you are not yourself taking action, but represent members who are, say, taking unofficial action, 'normal arrangements for time off with pay should apply'.

It is interesting to note that in the Code and this part of the EP Act, industrial action is regarded as a trade-union activity. This is in contrast to the approach of the EAT in *Cruickshank v Hobbs* (page 178) where former strikers were selected for redundancy, and were thereby victimised for taking part in an official dispute.

If your boss refuses time off

If you don't get time off when you want it, or if you are an official and don't get paid properly, you can claim to an industrial tribunal **within three months** of the date your boss refused your claim. See page 357 for the procedure.

If the claim is not settled with the help of ACAS the tribunal has power to award any compensation it considers is just, bearing in mind

1. your boss's 'default' in failing to allow time off; and

2. any loss you suffered as a result

There is thus a **penal** element in this remedy.

If your boss allows you time off as an official, but does not pay you properly, the tribunal can order him to pay up.

In proceedings before a tribunal, the Code must be taken into consideration.

Negotiating time off

The Act and the Code give progressive rights to union officials and members. Of course, arrangements for time off are best negotiated between management and unions as basic parts of a recognition and procedure agreement. Failure to allow time off is ideally dealt with at workplace level as a breach of agreement.

Your rights within the union

Internal activities in your union are affected by the rule-book, by statute and by the rules judges have made. When you join you enter into a contract with the union, the terms of which are found in the rule-book. Like any other contract, the courts can interpret and enforce it. Unlike a contract of employment though, where only damages can be ordered, the parties can be ordered actually to carry out the terms of the contract.

Rules covering eligibility, discipline, elections and other matters can all be enforced by individual members. It is interesting to note that while unions want the law to recognise collective rights, rule-books don't usually give rights to groups within unions. Claims (for breach of contract or for a declaration of your rights) have to be brought in the civil courts. Legal representation under the Legal Aid scheme is available in appropriate cases. (See page 354.)

The effect of the rule-book and statute can be summarised as follows:

1. The rule-book, and custom and practice which is well known and not inconsistent with it, are the basis of your relationship with the union.

2. You have the right not to be discriminated against on the grounds of sex, marriage, race or Common Market nationality.

3. The rule-book is subject to the 'rules of natural justice' so that if you are liable to discipline you must be given

    a. notice of the charge against you

    b. time to prepare your case

    c. an opportunity to state your case

    d. a fair hearing before an impartial body

Rules providing for automatic termination without the above are not enforceable.

4. Procedures laid down in the rule-book must be followed by the union. Although there is no requirement that you must exhaust the internal procedures before complaining to a court, you will in practice have to justify yourself if you have not followed procedure.

5. A union decision said to be final and binding cannot deprive you of your right to go to court, but if the union behaved fairly and followed procedure the courts have no authority to interfere.

6. You have the right to complain to the Independent Review Committee (IRC) of the TUC – see below.

7. You have the right to leave the union at any time provided you give reasonable notice and comply with any reasonable conditions (TULR Act section 7). A condition that you pay arrears, or do not join another TUC-affiliated union contrary to the Bridlington Agreement, might be reasonable.

8. You have the right under the Trade Union Act 1913 to refuse to contribute to the union's political fund, if it has one, and you must not be prejudiced if you do opt out. You can make a complaint to the Certification Officer.

9. You have rights if your union amalgamates with another, including the right to be balloted.

In addition to the above summary, the judges have successfully introduced a number of other restrictions on trade-union affairs. These are less clear-cut, and more controversial, as statements of what the law is. Lord Denning has overturned democratically-approved rules and decisions of union conferences and committees on grounds which are probably (not certainly) invalid since the 1976 amendment to the TULR Act. He has even given a **potential** member the right to be admitted to the Jockey Club and, by extension, to unions – *Nagle v Feilden* 1966 (CA). However laudable this might be in some unions, the legal basis for the decision was a case of 1665 and cannot be relied on.

Independent Review Committee (IRC)

The IRC considers appeals by individual workers who have been *sacked* as a result of being expelled from, or of having been refused admission to, a union in a situation where trade-union membership is a condition of employment. Although set up under the auspices of the TUC, the three members of the IRC were appointed after consultation with the Employment Secretary.

The Committee's procedure is:

1. You complain to the Secretary at Congress House, Great Russell Street, London WC1.

2. The Committee must be satisfied, before considering an appeal, that you have been dismissed and have exhausted all internal union procedures.

3. The Committee will discuss the case with the union and you, and will try to resolve the matter by agreement.

4. If agreement cannot be reached the Committee will

make a recommendation about whether or not you should be admitted to the union, or, if you have been expelled, whether or not you should be taken back into the union and, if so, upon what conditions. There is then a 'clear responsibility' on the part of the union concerned to act upon such a recommendation.

Inter-union relations

The TUC has drawn up a set of rules, known as the Bridlington Principles, concerning inter-union relations. They require every union to ask all applicants for membership if they are or have recently been a union member. The new union must then ask the old union if the member resigned, is clear on the books, is under discipline or should not be accepted. If the old union objects, the matter can be resolved by using a TUC Disputes Committee, any decision of which is 'morally binding' on the unions.

Dual membership is usually permitted only if both unions agree.

A union should not accept any member who is in arrears or involved in an industrial dispute, nor should it start organising workers at any establishment in grades where another union has a majority of the employees *and* negotiates for them.

In *Shaw v Marley Tile Co* (1978) an AUEW shop steward took up a member's pay grievance and met management, who didn't recognise him or the union. He called a meeting of the fitters, which meant a stoppage of one hour. The EAT said handling the grievance during working hours *was* a protected union activity and (by a 2-1 majority) the steward had the implied consent of management, arising out of the informal relationships at work, to hold the mass meeting.

14.

Recognition

Legal methods of getting your union recognised by your employer / what is meant by recognition / how to tell whether your boss is negotiating seriously / what to do if he isn't / the legal advantages of recognition / which employers can be required to recognise a union / the procedure under the Employment Protection Act / a summary / and an assessment of how effective the right to recognition is.

Workers can guarantee all their rights by means of trade-union organisation, but to be effective a union needs to be recognised as the workers' negotiating body.

Recognition of your union is the essential first step towards attacking management's right to decide everything. The traditional ways of achieving recognition, through organisation, agitation and industrial action, are the best. But if these don't work, you can use the Employment Protection Act (EP Act). Even this does not guarantee you will get recognition, because although your boss can be ordered to pay heavily for refusing it, many employers would prefer to pay than grant recognition.

Recognition is not an end in itself. It is a way of ensuring you get the benefits you can negotiate through collective bargaining. Fighting for recognition is also an education in building an organisation and in learning what trade unionism is about. It often helps to strengthen the union.

Where to find the law

You find the right to recognition in the Employment Protection Act 1975 (EP Act) sections 11–16; the scope of collective bargaining is set by the Trade Union and Labour Relations Act (TULR Act) section 29.

What does recognition mean?

Section 11 of the EP Act entitles an independent trade union to claim recognition 'to any extent'. If your union is already recognised for negotiating certain things, such as individual grievances and discipline but not wages or pensions, or is already recognised for certain groups of workers, you can claim for **further recognition**'.

In fact, there is a limit to the extent to which employers have to recognise a union. The EP Act talks about recognition by an employer or associated employers 'for the purposes of collective bargaining'. This is defined as **negotiations related to or connected with** any of the matters listed in section 29 of the Trade Union and Labour Relations Act.

These are:

a. terms and conditions of employment, or the physical conditions in which any workers are required to work

b. engagement or non-engagement, or termination or suspension of employment or the duties of employment, of one or more workers

c. allocation of work or the duties of employment as between workers or groups of workers

d. matters of discipline

e. the membership or non-membership of a trade union on the part of a worker

f. facilities for officials of trade unions; and

g. machinery for negotiation or consultation, and other procedures, relating to any of the foregoing matters, including the recognition by employers or employers' associations of the right of a trade union to represent workers in any such negotiation or consultation or in the carrying out of such procedures.

This list is important because it defines the scope of **collective agreements, disclosure of information and industrial action**. The Advisory, Conciliation and Arbitration Service (ACAS) is under a duty to promote and improve industrial relations (EP Act 1975 section 1) so it could give negotiating rights on take-overs, investment and marketing since these are becoming collective bargaining issues. These subjects are anyway 're-lated to' terms and conditions of workers in that they affect job security. While terms of employment means contractual terms, conditions has 'a very wide meaning'. Lord Denning said, in *BBC v Hearn* (see page 301) that it includes **everything understood and applied by the parties in practice**, or **habitually** or **by common consent**, without ever being incorporated into the contract.

Recognition means you are entitled to negotiate

The EP Act 1975 says that collective bargaining involves **negotiations** (section 126), so if your union is only **consulted** on certain issues, it can claim negotiating rights.

Consultation requires employers to give the union full details of their proposals, to consider union representations and to reply to them giving any reasons for rejecting them (see chapter 20 on redundancies). In **negotiations** the union is much less passive.

The law does not define negotiations. If you feel your boss is only going through the motions of negotiation you can claim he is not recognising the union. Do this if he is not negotiating properly – whatever he may claim. As ACAS and the Central Arbitration Committee (CAC) begin to hear complaints they will start drawing up rules by which employers' behaviour can be judged. In the meantime, American unions' experience can give a useful indication of what is required.

Some sort of duty to negotiate was first imposed in the USA in 1917 in order to prevent disruption of arms manufacture. Now it is embodied in statute as a 'duty to bargain in good faith'. The following broad principles have been adopted and these could become applicable in Britain. An employer must:

■ genuinely be seeking an agreement

■ give any information requested that is in accordance with good industrial relations and which the union needs for bargaining (compare chapter 16)

■ not undermine the union's representative by dealing directly with individual members or failing to give notice of proposed changes, redundancies etc.

■ not act unilaterally by, for example, giving a wage increase or changing conditions during negotiations

■ negotiate reasonably, not simply 'go through the motions' – that is, your employer must be prepared to compromise, put counter-proposals, give reasons, act promptly

■ give negotiators authority to settle

■ not impose conditions at the start of negotiations, for example, that the union drop outstanding grievances

■ not pre-empt the union's claim by putting forward his own offer based on research and what he considers is 'best' for you. This illegal strategy was adopted at General Electric after it suffered a crippling strike in 1946.

So **if your union is recognised** – either voluntarily, or on the recommendation of ACAS – **and your boss resorts to any of the above tactics, the union should claim that he is not 'ready and willing' to negotiate**. This initiates the EP Act procedure (see below).

The legal advantages of recognition

In law an independent trade union which is recognised, and its members, gain a number of important advantages. Only a **recognised** independent union can demand:

■ disclosure of information under the EP Act, and be given it under the Industry Act (see page 263)

■ to be consulted over proposed redundancies (see chapter 20)

■ time off for its representatives and members (see page 232)

■ consultation on occupational pension schemes (and 50 per cent representation on trustee boards when this becomes a legal requirement).

These rights apply both if you are recognised voluntarily, and if ACAS has recommended recognition.

Which employers are liable?

Many employers in the public sector are required to recognise appropriate trade unions by law. All nationalised industries do, as does the government itself. Government contractors are required by the Fair Wages Resolution (FWR) to allow their workers the freedom to join unions (although there is no obligation to recognise them when they do).

Claims for recognition can be made against any employer, or two or more **associated employers**. You cannot claim against an employers' federation or go for recognition throughout a whole industry, so you have to force the issue by getting recognition the long way round from individual plants or employers. A union can claim recognition throughout the whole of a *group* of associated employers without the necessity for showing membership in every company or plant.

Claims can be made against the Crown and National Health Service employers, and ACAS can make a recommendation. But if the Crown employer does not act on the recommendation, there is no legal way to force it to do so.

Workers who are not employees can claim recognition for their union. Self-employed actors, musicians, draughtsmen and building workers for example, can claim and ACAS can make a recommendation. But the procedure stops there, so enforcement is impossible despite the recommendation. The Lump can therefore survive a recommendation of union recognition.

Procedure for claiming recognition

Sections 11–16 of the EP Act 1975 lay down the procedure a union must follow to get a recommendation for recognition. It is cumbersome and slow and its general effectiveness is assessed at the end of this chapter. Diagram 7 shows the steps in the legal procedure.

Step 1: Reference

An independent union, or several, can apply to the local office of ACAS for recognition by an employer or group of associated employers. Form ACAS 34 (see page 381) should be used. You do not need a specific percentage of membership. USDAW succeeded with 140 out of 700 eligible workers at the British Shoe Corporation.

You can claim *further* recognition if your union is already recognised for some issues or groups of workers. In 1976 only two out of 461 claims were for further recognition – negotiating rights on pensions and a house purchase scheme. **Employers** have no right to apply to ACAS for recognition of a union. They might want to do this to try to choose the less militant of two competing unions. A claim can be made even if another union is already recognised, but TUC unions will be subject to the Bridlington Agreement. (See page 239). The application is in the union's name and must be made by an official authorised to make such a claim, so you should involve your full-time officials.

In making your application, it is important to be clear about the scope of the group you are claiming for. Don't draft your claim wider than you need, because if you include groups where you do not have significant support, you will

Diagram 7 **Recognition Procedure**

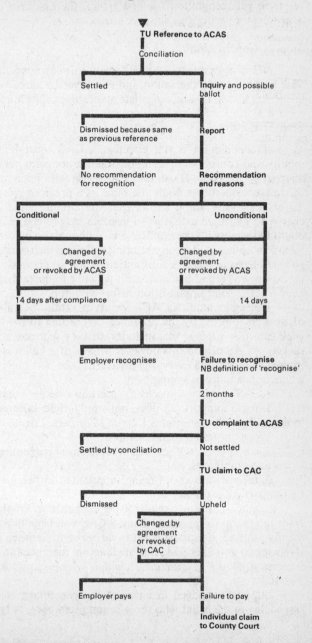

dilute the claim of the groups where you do. In practice, it is better to get recognition for one group, then make a claim later for other groups as support grows.

Step 2: Conciliation

ACAS attempts to get a settlement through conciliation. This means getting the union and employer to agree voluntarily. ACAS will try and conciliate at all stages of its inquiries.

Step 3: Inquiry

If conciliation is not effective, ACAS must hold an inquiry and consult any person or organisation who might be affected by the issue. It can refuse to go on with its inquiry if the reference is substantially the same as a previous reference 'unless the trade union shows that the circumstances have changed to such an extent as to justify a new reference'. This ought to stop premature applications. Although no percentage membership is required, if you bring a claim which is rejected you will have to prove a substantial change in circumstances if you want a second try later. So it is better to make sure you have a fairly solid organisation before you apply.

During its inquiries, ACAS must ascertain the opinions of workers affected by the reference. According to the *Grunwick* case (see page 7) this includes strikers who have been sacked. ACAS can do this however it likes. If a ballot is used it must be secret and every one invited to take part must have a fair opportunity of voting.

ACAS's main purpose is to ascertain whether the union has adequate support. It does not apply rigid criteria but looks at three things (ACAS Report 1976 para 23):

1. current union membership
2. employees' wishes about collective bargaining on terms and conditions, and
3. their wishes about being represented in negotiations by the particular union

Research has shown that if 50 per cent or more employees want the union to represent them, ACAS will usually recommend it, but not if support is below 40 per cent. Between those levels it can go either way, although actual membership is an important factor (*Industrial Relations Review and Report* No. 169)

Support is judged in terms of the percentage **of those responding to the ballot** who show union preference. A typical ballot would include a section similar to this:

Question	Yes	No
1. Do you want a trade union to negotiate with your employer about your pay and conditions of employment?	☐	☐
2. Do you want the XYZ Union to negotiate with your employer about your conditions of employment?	☐	☐
3. Are you a member of the XYZ Union?	☐	☐
4. If the XYZ Union were recognised for negotiations, would you join?	☐	☐

If it helps, the questions can be written in several languages.

Employer pressure at this stage would constitute unfairness. ACAS must tell the union(s) and employer(s), and consider their views about, which groups of workers are to be balloted and what the questions will be. Since ACAS will already have formed an opinion about which group should be asked what questions, the union must **make clear any objection it has**.

Step 4: Report

This is the stage when ACAS commits itself. If the union has not withdrawn, and there has been no settlement, ACAS *must* make a written report. This must include its findings, any advice it gives, and the reasons for making or not making any recommendation for recognition of a union. The report is approved or amended at national level by the ACAS Council, often causing delay.

A recommendation must specify:

1. the employer(s) and union(s) to which it relates

2. the description of workers covered, for example, whether they are confined to a particular plant or work throughout the company

3. whether it is for recognition in general, or only for a specified subject

4. the levels at which recognition will take place, for example, whether the union negotiates at national, local or lay official level

5. any conditions which ACAS requires the union to comply with, for example, requiring it to reach or maintain a specific percentage of membership, or to get members in other locations of the same company

These are the most important industrial relations issues ACAS has to deal with and it must deal with them publicly, since reasons have to be given – at least for making or refusing the recommendation.

The recommendation takes effect 14 days after it is received by the employer, or 14 days after ACAS notifies the employer that the union has satisfied the specified conditions.

There is no time limit on the recommendation, which lasts forever or until varied (see Step 4A). Subsequent references can be refused if the applicant union cannot show a change in circumstances.

Step 4A: Variation

An ACAS recommendation can be changed if both the employer *and* the recommended union agree. It can also be changed as a result of a joint application by the union and the employer, or of either one of them. In other words, the employer is given the right to initiate a reference to ACAS for a change in the recommendation.

As with an original reference ACAS has a duty to inquire and report. When the issue being investigated is the same as under an earlier reference ACAS can decide to go ahead only if circumstances have changed or new information has come to light.

Step 5: Complaint

If your employer still refuses to recognise you, that is, to negotiate properly (see page 242 above), the union can complain to ACAS, but not until **two months** after the recommendation comes into force.

Step 6: Conciliation

ACAS is then obliged to try to obtain a settlement. It is difficult to see how conciliation at this stage could get a recalcitrant employer to negotiate.

Step 7: Claim

If there is no settlement, the union must now apply to the CAC. The union claims that the employer is still not recognising the union – properly or at all – *and* makes a claim for every worker covered by the recommendation to have certain new terms or conditions of employment. You can include a claim for any conditions which you could have asked for if you were in negotiations – wages, hours, pensions, guaranteed earnings, additional notice and redundancy payments (useful if redundancy has been threatened). The union could even ask for union membership to be a condition of employment or a contractual right to have the union recognised but the CAC rejected one such claim (Phoenix Timber).

The CAC holds a hearing, listens to the union and the employer, and decides whether or not the employer has failed to negotiate. If the union wins, the CAC can then decide to give every employee the terms claimed by the union or any terms the CAC thinks fit. This automatically changes every affected employee's contract and becomes legally binding on the employer. **Backdating to any date is possible.** There is no appeal against a CAC decision, unless it goes outside its terms of reference.

The obvious difficulty here, as shown in the *Grunwick* case, see page 7, is that if the union members strike and are sacked, a change in conditions of employment will benefit only the scabs.

Step 7A: Variation

There are two ways a CAC award can be changed:

1. by agreement between the employer and 'the union for the time being representing the employee'. This means that if a worker changes union the new union and the employer could change the agreement. So watch out for shady deals with a new union.

2. by individual agreement between the employer and employee, provided this improves on the CAC award.

Step 8: County Court Claim

If at the end of all this your boss still refuses to negotiate with your union an individual member of the union can claim to a county court for breach of contract. The union has no right to bring the case in its own name though it would certainly give legal aid.

Because in the end it is only the individual who can bring a claim for breach of contract it is important for the union to claim, as the contractual right of each member, that the employer recognises the union.

Summary

1. Recognition means being ready and willing to negotiate.

2. An independent trade union can claim legal recognition if an employer:

    a. refuses to recognise the union at all

    b. recognises the union merely for consultation, discussion or communication

    c. negotiates only on some issues, not others; or

    d. refuses to recognise the union for any particular group of workers

3. A claim can be made against any employer, or group of associated employers, but final enforcement is not available against the Crown, NHS and employers of self-employed workers.

4. ACAS can make a recommendation and the CAC can order an employer to accept the union's claim for improvements in workers' conditions of employment, which can include such things as pay, holidays, hours and pensions.

5. While ACAS is investigating, you are not prevented from taking industrial action.

How effective is the procedure?

There is no short cut to union recognition. It can only come with solid membership figures. A legal right to recognition is an effective alternative only where organisation and industrial pressure are not sufficient or, rarely, not appropriate.

For example, in the Grunwick dispute, see page 7, all APEX members had been sacked so the union had to use ACAS **as well as** picketing and blacking. Or you may have low membership but know that many workers are showing interest and an *immediate* display of industrial action might turn potential members against you. Or you may not have sufficient members, or support among members, to make a strike effective. If a strike is called in this situation there is a risk that the union will be discredited.

The EP Act procedure is full of problems which militate **against** its effectiveness and so reinforce the need to rely on organisation and industrial strength.

Firstly, the procedure is so long-winded that many employers will be able to frustrate a claim by refusing recognition and by forcing a union through all the legal hoops. When a union starts recruiting it needs to show results if it is to keep and expand the membership. Often workers join in response to a specific management move or out of a sudden fear of losing their jobs. If the union does not get recognition quickly, support will dwindle and management can pick off the activists. **A slow procedure is no procedure.**

Nevertheless, with ACAS receiving claims at the rate of 40 a month in 1976, delays are inevitable. By the end of 1977, it had published only 93 reports out of 1037 applications. **It is not unusual for the procedure to take a year.**

Second, ACAS's scope for recommending recognition could be limited if the courts begin to narrow the definition of collective bargaining, and claims for recognition throughout a multi-employer industry are excluded.

Third, the punishments for an employer who persistently refuses to negotiate are very weak. This will encourage big employers to resist ACAS and CAC awards. Union organisation is weakened by the necessity for an individual county court claim to be brought by each worker. And even this may still not lead to recognition. According to a survey by *Industrial Relations Review and Report* (No. 169) only 10 agreements had been made following 63 ACAS recommendations out of the first 93 reports.

So what is needed? **Fast, effective action by independent unions.**

15.

Collective Agreements

The definition of a collective agreement /
legal enforcement / no-strike clauses / national
and local agreements / the closed shop /
attempts to restrict it / the legal definition /
points to watch in making a closed shop
agreement / the legal consequences.

Collective agreements between unions and employers
cover two-thirds of the working population, although only 50
per cent of workers are trade unionists. This is because agreements are almost invariably made to cover *all* workers in a
plant or district or industry. Agreements and custom and
practice accepted by management and unions are the basis of
industrial relations. They are the vehicle for union organisation
and pressure.

A closed shop can be established by a formal agreement
with management or by accepted custom, so it is included here
as a special form of collective agreement.

Where to find the law

Collective agreements and the closed shop are dealt with
in the Trade Union and Labour Relations Act 1974 (TULR
Act) sections 30, 29 (1) and 18.

The legal definition

Collective agreements are defined by section 30 of the
TULR Act as agreements *or arrangements* made between
unions and employers which relate to any of the issues listed
on page 241, and in connection with which a trade dispute
can arise. The courts say these must be given a 'very wide
meaning' so they cover almost all the matters that unions
want to bargain about. Only agreements made by or on

behalf of a trade union are within the definition. The agreement can be in writing or can exist as an informal 'arrangement'. The legal definition is important if the question of enforcement arises.

Legal enforcement

There are two questions about legal enforcement:

1. Can the agreement be enforced in the courts by the employer or the union which made it?

2. Can parts of the agreement become enforceable in the courts by individual workers covered by it?

Enforcement by the employer or union

An agreement made today between an employer or federation on the one hand and a union or workers acting on behalf of the union on the other is not legally binding. This means your union or shop stewards' committee cannot be sued if it breaks an agreement by, say, calling a strike in breach of procedure or making a claim for higher wages before the appointed settlement date.

There are three types of agreement:

a. Agreements made before December 1971 and after 16 September 1974, that is, outside the period covered by the Industrial Relations Act (IR Act). These are not legally binding unless they are **in writing** and specifically say they *are* legally binding.

b. Agreements made between the above dates. These *are* legally binding unless they contain a clause saying they aren't.

c. Agreements which don't count as collective agreements, for example because they deal with things outside the list on page 241, or because they are not made on behalf of a union. These *may* be legally binding, so the union should always insert a clause saying they are not intended to be.

The protection of unions against legal action, for example, for recommending a strike or blacking (see page 299) does not apply to breach of contract. A legally enforceable collective agreement is a contract, so the union can be sued for damages if, for example, it calls a strike in breach of an agreed procedure in a legally enforceable agreement.

Enforcement by individual workers

Some parts of collective agreements can be binding on individual workers covered by them – see page 32. An agreement for wages or hours negotiated between your union and your boss is not enforceable by either against the other, but usually *you* can sue your boss if he does not follow it. This is because the agreement has changed your individual contract, and you as an individual (or your boss) can go to court to enforce it.

No-strike clauses

Any particular part of an agreement can be made legally binding. Usually clauses dealing, for example, with wages, hours or holidays, will be binding on individual workers and their employer, even though the collective agreement itself is not legally binding between the union and the employer. If the agreement contains a clause which restricts (*or has the effect* of restricting) industrial action, or restricts it until procedure is exhausted or notice given, section 18 of the TULR Act steps in. This part of a collective agreement cannot be binding on individual workers unless:

■ it is in writing;

■ it specifically says that this restriction is part of every worker's own contract;

■ it is reasonably accessible to every worker;

■ it is signed by *independent* trade unions; and

■ each worker's own contract incorporates this restriction (either expressly or by implication).

This is to protect every worker's right to strike, and any workers who may be tied down by an employer-dominated staff association which attempts to stop them striking.

National and local agreements

As far as the law is concerned it does not matter whether agreements are made at national, local, company or plant level. Nor does it matter whether bargaining is done in a joint council with decisions made 'jointly', or in direct negotiations between, for example, the Confederation of Shipbuilding and Engineering Unions and the Engineering Employers' Federation. Generally, a local agreement will override an existing national agreement. This almost always happens in engineering, construction and many other industries, so local modifications should be given precedence. However the courts are erratic on this question and have denied workers the right to have an effective local agreement.

> John Mercer, a gas conversion fitter, worked 54 hours a
> week and this was provided for in a local agreement for
> the North East. The national agreement signed by the
> GMWU and the employers' association provided for a
> 40-hour week. He subsequently received a written
> statement of his contract, which followed the national
> rather than the local agreement. He signed it. When
> John Mercer claimed redundancy pay based on his 54-
> hour week, the Court of Appeal said the national agree-
> ment was the one to be followed. The court said John
> had to work the 14 hours' overtime if required, but his
> boss wasn't legally bound to provide more than 40 hours.
> Only if the overtime is **guaranteed** does it count for
> statutory purposes. *Gascol v Mercer* 1974 (CA)

It is not too cynical to say that when there is a clash
between a national and a local agreement the courts have
generally said that **the agreement less favourable to the worker
is the one that is binding. In order to avoid problems, write into
your local agreement 'Insofar as this agreement is more favourable than any national agreement, this local agreement is to take
precedence',** or vice versa if appropriate.

Conditions agreed at Wages Councils and Statutory
JICs are dealt with in chapter 17.

The closed shop

Attempts at legal restraint

Closed shops exist in many industries. They vary from
strict pre-entry shops requiring union membership before you
can apply for a job – the merchant navy, printing and entertainment, for example – to loose understandings that life
would be difficult if non-members were allowed to continue
working after a certain period of time. The (Donovan) Royal
Commission on Trade Unions and Employers' Associations
in 1968 adopted the following definition of a closed shop:

> a situation in which employees come to realise that a
> particular job is only to be obtained and retained if they
> become and remain members of one of a specified
> number of trade unions.

The spirit of the description is now embodied in the
TULR Act.

By imposing strict conditions the Tories tried to make
closed shops illegal in almost every industry. They introduced
the 'agency shop' which restricted the privilege to **registered**
unions and allowed exceptions to union membership on

'reasonable grounds'. They see the closed shop as a serious restraint on management prerogatives:

> In a true 'closed shop' the union has a powerful say – if not control – in the recruitment of labour ... Furthermore, since trade unions – and in many trades, local branches or chapels – often make their own 'working rules', this situation can mean that production methods, job allocation and general conditions of work are controlled more by employees than by management.
> *Fair Deal at Work. The Conservative approach to modern industrial relations*, 1968, p. 24.

In short, the closed shop 'places too much economic power in the hands of trade unions'.

It is frequently assumed that there is a logical relationship between the right not to be a union member, and the right to be one. But as the Donovan Commission said:

> the two are not truly comparable. The former condition is designed to frustrate the development of collective bargaining, which it is public policy to promote, whereas no such objection applies to the latter. (para. 599)

Under present law the only grounds for refusing to be a member of a union in a closed shop situation are religious objections.

In the years following the repeal of the IR Act, closed shop agreements have proliferated, either as new arrangements or as revivals of pre-1971 agreements. The public sector has been increasingly active. Agreements and arrangements are now operating in electricity supply, gas, British Rail, London Transport, and many local authorities, together with traditional areas such as coal mining and the docks. Despite their failure to shake workers' solidarity, or even to convince managements of the need to break up the closed shop, the Tories (aided by Liberals) tried to wreck the Labour proposals in the TULR Act.

The legal definition

The law does not use the phrase 'closed shop'. It is known as a **union membership agreement** (UMA). A union membership agreement under section 30 of the TULR Act is one which

> **a.** is made, or exists, between one or more independent trade unions, and employers or employers' associations

b. relates to an identifiable class of employee; and

c. has the practical effect of requiring employees of that class to be members of one of the unions which is a party to the agreement, or of any other union specified by the parties

The only exemption is for those who 'genuinely object on grounds of religious belief to being a member of any trade union whatsoever' (TULR Act schedule 1 para. 5). Quite why religion should continue to have such primacy in an increasingly secular society is difficult to understand and the TUC were opposed to this exception. No definition is given, so an adherent to any religious faith who could substantiate his faith's objection to trade unionism might prove his dismissal was unfair. In practice, Jehovah's Witnesses, Plymouth Brethren, Christadelphians and those who believe that they should 'be not unequally yoked with unbelievers' (2 Corinthians 6: 14) will be likely to prove their objection. A railwayman who refused to join the NUR because he was a Jehovah's Witness successfully claimed that it was his **own** belief, not that of his sect, that was the most important. *Saggars v British Rail* 1977 (EAT)

Points to watch

■ There is no need for an explicit written or oral agreement. Long-established custom and practice is sufficient, but obviously a written agreement creates less uncertainty.

■ There can be any number of unions but they must **all** be independent – if a non-certified staff association is included, this will wreck the agreement.

■ It does not matter how you define your 'class of employees'. You can do it by grading, or skill or personal characteristics or whatever other system you choose. You can draw your boundaries to exclude supervisory staff, or members of other unions at a given time, or even workers whom you know will refuse to join, for example by describing them or even naming them.

■ Union membership need not be a specific condition of employment, but it is a good idea to make it one, just to be sure.

■ A **specified** union is one which is: a party (that is, a signatory to a written agreement); or is mentioned in the agreement as acceptable; or is not mentioned but nevertheless is 'treated by the parties as equivalent', or is recommended for recognition by ACAS; or has applied to ACAS for recognition.

> **Example:** The TGWU signs an agreement with XYZ Ltd for the process workers. It is a *party* to the agreement. The agreement allows membership of the AUEW, but the TGWU negotiates for them. AUEW is *'specified'*. Occasionally, EETPU fitters do work in the shop. No one wants to mention them in the agreement but the TGWU and XYZ Ltd treat them as *'equivalent'* to being specified. So the valid TGWU closed shop is not prejudiced by the other two unions.

Once you have defined your boundaries, **it is crucial that the agreement is enforced uniformly** as the case involving Ferrybridge C power station in Yorkshire shows.

> Six employees of the CEGB refused to join any of the four unions which had signed the Electricity Supply NJIC agreement. They were members of the Electricity Supply Union (ESU) which had for some time been demanding recognition, and canvassing support against the TUC unions, on the ostensible basis of wanting a single union for electricity supply. The ESU is affiliated to the Confederation of Employee Organisations and both bodies are actively supported by Conservative Central Office. The men were told they would be sacked if they did not join one of the TUC unions which had signed the agreement, or apply for exemption on religious grounds. They refused, were sacked and claimed unfair dismissal. Following a 14 day hearing, the Leeds tribunal accepted their arguments. The NJIC agreement was valid, the tribunal said, but because there were members of the Boilermakers' Society in another plant, and possibly other non-unionists elsewhere, the CEGB could not say that they had established the *practice* of rigorous enforcement of the agreement. The tribunal said the Ferrybridge six were being picked on because they were active in the ESU. They got substantial compensation. *Sarvent v CEGB* 1976 (IT)

Although the law has now changed slightly, the lesson of *Ferrybridge* is that **if you have a closed shop you must secure 100 per cent compliance with it**. Stewards must regularly have card checks of members, and if warnings to non-members are not immediately effective, they must report breaches of the agreement to management. Stewards should not turn a blind eye to non-compliance in individual cases as this will affect the 'practice' of the agreement and could, as at Ferrybridge, jeopardise any action taken under it.

The legal consequences

A valid closed shop agreement affects workers' legal rights in three broad areas: new employees can be refused a job if they are unlikely to join the union; dismissal of non-members is fair; and the right to take part in activities of a non-specified independent union are modified. The detailed consequences of a closed shop are:

1. New and existing employees must join the union (TULR Act schedule 1 para. 6).

2. The only workers who can refuse to join are those who object on religious grounds to joining any union, and those specifically excluded from the agreement (TULR Act as above).

3. Otherwise, dismissal for not belonging is automatically fair, that is, there is no question of 'reasonableness' (TULR Act as above). But a sacking *may* be unfair if management fail to follow any agreed procedure for dealing with non-members. *Jeffrey v Laurence Scott* 1977 (EAT)

4. There is no obligation to take part in the union's activities, although a failure to attend a compulsory union meeting (for instance, in journalism) might result in pressure to dismiss. Such a dismissal could be tested for reasonableness by a tribunal.

5. It is not illegal for employers to treat remaining non-members less favourably than members (that is, by victimisation) unless they are religious objectors (EP Act section 53 (4)).

6. Provided you are a member of a union specified in the agreement, dismissal for being a member of another independent trade union (that is, one having dual membership), or taking part in its activities at an appropriate time, is automatically unfair (TULR Act, as above).

7. In the same situation, victimisation for taking part in the other union's **activities at the workplace** is lawful (EP Act section 53 (4)) but victimisation simply for being a member is unlawful.

8. If any dismissal *is* held to be unfair, it is management and not the union which is liable. But a tribunal would almost certainly not order reinstatement if there were a threat of industrial action. Compensation is the usual remedy.

While you remain a member of the union specified in the agreement you retain your basic trade-union rights. If a non-TUC union which has been certified as independent tries to gain a foothold, so long as its members stay in the specified union, they are free to refer a claim for recognition to ACAS.

And because the definition of 'specified union' includes one which is **recommended** or **being investigated** by ACAS (see page 257) the members of that union acquire the full rights to organise.

16.

Disclosure of Information

Your right to get information from your employer / financial information companies must give under company law / information employers must give for bargaining under the Employment Protection Act / and for planning under the Industry Act / who can claim / what kind of information / the exceptions / the procedures / and their effectiveness / information relevant to health, safety and welfare / and trade union demands.

Disclosure of information to trade unions is often confused with discussions on workers' participation and industrial democracy. In fact these are entirely separate issues. Disclosure of information is an integral part of collective bargaining between unions and employers, and does not necessarily erode the conflict between them. Indeed information discovered about the company has always been an essential weapon for trade unionists in any struggle. Employers' reluctance to divulge information is an admission of conflict. This chapter looks at disclosure of information, and not at the proposals for industrial democracy.

Disclosure is not an end in itself. It is a step towards giving the unions power to discuss issues from the same background of knowledge as management, and thereby to spot management's half-truths, concealment and deceit. The right to know what's going on at work is a basic demand. The law recognises this right only to a very limited degree.

For this reason, unions need to demand information, and force management to agree to regular disclosure of information. Targets for union demands are dealt with at the end of the chapter,

Where to find the law

The law requires information to be made available in the following ways:

Financial information	— Companies Acts 1948–67
Information for bargaining	— Employment Protection Act 1975 (EP Act) sections 17–21
Information for planning	— Industry Act 1975 sections 27–34
Information for health safety and welfare	— Health and Safety at Work Act (HSW Act) sections 2, 3, 28, 79
Consultation about redundancies	— EP Act section 99 (see chapter 10)
Particulars of your contract of employment	— Contracts of Employment Act 1972 section 4 (see page 29)

Diagram 8 on pages 268–9 sets out the various procedures that you have to follow in order to get the data you want.

Financial information

The most complete guide to finding and using financial information is Christopher Hird's *Your Employer's Profits*, Pluto 1975, in this series of Workers' Handbooks. A full list of what every limited company is obliged to disclose annually under the Companies Acts 1948–67 is given in Appendix 2 of that handbook. The annual balance sheet and profit and loss account must be prepared by independent auditors *for the shareholders* and this is open to inspection by the public at Companies House (addresses on page 400).

The Registrar does not, however, keep the records up to date. For example, in 1975, 29 per cent of the 643,000 limited companies registered were in default. But only 989 were prosecuted.

Local authorities, nationalised industries and charities are required to render annual accounts too.

The Government has proposed changes in company law to require companies to include an 'employment statement' in annual reports. (*The Aims and Scope of Company Reports*, HMSO, July 1977). If enacted these proposals would mean that information on strikes, pensions, collective bargaining, training and labour turnover would have to be given annually.

Information for bargaining

Section 17 of the EP Act imposes a duty on employers to provide unions they recognise with information for bargaining. The Advisory, Conciliation and Arbitration Service (ACAS) has published a Code of Practice giving guidelines on what should, and should not, be disclosed.

Who can demand disclosure?

An independent trade union recognised by an employer can request information. So can one which has been *recommended* for recognition by ACAS. The information must be given to representatives who are *authorised to carry on collective bargaining*, such as full-time officials or shop stewards. The union must be recognised for the group of workers which is making the request. Employers have to disclose information only if requested to. Your employer can get you to put your request in writing and it is always best to do this anyway.

The Crown and the NHS are covered by the same duty, and can be told by the Central Arbitration Committee (CAC) to disclose information, but there is no way of enforcing this.

What information?

Under section 17 of the EP Act 1975 your employer must disclose information which satisfies all the following four conditions:

1. The information is needed for any stage of negotiations.

2. Without it the union representatives would be seriously impeded in negotiating.

3. Good industrial relations practice requires the employer to give this sort of information to the union to help it in negotiations.

4. The information must be in his or an associated employer's possession.

The information is to be made available *for all the stages of collective bargaining*. As preparing for negotiations is part of collective bargaining you can start collecting and preparing data long before the negotiations begin. The legal scope of bargaining issues is given on page 241. Employers may argue that mergers, pricing, marketing, investment, research and development are not covered by the legal definition. But 'conditions of employment' is probably wide enough to include these subjects.

The CAC will be the judge of this and of what constitutes *serious impediment*, but no criteria are laid down. It will also judge *good industrial relations practice*, for which the Code of Practice sets guidelines. (See page 16 for the effect of codes).

Refusal to give information to a union recommended by ACAS could also be grounds for a claim under the **recognition procedures** (see Chapter 14) to the effect that your employer was not negotiating properly.

The Code lists the following data that should be given.

Pay and benefits: principles and structure of payment systems; job evaluation systems and grading criteria; earnings and hours analysed according to work-group, grade, plant, sex, outworkers and homeworkers, department or division, giving – where appropriate – distributions and make up of pay, showing any additions to basic rate or salary; total pay bill; details of fringe benefits and non-wage labour costs.

Conditions of service: policies on recruitment, redeployment, redundancy, training, equal opportunity and promotion; appraisal systems; health, welfare and safety matters.

Manpower: numbers employed analysed according to grade, department, location, age and sex; labour turnover; absenteeism; overtime and short time; manning standards; planned changes in work methods, materials, equipment or organisation; available manpower plans; investment plans.

Performance: productivity and efficiency data; savings from increased productivity and output; return on capital invested; sales and state of order book.

Financial: cost structures; gross and net profits; sources of earnings; assets; liabilities; allocation of profits; details of government financial assistance; transfer prices; loans to parent companies and interest charged.

This list is *not exhaustive*, nor is it mandatory. It is useful as a checklist when drawing up your basic demands. The TUC has also drawn up a checklist – see page 272.

You can use the EP Act to get financial information from organisations not covered by the Companies Acts, such as **associated** and **subsidiary** companies, local authorities, charities and private companies.

What are the exceptions?

The Act and the Code are riddled with exceptions. Obstructive employers with sharp advisers will be anxious to exploit them. There are six specific situations (section 19) where there is **no obligation to disclose**. These cover information which:

1. it would be against the interest of national security to disclose;

2. your boss is under a **statutory** obligation to keep secret;

3. 'has been communicated to the employer in confidence';

4. relates to a specific individual who does not want it disclosed;

5. 'would cause substantial injury to the employer's undertaking for reasons other than its effect on collective bargaining';

6. is obtained for the purpose of legal proceedings.

National security can be pleaded by any employer. If it is backed up with a certificate from a government ministry, it cannot be challenged in any way. People who work for the Crown, the NHS and government contractors are most vulnerable.

The **confidentiality** and **substantial injury** exceptions are full of difficulty for unions. Information about takeovers, expansion, capital spending, investment, and research and development might be wrapped up in these two exclusions. These are not, however, mentioned in the Code. The examples given in it are the cost of individual products, *detailed* analysis of proposed investment, marketing and pricing policies, price quotas, and the make-up of tender prices.

The Code says that your employer must explain his reasons in detail and he must be able to substantiate them at an inquiry by ACAS or the CAC. The burden of proof is on your employer, who will not be allowed to get away with sticking 'confidential' labels on all his documents, or with over-reacting to the prospect of injury to his business. The Act excludes information which *would* cause substantial injury, not that which *could possibly* cause it.

Packaging the information

You can ask your boss to disclose information, or to confirm it, in writing. But you have no right to have the data audited either by independent examiners, or by union-appointed auditors. Nor is your employer required to allow you to inspect any document, or to make a copy. So you have to accept management's written assurance as to what a document contains. There is no obligation on your employer to disclose matters which are relevant, but merely *incidental* to the data requested. For example, you may be given raw figures from a management consultant's report, without the consultant's comments and opinions.

Your boss can get out of providing information if this 'would involve an amount of work or expenditure out of reasonable proportion to the value of the information in the conduct of collective bargaining'.

The law treats shareholders much more seriously than it treats unions. Shareholders' information is packaged according to the Companies Acts and it must be prepared and certified by independent accountants.

How to claim

Diagram 8 on pages 268–9 shows the procedure for making a legal claim for information. It is similar to the recognition procedure, only even more cumbersome.

Step 1: Complaint

The union complains in writing to the CAC if, following a written request, management

1. refuses to provide information, quoting one of the defences, for instance 'substantial injury'; or
2. provides inadequate information; or
3. provides information which the union does not think is correct.

The CAC may (but is not obliged to) ask ACAS to conciliate. If there is no conciliation, or if there is no settlement, the CAC must hear the complaint. Any person or organisation having an interest in the complaint is entitled to a say – for example, other unions. Employers' claims for exemption, and defences, have to be proved at this stage.

Step 2: Declaration

If the union wins, the CAC must specify the information, the date on which it was refused by the employer, and the date by which it must be disclosed.

Step 3: Further complaint

If your employer still refuses to disclose the information the union complains *again* to the CAC. The CAC hears the complaint and gives its reasons for any finding it makes. In addition the union can **claim improved terms and conditions** for a particular group of employees. This may be a money claim, **or a claim for specific information to be given to each worker**. This is most important because if it is accepted, it can be enforced in the courts (see below). The CAC may tell the employer to observe either the terms and conditions claimed by the union, or any terms it considers appropriate. Any award the CAC makes takes effect as a term of every individual worker's contract of employment. The award can only be made for those workers and for those terms and conditions for which the union is recognised.

Step 3A: Variation

Awards of the CAC can be varied by agreement or by the CAC – see page 249.

Step 4: County Court Claim

If your employer still refuses to pay money or observe conditions (for example, to disclose certain information) awarded by the CAC each individual worker can present a claim in a county court for breach of contract – see page 249.

How effective are these rights?

Even after going through all these steps your boss can still get away with refusing to give you the information. It is left to the individual worker, and not the union, to take the final steps of enforcement.

The Act preserves managerial secrecy. Only information in the possession of your company or group need be given. You do not get to see the original sources and cannot verify the facts by independent audit. You must know the data exists in order to request it, so you cannot rummage for it; and your boss can say it will cost too much to prepare. The Act and

Diagram 8 **Procedures for obtaining information**

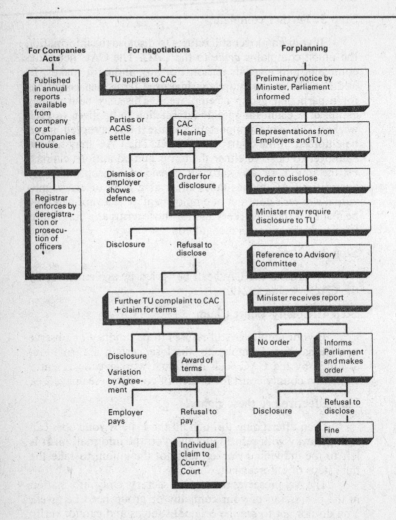

For Companies Acts

Published in annual reports available from company or at Companies House

Registrar enforces by deregistration or prosecution of officers

For negotiations

TU applies to CAC

Parties or ACAS settle

CAC Hearing

Dismiss or employer shows defence

Order for disclosure

Disclosure

Refusal to disclose

Further TU complaint to CAC + claim for terms

Disclosure

Award of terms

Variation by Agreement

Employer pays

Refusal to pay

Individual claim to County Court

For planning

Preliminary notice by Minister, Parliament informed

Representations from Employers and TU

Order to disclose

Minister may require disclosure to TU

Reference to Advisory Committee

Minister receives report

No order

Informs Parliament and makes order

Disclosure

Refusal to disclose

Fine

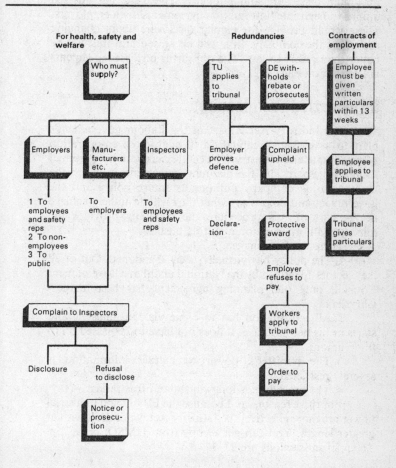

For health, safety and welfare

Who must supply?

Employers — Manufacturers etc. — Inspectors

1 To employees and safety reps
2 To non-employees
3 To public

To employers

To employees and safety reps

Complain to Inspectors

Disclosure — Refusal to disclose

Notice or prosecution

Redundancies

TU applies to tribunal — DE withholds rebate or prosecutes

Employer proves defence — Complaint upheld

Declaration — Protective award

Employer refuses to pay

Workers apply to tribunal

Order to pay

Contracts of employment

Employee must be given written particulars within 13 weeks

Employee applies to tribunal

Tribunal gives particulars

Code give unions no effective right to challenge traditional management prerogatives.

But the Act and Code are not entirely worthless; a little knowledge is better than none. Your union does have rights and, weak as they are, they should be used to obtain maximum disclosure and publicity. The TUC has advised unions to negotiate 'information agreements' with employers. These would provide for regular disclosure about changing aspects of the company. In a well organised firm this will be better than resort to law. The objectives of these agreements are set out on page 272.

Information for planning

The Industry Act is part of the Labour government's plan to save British capitalism through close co-operation between state and industry. The centrepieces are the National Enterprise Board and the planning agreement, in which the manufacturing company outlines its future policy and the government and unions say what they will do to help achieve it. As part of this procedure the company provides the minister with information about its business.

There are four snags.

1. The policy has virtually been abandoned. Out of 32 'key sectors' identified by the National Economic Development Council, only one planning agreement has been made – Chryslers.

2. All information has to come via the minister, and starts as his/her initiative. It does not have to be passed on to trade unions.

3. The minister's power to extract information is severely restricted.

4. The procedure is longwinded and frustrating.

For these reasons and because the EP Act and industrial power are more effective, the Industry Act is not dealt with at greater length. You can get a copy from HMSO, price 75p. The relevant sections are 27–34.

Health, safety and welfare

The Health and Safety at Work Act 1974 (HSW Act) imposes obligations on employers and others to disclose information on health, safety and welfare. The Health and Safety Commission has published Regulations, a Code of

Practice and guidance notes. All these, and how to use them in the drive for information on hazards, are dealt with in Patrick Kinnersly's *The Hazards of Work*, second edition, Pluto 1979, in this Workers' Handbook series. So, only the bones of the disclosure provisions are dealt with here.

Disclosure by employers

Your boss is meant to provide whatever information is necessary to ensure, as far as is reasonably practicable, your health and safety while at work. If you are a union **safety representative** the Commission's Code requires management to give the information you need to carry out your work, including information about: plans, performance and changes affecting health and safety; hazards from plant including information provided by manufacturers and suppliers; precautions; accidents, diseases and near-misses; measurements and samples.

You can inspect documents which the law requires employers to keep – about accidents, dangerous near-misses and hours of women workers. Employers must give information **to the public** who may be affected by their business (section 3), but for this the business must be 'prescribed'. None has been – pressure from people living close to a noxious plant could lead to information under this section.

Employers must also give information to the **Health and Safety Inspectors,** who have power to order disclosure.

Section 79 of the HSW Act changes the Companies Acts. When the change takes effect companies must include information on health and safety in annual reports.

Disclosure by manufacturers and others

Under section 6, manufacturers, designers, importers and suppliers of any product used at work must make available adequate information 'about the use for which it is designed and has been tested, and about any conditions necessary to ensure that, when put to that use, it will be safe and without risks to health'.

This information is usually given to employers, not to the workers who are exposed to the risks. But the section says that the information must be available 'in connection with the use of the article at work' so workers and safety representatives can get their employers to disclose this data to them.

Disclosure by inspectors

Inspectors are required to contact workers' representatives at every workplace they visit. Inspectors must keep workers and safety representatives informed about health, safety and welfare matters affecting them. This means factual information (not opinions) about the premises and activities going on there, and action (s)he has taken (section 28).

Trade union demands

The ACAS Code favours the negotiation of information agreements, which would ensure that specific or general information is made available on a regular basis to recognised unions, and in an agreed form. Although the Code follows the narrow contours of the EP Act the principle of bargaining for information could be adopted. Failure to agree should be dealt with in the same way as any other failure to agree under your procedures.

So what demands should a union make?

There is no point in asking for information you don't need or can't cope with. The important thing is to fight for the **right** to any information, in any form, whenever you want it.

The TUC set out a shopping list in its negotiator's guide *Good Industrial Relations* (1971) under the following headings:

Manpower: Numbers of employees by job description; rates of turnover, short-time, absenteeism, sickness and accidents; details of existing provisions for security, sickness, accidents, recruitment, training, redeployment, promotion and redundancy.

Financial: Sales turnover, by main activities; home and export sales; non-trading income including income from investments and overseas earnings; pricing policy.

Costs: Distribution and sales; production costs; administrative and overhead costs; costs of materials and machinery; labour costs including social security payments; costs of management and supervision.

Incomes: Directors' remuneration; wages and salaries; make-up of pay – negotiated rates, payment-by-results, overtime and bonuses.

Profits: Before and after tax and taking into account government allowances, grants and subsidies; distribution and retentions.

Performance indicators: Unit costs, output per worker, return on capital employed, value added etc.

Worth of company: Details of growth and up-to-date value of fixed assets and stocks; growth and realisable value of trade investments.

Prospects and plans: Details of new enterprises and locations; prospective close-downs; mergers and take-overs.

Trading and sales plans: Investment plans including research and development.

Manpower plans: Plans for recruitment, selection and training; promotion, regrading and redeployment; short-time and redundancy provisions.

A description of the company's activities and structure: Details of holding companies and subsidiaries; organisational and managerial structure; outside contracts.

Details of ownership: Directors and shareholders in the company and in holding companies; beneficial control of nominee shareholdings.

To these can be added details of **overseas associates** and **subsidiaries** (particularly important as company law does not require complete data about subsidiaries of a group); labour costs such as a breakdown of all wages by grade and number of employees; names and formulas of all products that might be harmful at work; nature and worth of all investments; sources and uses of all funds; injuries and disease statistics.

Crucial to these demands is the target of **independent audit** for all the information given. Many unions have facilities in their research departments for analysing technical financial data – the GMWU has a qualified accountant, and the AUEW, ASTMS, and Labour Research Department all provide expert analysis.

Conclusion

Beyond the workplace-level, an immediate demand is for changes in company law to widen the scope of information companies must give (see page 262) and to ensure **rigid adherence** to reporting obligations. Independent audit of **all information for unions,** must be provided.

These proposals will be strongly resisted. **So the fight for the right to know must go on at individual workplaces and throughout multi-plant companies.**

17.
The Going Rate

Your legal right to get the terms and conditions set by collective agreements / or as favourable as the general level observed by employers in your area / how to claim this right / the obligations imposed on government contractors by the Fair Wages Resolution / and on nationalised and licensed industries / the nature of Wages Councils and Statutory JICs / and how to get the going rate in these industries.

Since 1891 there have been measures designed to assist workers obtain terms and conditions which are fair in comparison with other workers in the same trade. The way in which it is done varies according to the legislation you are claiming under, and the shades of difference are important to any union claiming the going rate for its members.

The law intervenes in five areas:

1. Where there are collective agreements between employers' associations and trade unions.

2. Where employers in a district have established a general level of 'fair' terms and conditions.

3. In companies which have contracts or sub-contracts with government departments.

4. In industries which receive government money or depend on licences issued by public bodies.

5. In industries covered by a Wages Council or Statutory Joint Industrial Council (JIC).

The laws can be especially useful during periods of pay restraint because they are usually exempted from incomes policy. Real advances in pay and conditions can be made, but the procedure is tortuous and it should not be regarded as a substitute for negotiation and industrial action in a period of free collective bargaining.

These laws look like a gift to the organised working class, but they serve employers' interests too. First, if employers are forced to concede wage increases, they do not want their competitors who do not recognise unions to obtain a price advantage in their products. Any employers' association in a trade covered by a collective agreement can bring a claim against an employer who is undercutting the negotiated rates and get an increase in wages for that employers' workers in just the same way as a union can. Second, although the government has required its contractors to pay fair wages since the last century, the rights of unions to demand observance of negotiated terms in all industries was given only during the first world war as a way of keeping down strikes.

Throughout this chapter an employer who is underpaying is described as 'the unfair employer'.

Where to find the law

Recognised terms and conditions: Employment Protection Act 1975 (EP Act 1975) Schedule 11; the Fair Wages Resolution of the House of Commons 1946; the following Acts: Road Haulage Wages (1938); Coal Industry Nationalisation (1946); Transport (1947, 1953); Electricity (1947); Gas, Agricultural Wages (1948); Civil Aviation, Air Corporations and NHS (Amendment) (1949); Atomic Energy (1954); Sugar (1956); Civil Aviation (Licensing), Road Traffic, Films (1960); TV (1964); Wages Councils (1959); EP Act Schedule 8 (for Statutory JICs).

Claims under Schedule 11 of the EP Act

Schedule 11 aims to improve the terms and conditions of most private and public sector workers. It does not apply to Crown employment, some NHS workers, some workers in road haulage, civil aviation, film-making and broadcasting, teachers or probation officers, whose conditions are subject to other Acts of Parliament. Workers covered by Wages Councils can use Schedule 11 and also the specific part of it dealt with on page 284.

Schedule 11 applies in two situations: **A.** where there are collective agreements between unions and an *employers' association* and **B.** where there is no collective bargaining with an *employers' association*.

A. Where there are collective agreements with an employers' association

Employers are obliged to observe terms and conditions not less favourable than those obtained through collective bargaining between independent trade unions and an *employers' association*. The obligation arises if *and only if* all the following seven conditions are met:

1. There is an agreement between one or more independent trade unions and an employers' association. A collective agreement with a single employer does not count, so if you do not negotiate with an association or federation, you will have to run your claim under **B.** below. National and local agreements and decisions of national and local joint councils and arbitration awards all count.

2. The agreement covers workers comparable to those employed by the unfair employer. This means they do similar work even though job-titles may be different. A 'broad approach' is taken by the Central Arbitration Committee (CAC) in dealing with this point. You can compare two groups of workers employed by the *same* employer – in order for example to try and close differentials – provided the agreement deals with conditions for comparable work.

3. The comparable workers are employed in the same trade or industry or a section of it as the unfair employer. For example, the CAC has decided that pattern makers are a section of the engineering industry, but that workers employed by the Bank of Pakistan in London are not in the same industry as those employed by the big clearing banks.

The main test of whether the industry is the same is the *general nature* of the unfair employer's business. But the CAC has said that this is not the only factor:

> It is perfectly possible . . . for a company to be engaged primarily in one industry and yet be engaged also in one or more other industries or sections of them.

For example, vehicle fitters working for Sunblest Bakery were held to be in a different industry from workers covered by the motor retailing and repair agreement – presumably because their boss sold bread not cars. **But you will do better if you can show that you belong to a self-contained section of industry which operates more or less independently within a different industry.**

Examples:

■ Engineer surveyors (who inspect plant and equipment) employed at STD Ltd, a subsidiary of Tube Investments making domestic and industrial appliances, got parity with similar workers employed by insurance companies, even though STD was itself in the broad engineering industry.

■ Maintenance workers at Blackpool Tower got parity with workers in the construction industry, even though the Tower itself is in the entertainment and leisure industry.

■ Fourteen drivers out of a team of 85 working on ICI contracts for Rankin Tankers got an increase of £16 a week. They drove oil tankers and so were in the oil transportation industry, not in *general* road haulage.

Other factors are: the work done by the employees, the products created by the employers, their membership or non-membership of employers' associations, the relationship to parent companies and industrial relations. You can try to show that all or any of these indicate that both employers are in the same trade, industry or section – and therefore that you are entitled to the higher rate paid by the other employer to comparable workers.

4. The agreement fixes terms and conditions. This includes wage rates, holidays, bonus, hours, pensions and other conditions. The agreement may fix minimum conditions.

5. The agreement applies either 'generally' or in the geographical district in which the unfair employer operates. You can compare with an agreement that applies throughout the UK, or in a major part of it like Scotland or England, or with a local agreement in a 'district' – like the West Midlands or Sheffield or a county. If locally agreed rates are better than national, you can use them provided the agreement meets the other conditions listed here.

6. The parties to the agreement represent a substantial proportion of employers and workers in the sector you are comparing. In other words, there must be a substantial proportion in the same trade or industry (or section) in the geographical area covered by the agreement, that is, nationally or in your local district.

7. The unfair employer is observing less favourable terms and conditions than those in the agreement. For this you must look at the whole package of conditions and not rely simply on an item-for-item comparison. The unfair employer can say that he is paying less in wages but he is giving longer holidays and better pensions. But he cannot trade off non-contractual or discretionary benefits. Cambion Electronic Products in Sheffield paid below engineering national rates and said that the difference was made up in free travel and an (ex gratia) profit-sharing scheme negotiated with a staff committee. The CAC said these were not relevant.

You should also compare wages at the same stage in the negotiating cycle, because a discrepancy may exist solely due to different annual settlement dates.

B. Where there are no collective agreements with an employers' association

Even if you cannot show an agreement with an employers' association, **employers are still obliged to observe fair terms and conditions**. To enforce this you must be able to show that the following four conditions are met:

1. There is a 'general level' of terms and conditions for comparable workers. The level can be set simply by a few employers offering more or less similar terms. They do not have to be aware they are doing so. The general level can be established by looking at a number of different employers paying rates or observing conditions better than yours. Their terms and conditions may be different from each other, but, taken together, the general level is higher. For example, their rates of pay are from 5–25 per cent higher or they give three to five days extra in holidays.

The 'general level' does not mean the highest level, but there is no legal definition – it may mean the average, the median, or be calculated using other statistical methods: clusters, division by quartiles. One employer paying higher rates may not often set a general level, but a few might be said to. It can also be set by collective agreements with individual employers rather than with an employers' association. This is an important advantage over category A. claims because it means that you may be able to compare with a single leading company in the area.

2. The general level is observed by employers in the same trade or industry (or section) in the same district. 'District' is not defined. The smaller the number of employers or employees in the trade, the bigger the district is. For example, the Highlands and Islands is a district. The CAC has, though, taken account of national comparisons in looking for a general level. It is arguable that for specialist skills, the district is the whole of the UK.

3. The circumstances of these employers are similar to those of the unfair employer. This condition is usually met simply by the fact that condition **2.** above is satisfied, but employers do try to argue against comparability on the grounds that the size of the establishment, its location and its profits are all different. Certainly the CAC should not allow employers to escape fair wages obligations in order to keep their profits up.

4. The unfair employer is on the whole observing less favourable terms and conditions. The comparison is easiest to make if time rates are compared with time rates, holidays with holidays and so on, but if different payment systems are in effect you can look at actual earnings. Comparison must be to the package of terms and conditions as a whole, but no guidance is given in Schedule 11 on whether you look at averages, medians or clusters of earnings. The only test is 'unfairness'.

Is this your problem . . . ?

There are two situations where it may be difficult to get the going rate.

1. There are collective agreements with an employers' association but they do not cover all terms and conditions. Schedule 11 operates if the agreement you are comparing deals, for example, only with time rates or minimum earnings levels, and says nothing of other conditions like bonus, piecework rates or pensions. You would draft your claim to say that, insofar as there *are* agreed terms, the unfair employer is not observing them, and insofar as there are *no* agreed terms, he is not observing the general level.

2. Where there are agreements with an employers' association but they provide minimum rates which are below those generally paid in the district. Sometimes strict application of *agreed* rates would frustrate the intention of the Act because it would not advance the cause of fair wages and would restrict the workers to wages, hours and conditions **less favourable** than the general level.

But the High Court has decided (against industrial common sense) that when agreements provide only *minimum* rates – as in engineering and construction – there is no claim:

In 1975 the minimum rate in the engineering industry was
£42 a week. Since that date, local bargaining had increased the minimum. Deltaflow Ltd paid above £42 but
less than the general level of wages in their district. The
CAC said that in reality £42 was not now the minimum
wage. But the High Court over-ruled this. Where there is
an agreed minimum wage, you can't bring a claim for a
(higher) general level of wages, even though the agreed
wage is unrealistic. *The Queen v CAC ex parte Deltaflow*
1977 (HC)

Who can claim under Schedule 11?

If you are claiming that an agreement is not being kept
to – **A.** above – you must be
  1. a party to the agreement, and
  2. either an independent trade union *or* an employers'
association.
  If you are claiming the general level of terms in the
industry – **B.** above – you must be
  1. a union or an employers' association, and
  2. have at least one member in the trade in the district.
  But if the unfair employer recognises an independent
union for the group of underpaid workers, only *that* union or
an employers' association can complain.

How to claim

  1. Lodge a claim with your employer – backdating of
an award is possible only to the date the employer was told of
the claim.
  2. Your union complains to ACAS. Form ACAS 72
(pages 382–3) should be used. If ACAS cannot settle it, the
Central Arbitration Committee convenes a hearing.
  3. The Committee may simply give advice, or it may
make an award which takes effect as part of every worker's
own contract (compare page 249).

The Fair Wages Resolution

What is the Resolution?

The Fair Wages Resolution of 1946 (FWR) is not an
Act of Parliament, but an instruction from the House of
Commons to government departments. Its origins lie in trade
union agitation against contractors to local authorities and
government departments. These employers, in order to obtain
contracts against fierce competition, would cut the wages of

their employees to the bone. This practice of 'sweating' was revealed in a series of reports by a Select Committee of the House of Lords during the late 1880s and early 1890s. The Committee found appalling conditions. A long trade-union campaign had some successes at local authority level, and culminated in the first Resolution of 1891.

Who is bound by the FWR?

The present FWR requires government contractors and sub-contractors to pay wages and observe terms and conditions that are not less favourable than:

1. those established by collective bargaining between organisations of employers and trade unions for the trade or industry in the district – clause 1(a); **or**

2. those observed by other employers whose general circumstances in the trade or industry in which the contractor is engaged are similar – clause 1(b).

The only difference between the FWR and the corresponding part of Schedule 11 is that under Schedule 11 the collective agreement setting the 'fair' standard can apply *either* in the same geographical district as the unfair employer or nationally. Under the Resolution, the agreement has to apply in the district in which the unfair employer actually operates. The conditions set by the agreement must be 'established' in this district. There has been a High Court ruling saying minimum rates are established, but the CAC has not followed this line and has treated terms as 'established' if they are the *actual* rates paid in the district.

The Resolution is incorporated into all government contracts. It also requires every employer who works for a government department to 'recognise the freedom of his work-people to be members of a trade union'. This does not mean the employer must recognise the union, but it is a rare example in labour law of a right to join a union. There have, however, been no successful cases on this clause. The contractor must display a copy of the Resolution in every workplace where work is being done on the contract. To get on the government's approved list of companies who may tender for work, an employer must declare that he has observed the Resolution for at least the previous three months. Contractors must ensure their sub-contractors observe it, and they must notify the government department, if required, of the contractors' names and addresses.

How to claim

There is no formal method of claiming, as there is under Schedule 11. If a contractor is not observing fair terms, anybody – a worker, the union or even another contractor – can complain to the DE. If not otherwise settled, the Employment Secretary will refer it to the CAC for a decision. If the complaint is upheld, the contractor will have broken his contract with the government department – since the FWR is a term of that contract.

The CAC strictly has no power to do anything more than declare whether the Resolution has been broken, but in practice it also makes an award, recommending terms for every worker's contract of employment.

Equally important for direct action is the fact that the **government contract can be cancelled**, so political pressure and publicity are effective methods of enforcing adherence to the FWR.

Since the introduction of the wider and more powerful Schedule 11, claims under the Resolution may become less important. Any claim that can be brought under the FWR can also be brought under Schedule 11, and unions have *direct* access to the CAC under Schedule 11.

Statutory fair wages

Some industries are covered by Acts of Parliament which demand that fair wages and conditions must apply. These include **nationalised industries and some in the private sector which have received government backing or which can only operate with a government licence**. Employers in these industries must observe terms and conditions that are set by collective agreements or are part of an identifiable 'general level'. There are Acts for the following industries: coal, gas, electricity, atomic energy, civil aviation, road transport, road haulage, beet sugar refining, TV, film-making and the NHS.

Local authorities are not specifically included, but in practice they often include the FWR as part of their contracts.

How to claim

The procedure varies from Act to Act, but generally unions and sometimes individual workers can complain to ACAS, who will normally refer it to the CAC. Contracts can be cancelled and licences withdrawn, and the CAC can make an award for improved terms and conditions of all relevant workers.

Wages Councils

In many industries where trade unionism is weak, Wages Councils, dating back to the Trade Boards first established in 1909, fix wages and other conditions. The industries covered include retailing, clothing manufacture, hotels, catering, agriculture (Wages Boards), road haulage and numerous small-scale and esoteric manufacturing industries. There are 47 altogether, covering about 3·6 million workers.

They are appointed by the Employment Secretary. The Council members include an equal number of representatives from unions which organise in the industry, and of employers, and one or more 'independent' members, who act as chairmen. Traditionally the councils were intended to provide minimum wages and holidays in unorganised industries and to give a stimulus to collective bargaining. They have been a dismal failure. Many workers are on, or marginally above, the very low Wages Council rates. Union organisation remains hopelessly poor – less than 4 per cent in the hotel industry, for example – and collective bargaining has, if anything, been stifled by Wages Councils. It is all too easy for employers to offer a pound or two above the rate and tell their workers they are paid more than the union could get them, for the unions, after all, are represented on the Councils.

Wages Councils can deal with wages rates, holidays and lodging allowances and any other terms and conditions of employment. A Wages Council order becomes the law of the land, and failure to observe the rates carries a penalty of a £100 fine. The DE has inspectors who can bring a criminal prosecution, and the courts can, in addition to imposing a fine, order arrears of wages for up to two years to be paid to any affected worker. (Arrears of up to six years can be obtained by a civil law suit.)

In 1975 arrears of £500,000 were collected. Underpayment and poor enforcement add insult to the injury of already low Wages Council rates. In 1976 the DE carried out a 'blitz' on Wages Council employers. Out of 3,000 establishments the inspectors visited, 27 per cent of them were underpaying. 1,659 workers shared £76,000 in back pay – over £45 each.

Power is given to the Employment Secretary to wind up any Wages Council if voluntary collective bargaining can take its place. But progress towards this has been slow.

Statutory Joint Industrial Councils

Section 90 of the EP Act enables a Wages Council to convert to a Statutory Joint Industrial Council (SJIC). It has the same powers to fix terms and conditions, with the same binding effect. **Unions and employers can make their own appointments and there are no independent members.**

Any attempt to bring the paternalistic Wages Council system out of the nineteenth century must be welcomed, and the TUC has long been advocating the substitution of voluntary collective bargaining. But it is very doubtful whether conversion to an SJIC is a step forward. It seems quite likely that, having once made the move from Wages Council to SJIC, the industry will languish in inactivity. Nothing short of voluntary collective bargaining without legal strings will encourage trade unionism in these industries.

The going rate in these industries

In industries covered by Wages Councils and SJICs Part 2 of Schedule 11 applies. It requires employers to pay at least the **lowest current rate** if the following five conditions are met:

1. The employer has employees within the scope of a Wages Council, SJIC or agricultural wages board.

2. An *independent* trade union has an agreement that covers a 'significant number of establishments' covered by the Council, either nationally or *in the particular district*.

3. This union has at least one member employed by the employer and covered by the Wages Council, SJIC or agricultural wages board.

4. The unfair employer's circumstances are similar to those of other establishments.

5. He is paying less than the lowest rate agreed within the last 12 months for workers of the same description.

The only terms and conditions that can be reported are **wages**, so it might be more advantageous to go for a general level of terms and conditions under the main provisions of Schedule 11.

An independent union can complain to ACAS (see

Form ACAS 73, pages 384–5), which must then refer it to the CAC. The CAC procedure and powers are similar to the main provisions of Schedule 11.

Summary

1. A union can claim that an employer is not paying the going rate for terms and conditions set by agreements **with an employers' association** – Schedule 11 para. 2(a).

2. If there are *no* agreements at all or agreements only **with individual employers**, a union can claim the going rate if there is a generally observed level of terms and conditions – Schedule 11 para. 2(b).

3. If agreements with an association do not cover all terms and conditions, a union might claim these actual rates.

4. The Fair Wages Resolution requires government contractors and sub-contractors to pay the going rate established in accordance with 1, and 2, (and probably 3) above.

5. Some government financed or licensed industries are specifically required by statute to pay the going rate, for instance coal, gas and road transport.

6. Wages Councils and SJICs set legally binding minimum terms and conditions. If collective agreements improve on these in respect of **wages**, these can become the going rate – Schedule 11 para. 15.

7. Claims are usually made to ACAS and referred to the CAC. A decision of the CAC is binding only in that particular case; previous cases are influential but are not binding precedents. The CAC can say that the going rate should now be part of every affected worker's contract.

18.

Industrial Action

The 'right to strike' / workers who have no
right / government emergency powers in
disputes / what industrial action means /
strikes, work-to-rule, go slow, blacking,
work-in / the purposes of industrial action /
whether action is official or unofficial / how
it affects your contract / discipline, sacking /
legal action against your union, and strike
leaders / injunctions / lockouts / how a strike
affects redundancy pay, social security
benefits, and continuity of employment / a
summary / and the demand for a legal right
to strike.

The right to strike

There is no positive right to strike in British law. There
are merely some defences and immunities that workers and
workers' leaders can use if employers try to take offensive
action in the courts as a result of a strike. From 1871, many
acts and agreements which are likely to occur during a strike,
and which would normally be illegal, have been blessed with a
legal immunity.

A number of attempts have been made by Parliament
and the judges to abolish these immunities and to make strike
activity unlawful. Following a strike in 1900 over victimisation
of a union activist, the Taff Vale Railway Company successfully sued the Amalgamated Society of Railway Servants for
£23,000 and £12,000 in legal costs. The 1906 Liberal government pressurised by new Labour MPs, overruled this by the
Trade Disputes Act 1906, which became the basis on which
unions and workers are relatively free to conduct industrial
action.

After the General Strike, the Tories tried to curtail so-called 'political' strikes and union activities by the Trade Disputes and Trade Unions Act 1927, which was not repealed until 1946. During the two world wars, there was a ban on strikes and lock-outs with compulsory arbitration as the alternative final step. Elements of the wartime orders continued until 1959.

During the late 1950s, with unemployment low and profits booming, employers were unable to resist many demands from unions for better terms and conditions. But occasionally they fought back and, with the help of the judges, restrained the ability of workers to conduct industrial action. Disputes over a closed shop at Heathrow Airport and recognition on the London waterfront and in Torquay hotels gave the judges the opportunity to create laws that jeopardised strike activity throughout industry. No dispute could be conducted without the threat of legal action hanging over the strikers.

In 1968, the Labour Cabinet introduced its White Paper *In Place of Strife* which contained proposals for plugging one of the loopholes found by the judges (on breaking commercial contracts), but which also sought compulsory ballots and cooling-off periods before strikes. It was opposed and defeated by the trade-union movement.

In 1971, the 'right to strike' was reduced still further. The Tories' Industrial Relations Act outlawed the calling of all industrial action short of a strike by any but a registered union, and the leaders of strikes called without notice were also threatened. Unions were ordered to pay compensation and fines, ballots were ordered, strikes postponed and workers imprisoned. Even after the Act was repealed, litigation continued until 1976 (against the TGWU) and the Tory and Liberal amendments to the repealing Act of 1974 were not deleted until 1976.

What we have now can in *no* sense be regarded as a right to strike and employers are still able to sack all workers engaged in any dispute. In 70 years no real advance has been made to guarantee the most fundamental of workers' rights. Worse, some statements by the courts under the Industrial Relations Act (IR Act) remain law and impose additional restrictions.

Workers denied 'the right to strike'

Although the right to strike exists only in the form of defences against some forms of legal action, some workers are specifically denied access to these. They are:

■ **Merchant seamen.** Many workers can be sued in the civil courts by their employers for breach of contract, but seamen are liable to **criminal** prosecution if they disobey orders at sea, or, by their absence, prevent a ship from sailing. The 1970 Merchant Shipping Act allows strikes only when your ship is safely moored in a UK port and you have then given 48-hours notice of your intention to terminate your contract. In other words, you can strike if you no longer work for your employer!

■ **The police.** Since the 1919 police strike was broken, the police have been denied the right to join a trade union – the Police Federation is not affiliated to the TUC and is not a trade union as such. It is a criminal offence to 'cause disaffection' or to induce a policeman to withhold his services or breach discipline. Governments play down the political implications of policemen being considered as workers (they are 'office-holders') and behaving as trade unionists. This makes it easy for employers and government to use them against other workers.

■ **The armed forces.** You can retain your union membership if you join the services but you must not be active. You cannot join a union while in service and it is a criminal offence to organise. The requirement of obedience effectively denies the freedom to strike. Again, the implications of a unionised soldiery are too much for the establishment to contemplate.

■ **Postal workers.** The Post Office Act 1953 makes it a criminal offence for postal workers wilfully to delay or detain a letter or parcel. They can get two years inside or a fine or both. Anyone (including a union) who tries to get postal workers to delay or detain letters or parcels also commits an offence. The Telegraph Act 1863 makes it an offence for Post Office workers to fail to deliver or transmit a message (for instance by phone or telegram) or to delay it. The penalty is up to a £20 fine.

These Acts can be enforced against Post Office workers by:

1. a prosecution by the police.

2. a complaint to the civil courts for an injunction to prevent a threatened offence. **Only** the Attorney-General or someone acting with his consent can do this.

> In 1977 the TUC called for a week of action against South Africa. The Post Office unions threatened to advise members to black communications to and from South Africa. John Gouriet, leader of the right-wing National Association for Freedom, asked the Attorney-General to stop the threatened boycott. When this was refused, Gouriet got an injunction in the Court of Appeal and the boycott was stopped. Months later, the House of Lords unanimously overturned this judgment saying that a private citizen could not, without the Attorney-General, intervene to stop a *threat* of action by postal workers. Nor could the Attorney-General's reason for refusing to intervene be questioned. Even if Gouriet had suffered *personally* (for example, by losing business) from the boycott, *he* could not sue the Post Office or the unions. They are exempt from civil liability. But if an offence was actually committed, the police could prosecute. *Gouriet v UPW* 1977 (HL)

Following threats of legal action against postal workers during the Grunwick dispute (see page 7), a private member's Bill was introduced in December 1977 to give them the right to strike.

Emergency powers

The government can intervene in any industrial dispute. Under the Emergency Powers Act 1920, the Queen can proclaim an emergency if there are events of such a nature 'as to be calculated, by interfering with the supply and distribution of food, water, fuel, or light, or with the means of locomotion, to deprive the community, or any substantial portion of the community of the essentials of life'. Use of the Act must be approved by Parliament and renewed monthly. The Act gives almost unlimited powers to the government to make orders, but it cannot ban strikes and picketing or introduce military and industrial conscription. Since troops can be and usually are moved in, the effectiveness of a strike can be substantially undermined.

An emergency has been proclaimed 11 times since 1920, including three times by Labour governments (1948 and 1949 – docks; 1966 – seamen) and five times by the Heath government (1970 and 1972 – docks; 1970 – electricity supply; 1972 and 1973 – miners).

What is industrial action?

Strikes

There is no all-purpose definition of industrial action. A **strike** is defined in the Contracts of Employment (CE Act) Schedule 1 para. 11 as:

> the cessation of work by a body of persons employed acting in combination, or a concerted refusal or a refusal under a common understanding of any number of persons employed to continue to work for an employer in consequence of a dispute, done as a means of compelling their employer or any person or body of persons employed, or to aid other employees in compelling their employer or any person or body of persons employed, to accept or not accept terms or conditions of or affecting their employment.

This definition is used to work out how long you have been continuously employed if you are claiming, say, redundancy pay and have ever been on strike. Any part of a week when you are on strike does not count.

Another definition is used when you claim social security benefits (see page 212). You are disqualified if you are involved in **'a stoppage of work due to a trade dispute'**. This includes lock-outs. Under the TULR Act (Schedule 1 para 7) there is nothing to stop employers sacking *all* workers who are engaged in **a strike or other industrial action**. This gives them a powerful weapon and the job of defining a strike is left to the judges.

The judges have gone further than the CE Act definition. Lord Denning, for example, in a commercial case about shipping delays said that there could be a strike even though there was no breach of contract. Dockers who quite lawfully refused to change to a 24-hour three-shift system and stuck to normal day work were held to be on strike – *Tramp Shipping Corp. v Greenwich Marine Inc.* 1975 (CA).

A strike is still a strike even if all the strikers have been dismissed, and it is a strike whether or not notice has been given.

Other industrial action

Problems of definition are even harder when looking at industrial action short of a strike. You can escape liability for going on strike if you give proper notice to terminate your contracts, but nothing can validate other industrial action. In a case following a refusal by clerical workers in the TGWU to do additional work connected with handling cargo for Iberia Airlines, Sir John Donaldson said:

> almost all forms of industrial pressure short of a strike fall within the definition . . . of irregular action short of a strike and a safe working rule is that there is no alternative to either striking or doing the full job which the employees are employed to do . . . Any concerted form of working without enthusiasm, or prolonged tea-breaks, or departure for the relief of natural pressures – the forms of industrial action are limited only by the ingenuity of mankind – all of them constitute irregular industrial action short of a strike and are prohibited with or without notice. *Seaboard World Airlines v TGWU* 1973 (NIRC)

A **ban on voluntary overtime** and a **withdrawal of goodwill** *may* count as industrial action even though you have not 'sold' these as part of your contract and cannot be said to be breaking it, but no court has ever made this illegal.

In 1972, a **work-to-rule** by the three rail unions was declared unlawful under the now-repealed IR Act, and a cooling-off period was ordered followed by a ballot (which went, predictably, against the employers and the Tory Employment Secretary).

Why should mere adherence to your employer's own rules be considered illegal? – a tricky problem for judges who insist on observance of rules. But they were undeterred and found that there is more to your contract than you think. Lord Denning said that the rule-book constituted lawful instructions which every worker had to obey and that it was a breach of contract to 'construe the rules unreasonably'. He said if any worker:

> with the others, takes steps wilfully to disrupt the undertaking to produce chaos so that it will not run as it should, then each one who is a party to those steps is guilty of a breach of his contract . . . what makes it wrong is the object with which it is done . . . it is the wilful disruption that is the breach. *Secretary of State for Employment v ASLEF* 1972 (CA)

Lord Justice Buckley went even further and revealed that 'the employee must serve the employer faithfully with a view to promoting those commercial interests for which he was employed'.

Lord Denning was prepared to say that whatever you do, whatever your contract says, you can be acting unlawfully in taking industrial action if you have a 'wilful' state of mind, including working only a 40-hour week. This is certainly wrong but, as they stand, the breadth of the implied terms – not wilfully to disrupt the undertaking and to promote its commercial interests – could possibly be used to justify mass sackings. So far, they haven't been.

Workers who left their work-benches and gathered round two machines to **stop them physically from being tested** were considered to have taken industrial action and were sacked. – *Thompson v Eaton Ltd* – see page 292.

A **go-slow** is a refusal to perform your contract efficiently and constitutes industrial action.

Blacking and **refusal to work with non-union labour** have been declared to be breaches of contract and unlawful industrial action. At a time of mass redundancy, TASS members at C. A. Parsons Ltd refused to handle work done by UKAPE members or to work with them. The NIRC ordered them to stop – *UKAPE v AUEW (TASS)* 1972 (NIRC).

Work-ins and occupations

At first sight there is no reason why a work-in should be unlawful – you are, after all, merely doing without supervision what you are employed to do and probably more efficiently. But if in a work-in or occupation you refuse to leave the plant or office, you will be disobeying lawful instructions.

That means you might be sacked, but in order to get you off the site your boss will have to start a claim for trespass. This has always been a **civil** matter, but since the introduction of new offences in the Criminal Law Act 1977, the police can intervene in a work-in or sit-in. The grounds on which they can do this are set out on page 313.

Picketing is dealt with in chapter 19.

The purposes of industrial action

It doesn't matter why you are taking industrial action – for industrial, social, political or sympathetic reasons – the rules on breach of contract and mass sackings are the same. When shop stewards, union officials and others call on workers to take industrial action, they are protected from most legal action only if there is a **trade dispute**. This is defined on page 301 and may exclude some strikes.

Official or unofficial?

With the sole exception of calculating your family's entitlement to social security benefits – which are reduced if you get strike pay – the law is not concerned with whether a strike is official or unofficial. But strikes in breach of procedure – that is, before the disputes machinery has been exhausted – are more likely to have legal consequences for the workers involved. These strikes will usually be unofficial.

How does industrial action affect your contract?

The law on strikes has been turbulent since the mid-1960s with decisions of the courts creating confusion and danger. Fleeting support for strikers in several judges' statements provided false hopes, and now the EAT has followed the reactionary and employer-dominated approach to the right to strike.

The law is still unclear, but the prevailing view might be summarised in this way:

1. Your contract of employment is not suspended during a strike.

2. This means that you usually commit a breach of contract when you strike or take other industrial action.

3. Usually, but not always, this breach will be so serious that your employer can discipline you for it. This means withholding wages, suing for breach of contract or giving you the sack.

4. During a strike there is nothing to stop your boss sacking all strikers.

5. If only some are sacked or not taken back after the dispute, they can claim unfair dismissal.

6. If the strike is in self-defence or a reaction to your boss's own serious breach of contract or deliberate provocation, it may count as (constructive) unfair dismissal by your employer before the strike started.

7. Giving strike notice does not normally help you.

Now, these rules are very complicated and depend on an interpretation of several important cases. The following questions usually arise in connection with strikes and other industrial action.

Is the contract suspended during a strike?

Contracts are not usually suspended during a strike – it is assumed that the obligations under them continue to be operative and if you do not turn up for work, you are breaking your contract in the most fundamental sense. **It's important to find some suspension if you are going to say that the normal contractual obligations do not apply.** But the courts during the 1970s and now the EAT do not recognise suspension of contracts. They say that in striking you are putting an end to the employer-employee relationship, terminating your contract.

In an NGA strike in 1975 over differentials, the Newspaper Publishers Association threatened dismissal if assurances of normal working were not given. The union tried to stop these threats being carried out, on the basis that it was industrial nonsense to say that a strike is equivalent to self-dismissal and anyway

> where an employee went on strike, that was no repudiation of his contract of employment. The whole point of striking ... was not that the striker wanted to terminate his contract of employment but that he wanted to continue it on better terms.

But Mr Justice Megarry said this proposition of the union was 'wholly untenable', and Lord Denning said the strike was at least a breach of contract.

If there is a procedure agreement providing that no industrial action will be taken until the procedure is exhausted and some notice is given, the courts might say that the workers' contracts are suspended until the strike is over. But they will only do that if the agreement is incorporated into every worker's contract – see page 254.

Is striking a breach of contract?

In almost every case, you break your contract if you go on strike. The EAT, adopting old master-servant rules, has said:

> We are satisfied that at common law an employer is entitled to dismiss summarily an employee who refuses to do any of the work which he has been engaged to do . . . the employee has 'disregarded the essential conditions of the contract of service.' *Simmons v Hoover* (see below)

What disciplinary action can be taken against strikers?

Because most strikes involve a breach of contract, employers often want to take action against strikers. They might withhold wages, sue for breach of contract or dismiss you.

Withholding wages

If you are on strike you will not get paid. Some agreements have made the boss pay up after the strike is settled. The attraction of less dramatic forms of industrial action, such as a work-to-rule or go-slow, is that you continue to be at work and to receive pay. But if the judgments in the 1972 rail work-to-rule case (see page 291) were taken literally, there is no right to pay. If you 'wilfully disrupt' your boss's business – and the judges will be quick to classify all industrial action in this way – you are behaving in a way that is inconsistent with *your* contract, so *his* obligations under it are offset. In practice, though, most employers do not reduce or refuse to pay wages during industrial action short of a strike unless the action has a direct effect on bonus or commission.

Suing for breach of contract

This was a favourite with the mine-owners and the National Coal Board. Any breach of any contract entitles the injured party to go to court to obtain damages to put him in the same position as if the contract had been properly carried out. The same applies to a contract of employment. A major difference is that the courts cannot directly order you or your boss to carry out the terms of the contract, that is, actually to force you to go back to work or your boss to employ you. (TULR Act section 16 see page 9.)

As your employer can sue for damages only, it will not be worthwhile. This form of legal action has been so discredited and the value of the damages, even if they are obtainable, is so small that employers have not used this remedy in any important dispute since 1956.

Sacking

The EAT has confirmed the old **common law** right of an employer to sack an employee without notice (or wages in lieu) when 'there was a settled, confirmed and continued intention on the part of the employee not to do any of the work which under his contract he had engaged to do'.

> Bill Simmons had worked for Hoovers in Perivale for 10
> years when a strike occurred in 1974. He was off sick at
> the time. When he recovered he notified Hoovers but did
> not return to work because of the strike. Just after
> Christmas he was given one week's notice of dismissal.
> He quickly found a new job and on the day he started it,
> the strike was settled. He claimed redundancy pay, but
> Hoovers said that the Redundancy Payments Act
> allowed them to refuse a payment to any worker whose
> contract entitled them to dismiss him instantly. And the
> strike amounted to such conduct. The EAT agreed.
> *Simmons v Hoover* 1976 (EAT)

The right to claim reinstatement or compensation under
the unfair dismissal law is limited – see below.

Can all strikers be sacked?

There is nothing to stop an employer sacking *all*
workers taking part in a strike or other industrial action.

Provided *all* are sacked, none of them can claim unfair
dismissal. The tribunal cannot even hear the claim. (TULR
Act schedule 1 para. 7.) The sacking must take place while the
action is continuing, and is unlawful if the strike is over or
the employer has been told it is over. (*Heath v Longman*
below.)

The judges' justification for allowing employers to
escape unfair dismissal claims, adopted by the EAT, is:

> to give a measure of protection to an employer if his
> business is faced with ruin by a strike. It enables him in
> those circumstances, if he cannot carry on the business
> without a labour force, to dismiss the labour force on
> strike; to take on another labour force without the
> stigma of its being unfair dismissal. *Heath v J F Longman
> Ltd.* 1973 (NIRC)

In other words, mass sacking followed by the employment of
scab labour is not unlawful. The purpose of the strike is quite
irrelevant. The only question is: did the employer sack all the
workers participating in the industrial action and has he
refused to re-engage all of them?

Employers frequently threaten, or actually carry out
mass sacking of strikers. Grunwicks sacked all APEX
strikers, then sacked the TGWU drivers who much later came
out in support. Tribunals turned away the sacked workers'
claims. Even though the motive for sacking was clearly
anti-union, the tribunals had no jurisdiction to hear the merits
of the cases.

In 1977, Bristows Helicopters in Scotland sacked all

pilots who supported a dismissed colleague. British Airways sent dismissal notices to AUEW workers on strike at Heathrow Airport. The Civil Aviation Authority gave notice to all air traffic control assistants who refused to stop their national work-to-rule. British Leyland sent dismissal notices to striking toolmakers.

The reason advanced for allowing employers to get away with this is that Parliament never intended industrial disputes to be assessed for reasonableness by courts and tribunals. But by giving *no* support to strikers whose employer has carried out mass sackings, the law supports the employer.

The lesson is clear to every employer. In any strike he can stop union activists by sacking all the workers. **This difficulty can only be overcome by ensuring absolute solidarity** and by keeping strike breakers out. Until we get a right to strike and suspension of contracts, this is the only way to tackle this employers' offensive.

What if only some strikers are sacked?

If only some of the strikers are sacked or if only some are taken back after the dispute, the rest can claim unfair dismissal. Your employer must say why he chose *you* for dismissal and must justify it. You cannot win your case just by showing you were picked out – your boss may go on to show that he sacked you for reasons not connected with the strike.

The fact that some workers initially take industrial action, then go back to work before the strike ends, doesn't mean that there has been no discrimination. If *any* worker who at *any* time took part in the action is taken back, the other workers can claim unfair dismissal.

> 53 women at a Tipton, W. Midlands, curtain manufacturers, came out on strike for recognition. After a few days two of the women went back. The rest were all sacked and claimed unfair dismissal. The High Court said that as two people who had, *at some time*, taken part in the action had been re-employed, the claim for the others succeeded. Furthermore they had been sacked because they had taken part in the activities (a strike) of the union. *Frank Jones (Tipton) Ltd v Stock* 1978 (HL)

What if the employer provokes the strike?

You may be able to claim reinstatement or compensation if you are sacked following a strike which your boss provoked. The EAT said in Bill Simmons's case:

> We should not be taken to be saying that all strikes are
> necessarily repudiatory*, though usually they will be. For
> example, it could hardly be said that a strike of employees
> in opposition to demands by an employer in breach of
> contract by him would be repudiatory. But what may be
> called a "real" strike in our judgment always will be.

What is a 'real' strike? From other decisions of the EAT it
seems that just about every strike is a 'real' strike and therefore
workers are exposed to dismissal. Legitimate self-defensive
reaction to employers' unreasonable demands is still likely to
be a 'real' strike. Take, for instance, the action of Bill
Thompson and five fellow engineering workers in Bolton who
objected to the introduction of new machines into their shop
without agreement – *Thompson v Eaton Ltd*. 1976 (EAT). A
dispute arose, management would not put the matter into
procedure, so six of the workers left their benches and
physically obstructed access to the machines until the manning
and testing arrangements had been agreed. The men were
warned, then sacked. They claimed unfair dismissal, but were
turned down because at the time of the dismissal they were **all**
taking part in industrial action.

The EAT recognised that management behaved
'obtusely' but agreed with this decision. The bench, consisting
of Mr Justice Phillips, Ms A. Taylor and Mr Albert Blyghton,
TGWU Legal Secretary, said the only circumstances in which
a strike was all right were

> where a strike or other industrial action has been pro-
> voked or even engineered by the employer in some gross
> manner. It seems to us very probable that in such circum-
> stances the provisions [that is, denying the right to claim
> unfair dismissal] would not apply.

It is difficult to see what could realistically be envisaged
as provocation if such high-handed unilateral action by
management escapes liability. This case underlines the point
that **you cannot hope to get support or even justice if you are
involved in litigation over a strike or industrial action.**

Does it make any difference if you give strike notice?

Giving strike notice can only be regarded as a tactic.
Use it if you think it is worthwhile for industrial reasons, but
in general it confers no legal benefit or immunity. From the

---

* repudiatory means that you are refusing to be bound by
your contract and terminate it by your action, for
instance, by not going to work.

courts' point of view, you are usually outlawed if you take industrial action of any sort.

This is because strike notice means that you are going either to break, to terminate or to suspend your contract. A breach of contract is still a breach even if you give your boss advance warning.

If you give the amount of notice necessary to terminate your contract and in fact terminate it, you are doing nothing unlawful. But it is totally unrealistic to do this, as it means that the workforce is split according to length of service and status (staff or hourly-paid) as different notice periods are required of different workers. It also means that you are jeopardising your continuity of employment and your right to claim unfair dismissal and redundancy pay, and you are disqualified for receiving unemployment benefit for six weeks following a resignation 'without just cause'. So **don't give strike notice in the form of notice to terminate your contract of employment.**

Suspension of contracts is not possible unless there is some form of agreement allowing for it.

The only way you can be sure that notice will not prejudice your contract is to provide in your collective agreements that a strike after due notice (whatever you agree) will be treated as suspension of each worker's contract, so the failure to work does not give your employer the right to sack.

Legal action against the union

A trade union cannot be sued in its own name for most civil wrongs (torts) (TULR Act section 14). It *can* be sued for civil wrongs involving personal injury or involving the use of its property. So it can be sued by people libelled in union literature or injured on union premises. **But** if the civil wrong was done 'in contemplation or furtherance of a trade dispute', the union cannot be sued at all. The union can't be sued, for example, for libellous slogans on pickets' placards during a trade dispute.

A union can commit crimes – as, for example, the UPW was alleged to have done when it threatened to black South African mail (see page 288). It can also be liable for breach of contract – for example, to its own employees or to printers, builders, cleaners and solicitors who do business with the union.

In practice, there is no scope for legal action against most unions involved in strike action. These immunities, though, have not prevented **officials** from being sued.

Legal action against 'strike leaders'

It is usually assumed by the media and politicians that strikes are 'led' and that there are 'ringleaders', the majority of workers being unwilling to take industrial action. In legal terms, this is translated into a search for those who ask others to break their contracts by taking industrial action, or by not fulfilling their commercial commitments. These include union executive committees, local officials, shop stewards and individual workers, for example on picket duty.

Protection in **civil** law is given to workers for all acts that are likely to arise in connection with industrial action, provided they are done **'in contemplation or furtherance of a trade dispute'**. This term is crucial and is explained below. The protection applies to all persons, whether or not they are employees, so union officials and workers in other industries are covered. The protection, which is found in section 13 of the TULR Act, means you can

1. Induce someone to break any contract, or interfere with it, or induce someone to interfere with it.

2. Threaten that any contract will be broken, or interfered with, or threaten to induce someone to break or interfere with any contact.

3. Interfere with someone's business or with his right to 'dispose of his capital or labour as he wills'.

4. Conspire to injure someone (non-physically) in a way which does not involve committing a tort.

5. Conspire to do something which is not a crime if only one person does it. (Conspiracy and Protection of Property Act 1875 section 3).

What all this means is that you can **post pickets, persuade fellow-workers not to work, ask drivers not to deliver, contact the supplying companies, ask customers and customers' workers to black goods and encourage sympathetic action. All provided you are 'acting in contemplation or furtherance of a trade dispute'.** There are a few loopholes here so the definition is important.

Trade Dispute

This must be a dispute which actually exists or is imminent. If you *think* a dispute may arise, you must wait until there is some real likelihood of it. The dispute must be between workers and employers or groups of them, or between workers and workers. Disputes with the government are covered if government workers are in dispute, or if a minister is represented on a Joint Council, or if (s)he has to be involved in settling any matter.

The dispute can be in the UK or abroad, so sympathetic action with foreign workers is covered. Wherever the dispute is, you must be acting in furtherance of it. The judges have refused to recognise some sympathetic action:

> In 1977 NUJ members were in dispute with the Daily Mirror. The leader of SOGAT, the printers' union, instructed his members at the Daily Express not to print extra copies of the Express. There is an agreement between unions and management on Fleet Street not to overprint during a dispute in another paper. The Express got an injunction against SOGAT on the grounds that the printers' refusal to handle extra papers was not taken **in furtherance of the NUJ's dispute**. They were required to print extra copies, even though this was in breach of the SOGAT agreement and SOGAT were thereby affected by the NUJ dispute. *Beaverbrook Newspapers v Keys* 1977 (HC)

In every case the dispute must be 'connected with' one of the list of matters given on page 241.

> The broadcasting unions refused to transmit the 1977 FA Cup Final to South Africa. The BBC applied for an injunction to stop the boycott. Mr Justice Pain (formerly a leading union QC) said there was a trade dispute and so he could not grant an injunction. The Court of Appeal overturned this judgment, saying the threat to black the transmission was 'coercive interference'. It could have developed into a trade dispute if the workers had said they wanted their contracts to include a term that they would not have to transmit to South Africa. But it hadn't reached that stage. The court did say that a dispute on a **matter of conscience** could, in some circumstances, be a trade dispute. But not in this case. *BBC v Hearn* 1977 (CA)

Political disputes would not usually come within the list on page 241, but they can often be manipulated to show an industrial connection.

> In 1973 the TUC called for a day of protest on 1 May against the Tories' incomes policy. 20 AUEW members,

some employed by the Ministry of Defence, claimed it was a political strike and tried to get the courts to call it off. Mr Justice Phillips said the strike wasn't strictly political because there was probably an 'infrastructure' of wage claims which were held up by the wages policy, so it was an industrial dispute. *Sherard v AUEW* 1973 (HC)

Lord Denning wanted to follow an earlier decision which declared the General Strike illegal because it was between the TUC and the government. But in the end he said that, as the government was the direct employer of at least some workers in the 1973 dispute, the strike was industrial. And Lord Justice Roskill said:

> It is all too easy for someone to talk of a strike as being a 'political strike' when what that person really means is that the object of the strike is something of which he as an individual subjectively disapproves.

A dispute between two groups of workers in pursuit of a personal grudge of a district committee member has been found to be outside the definition of furthering a trade dispute.

On the whole, therefore, **almost all non-violent actions taken during a dispute will be protected.** In practice, **no civil actions can be brought against strike leaders and those active in furthering strike action.** But this still leaves individual strikers open to legal action for breach of contract or sacking, and the problems faced by pickets are still unsolved.

Injunctions

An injunction (or an interdict in Scotland) is an order of a court requiring someone to do or not to do something. It is normally intended to preserve the status quo pending a full legal trial and can be issued very quickly, often without the person against whom it is issued having a chance to be present. This is an 'ex parte' injunction. During the 1960s and under the IR Act, it was a favourite tactic of employers in stopping union officials and shop stewards calling for industrial action on behalf of their members. They were often successful.

If a person can show a judge that **1.** he has a serious issue that he wants to bring to court, and **2.** the 'balance of convenience' in preserving the status quo is in his favour, the judge **may** order an injunction to stop a particular event occurring until the 'serious issue' has been decided finally. Because of the speed at which strikes progress, it is a powerful tool for employers. But in trade disputes it is now restricted by statute.

Strike leaders are the main targets for injunctions. Employers cannot get an injunction to stop individual workers from breaking their contracts by striking (see page 295). In a dispute injunctions cannot be issued against unions themselves, since unions cannot generally be sued. Section 17 of the TULR Act says that if it looks as though someone is likely to claim that he is 'acting in contemplation of or furtherance of a trade dispute', the court must give him every opportunity to attend. If an injunction is to be granted, the court (except in Scotland) must consider whether it is *likely* that the person involved will succeed in showing (s)he has the defence of acting in a trade dispute.

On paper it is highly improbable that injunctions can be used to crush a strike. But by granting injunctions against union leaders, the judges have got round the TULR Act's protections preventing action by broadcasting unions (see page 301) and stopping NUPE action against public expenditure cuts in Scotland in 1977.

Lock-outs

The employer's crudest weapon is the lock-out. Because he controls the plant, premises and pay, the employer's opportunities for exerting pressure are unlimited; he rarely needs a full lock-out. A lock-out is defined in the CE Act as the closing of a workplace, or suspension of work, or refusal to continue employing people because of a dispute, done with a view to *either* compelling workers to accept terms and conditions *or* to helping another employer. Unless the employer gives the notice necessary to terminate every worker's contract of employment, or there is a provision in a collective agreement, a lock-out is a breach of contract but **not necessarily equivalent to a sacking**.

> Ten lorry drivers, members of the TGWU, held a one-day strike for better wages in August. The next day the boss refused to give them any work until they signed an agreement that effectively reduced the wages of eight of them by substituting the bonus scheme for a percentage increase. They refused and were locked out. Seven weeks later in October they were given their cards. The NIRC said they were dismissed *in October* because of redundancy and were entitled to payment. The lock-out in August did not amount to a sacking. *Davis Transport v Chattaway* 1972 (NIRC)

This is obviously the right way to look at lock-outs, and strikes should be treated in the same way. But, as we have seen, other courts have been quick to say that strikes don't suspend contracts but terminate them.

Dismissal of *all* workers by means of a lock-out and refusal to re-engage *any* of them means that tribunals cannot even *consider* a claim of unfair dismissal (page 296). But if there is no real dispute – if, for example, management closes the gates one day – the lock-out constitutes unfair dismissal. A court might uphold a union claim for an injunction in this situation, although this has not yet been tried.

A lock-out without notices equivalent to every worker's appropriate entitlement is a breach of contract and wages in lieu can be claimed.

Strikes and redundancy

If you are given notice that you are being made redundant and decide to strike to oppose the plan, you will not prejudice your right to a redundancy payment if the strike fails to stop the redundancies. (Redundancy Payments Act (RP Act) section 10). Your boss can require you to return to work after the strike to work out the balance of your notice. The same is probably true if you sit-in, as the definition of a strike (see page 290) seems to include a sit-in. It may not include a **work-in** or other industrial action. In this case, section 10 gives a tribunal **discretion** to order your boss to make a redundancy payment or part of one.

A frequent ploy used by employers is to threaten redundancy during the course of a strike, saying that the strike has caused a reduction in the need for particular kinds of work. He may have lost customers, for example. If this happens, you are in trouble. Striking is almost always a serious breach of contract. An employer can avoid making a redundancy payment if he sacks a worker who has committed gross misconduct. (RP Act section 2.) A strike may amount to this. (See *Simmons v Hoover* page 296.)

This gives a free hand to employers contemplating mass redundancies. All they have to do is spread a few rumours, wait for a strike and then sack all the workforce. As the strike is misconduct, there is no need to pay redundancy. And as all the workers are sacked, none can claim unfair dismissal. Since gross misconduct entitles the employer to dismiss instantly, you do not get your notice or wages in lieu. **This**

power has been in employers' hands since 1965, and the labour movement has taken no steps to remove it.

If you are made redundant *after* the strike is over, you can claim redundancy pay. For example, if your boss loses customers during the strike and has to make people redundant, the fact that you have been on strike does not prejudice your right to pay. Selection of former strikers for redundancy has been held to be fair. (See *Cruickshank v Hobbs* page 178.)

Strikes and social security

Social security benefits can be denied to workers involved in strikes and lock-outs. Supplementary benefits can be made to their dependents.

You cannot get unemployment or social security benefits if you are on strike or are laid off because of a stoppage due to a trade dispute at your place of employment in which you are participating or directly interested. See page 212.

Strikes and continuity of employment

The basic rule is that a week during any part of which you were on strike does not count in adding up your total continuous service, but it does not break it either. How you calculate your length of continuous employment for redundancy, maternity, compensation and other purposes is dealt with in chapter 21.

Summary

As we have seen, strike activity is surrounded by legal restrictions. The initiative to take legal action lies almost exclusively with employers and it is up to them to decide what to do. There is no guarantee that strikers will be in the clear legally, whatever they do. **The extent to which employers launch legal offensives depends on their financial strength, the availability of substitute labour, the political climate, public feeling and the solidarity of the strikers and their supporters.** The following broad rules sum up the position of workers in dispute:

1. Most strikes involve breaches of contract. The only exceptions are:

    a. strikes where you have given proper notice and resign.

b. strikes which have been deliberately provoked or engineered by employers, or where the employers have seriously broken their contracts with you.

c. strikes in which contracts of employment are regarded as suspended.

2. Almost all other industrial action involves breaches of contract. The only probable exceptions are:

a. a ban on voluntary overtime;

b. a withdrawal of goodwill;

but even these might be considered as 'wilful disruption' and hence a breach (unlikely).

3. Breach of contract in these circumstances usually, but not always, entitles your employer to sack you without notice or wages in lieu.

4. He can, alternatively, sue you for breach of contract but in practice never will.

5. Provided *all* the workers who ever took part in the industrial action are sacked, no one can make a claim. But if there is some discrimination, the victims can claim unfair dismissal.

6. Anyone, whether fellow-workers, shop stewards or union officials, can ask people to break any contracts during a trade dispute. So sympathetic action and blacking can be encouraged.

7. There are restrictions on employers getting injunctions during a trade dispute.

8. Unions cannot be sued for civil wrongs committed in a dispute.

The need for a right to strike

The right to terminate your contract in the way the contract stipulates can in no sense be described as a right to strike. Workers' rights are undermined by: the courts regarding almost all forms of industrial action as breaches of contract, employers' right to dismiss strikers for 'misconduct', employers' freedom to carry out mass sackings. There is no point in the law giving workers the right to notice, maternity leave, time off and so on if it does not give them the right to withdraw their labour to get these rights.

We need:

1. A legal right to strike.

2. In any strike contracts of employment should automatically be suspended, to be resumed after the dispute is settled. **This is what both sides of industry intend anyway.**

3. The employers' right to dismiss for misconduct should be expressly excluded during strikes and other industrial action, if the misconduct is part of the industrial action – that is, a failure to work or a work-to-rule.

4. Schedule 1 para. 7 of the TULR Act, which leaves employers able to sack all workers engaged in industrial action, should be repealed.

19.

Picketing, Occupations and Public Meetings

The absence of legal rights / legal actions that can be used against you if you picket or occupy or demonstrate / criminal and civil liability / how to organise industrial picketing / non-industrial picketing / what to do in an occupation / police powers in public meetings and demonstrations / and a summary

There is no positive legal right to freedom of speech, to demonstrate, to picket or to hold public meetings in Britain. There is no written constitution guaranteeing these freedoms, so, in exercising what should be your rights, you are at the mercy of the police and the judges. The police have very wide powers to 'execute their duty' in preventing what they see as potential disturbances. In addition, employers, landlords and their agents, local authorities and embassies, when confronted by a well-organised picket, may rush to the courts and will be treated sympathetically by the judges. Lord Chief Justice Hewart said in 1936:

> English law does not recognise any special right of public meeting either for a political or any other purpose. The right of assembly . . . is nothing more than a view taken by the courts.

Still, if you know your rights on a picket-line or a demonstration, you may be able to put the police on their best behaviour or even get a policeman to reverse a decision.

Pickets in an industrial dispute are given a very limited protection against some legal threats. But in practice non-prosecution of pickets is due to police toleration of them, rather than the existence of a 'right to picket'.

Where to find the law

The main statutes the police can use against you are: Highways Act 1959 section 121 (obstruction); Police Act 1964 section 51 (obstructing the police); Conspiracy and Protection of Property Act 1875 section 7 (intimidation); Public Order Act 1936 (offensive or racist language); Prevention of Crime Act 1953 section 1 (offensive weapon); Criminal Law Act 1977 sections 1–11 (conspiracy, entering property, obstructing court officers). See also Trade Union and Labour Relations Act 1974 (TULR Act) Section 15.

Summary of main legal threats

Criminal Offences

Obstruction

Section 121 of the Highways Act 1959 says that anyone who, without lawful authority or excuse, wilfully obstructs the highway commits an offence and can be arrested without a warrant. There is scope for arguing that you are protected as long as you use the highway reasonably. Lord Chief Justice Parker said in *Nagy v Weston* (1965):

> It depends on all the circumstances, including the length of time the obstruction continues, the place where it occurs, the purpose for which it is done and, of course, whether it does in fact cause an actual as opposed to a potential obstruction.

In practice this approach appears too liberal, since many campaigners have been convicted for doing nothing more than causing a technical breach of section 121. You can argue reasonableness, but the Act makes *any* wilful obstruction illegal. The maximum penalty is a £50 fine.

Public nuisance

Behaviour that materially affects 'the reasonable comfort and convenience of life of a class of Her Majesty's subjects' is a public nuisance **at common law**, and a **prosecution** can be brought. Or the Attorney-General can ask for a civil injunction to get the nuisance stopped. There must be discomfort to a class of persons, such as a group of shopkeepers or residents affected by picketing. An individual can do nothing if (s)he is just obstructed by a picket, but if (s)he is actually injured, (s)he can sue for damages in the civil courts or ask the police to prosecute. Local authorities are given wide powers by the Control of Pollution Act 1974. They could serve a notice on a **noisy** picket or public meeting and have the noise stopped.

Obstructing the police

Section 51 of the Police Act 1964 says that it is an offence to assault a constable carrying out his duty, for which you can get two years inside and an unlimited fine. If you 'resist or wilfully obstruct', you can get one month inside and a £200 fine.

The officer must be doing his duty – if he tells you to move on, it must be because, for instance, you are causing an unreasonable obstruction, or because he considers there are reasonable grounds for saying that some disruption (a 'breach of the peace') is genuinely likely to occur if you don't. The scope of his duty is very wide.

> In 1934, a woman was held to have obstructed the police when she held a meeting of unemployed workers outside a means test centre after being told to hold it elsewhere. It was alleged that a similar meeting 14 months earlier had led to a disturbance, so the police were acting to stop a breach of the peace. The disturbance was that workers had sung 'The Red Flag'. *Duncan v Jones* 1936 (HC)

A policeman has no right to detain you for questioning, so if you resist this with reasonable force you are, unless arrested, not interfering with the exercise of his duty.

Intimidation, following and watching

Section 7 of the Conspiracy and Protection of Property Act 1875 says that it is an offence if you 'wrongfully and without legal authority' use violence against or intimidate a person or his family, persistently follow him around or 'watch and beset' his house or business premises, with a view to compelling him to do or not do something he has a legal right not to do or do. This section was used extensively in 1926. Charges of intimidation were brought against 12 building workers in Flint following a national strike in 1972. They were all acquitted. The Shrewsbury pickets (see below) were convicted of **conspiracy** to intimidate, that is, the Act was used as a peg on which to hang the conspiracy charge.

Non-violent industrial picketing is protected against

charges of following and watching and besetting by the TULR Act. Non-industrial picketing isn't – see the Prebbles tenants' case, *Hubbard v Pitt* (page 319 below).

Conspiracy

This offence was created by the judges and added to by them over the years without an Act of Parliament. In other words, it was a common law offence, for which the punishment was unlimited. The Criminal Law Act 1977 makes conspiracy a statutory offence, although some common law conspiracies remain.

Conspiracy is an agreement by two or more people 'that a course of conduct shall be pursued which will necessarily . . . involve the commission of any offence . . . if the agreement is carried out in accordance with their intentions'.

It is the **agreement** that has always worried the ruling class. Organisations of workers represent a threat – whether or not you carry out your agreed aim, you are guilty of an offence.

If, during an industrial dispute, you agree to do something unlawful at **civil** law – to break a contract or to cause a nuisance – you cannot be prosecuted for conspiracy. Agreements to do something criminal are unprotected unless the criminal act itself does not carry a penalty of imprisonment. So you can't be charged with **conspiracy to cause an obstruction** if you agree to picket.

Since the 1977 Act you can't get more for *conspiring* to do something illegal than you could get if you were convicted of doing the act itself. If you carry out your agreement, there is nothing to stop the prosecution charging you with conspiracy *and* with the offence itself. During the Tory administration of 1970–74, several outrageous prosecutions were brought – including the trial of the Shrewsbury pickets:

> Between July and September 1972 there was a national strike of building workers for higher wages. During the strike self-employed Lump labour continued to work. The strike action committee in Chester and North Wales organised coaches to transport strikers to picket building sites where Lump labour and others were still at work. Six shop stewards on the committee were arrested in Shrewsbury while on a flying picket. 13 months later they came before Mr Justice Mais and a jury at Shrewsbury, facing 42 charges. Only three were proceeded with. The others -- intimidation, damage to property, threatening behaviour and assault were 'left on the file'. All six workers were convicted of unlawful assault and each got

two years' suspended sentence. John Jones, Eric
Tomlinson and Dennis Warren were convicted by a
majority of 10–2 of **conspiracy** to intimidate workers to
abstain from working, and unanimously of affray. They
got a total of 9 months, 2 years and 3 years respectively.
The Court of Appeal quashed the affray convictions but
upheld the rest. The three men served their full sentences,
despite massive rank-and-file pressure and some corridor
lobbying by the TUC for their release. *The Queen v Jones
and Others* 1974 (CA)

The following points can be made about the case:

1. The charges were not brought until long after the
strike, following instructions by Robert Carr, the then Home
Secretary, to get tough in industrial disputes.

2. Charges of actual assault and intimidation were
brought in a similar earlier trial in Flint and the men acquitted.
These charges were not pressed at Shrewsbury.

3. Instead, **conspiracy** charges were used, making the
prosecution's job easier. Hearsay evidence and evidence against
others can be introduced. The judge could also pass sentences
much higher than could be passed for intimidation. (The 1977
Act restricts this right.)

4. By the time the final appeals were heard in March
1974, Labour was already in office. Roy Jenkins, the Home
Secretary, thereafter steadfastly refused to free the pickets.

5. Demands by the TUC for a right to picket and to stop
vehicles were ignored by the Labour government.

6. Only in 1977 did the Inland Revenue take firm
measures to control tax evasion by Lump labour.

7. UCATT and the TGWU, whose members were in
gaol, and the TUC, refused demands for official industrial
action to free them.

Offences under the Public Order Act 1936

Section 5 was amended by the Race Relations Act 1976.
It is an offence, punishable by two years inside and an unlimited fine, for anyone in a public place or public meeting to
use threatening, abusive or insulting words or behaviour, or to
distribute or display anything threatening, abusive or insulting,
with the **intention** or **likelihood** of provoking a breach of the
peace or stirring up racial hatred. Colin Jordan and John
Tyndall were convicted for saying 'Hitler was right' in
Trafalgar Square in 1962, because this led 'hooligans', that is,
anti-fascists, to break up the meeting.

On the directions of Judge McKinnon, John Kingsley

Read was acquitted in 1978 of similar charges following a National Party speech when he talked of 'niggers, wogs and coons' and said 'a million to go' following the murder of a young Asian. McKinnon said this wasn't racist!

Possessing an offensive weapon

Section 1 of the Prevention of Crime Act 1953 creates the offence of carrying an offensive weapon in a public place 'without lawful authority or reasonable excuse'. Unusually in English and Scots law, it is down to the accused to prove (s)he had an excuse or had no intention of using it as a weapon. Since 'offensive weapon' would include acid, pepper, workers' tools, placards and even, as was alleged in a 1975 prosecution of Newcastle building workers, a shoe, the scope for police harassment in a demonstration or picket-line is very wide.

Criminal trespass

Trespass has always been a common law civil wrong. In the past, occasionally, it was also a crime – on railways, public utilities and in the vicinity of explosives factories, and if there is an intention to steal, rape or injure. If you squat or sit-in and refuse to leave, or enter premises without permission, you are a trespasser. You need not do any damage or cause any loss to the normal occupier.

In the last few years, as the courts have realised how squatting and occupations threaten property rights, they have developed special rules of civil procedure (see below). Parliament has also passed the Criminal Law Act 1977 which contains serious restrictions on direct action.

This creates the following new criminal offences:

1. Violent entry

It is illegal to use or threaten violence to secure entry to any premises if there is someone present on the premises and you know this. Violence or the threat of it can be directed against people or property. The maximum sentence is two years inside after trial by a jury.

2. Remaining on property

It is an offence to fail to leave premises when requested to do so by a 'displaced residential occupier' or by a person who has bought the premises, provided you entered the premises as a trespasser. Residential occupation is not defined and might be proved by a landlord who doesn't actually live on the premises, but leaves some furniture and occasionally visits them.

You could get six months inside and a £1,000 fine for this offence. You have no right to a jury trial.

3. Trespassing with an offensive weapon

If you have entered any premises as a trespasser and have an 'offensive weapon' with you, you could get two years inside and a fine, after a jury trial. Offensive weapon is widely interpreted – see above.

4. Trespassing in embassies

This is designed to prevent direct action against offensive foreign governments and follows protests in the embassies of Iran, Syria, Cuba, Bangladesh and Libya. You could get one year in prison after a jury trial.

5. Resisting bailiffs

If your employer or landlord gets a civil court order to evict you, it must be enforced by a court officer. This is either a full-time bailiff or one **authorised for this occasion** – which could mean an employee or agent of your boss. If you resist or wilfully obstruct him, you could get six months inside and a £1,000 fine. You have no right to a jury trial.

A policeman in uniform can arrest you without a warrant if he has reasonable grounds for believing you have committed any of these five offences. In order to arrest you for one of these offences he can also enter and search any premises without a warrant if he suspects that you are there.

Civil liability

Civil trespass

New procedures in the High Court (Order 113) and the County Court (Order 26) have been introduced to make it easy for property-owners and occupiers to evict you. Civil writs for possession can be served on *unnamed persons*, they need not be given to you *personally* and can be left in a bag at a factory gate. If orders for possession are obtained against a group of workers, they can be used against a completely different group if the composition has changed by the time the bailiffs arrive, even though the order was not made against them and they have had no opportunity to state their case.

Trespass to the highway

Committed by anyone who uses the highway in an unreasonable manner, that is, for anything other than travelling along. Industrial pickets are protected from this law. People taking part in unlawful or disorderly public meetings are not. Local authorities usually own the highway and, although they rarely sue, they might resort to suing for trespass if their **own** offices were continuously picketed.

Nuisance

For private nuisance there must be some interference with someone's enjoyment of their *land*. Smells, smoke, noise, vibration, queues, cars can all be a nuisance, as can a large demonstration or public meeting. Actual damage need not be proved – it is enough for someone to say he objects to a particular activity because it diminishes his enjoyment of his land and thereby causes him a 'loss'. Damages and injunctions can be awarded.

The way in which all these legal threats affect picketing, occupations and meetings is dealt with in the following sections.

Industrial picketing

The only time the law gives you a written right to engage in protest activities in a public place is when you are picketing in connection with a trade dispute. Since the Trade Disputes Act of 1906 there has been a clear right, on paper at least, to picket. **It is severely restricted by the criminal law and by the judges.** What protection we now have is given by section 15 of the TULR Act which says:

> It shall be lawful for one or more persons in contemplation or furtherance of a trade dispute to attend at or near – **A.** a place where another person works or carries on business; or **B.** any other place where another person happens to be, not being a place where he resides, for the purpose only of peacefully obtaining or communicating information, or peacefully persuading any person to work or abstain from working.

While this looks like a fairly broad right there are many restraints and the right can be summarised as follows:

1. The picketing (which, incidentally, is not defined)

must be in connection with a trade dispute that **exists** or is **imminent**. (See page 301 for what this means.)

2. You may attend a place for the specified purposes only. If what you do goes beyond mere attendance for the specified purposes you lose the cover of the Act. So if you try to **stop vehicles** or people who do not want to be informed or persuaded by you, you are exceeding the permitted purposes.

3. You can give or seek information, and you can persuade people not to work (and to work!). You are *not* covered as a picket if you try to persuade consumers not to use a product or workers to black a product.

4. The site of the picket can be anywhere except the residence of the person you are picketing. If the premises you are picketing are both commercial and residential, you are protected, as the right applies to any workplace and is not excluded simply because hotel workers, school and factory caretakers, or even managing directors, live there. It does not protect pickets once they are on private premises, for example, during a sit-in. Employers can use the civil law of trespass or the Criminal Law Act 1977 to evict them.

5. The police may always intervene under one of the criminal Acts listed above. If you create an unreasonable obstruction, or a potential disturbance, or in any other way exceed the narrow right of attendance for the specified purposes, you are open to various **civil** liabilities and it is more likely that the police will intervene to enforce the **criminal** law.

There are four detailed problems that you will need to know about if you are running a picket.

1. moving pickets
2. numbers of pickets
3. stopping vehicles and people
4. police consent

Moving pickets

As the highway is to be used for travelling along, you might think it would be lawful to do this carrying placards. This idea occurred to the chairman of a technicians' strike committee during an official dispute at English Electric in 1964.

Harold Tynan was leading about forty pickets in a circle outside the directors' and visitors' entrance on the East Lancs Road, Liverpool. He was told to stop the circling and, when he refused, he was arrested for obstructing a policeman in the execution of his duty (and also for intimidation, but this was not proved). The full-time ('stipendiary') magistrate, the Liverpool Recorder and the High Court all upheld the police decision. It was an obstruction of the highway, and so the police were entitled to break the picket up. The pickets had intended to seal off the entrance so **their purposes exceeded those of information and peaceful persuasion.** *Tynan v Balmer* 1966 (HC)

So moving pickets have no special advantage.

Number of pickets

The law does not stipulate how many pickets are lawful, but the police have the power to limit the size of a picket if they anticipate that a breach of the peace will occur. Police, judges and employers know that the larger the picket-line, the more effective it will be in furthering industrial action. The Liverpool Recorder in *Tynan v Balmer* said:

> I can quite see the value, from the point of view of advertising the strike and underlining the number of people involved and demonstrating their solidarity, of having a substantial number of people near the prestige entrance, but forty seems to me to be a number far in excess of what was reasonably required.

He wanted to see only two or three, so he allowed the leader to be fined.

In *Piddington v Bates* 1960 (HC) a policeman restricted the number of pickets at a plant on strike to two on each entrance. When a worker tried to join the line, he was arrested for obstructing the policeman in the execution of his duty. The courts upheld this decision but refused to make a ruling that two pickets are sufficient in *any* situation. Lord Chief Justice Parker said it was up to the discretion of local police in every case. This means that a local police force can't make a general ruling about the number of pickets *in advance*.

In 1974, the NUM posted a maximum of six accredited pickets on each pit. This not only dissuaded entrants, but also deprived the police of an excuse to intervene. Naturally, though, a miners' strike effectively closes all pits and the need for pickets at these sites is less pressing than at power stations, rail yards and docks.

Mass picketing, such as was seen at Saltley coke-works in 1972, at Shrewsbury during the 1972 national building strike and at Grunwicks, has been very successful. The law does not expressly say how many pickets you can have, but nor does it allow an unlimited number. Lord Reid said in John Broome's case (below):

> The section (now section 15) does not limit the number
> of pickets and no limitation of numbers can be im-
> plied ... But ... it would not be difficult to infer as a
> matter of fact that pickets who assemble in unreasonably
> large numbers do have the purpose of preventing free
> passage.

In other words there comes a time when the mere size
of the picket deprives it of its limited protection. However, it
is at this stage that mass arrests become impracticable. For
this reason and because it is a demonstration of solidarity,
mass picketing is usually the most effective method.

Stopping vehicles and people

The right to attend to communicate information, and
to persuade someone not to work, does not extend to stopping
vehicles and people who do not want to stop.

> During the 1972 building workers' strike, John Broome, a
> union official, held up a placard and stood in front of a
> lorry which was trying to enter a site. The lorry driver
> stopped and listened and then tried to manoeuvre round
> the picket. A policeman arrived and Broome was arrested
> for obstructing the highway. The magistrates found that
> the whole operation took only nine minutes, that this was
> a reasonable period of time and that otherwise the right
> to picket was meaningless. The House of Lords over-
> turned the decision, saying he lost the protection of the
> Act when he tried to do more than 'peacefully persuade',
> that is, when he stopped the vehicle. *Broome v DPP* 1974
> (HL)

The judges in this case were divided about the scope of
the right to persuade. Lord Reid, for instance, said that you
have the right to stand about and try to persuade people, and
even to walk along with them, but if the person decides he has
heard enough, or does not want to listen at all, you have no
right to detain him. Nor can you stand in the road and halt a
vehicle.

If the police **prevent you from communicating** with
people, there is nothing you can do to exercise your right to
persuade:

> Peter Kavanagh, a former TGWU official, was outside
> St Thomas's Hospital building site in 1973 during an
> electricians' strike. Scab labour was being used and when
> a coach-load of blacklegs left the site, the police formed
> a cordon and **refused to allow even the four official pickets
> to speak to them.** Kavanagh tried to push through and
> when stopped, punched a policeman. He was fined £20
> for assaulting and obstructing a policeman, who was

executing his duty to prevent a breach of the peace.
Kavanagh v Hiscock 1974. (HC)

Identical tactics were used daily by the police in 1977 at Grunwicks. (See page 7.)

So, by trying to stop a vehicle and by trying simply to speak to blackleg workers when the police deny you access to them, you lose the limited protection of the Act. You are liable to some or all of the civil and criminal actions described at the beginning of this chapter.

Police consent

As we have seen, the police have substantial control over pickets. Often small numbers of officially accredited pickets are left alone. But even if you escape interference by the police, civil injunctions are still possible, as happened in *Hubbard v Pitt*, where a tenants' group mounted a picket with the full knowledge of the police who did not intervene at all (see below). And an orderly picket can become the source of individual prosecutions if one policeman decides to exercise his authority at any particular time – see *Tynan v Balmer* (page 316).

Non-industrial picketing

If you think your rights to picket in industrial disputes are puny, they are almost non-existent where there is no trade dispute. Consumers protesting against a store, women campaigning against discrimination in banking and insurance, parents protesting against a school's policy, voters complaining of cuts in public expenditure, tenants seeking to expose racketeering – none of these groups has a right to picket under the TULR Act. Whether or not they have any *other* right is unclear, and depends on an interpretation of one case.

Hubbard v Pitt was heard in 1975 by the Court of Appeal but as it was about an application for a temporary injunction, it was not a full hearing. So the judges were only giving a preliminary view. But, as with most injunctions, the preliminary judgment decided the whole issue.

James Pitt and nine others objected to the property speculation going on in London in the early 1970s. In Islington a tenants' group picketed the offices of Prebbles, an estate agent which they claimed had been harassing and winkling out tenants. They were there on Saturday mornings, in numbers of up to eight. The picket was orderly and aimed to give information to passers-by. The

> firm claimed the picket was a private nuisance and asked
> for an injunction to stop it. This was granted because a
> 'serious question' had arisen concerning their property
> rights. The pickets had no protection under any Act, so
> they were banned until the serious question could be
> tried. *Hubbard v Pitt* 1975 (CA)

The Court of Appeal confirmed the injunction by a
two-to-one majority. The majority said the presence of the
pickets constituted a nuisance because they were 'watching
and besetting' the office with a view to compelling people not
to do something they had a right to do. In slapping on the
injunction, the judges said that the **interference with free
speech was a minimal worry compared with the possible loss to
the agent's business**. The judges said the pickets might not be
able to pay for any losses Prebbles might suffer, but Prebbles
could afford to compensate the pickets for any loss *they* might
suffer for interference with their free speech if Prebbles lost the
case. So the 'balance of convenience' lay with granting an
injunction.

But Lord Denning did not agree, and what he said *may*
provide the basis of a **common law right to picket** in non-
industrial situations. What he said was:

> There was no obstruction, no violence, no intimidation, no
> molestation, no noise, no smells, nothing except a group of
> six or seven people standing about with placards outside
> [Prebbles'] premises all quite orderly and well-behaved.
> That cannot be said to be a nuisance at common law.

In other words, **orderly picketing even if done with the intention
of compelling someone not to do what he has a lawful right to do,
is acceptable** if this interpretation of the law is subsequently
followed.

Occupations

The Criminal Law Act 1977 and the procedures in the
civil courts make it easy for the police and the courts to
support employers against workers who are occupying a plant.
The offence of violent entry is committed if someone – a
security guard for instance – *believes* violence has been
threatened. Sheer numbers of workers might constitute a
threat. Entry from one part of a plant to another – for example from the shopfloor to the administration offices –
might make you a trespasser. You are then guilty of remaining
there after being told to leave.

Many items found in a factory could become offensive weapons in the imagination of the police and judges. Lying down in front of your boss's agents, authorised by a court to serve an eviction order, means you are committing an offence. The new powers of the police to intervene on suspicion of any of these offences means that occupations have become a public rather than a private industrial matter.

You can minimise the threat of police intervention in an occupation, or stall it temporarily, if you:

1. stay on the part of the plant where you are entitled to be.

2. don't enter residential areas unless the workers who live there agree, for example, in hotels, ships, farms.

3. don't carry tools or anything that could remotely be considered 'offensive'.

4. gain entry with a key, or by consent of someone inside.

5. don't enter in such large numbers, or in such an aggressive way that a charge of threatened violence is credible.

6. don't damage any property or plant while the occupation is on.

7. If the bailiffs do get in, demand to see credentials and a court order. Bear in mind that only police **in uniform** can intervene without a warrant, and they must have reasonable suspicion that an offence under the Act has been committed – ask them to specify their grounds.

Public meetings and demonstrations

Many workers talk of the right of free speech. But as it is not a right contained in any Act of Parliament, it is elastic and easily manipulated by the police and judges. There is, for instance, no general right to hold a meeting in a public place. The only time you can **demand** premises from a local authority is on behalf of a candidate in a parliamentary or local government election. (Representation of the People Act 1949).

In some towns the police control the holding of meetings because local by-laws require that police permission must be obtained before a meeting can take place – in many parks, for example. In fact, though, if there is no by-law, public meetings cannot be banned in advance by the police. Demonstrations can. However, some **civil** liability may be incurred if you use a roadway for a public meeting, because roadways are usually owned by local authorities who make them available for 'reasonable use', by people, which means for passing to and fro along. If you do anything in excess of this 'privilege', you can be sued by the local authority for **trespass to the highway** (page 315). In practice this power isn't used and it is the police who break up meetings.

On what basis can they do this? It is usually to prevent a breach of the peace, or an obstruction. In one case police who entered **private** premises and broke up a public meeting acted lawfully. It is not clear whether they can do so if they merely suspect a breach of the peace – they probably can't – or whether there must be a suspicion of sedition, that is, serious anti-government agitation. If a breach of the peace – any disruption – actually occurs, the police can enter premises and put it down. The police can intervene in a meeting wherever a breach of the Public Order Act (above) occurs, or where it is expected to occur.

A **demonstration** is technically a reasonable use of the highway. Each participant is doing what (s)he is entitled to do on the highway, that is to walk along it. But the police can intervene on the grounds of obstruction, and if you do not do as you are told you are obstructing the police in the execution of their duty.

In addition, the Public Order Act, passed to try to stamp out Fascist marches, allows the police to lay down the route that must be followed by a demonstration if there is a risk of serious disorder. If that is considered inadequate they can ask the appropriate local authority (Home Secretary in the Metropolitan Police area) to ban certain demonstrations for up to three months. The police refused to ban National Front marches in Lewisham and Ladywood in 1977, despite pleas for these Acts to be enforced. However, in order to prevent a National Front march in Manchester in 1977 the police used the Public Order Act, for the first time in recent years, to ban *all* marches for five weeks.

A failure to observe directions or a ban would mean prosecution for unlawful assembly, obstructing the police and worse. Forty Right to Work marchers were prosecuted in 1976–77 following contradictory police instructions when they marched through Hendon, North London.

What happens if you meet a counter-demonstration which tries to disrupt your demo or meeting? The law is unclear. But in 1902 a Liverpool Orangeman was 'bound over to keep the peace' when he led a march into a Catholic area and caused a disturbance. He was found to have known that disruption would be obvious, **because he used insulting language and behaviour**. (*Wise v Dunning*). National Front marchers in immigrant areas could be charged with this. If they actually assault people, they can be charged with various offences.

Summary

1. You have no positive right to picket, sit-in, demonstrate or hold public meetings.

2. You have a very limited protection from some **civil** liability if you are picketing in an industrial dispute.

3. Non-industrial picketing is not protected, but it is **arguable** that there is a limited common law right.

4. Police discretion to intervene, to control the number and location of pickets is very wide. They have total power over pickets.

5. In practice, agreement with the police on numbers has been effective. **The most effective picketing method is mass picketing.**

6. The Criminal Law Act is a disincentive to workers occupying a workplace and the police have wide powers to intervene on suspicion without a warrant.

7. The civil law is not as quick, but can be used by property owners against pickets, and against workers occupying a workplace.

8. Police powers to ban or re-route a march are extensive.

20.
Saving Jobs

Direct action to prevent redundancies / using the law if direct action fails / your union's right to be consulted / which employers must consult / what consultation means / when it must begin / how employers can get out of consulting / how to claim a protective award / your boss's duty to notify the Department of Employment / government measures to reduce unemployment / a summary / and what to demand if redundancy is threatened.

Direct action by many workers in the 1960s forced government and managements to acknowledge that their policies meant mass sackings. The White Paper *In Place of Strife* conceded:

> The disparity of power between employee and employer, though much reduced, still persists, particularly in areas where trade unionism is weak. Lock-outs are now almost unknown, but in their place has come the new threat of widespread redundancies as industry is restructured and mergers multiply.

Still, no action was taken to require employers to negotiate with unions or to inform the Department of Employment (DE) about proposed redundancies until 1975. Workers have no right to work and government agencies have no power to veto sackings. Instead the EP Act gives workers a right to (limited) monetary compensation and the DE can withhold a fraction of employers' rebates of redundancy pay.

Sometimes workers have done better themselves:

■ In 1971 shipyard workers started a work-in on the Clyde and forced the government to keep Upper Clyde Shipbuilders going.

■ An 18-month work-in at Fisher-Bendix in Kirkby forced the government to give support to keep the factory going as a workers' co-operative. The financial targets set for it were quite unrealistic, especially as under private ownership it had failed four times, but the co-op succeeded in staying afloat.

■ Many jobs were saved when workers making motor-bikes in Meriden occupied the plant and forced the government to give aid to their workers' co-operative.

Your first response to all redundancies must be resistance. Only if all your efforts fail do you need to look at the statutory methods of fighting.

Your rights to notice, redundancy pay, protection against your boss's bankruptcy and unemployment benefit are dealt with in chapters 10, 11 and 12. This chapter deals with action your union can take.

Throughout, the definition of redundancy is the same as that used in chapter 11.

Where to find the law

Sections 99–107 of the Employment Protection Act 1975 (EP Act) deal with consultation and notification.

The union's right to be consulted

Section 99 of the EP Act requires employers to consult recognised independent unions about **every** proposed redundancy. So long as the union is recognised for workers of the description the employer proposes to sack, union representatives (full-time, or lay if they are recognised for negotiations) must be consulted. It does not matter whether the proposals relate to members of the same or another union, or non-members, or to workers of the same description in another location.

A union is recognised if the employer negotiates with it over any of the list of matters set out on page 241. There doesn't have to be a formal agreement – recognition can be inferred from the conduct of the union and the employer, provided this clearly shows the intention to recognise:

A TGWU member was sacked by a Scottish haulage firm. Trade unionists on the docks blacked the company. A union official offered to lift the blacking if the member was re-instated and this was agreed. Later three union members

> were made redundant. When the TGWU claimed under section 99 the EAT said the union was not recognised, and recognition could not be inferred from the earlier meeting as **the employer never intended it**. *TGWU v Andrew Dyer* 1977 (EAT)

An employer who belongs to an employers' association which negotiates with a union does not *necessarily* recognise the union, according to the EAT. It is an important factor, but the union will need to show that **the employer** (not just the association) negotiates with the union.

Who is covered?

The Act applies to all workers threatened with redundancy whether or not they are entitled to redundancy pay. **So workers with less than two years' service, and part-timers are covered.**

The Act applies to all employers except the Crown, some parts of the National Health Service, the police and the armed forces, and employers of: self-employed workers, registered dockers, share fishermen, workers who ordinarily work outside Great Britain, merchant seamen, workers covered by an agreement approved by the Employment Secretary, and short-term workers. This last group is a major escape route for employers.

Short-term workers according to section 119 are: **1.** workers on fixed term (that is, unalterable) contracts of 12 or less weeks; **2.** workers taken on to do a specific task which is not expected to last more than 12 weeks. If in either of these cases they actually work more than 12 weeks, they are protected. Clearly many workers will be excluded in jobs with fluctuating prospects such as building, catering, shipbuilding, ship repair and supply teaching.

An employer claiming to be exempt must prove it. This means showing that the duration of the work was fully explained at the point of hire, or that the workers must have known there was a custom and practice of short-term contracts.

> Swan Hunters took on 17 painters to paint a ship. They were told they would be on 'short-term contracts' but this was not fully explained. Their union was told the job would last only three-to-four weeks, and the DE was notified. All the painters were sacked within four weeks and UCATT claimed the employers had failed to consult them. The Newcastle tribunal said the union and the DE had been notified of the hiring, and as shiprepair is a 'type of "in and out" occupation', the men must have

known they were on short-term contracts. *UCATT v Swan Hunters Shiprepairers (Tyne) Ltd.* 1976 (IT)

Abuses of the Act are common in these vulnerable trades, with employers taking on workers for 12 weeks, sacking them, and later re-engaging them. **Remember** you are considered to have been employed continuously unless you are unemployed for a whole week, Sunday to Saturday. And in any event you might be able to show this was absence due to a 'temporary cessation of work'. (See chapter 21).

What is consultation?

The EP Act requires consultation not negotiation. But if your union is recommended by ACAS for recognition for collective bargaining your boss must **negotiate** or risk a claim for failing to recognise you. Consultation is a lighter responsibility. Section 99 says it means giving **in writing** to the union:

1. the reasons for the proposals, for instance, lack of orders, automation.
2. the numbers and descriptions (that is, what they do) of those affected, for example, by department, skill, shift.
3. the *total* number of workers in those descriptions.
4. how the employer proposes to select them, for example, last-in-first-out, age.
5. how the employer proposes to carry out the sacking, for instance, timing, calling for volunteers, methods of payment.

After this, your boss *must*

1. consider the points made by the union; and
2. reply to them, giving reasons for any he rejects.

When must consultation begin?

Consultation over any redundancy must begin 'at the earliest opportunity'. When **mass sackings** are proposed the following timetable must be observed as a **minimum**:

■ If 100 or more workers are to be sacked at one establishment over a period of up to 90 days: consult at least **90 days** before the first sacking;

■ If 10 or more (but less than 100) workers are to be sacked at one establishment over a period of up to 30 days: consult at least **60 days** before the first sacking. This means employers must give information and begin consultation as soon as they **propose** to make cuts. A Nottingham tribunal has said:

> Indeed until that information is supplied there is probably
> not a great deal of point in entering into consultation
> because the information is what the trade union needs in
> order to consult with the employers. *EESA v Ashwell
> Scott* 1976 (IT)

If your boss ignores this timetable, all workers sacked can get
compensation.

> **Example:** if the board of XYZ Ltd wants to sack 50
> workers during September the following minimum
> timetable must be followed:
> 1 **July** – Board meets and decides in principle on 50
>   redundancies. Notifies local union official and shop
>   steward by letter.
> 3 **July** – Union receives letter. Demands disclosure of
>   relevant information.
> 5 **July** – Employer sends information.
> 7 **July** – Union receives it. Makes representations and
>   seeks meeting.
> 7 **September** – First dismissal can take effect, that is, 60
>   days after full information given to union.

Problems

1. The consultation period

The earliest date on which notice of dismissal can be
given to each employee is 7 July. Notice can run concurrently
with the consultation period, so many employers give notice
to employees and union on the same date or a day later. Of this
the EAT has said:

> there is nothing prevent it, but that, if it is done, it may
> well be the case that . . . there has never been any meaning-
> ful consultation by the employer such as is required by
> section 99, in which case that will be a ground of complaint.
> *NUT v Avon County Council* 1978 (EAT)

If management have decided who must go and given
them their notices before the union is informed, they cannot
say the sackings are 'proposals'. The earliest opportunity for
consultation is the date the decision in principle, as opposed
to the final decision, was made. In industries like construction,
where eventual redundancy on a site is obvious from the outset,
consultation should occur when the workforce is at its peak,
hiring has ceased, and shrinkage is inevitable.

> Four UCATT members worked on a site where, at peak,
> there were 50 workers. In March 1976, 29 were made
> redundant. On 14 April the four were told there was no

more work, given a week's notice, and their convener was informed. UCATT claimed they had not been properly consulted. The London tribunal agreed, saying that consultation must begin 'when the tide has turned and the work has actually begun to run out'. But it exercised its 'discretion' not to award the men any money, as the employer was not seriously 'in default'. *UCATT v G. Ellison Carpentry Contractors* 1976 (IT)

In cases where there is only a **remote possibility** of redundancy, consultation is not required until a decision has been made to dismiss. In 1976 NUPE complained because General Cleaning Contractors failed to consult them over the possibility that 96 redundancies might occur if GCC failed to get its contract with Barking Hospital renewed. The London tribunal said consultation was not required until the tender had been turned down by the hospital.

The duty to consult the union would obviously arise earlier if the contract was *likely* to be terminated. Unions should demand full details about all renewable contracts.

2. The date of dismissal

Consultation must begin as soon as possible before the first dismissal takes effect. This means the date of the first sacking, if you are given your legal notice. If you are given money in lieu of notice your dismissal takes effect on the day you leave. So your boss can't claim that the notice-period is part of the consultation period unless you are still working. In *NUT v Avon County Council* (above) the EAT even said that consultation must begin 90 (or 60) days **before the first dismissal notice is sent.**

3. The definition of establishment

Local authorities, nationalised industries and others proposing cuts across the board in a number of departments may try to escape or reduce their obligations by saying each department is a separate establishment – even though all the departments belong to one enterprise. Geographical separation is not conclusive. A chain of bakery shops, and 20 British Gas depots in the south-east have been held to be single establishments.

4. Timing

Section 99 states that if your boss begins consultation, for example, over 50 redundancies and then decides to sack a *further* 50, he does not have to give the 90-day warning that

330 / Rights at Work

would be required if he had proposed 100 redundancies straight off. If this happens you can claim that the union was not given the full information in the first place, and so the consultation period did not begin until the second series of redundancies was announced.

If 20 redundancies are proposed during a period of **90 days,** your boss must consult at the earliest opportunity. If any 10 fall during any 30-day period, the legal minimum of 60 days consultation must begin.

Employers' defences

Employers can get out of the following obligations if they can show (and it is up to *them* to prove it) that there were **'special circumstances'** which made it **'not reasonably practicable to comply'.**

■ To consult at the earliest opportunity
■ To give the specified information
■ To consider and reply to the union's points

If your boss proves this, he must still show he took all reasonable steps to keep the rules.

The following examples show the way in which employers' claims of 'special circumstances' have been treated:

1. If a Receiver is called in, it is unlikely that section 99 will be applied meticulously. Insolvency is not on its own a reason for escaping consultation, but it *may* be if your employer delays in order to preserve a fraction of the assets, or to avoid liquidation.

2. A company failed to apply for government aid to avert redundancy. But the tribunal still said it had done everything practicable to consult.

3. A company can't escape its obligations simply by writing to the head office of the union concerned.

4. An employer can't claim the effect the news would have on the workforce as a reason for not keeping to the timetable.

How to claim

A recognised independent union which has not been consulted can complain to an industrial tribunal **within three months** of a dismissal taking place. (See page 357). It can also complain about a **threatened** sacking but, as we shall see, there may be a disadvantage in doing this when it comes to getting compensation.

If the tribunal agrees with the union, it will say consultation should take place, or information should be given. It *may* also make a **protective award**.

Compensation

A **protective award** requires your boss to pay your wages for a 'protected' period of time. The award:

■ specifies the workers covered;

■ says that your boss has sacked, or plans to sack, some of these workers on the grounds of redundancy; and

■ says that your boss failed to carry out properly the section 99 procedures for consultation, information or representation on particular sackings or proposed sackings.

The length of the protected period is decided by the tribunal but it cannot exceed the minimum consultation period. So the maximum you can get is:

■ **90 days** if 100 or more workers are to be sacked within 90 days.

■ **60 days** if 10 or more workers are to be sacked within 30 days.

■ **28 days** in any other case (that is, if less than 10 workers are involved).

The actual length of time depends on what the tribunal considers fair after taking account of the seriousness of the employer's failure to comply with any requirement of section 99. **The aim is to penalise your employer for failing to adhere to section 99.** But tribunals and the EAT have, however, taken more notice of the amount of money workers have lost.

You should bear in mind three further points. **1.** The amount of money awarded is based on a 'week's pay', not earnings. (See chapter 21). **2.** The date on which the protected period must begin is either the date of the first dismissal, or the date of the award. **3. Earnings and notice money coming from your boss can be used to offset the obligation to pay during the protected period.**

This means you are better off if your union waits until near the three-month deadline for submitting claims. Although sackings may have taken place, a protective award will actually mean something in money terms. Because you are less likely to be working, or receiving money in lieu of notice, your protective award will not have to be offset.

If you are offered different work, or work on different terms, during the protected period, you are entitled to a trial period of four weeks. If the job turns out to be unsuitable and you leave, or if you turn down the opportunity in the first place, you still get your protective award.

If your boss fails to pay you as ordered, you have **three months** in which to complain to a tribunal (see page 357). This has to be **your** claim, not the union's, although the union should represent you.

Redundancy pay and unfair dismissal

Don't forget . . . that you are still entitled to your full redundancy pay if you have two years' continuous service. This is not affected by consultation. And a failure to consult or warn about redundancy will often be grounds in itself for an **additional** claim of unfair dismissal – see page 178.

Notifying the DE

The Department of Employment must be notified about mass sackings. Section 100 of the EP Act lays down a timetable similar to section 99 with two differences. There is no overriding requirement to notify 'at the earliest opportunity'. And while an employer who sacks less than 10 workers without union consultation can be ordered to pay a protective award for 28 days, the obligation to notify the DE arises only when 10 or more redundancies are planned.

Notification must be in writing. Form HR1 (see pages 386–9) required by the DE asks for the same kind of information as must be given to unions. If a union is recognised, the form must name the union, say when consultation began, and a copy must be given to the union. This notice is in addition to the employer's claim for a rebate for redundancy pay. If you discover that this claim is made at the same time, it will be clear that the dismissals were fixed and proper consultation was not held **prior** to this decision being made.

Again employers can escape liability on the grounds of 'special circumstances'. Failure to comply entitles the DE to withhold up to one-tenth of any redundancy rebate, or to prosecute for a fine of up to £400. Neither is particularly onerous, and for workers who have less than two years' service, there is no rebate to withhold anyway. The DE is slow to take action. In the first 18 months there were no prosecutions and rebates were withheld on only 169 occasions; the amount withheld averaged £91. Employers, but not unions, can appeal to an industrial tribunal about the amount of any rebate withheld.

Government measures to reduce unemployment

By May 1978 the Labour government had introduced no less than seven new measures to alleviate unemployment. Most of them were not intended to last beyond the end of 1977 but they have been continued.

Four were introduced specifically to help young people – the Youth Employment Subsidy, Youth Opportunities Programme, Special Temporary Employment Programme and Community Industry. The Regional Employment Premium (wound up in 1977) and the Small Firms Employment Subsidy are available only in assisted areas. Job Release enables people to retire at 64 (or 59 for women). The Temporary Employment Subsidy is the one most likely to be useful in a threatened redundancy. It operates as a £20 per week payment to employers threatening 10 or more redundancies within 90 days, for each worker kept on. It can run for one year initially and can be extended after that.

Details of the present availability of any of these schemes can be obtained from any DE office, Job Centre or Careers Office. The result is that if you are threatened with redundancy, or out of work, there is a possibility of your getting some subsidised work for some time, particularly if you are under 20. But many workers, not just the proverbial cynics, would say there would be no need for such a panoply of elaborate short-term schemes if the government had put employment as a first priority.

Finally, there are powers in the 1972 and 1975 Industry Acts to give aid to, or take over, sectors of industry. Section 3 of the 1975 Act, for example, says one of the purposes of the National Enterprise Board is 'the provision, maintenance or safeguarding of productive employment'.

Summary

1. A recognised union must be consulted about **every** redundancy at the earliest opportunity.

2. If 10 or more workers are to be sacked, the union must be consulted and the DE notified 60 days before the first sacking. If 100 or more workers are to be sacked, the period is 90 days.

3. Information must be disclosed and the union's views considered before any **final** decision is made.

4. The union can claim a **protective award** for workers when there has been a failure to consult.

5. The DE can prosecute, or part-withhold redundancy rebates, if there has been inadequate notification.

6. If redundancy cannot be attacked by direct action or through the legal procedure, there are a number of government schemes for saving jobs.

What to do if redundancy is threatened

As basic measures to prevent redundancies you should make the following demands to your employer:

1. Discharge sub-contract labour and agency staff on site and withdraw work sent to outside contractors;

2. Consider transfer of workers to other departments and changes in working arrangements;

3. Restrict overtime;

4. Consider short-time working to cover temporary fluctuations;

5. Retrain employees in skills still needed;

6. Stop recruitment;

7. Consider work-sharing by reduction in hours or other means;

8. Retire workers over retirement age;

9. Consider what alternative products could be made.

If these measures fail, resort to –

10. Applying for government assistance;

11. Early retirement with full pension;

12. Dismissal of non-unionists;

13. Voluntary redundancies;

14. An agreed procedure, for instance, last-in, first-out, and the statutory procedure of consultation with recognised unions, and notification to the Department of Employment.

Part Four: Making a Claim

21.

Doing the Sums

How to work out your claim / the definition of continuous employment / why it's important / the effect of working less than 16 hours a week / and of breaks in your contract / a summary of the basic rules on continuity / calculating 'a week's pay' / why it's important / a summary of the rules for different groups of workers / using the formula for working out compensation for unfair dismissal / redundancy pay and basic awards for unfair dismissal / a ready reckoner / an example of unfair dismissal compensation / and a summary.

Before rushing off to a tribunal to enforce any of the rights mentioned in this handbook you should ensure that you are entitled **in law** to make a claim, and work out what the claim is worth. In any event, knowing the answer to both these questions will give you the basis on which to negotiate with management, ask workmates to support you, and deal with ACAS in conciliation.

The two calculations you must make are:

1. the length of your continuous employment; and
2. the amount of your week's pay.

In everyday industrial relations these sums should not prove difficult to do. But in legal terms they present great complexity, and involve the most convoluted and inaccessible parts of the legislation. As a result, many injustices have occurred. John Mercer, for example, the gas fitter who always worked 54 hours a week got redundancy pay on the basis of only 40 (see page 255).

The TUC's request for simplification in this area has been denied. Governments have refused to modify the strictness of the continuity of employment rules, where a break of a week can deprive you of all your statutory rights. And demands for redundancy pay to be based on earnings instead of 'a week's pay' have consistently been turned down.

Where to find the law

Continuous employment – Contracts of Employment Act 1972 (CE Act) Schedule 1; 'a week's pay' – Employment Protection Act 1975 (EP Act) Schedule 4; redundancy pay – Redundancy Payments Act 1965 (RP Act) Schedule 1; compensation for unfair dismissal – EP Act sections 72–77.

Continuous employment

When considering a claim to your employer or a tribunal you should first use the **Workers' Rights Checklist** on page x. Find out whether you need to have worked for a specified period in order to make the claim. Most rights require this – unfair dismissal, redundancy, maternity, notice and guaranteed wages, for example. Others such as discrimination, dismissal for union activity, equal pay and time off are available to **all** employees irrespective of length of service.

The rules for calculating **continuous employment** are important for two reasons. **Firstly,** a break in continuity deprives you of your rights. Once you have continuous employment for the requisite period, you are protected until there is a break. **Secondly,** the value of some of your rights depends on the length of your continuous employment. Redundancy pay, the basic award in unfair dismissal claims, and notice money all increase with service.

In all the Acts there is a presumption in your favour that employment is continuous. If your boss says that continuity is broken, he must overcome this presumption and prove the point. Continuity runs while you are with the **same employer** and also if the **business is taken over**, or you **transfer to an associated employer**. The presumption applies even if you have worked for **several employers** – *Evendon v Guildford Football Club* 1975 (CA)

Continuous employment depends on your working, or contracting to work, a specified number of hours each week AND on there being no gaps in the period covered by your contract. Sections **1–4** below deal with hours; section **5** with gaps. Many 'part-timers' have full legal rights.

1. Your contract requires you to work 16 or more hours each week

While your contract lasts, your continuity is preserved. It doesn't matter whether you *actually* work 16 hours or not, since you are governed by a contract that **normally** requires it.

This can mean many things. In some jobs you can count hours when you are working beyond the minimum laid down in your written contract. A part-time teacher, for example, was able to claim unfair dismissal because in order to mark books and prepare lessons she had to work outside school hours. These necessary extra hours were added to her contracted hours so she could bring her claim – *Lake v Essex County Council* 1977 (EAT)

And a retained fireman, who was on stand-by duty 102 hours a week, got redundancy pay by saying that he was employed not merely when he was actually called out but for the whole of the 102 hours – *Bullock v Merseyside County Council* 1977 (EAT)

2. Your contract requires you to work less than 16 hours

Continuity is broken if you don't work 16 hours in any week (but see section 4 below). However, if you *actually* work 16 or more hours, you can start to build up continuity.

Example: you provide school meals five days a week for three hours a day. But you work half an hour overtime each day. You have continuous employment because you actually work at least 16 hours a week.

3. Your contractual hours are reduced below 16 hours a week

If your hours are reduced to **less than eight** you lose all your rights unless you actually worked 16 or more hours each week. But if the reduction is to somewhere **between 16 and eight** hours, you are protected in two ways.

a. Any periods of up to 26 short weeks you work on this contract count as weeks of 16 hours, even though you are not contracted to work them nor in fact work them.

b. After that, any rights you have become entitled to by length of service are **preserved**. You can count weeks either because **you were on a contract for 16 or more hours a week**, or because **they are part of a 26-week period that counts in a. above. Once you have become entitled to any right, it is preserved so long as you keep working eight or more hours a week, or are on a contract to do so.**

> **Example:** you start work on 1 January 1974 at 40 hours a week. On 1 March 1976 you ask to work part-time at 15 hours a week because of family commitments. On 1 March 1977 you are made redundant. You have **three years'** continuous employment and get three weeks' notice, and redundancy pay based on three years. This is because you had **already become entitled to notice and redundancy rights before the reduction in hours,** that is, after four weeks for notice, and after 104 weeks for redundancy.

4. You work eight hours a week for five years

Long-standing part-timers are treated as if they had worked 16 hours or more. If you have worked for less than 16 hours, but at least eight, **for five years**, you have the same rights as full-timers.

> **Example:** you are an office cleaner working for two hours on five nights a week. Until you have done this for five years, you do *not* have 'continuous employment' and can't use any of the rights that depend on it. But after five years you have the full protection of all statutory rights in the **Checklist** on page x.

5. There is a temporary gap in your continuity

A week in which **you are not covered by a contract at all** breaks your continuity. If you **resign** or **are sacked** and then come back after a week or more you lose all your continuity. The exceptions to this rule are when your contract is terminated because of: **1.** sickness, **2.** pregnancy, **3.** temporary cessation of work, **4.** agreement or custom, **5.** unfair dismissal, or **6.** industrial action.

If you are in doubt about your continuity, an assurance from your boss, given at any time, is sufficient to preserve your rights. If your boss says your continuity is intact, he can't deny it if some time later you have cause to claim redundancy pay or other rights. (*Evendon v Guildford* above.)

1. Sickness and injury

Provided you are taken back within 26 weeks of your termination, and the reason for the absence was that you were sick or injured, your continuity is not broken. The weeks off are added to the weeks during which your contract exists.

2. Pregnancy

The same is true if the reason is pregnancy. Continuity is anyway preserved for women who are entitled to the full EP Act rights, if they return to work within 29 weeks of the week of confinement. The right here is useful for women who are not entitled to the full EP Act rights – because, for example, they do not have two years' continuous employment.

Example: you join the firm as a typist on 1 June 1976 and want to take maternity leave on 1 June 1977. The firm doesn't have an agreement on this, and you don't have the two years necessary for maternity rights under the EP Act. So on 1 June 1977 you resign and have your baby in September. On 5 November the firm is advertising for a typist and you are accepted back. The weeks of absence **count** and you have **continuity** as though you had never left.

3. Temporary cessation of work

Normally your contract continues during a temporary lay-off, even if you are claiming unemployment or social security benefit. When you are laid off and your contract is **terminated** you can still claim continuity if you are subsequently taken back. There must be a **cessation**, it must be the **cause of the absence** and it must be **temporary**. In looking at these rules you must as Mr Justice Phillips said, do so 'as the historian of a completed chapter of events, and not as a journalist describing events as they occur from day to day'.

Blackburns closed their engineering works in 1963. D. Crown who had 15 years' service found work in one firm, then another, for two years. S. Miller had 15 years' service but he was out of work for 21 months. In 1965, both were offered work with Bentleys. Bentleys and

Blackburns were associated employers. The men were made redundant in 1974 and claimed payments based on unbroken continuity of employment from their first days at Blackburns. The High Court said that the periods of two years and 21 months were absences due to a 'temporary cessation of work'. Important factors were: length of service, duration of the gap, the nature of their work and what was said on re-engagement. *Bentley Engineering v Crown* 1976 (HC)

4. Agreement or custom

In some industries you are by custom and practice regarded as continuing in employment even if your contract is terminated. For instance, you might be 'loaned' by your boss to another employer. You might, on the other hand, ask for time off during which you may be regarded as still in employment even though no contract exists. In these situations, you don't forfeit your rights if you are regarded as continuing in employment 'for all or any purposes'.

Ms Moore worked as a doubler in a Glasgow factory. Her son had a serious accident and she left work for three months in 1968 to look after him. She told her supervisor that she didn't know how long she would be off but she hoped to return. Clarksons kept her cards. In 1970 she was made redundant. The President of the Scottish tribunals said there was no break in her continuity. There was an arrangement that **suspended the contract** until her domestic situation allowed her to return. *Moore v James Clarkson & Co.* 1970 (IT)

If your pension or other benefits continue while you are away or if your 'cards' (nowadays your P45 and contribution record) are kept you can say your contract is continuing. But if there is no formal relationship between you, it will be difficult to establish continuity.

A Derbyshire County cricketer played for his club from March to September each year and worked for Pontins travel agency in the winter. Each March he got his cards and P45 from the agency. He got no money from Pontins during the summer, but was re-engaged each autumn. The Derby tribunal said he did not have continuity of employment with Pontins. He was not regarded as employed by them during the cricket season. *Rhodes v Pontins Ltd* 1971 (IT)

5. Re-engagement after unfair dismissal

If you are sacked and reinstated in your old job, or re-engaged by your employer, or an associated employer, you preserve your continuity. Provided you make a complaint of

unfair dismissal and are taken back following **conciliation by ACAS** or **a tribunal order**, your period off work counts. But not otherwise, unless your boss agrees this.

6. Industrial action

Lock-outs don't break your continuity. All the time during which you are locked-out counts.

Strikes, however, are treated differently. These don't break your continuity. But if you were on strike for any part of a week, *that* week does not count towards your total service.

Example: you joined the company on 10 March 1974 and were made redundant 10 April 1977. You would expect redundancy pay and notice based on three years' continuous employment. But on 10 May 1976 you took part in a 10-week strike. Your continuity is not broken, but your service is reduced by 10 weeks. So you get redundancy pay and notice based on two years and 46 weeks.

Preservation of continuity in a strike is an important right. Without it even short strikes would jeopardise every striker's accrued legal protections.

Remember: in all the above six cases we are talking about a period when you are not covered by a contract, and do not have your boss's assurance that continuity is unbroken. If you are covered by a contract or have an assurance, continuity is preserved.

Summary of continuous employment rules

1. Every week counts in which you work, or have a contract to work, at least 16 hours.

2. Any week in which you have a contract which requires less than 16 hours breaks continuity unless

    a. you actually work 16 or more hours;

    b. you have worked 8 or more hours for 5 years; or

    c. you have been reduced *from* 16 or more hours *to* 8 or more.

3. Once you have built up enough continuous employment to entitle you to any particular right, that right is preserved so long as you work, or are contracted to work, at least 8 hours a week.

4. Any week in which you have *no* contract and you do not work breaks continuity unless you return to work

a. after being sick for 26 or less weeks;

b. after being away for 26 or less weeks because of pregnancy, and you are not entitled to the full EP Act right;

c. after a temporary cessation of work;

d. after a period during which you are regarded by agreement or custom as having continuity;

e. after claiming unfair dismissal;

f. after a strike or lock-out.

'A week's pay'

The starting point for determining the amount of pay to be given in compensation under many parts of the legislation is Schedule 4 of the EP Act. This lays down an absurdly artificial formula for finding out basic weekly pay. It is used for calculating: **redundancy, notice** and **maternity pay**, wages during **medical suspension** and **while looking for work** in a redundancy situation, the amount of a **protective award** when your employer has not followed the procedure for handling redundancies, and the '**basic award**' made in a finding of unfair dismissal. The amount payable for any of these rights often bears very little resemblance to industrial reality, particularly with regard to overtime. Nevertheless, the rules are rigid. In this handbook 'a week's pay' refers to pay calculated in accordance with this chapter.

Before you can find out what your week's pay is, you must ask what the method of calculating your wages is. In other words, **1.** whether you have no normal hours or **2.** whether you work normal hours, and if you work normal hours, whether you are a time-worker, piece-worker, or shift-worker. They all have different rules which are found in Schedule 2 of the CE Act and Schedule 4 of the EP Act.

Workers with no normal hours

There is a small group of people – union officials, commercial travellers and college lecturers for example – who work on a no-fixed-hours contract. If they are made redundant their weekly pay is determined by reference to the average weekly pay in the last 12 weeks. If they are dismissed for **redundancy** and are given proper notice, the 12 weeks dates back from the date notice was given. If no notice was given, or if inadequate notice was given, the 12 weeks is taken from the date of termination. For pay during **maternity**, and **medical**

suspension, the calculation date is the date immediately preceding the date of absence. For **notice pay**, it is the date preceding the date notice was given.

Workers with normal hours

If you have a set number of hours each week, beyond which you are regarded as working overtime (whether or not you get a premium), you have 'normal hours'. Most workers come into this definition and fall into one of the following categories.

1. Straight time-workers

If you are not on shift-work, and receive wages that do not vary with the amount of work done, that is, you are a straight time-worker, calculate your week's pay by reference to the amount received in the last week before notice was given in cases of redundancy, dismissal etc., and before absence began in cases of maternity and medical suspension.

2. Piece-workers

If the amount of pay varies according to the amount of work done, that is, because of piece-work or variable bonus or commission, a week's pay is worked out by reference to the 12 weeks preceding the date on which notice of redundancy or dismissal was given, or before the date on which maternity leave or medical suspension began.

Any hours that were worked at overtime rate are included but the overtime premium is disregarded. The average weekly rate can therefore be determined by dividing the 12 weeks' pay by 12. If there are short weeks because, say, of lay-off or sickness, go back further and find 12 full weeks.

3. Shift workers

If you are on shifts and your pay varies according to the day of the week on which you work, you calculate your week's pay in the same way as **2.** above.

4. New starters

If you have not worked for 12 weeks you take a figure which fairly represents a week's pay. Look at the amount received and rates paid to similar workers inside and outside the company.

What is included in a week's pay?

Not all forms of payment qualify to be included in a week's pay. The most unjust exception is **non-contractual overtime**. Overtime which is obligatory on both employee *and* employer will count, but no other. So if your normal working hours are 40, with five hours' conditioned overtime **and the employer is obliged to make payments in respect of these five hours whether or not work is given**, then these 45 hours will be included. However, when there is a stipulation to work overtime 'as and when required by the employer to do so', **you** are obliged to work reasonable overtime, but **your boss** is under no obligation to give you any. So even **regular** overtime of this kind does *not* count towards a week's pay. **There must be a mutual obligation to provide, and to work, overtime if it is to qualify**, as John Mercer found out (page 255).

A **bonus** will qualify if it is contractual. **Tips** and payments from people other than your employer cannot be included except in one narrow case. If your boss takes a certain percentage off his customers and puts it in a tronc, in the hotel trade for example, and this is then paid out amongst the workers concerned, this will qualify as part of a week's pay. However, if it is given by a customer direct to you it will *not* qualify. **Lodging allowances** do not qualify if, for example, they go with the job. If you live above the shop and get a free flat you cannot include the value of this flat in your week's pay. **Expenses** only qualify in so far as they represent a **profit** to you. If they are a genuine estimate of what you are likely to spend, they will not qualify; but if there is an element of profit involved then it can be taken to be part of a week's pay. It will of course have tax consequences each week in this case! Payments for **travelling time** do not qualify, nor do **benefits in kind** even if they can be assessed in value. Cars, for example, cannot be part of 'a week's pay'. But **mobility** payments are. **Threshold** and **cost-of-living payments** count.

Summary of rules for working out a week's pay

The precise formula is explained in Schedule C of the leaflet 'Contracts of Employment Act', available free at DE offices. The following are offered as reasonable rules-of-thumb which will bring you very close to your actual entitlement:

1. If you have no fixed hours:

    a. Count back the last 12 weeks you actually worked before notice was given.

    b. Add all gross pay.

    c. Divide **b.** by 12 to give average weekly pay. This is a week's pay.

2. If you are a time-worker:

    a. Find gross pay for all hours worked, excluding pay for non-contractual overtime, in the week before notice was given.

    b. This is a week's pay.

3. If you are a shift worker, or are paid by the piece, commission, bonus:

    a. Count back the last 12 weeks you actually worked before notice was given.

    b. Add all gross pay excluding pay for non-contractual overtime.

    c. Add all hours excluding non-contractual overtime.

    d. Divide **b.** by **c.** to give average hourly rate.

    e. Divide **c.** by 12 to give average weekly hours.

    f. Multiply **d.** by **e.** to give a week's pay.

Why is a week's pay important?

All the rights in the **Checklist** require a calculation based on a week's pay. The only exception is compensation for victimisation for union activity. Some *also* take account of **earnings** – unfair dismissal, time off for union representatives, and guarantees when your employer goes bust. Two rights provide automatic compensation based on a combination of length of continuous employment, amount of a week's pay, and age. These are **redundancy pay** and the **basic award** in unfair dismissal cases.

Compensation for unfair dismissal

We have seen (page 182) that if you win a case of unfair dismissal and are not reinstated or re-engaged your compensation may consist of

1. Basic award	maximum	£3,000
2. Compensatory award	maximum	£5,200
3. Additional award (or £2,600 depending on reasons)	maximum	£5,200
	Total	£13,400

This section deals with compensatory and additional awards. Basic awards are explained in the next section. All these amounts can be increased each year by the Employment Secretary.

What is included in the compensation?

You can claim compensation for:

■ loss of **net** earnings from the date of dismissal to date of hearing and loss of benefits, for instance, a bonus that you would have received.

■ loss of future net earnings if you are likely to be un-employed or working for less money.

■ loss of expected benefits, for example, increments or annual pay settlements.

■ expenses in looking for work.

■ loss of pension rights.

■ loss of unfair dismissal protection (usually half a week's pay).

■ losses arising out of the **manner** of dismissal, for example if you are now blacklisted because of being an active trade unionist.

■ loss of a right to a period of notice (that is, if you were entitled to four weeks but in your new job you only get one week).

■ loss of right to higher redundancy pay than is given by law, that is, if better rights are given in a collective agreement.

For some of the above losses, the tribunal will have to estimate the amount. It will have to decide how long you are likely to be out of work, how much social security money you will get and how much you are likely to earn when you do get a job. You will have to produce evidence to back up your view on all these questions.

The tribunal can order your boss to pay whatever it considers just and equitable. It can award you nothing, or up to 104 weeks' pay (£5,200 maximum).

The tribunal must take account of any wages you receive from any source. If you get money in lieu of notice, or an ex gratia payment, this is subtracted from your boss's total bill. So are earnings from other employers. **If you are sacked without proper notice**, the tribunal should ensure that you get at least as much as your proper notice money. This is the 'irreducible minimum' that must be given in accordance with 'good industrial practice', and the net amount should be paid regardless of earnings received from other sources – *Vaughan v Weighpack* 1974 (NIRC)

Social security payments

The tribunal must deduct from the total bill any social security payments you will receive *after* the date of the decision. For social security payments received between the date of sacking and the date of the tribunal's decision, the tribunal must go through a complicated process to enable the DHSS to recoup these payments from your boss. In other words, your boss, not the DHSS, must bear the cost of your being out of work, at least up to the date of the decision. After that date, your boss's compensation bill is reduced by the amount you get from social security payments.

The tribunal must say how much compensation is attributable to the period leading up to the date of its decision, that is, how much your net loss is for this period. It will then notify the DE who will check with the DHSS on how much you have received. The DE may then deliver a bill to your boss. Your boss must pay the bill, which consists of the amount of your social security pay, to the DE. Only then can he pay **you** the balance. The delays and complications that can arise are formidable!

Did you contribute to your own dismissal?

The tribunal can reduce your compensation by any amount it considers just and equitable if you have to any extent caused or contributed to your own dismissal. If it finds you were as much to blame as your boss, it might reduce your money by 50 per cent. For example, you may have been to blame in failing to repair a machine properly, but your boss may have given you no warnings or taken too drastic action.

The House of Lords has said that there is nothing to stop the tribunal reducing your money by 100 per cent (*Devis v Atkins* page 170). In practice, reductions of over 80 per cent are highly exceptional.

Employers frequently try to reduce their compensation bill by saying you were partly to blame.

Did you try to reduce your losses?

The tribunal can also reduce your compensation if it finds that you failed to 'mitigate your loss'. You can't sit back and do nothing, waiting for your case to be heard. You must be seen to be taking all the steps that a reasonable person would if (s)he had no hope of getting the job back. You should register as unemployed and actively look for jobs while your case is pending.

Again, employers will often produce evidence such as newspaper advertisements to show that jobs are plentiful and that you haven't tried hard to reduce your losses. You will have to bring evidence of the jobs you have applied for to combat this.

Additional compensation for unfair dismissal

If the tribunal orders your boss to reinstate or re-engage you, you can complain to the tribunal if the terms of the order aren't carried out to the letter. If the tribunal agrees with you it can order your boss to pay an **additional** amount of between 13 and 26 weeks' pay up to a maximum of £2,600.

If you have been unfairly dismissed for a reason connected with race or sex discrimination, or trade-union membership, the tribunal must order an additional amount of between 26 and 52 weeks, up to a maximum of £5,200.

Basic award for unfair dismissal and redundancy pay

If you are unfairly dismissed the tribunal must order your boss to pay you **a basic award**. The calculation for this and for **redundancy pay** is the same.

The formula for deciding how many weeks' pay you get is as follows:

If you were aged	but less than	number of weeks' pay for each year
	18	0
18	22	$\frac{1}{2}$
22	41	1
41	65	$1\frac{1}{2}$

Ready Reckoner for basic awards and redundancy pay

To use the Table

1. Read off employee's age and number of complete years service. Any week which began before the employee attained the age of 18 does not count. The table will then show **how many weeks pay** the employee is entitled to. For definition of a week's pay, *see* appendix D of the booklet *The Redundancy Payments Scheme*.

2. For a woman aged between 59 and 60, and a man aged between 64 and 65, the cash amount due is to be reduced by one-twelfth for every complete month by which the age exceeds 59 or 64 respectively.

AGE (years)	SERVICE (years) 2	3	4	5	6	7	8	9	10	11	12	13	14	15	16	17	18	19	20
20	1	1	1	1	—														
21	1	1½	1½	1½	1½	—													
22	1	1½	2	2	2	—													
23	1½	2	2½	3	3	3	3	—											
24	2	2½	3	3½	4	4	4	4	—										
25	2	3	3½	4	4½	5	5	5	5	—									
26	2	3	4	4½	5	5½	6	6	6	6	—								
27	2	3	4	5	5½	6	6½	7	7	7	7	—							
28	2	3	4	5	6	6½	7	7½	8	8	8	8	—						
29	2	3	4	5	6	7	7½	8	8½	9	9	9	9	—					
30	2	3	4	5	6	7	8	8½	9	9½	10	10	10	10	—				
31	2	3	4	5	6	7	8	9	9½	10	10½	11	11	11	11	—			
32	2	3	4	5	6	7	8	9	10	10½	11	11½	12	12	12	12	—		
33	2	3	4	5	6	7	8	9	10	11	11½	12	12½	13	13	13	13	—	
34	2	3	4	5	6	7	8	9	10	11	12	12½	13	13½	14	14	14	14	—
35	2	3	4	5	6	7	8	9	10	11	12	13	13½	14	14½	15	15	15	15
36	2	3	4	5	6	7	8	9	10	11	12	13	14	14½	15	15½	16	16	16
37	2	3	4	5	6	7	8	9	10	11	12	13	14	15	15½	16	16½	17	17
38	2	3	4	5	6	7	8	9	10	11	12	13	14	15	16	16½	17	17½	18
39	2	3	4	5	6	7	8	9	10	11	12	13	14	15	16	17	17½	18	18½
40	2	3	4	5	6	7	8	9	10	11	12	13	14	15	16	17	18	18½	19
41	2	3	4	5	6	7	8	9	10	11	12	13	14	15	16	17	18	19	19½
42	2½	3½	4½	5½	6½	7½	8½	9½	10½	11½	12½	13½	14½	15½	16½	17½	18½	19½	20½
43	3	4	5	6	7	8	9	10	11	12	13	14	15	16	17	18	19	20	21
44	3	4½	5½	6½	7½	8½	9½	10½	11½	12½	13½	14½	15½	16½	17½	18½	19½	20½	21½
45	3	4½	6	7	8	9	10	11	12	13	14	15	16	17	18	19	20	21	22
46	3	4½	6	7½	8½	9½	10½	11½	12½	13½	14½	15½	16½	17½	18½	19½	20½	21½	22½
47	3	4½	6	7½	9	10	11	12	13	14	15	16	17	18	19	20	21	22	23
48	3	4½	6	7½	9	10½	11½	12½	13½	14½	15½	16½	17½	18½	19½	20½	21½	22½	23½
49	3	4½	6	7½	9	10½	12	13	14	15	16	17	18	19	20	21	22	23	24
50	3	4½	6	7½	9	10½	12	13½	14½	15½	16½	17½	18½	19½	20½	21½	22½	23½	24½
51	3	4½	6	7½	9	10½	12	13½	15	16	17	18	19	20	21	22	23	24	25
52	3	4½	6	7½	9	10½	12	13½	15	16½	17½	18½	19½	20½	21½	22½	23½	24½	25½
53	3	4½	6	7½	9	10½	12	13½	15	16½	18	19	20	21	22	23	24	25	26
54	3	4½	6	7½	9	10½	12	13½	15	16½	18	19½	20½	21½	22½	23½	24½	25½	26½
55	3	4½	6	7½	9	10½	12	13½	15	16½	18	19½	21	22	23	24	25	26	27
56	3	4½	6	7½	9	10½	12	13½	15	16½	18	19½	21	22½	23½	24½	25½	26½	27½
57	3	4½	6	7½	9	10½	12	13½	15	16½	18	19½	21	22½	24	25	26	27	28
58	3	4½	6	7½	9	10½	12	13½	15	16½	18	19½	21	22½	24	25½	26½	27½	28½
59	3	4½	6	7½	9	10½	12	13½	15	16½	18	19½	21	22½	24	25½	27	28	29
60 *(men only)*	3	4½	6	7½	9	10½	12	13½	15	16½	18	19½	21	22½	24	25½	27	28½	29½
61 *(men only)*	3	4½	6	7½	9	10½	12	13½	15	16½	18	19½	21	22½	24	25½	27	28½	30
62 *(men only)*	3	4½	6	7½	9	10½	12	13½	15	16½	18	19½	21	22½	24	25½	27	28½	30
63 *(men only)*	3	4½	6	7½	9	10½	12	13½	15	16½	18	19½	21	22½	24	25½	27	28½	30
64 *(men only)*	3	4½	6	7½	9	10½	12	13½	15	16½	18	19½	21	22½	24	25½	27	28½	30

The Ready Reckoner on page 349 shows how this formula works out in practice.

Example: you were dismissed at 50 having worked for 15 years continuously. You are entitled to 19½ weeks' pay. This is made up of 6 years at 1 week (that is, under the age of 41) and 9 years at 1½ weeks (for the years over the age of 41).

This formula is subject to some restrictions:

1. If you are 64 (59 for women) your entitlement goes down by 1/12th for each month after your 64th (59th) birthday.

2. Only 20 years can be counted. So working back from the date of dismissal and taking your most valuable years (that is, those when you were 41 or over), the highest number of weeks' pay you can get is 30.

3. The maximum allowable for a week's pay is £100, although the Employment Secretary must review this limit each year (EP Act section 86). If your week's pay is over £100, only £100 counts.

4. In basic awards (but not redundancy pay), you *must* be given two weeks' pay. This is your irreducible minimum; 5 below is the only exception. So workers between the ages of 16 and 23 still get two weeks' pay.

5. If you get redundancy pay, this is offset against your basic award. So is any compensation you get under the SD Act or RR Act for loss of redundancy rights.

6. Your basic award can be reduced if the tribunal thinks you were partly to blame, or you didn't mitigate your losses.

Example of unfair dismissal compensation

The example is based on the following assumptions:

1. You were born in 1927.

2. You started with XYZ Ltd on 30 March 1967.

3. You were sacked without notice on 30 July 1977.

4. You earned £75 a week gross, £5 of which was voluntary overtime. You took home £60 net.

5. You got an ex gratia payment of £100.

6. You were disqualified for unemployment benefit for six weeks but got supplementary benefit at £15 a week.

7. You then got unemployment benefit at £20 a week.

8. Your case was heard on 30 October 1977.

9. The tribunal found that you would not get work until about 1 January 1978. You would probably get only £70 a week because you would not have seniority.

A. Compensatory award

1. Loss of net earnings from 30.7.77 to 30.10.77
    13 weeks at £60   = £780

    Loss of half yearly bonus payable
    1.10.77   =   50
                         ——
                      830
    Less ex gratia payment   — 100   = £730*

2. Loss of earnings from 30.10.77 to 1.1.78
    9 weeks at £60   = 540
    Less unemployment benefit
    9 weeks at £20   — 180 = 360

3. Loss of earnings from 1.1.78 for 1 year (say)
    52 weeks at £5   =   260

4. Expenses looking for work   20

5. Loss of pension rights (say)   500

6. Loss of unfair dismissal protection (say)
    ½ week at £60   =   30

7. Loss of right to 10 weeks notice (say)
    5 weeks at £70   =   350

8. Loss of rights to negotiated redundancy pay (say) 50
                         ——
                Total 1–8 £2,600

9. Less 20 per cent contributory fault   — 520
                         ——
        Total 1–8 minus 9 £2,080

---

* In practice the tribunal will itemise this as the 'prescribed amount'. The DE can recoup from your boss the equivalent social security benefits you have received. Your boss must then pay you the balance.

B. Basic award

10. 2 weeks at £70		=		140
11. 8 weeks at £70		=	560	
Less 20 per cent contributory fault		−	112	= 448

Total 10–11   £588

C. Additional award

Nil   =   000

     2,080

     588

Grand Total A+B+C   £2,668

Summary

1. Before you negotiate or make a claim for any worker's right, check that you have continuous employment for the requisite period. Most rights require a minimum period of service.

2. To calculate what compensation you need, you usually have to calculate 'a week's pay'.

3. For unfair dismissal you can get compensation for your losses, an additional award if your boss refuses to comply with a tribunal order, and a basic award.

4. The basic award and redundancy pay are based on the same formula. This takes account of your age, length of continuous employment and a week's pay.

22.

Going to a Tribunal

Bringing a legal claim / preliminary steps /
legal advice and representation / costs /
documents you need / time limits / test cases /
witnesses / conciliation / settlement / hearings /
enforcement / reviews and appeals / and a
summary.

If you are sacked, made redundant, discriminated
against or denied almost any right in Part Two of this handbook, and you can't assert your rights at workplace level, you
will have to consider taking legal action.

The procedure described in this chapter relates to an
industrial tribunal. If you are exercising your right to social
security benefits, disputed claims go to a Local Tribunal or a
Medical Appeal Tribunal. Disputed claims for supplementary
benefit go to a Supplementary Benefit Appeal Tribunal. If you
are claiming that a civil wrong has been done to you, for
example, that you have been injured by your employer's
negligence, or that you are threatened with eviction from a
flat that goes with your job, you go to a county court or the
High Court, depending on the amount of money involved.

Where to find the law

Powers of tribunals are found in the Industrial Tribunals (Labour Relations) Regulations SI 1974 No. 1386 and
1387 (Scotland), and SI 1976 No. 661; and the Employment
Appeal Tribunal Rules SI 1976 No. 322.

Preliminary steps

There are four preliminary matters that you must check
before you start. Using the **Workers' Rights Checklist** on page
x, make sure:

1. that you have worked for the minimum number of weeks required for making a claim;

2. that you have worked, or normally would have worked, for the appropriate number of hours in each of those weeks;

3. that your service is unbroken except by illness, holidays, absence with leave or maternity; and

4. that you are within the time limit for making a complaint.

You may need advice in deciding whether you have met the above conditions.

Advice and representation

Unions

The most obvious source of help is your union. Its officials should provide advice and representation, and will be most able to get your rights without going to a tribunal. Unions have different procedures but the TUC has recommended that a special **internal** application form be printed by each union. Ask your union rep or local official how to apply for advice and assistance. Once you apply make sure the application has been received and acted upon.

Some unions require you to send the originating application **form IT1** (see below) to the tribunal yourself. In this case, it is still important to contact your official to get advice on how to fill it in.

Legal Aid

If you are not in a union, your scope is limited.

Legal assistance is available on what is known as the Law Society's **green form** (pink, in Scotland) for general advice. You have the right to £25 worth (sometimes more) of a solicitor's time to be given free, or at a discount, according to your means. Means are assessed by reference to your savings and to your disposable income. Disposable income is what you have left after deductions and rent, and after dependants are taken into account. Generally speaking, you are entitled if you are out of work. Not all solicitors give legal assistance on the green form – ask and make sure before you get an interview. Also ask if they have experience of industrial tribunal matters, as many solicitors are new to this kind of case.

If you don't qualify for free or cheap legal advice and assistance you can usually get half an hour's advice for £5 from most solicitors. Ask for a 'fixed fee interview'. The Legal Aid Solicitors' List, available in public libraries and Citizen's Advice Bureaux, gives the names and addresses of solicitors on a local basis, and the subjects they specialise in.

Legal Aid is not available for **representation** at a tribunal. This is a major denial of rights to many working people. But solicitors can use the green form to:

- give advice
- fill in your tribunal application form
- prepare evidence
- write letters
- tell you how to present your case
- get counsel's opinion on difficult points (the £25 limit can be raised for this)

Law Centres in London and other big cities will help you without charge and will often represent you. Citizen's Advice Bureaux give basic advice but often have no industrial experience. They can advise you where to get more help.

Equality Commissions

You can sometimes get legal assistance from the Commission for Racial Equality or the Equal Opportunities Commission in discrimination cases.

ACAS

You can get advice free from ACAS. Addresses on page 399. See also **conciliation** below.

Other representation

At the hearing you can be represented by **anyone you like** – a lawyer, union official, or a friend – or you can present your own case. A 1974 survey showed that in 53 per cent of cases the applicant had no representation but those who did clearly fared better.

Costs

It is important to mention costs at this stage because they are frequently referred to by employers right from the moment you consider claiming against them. In fact, **there is almost no chance of a tribunal ordering you to pay your boss's costs.** It has power to do so *only* if it is of the opinion that you acted 'frivolously or vexatiously', or if you have postponed the dates of a hearing (see below).

A tribunal will not make you pay costs simply because you are bringing a case that turns out to be hopeless. Some employers' solicitors (in particular, one London firm acting for a large hotel and leisure group usually against non-unionists) frequently make the threat of costs.

If you are claiming a right which is not available to you because, say, you have not worked enough weeks, it is just possible to envisage a tribunal making an order for costs. But the tribunal secretary will write to· you in confidence and explain the law so you will be aware of the possible threat. An order for costs will not be made unless your employer asks for it.

These are the *only* circumstances in which the possibility of costs can arise. In practice it can be disregarded. If you are extremely unlucky and also not represented by a union (which would bear the costs) you would have to pay all or part of the other side's costs. These may be set at a fixed amount or assessed by a court official.

Documents

Questionnaire

If you are thinking of pushing a claim of sex or race discrimination you can use a question-and-answer form (pages 376–8) to get information from an employer before you take action. The answers will form part of the evidence at the hearing. Although employers aren't obliged to answer, their failure to do so can be noted and inferences can be drawn by the tribunal.

Originating Application

No formal document is necessary to make a claim. If you write giving the following basic information, your claim is a valid originating application.

1. your name and address.
2. the name and address of the person or company you are claiming against.
3. the grounds on which you are making a claim.

Most applicants use the official Form IT1.

Originating Application – Form IT1

This is the basic document for all industrial tribunal claims. It is available from union and DE offices and a specimen is shown on pages 372–3. If you are getting assistance, fill in the form with the help of your representative. The form is not in duplicate so ask for two copies and keep one for yourself or your representative.

As a general rule it is better to say little rather than a lot on the form, so that you are not tied down later, or tripped up in fine distinctions such as those in redundancy and unfair dismissal. If you have given too little information, the employer can always ask for further particulars (see below).

Time limits

The form must be sent to the Central Office of the Industrial Tribunals in London, Glasgow or Belfast, according to where the case arose. Addresses on page 400. It can be sent by you or your representative, but should be signed by you. It must be **received** by the Central Office within the time limit.

> **Example**: You are sacked without notice on 15 September. You have three months to claim. Your application must reach Central Office on or before 14 December. If 14 December is a weekend or holiday, it could be delivered on the next working day.

The tribunal has discretion in most claims to extend the time limit if it is satisfied

1. that it wasn't reasonably practicable for you to make the application within the time limit *and*

2. that when you were able to make the application, you did so within a further reasonable period.

Don't delay making your claim. You can always ask for postponements of the hearing if you have a good reason.

The tribunal is unlikely to extend the time limit if the delay is caused by: bad advice or default by your representative, or the fact that you were **pursuing negotiations or going through procedure**, or that you didn't know of your right to claim. It might extend it if you have been ill, or if your boss asked you to hold back pending negotiations.

The deadline for most claims can be extended. For redundancy pay it can be extended by six months. For equal pay, there is no power to extend the deadline beyond six months after you leave the employment.

Action by the tribunal

The Central Office allocates your claim to a regional office to whom all further correspondence should be sent. If the regional secretary considers that the tribunal has no power to deal with your claim, (s)he will write to you saying this. For example, (s)he would do this if you hadn't worked long enough to claim redundancy pay.

When your claim is registered, the tribunal notifies the other party who has 14 days in which to file the Respondent's Reply on Form IT3 (see page 374). A copy is sent to you by the tribunal. You are given 14 days' notice of the date set for the hearing. If you have named a representative, that person will receive the reply and notice of hearing and must notify you and all of your witnesses.

Further particulars

Either party can ask for more details about the other's case. You can ask about names, places, written documents, dates, numbers of male and female employees, or anything else that may help your case. If you disbelieve that there is a redundancy situation you can ask to see the accounts, order books and stocklists. If you think you have been selected unfairly for dismissal, ask for a breakdown of all employees by grade and length of service. If you are alleging sex or race discrimination, ask for details of applicants for jobs or for promotion over a period of time.

You write direct to your employers or the person representing them. Give them a time-limit of say, seven or 14 days in which to comply with your request. You could even ask for the **managing director** to bring the order-books to the hearing. If they refuse, or do not reply, write direct to the secretary at the tribunal office which is dealing with the case, enclosing a copy of your original letter to your employers, and ask for an **order** to be issued. The chairman of the tribunal may grant this request and if so the order will be sent to you, or your representative. You must then write to the employers or their representative enclosing the order and asking for the information to be provided. Send it by recorded delivery so you know it has been received.

Sometimes, employers' solicitors will say that the documents you are looking for can be inspected at their offices, and they will produce them at the hearing. You can always ask them if they will send you a photocopy. If they ask you about, say, your attempts to find a new job or your present wages, and you want to stall, you can allow these to be inspected by appointment during certain hours at your union or solicitor's office. Anyone refusing to comply with a tribunal order can be fined up to £100. Their claim or defence can also be struck out.

Amendment

If you want to add or delete something, write to the secretary at the tribunal office, explaining the amendment and asking for 'leave to amend' your application form; and send a copy to the employers' representative.

Documents for the hearing

If a hearing is inevitable, you will be asked by the tribunal to bring with you your wage slips, contract, agreements and other documents relating to your work with your employer, and, if you have been sacked, relating to your present work or the period while you were out of work. This would include details of social security payments, wages earned, and money in lieu of notice. It is a good idea to bring any letters from employers you have applied to, and copies of advertisements you have followed up. These will show you have been trying to get work and will favourably affect the amount of any compensation you may get.

Any documents or collective agreement – for example one which contains a disciplinary procedure, or equal opportunity clause – that you want to use should be photocopied, if possible five times. This means that you have copies for your representative, the employers, your witness and the three tribunal members. Some documents will be uncontroversial and the other side will not object. You can even draw up a jointly agreed 'bundle' of relevant documents. But if you don't agree to, say, a management report being submitted because you think it was made after your sacking you can object at the hearing.

Test cases

Test cases are not provided for in tribunals. If you and a number of other workers have an identical dispute over equal pay or mass sackings you must all file individual claims. Clearly this is unsatisfactory; if the issue in each case is precisely the same your union may want to try one test case.

This can be agreed informally between the union and the employer, with both sides agreeing to follow the result. But it can't prevent you bringing your own claim and, conversely, your employer can't be forced in law to accept the test case as binding on him. Obviously, if you won your test case, it would be foolish for your boss to resist other cases on the same facts, and costs might even be awarded against him.

In a genuine attempt to save time and expense the union could agree to treat one case as a test case but 'without prejudice to each member's right to bring his or her own claim'. If you are in any doubt about the suitability of the test case chosen – for example if it isn't quite the same as your own – get your union to register a claim for you. You need not proceed with it, and can get the tribunal to wait until the test case is decided before hearing yours. If no claim is registered, you may find you are time-barred, so **all claims should be registered even if a test case is being tried.**

The failure of the tribunal regulations to provide for test cases, or for a union or women's group to bring a claim, necessarily creates inconvenience. It reflects yet again the individualistic view Parliament takes of industrial disputes and the desire to discourage workers from gaining advantages through organisation.

Witnesses

You can bring any witnesses you choose, and in any order you choose. You will usually be a witness yourself. If your union official has been involved at workplace level in your dispute, and is also presenting your case, (s)he can appear as a witness if you think it helps your case. Get a full statement from each of your witnesses so that you know the basic ingredients of what they are going to say. They can see and sign the statement but can't take it into the witness-box.

Witnesses are paid some travelling expenses, loss of earnings and subsistence by the tribunal. Tell your witnesses this. They must be allowed time off to attend. Victimisation of a fellow-worker who gives evidence for you would amount to criminal interference.

A witness who is not prepared to attend can be ordered to do so. The procedure is the same as for obtaining an order for further particulars or documents. You should be wary, though, of calling a witness who is unwilling to come, as his or her evidence may turn out to be different from what you expected. But if their evidence is important to your case, call them.

You are not obliged to tell the tribunal or the other side the names of your witnesses. And even if you do tell them, you can change your mind at any time, even during the hearing.

Conciliation

A feature of almost all individual complaints to an industrial tribunal is the existence of facilities for conciliation. ACAS get a copy of every form except those claiming redundancy pay only. ACAS will act if both parties request, or if the conciliation officer assigned to the case thinks there is a reasonable prospect of settlement. Either party can ask for conciliation after a dismissal has taken place but before a claim is presented (TULR Act schedule 1 para. 26) and *in practice* either party can ask the conciliation officer to intervene at any stage.

You won't know who has been assigned to the case and you can't find out from the tribunal office. Often the conciliation officer makes contact in person or by phone with you, or with your representative if you have nominated one. If you want immediate help, contact the regional office of ACAS (addresses on page 399) quoting the number of your case.

In dismissal cases, ACAS's primary duty is to try to get you reinstated, preferably using any agreed procedures. Failing that, re-engagement and compensation must be tried. (TULR Act schedule 1 para. 26).

If you are not represented, ACAS can be very useful as you may find it difficult or be unwilling to talk to the other side. If you are represented by a union official it is less likely that you will need ACAS, as the official can talk direct to management or their representative. If you are represented by a lawyer, ACAS can be a useful intermediary by providing industrial experience in discussions of a settlement.

The ACAS officers responsible for conciliation of individual cases are in a different branch from those who conciliate in strikes. They are expected to know the law and in practice help both parties to reach a settlement by suggesting from experience the possible outcome of the case if it goes to a tribunal. They are supposed to be impartial, and to seek simply to get a settlement. In fact, they often go further than this. Although they are not supposed to suggest figures for compensation, they sometimes do.

It is a good idea to give the conciliation officer a detailed breakdown of the money you are claiming (see page 346). It is also useful to ask for your job back, even if you are not keen, because it looks better to the tribunal if your boss turns you down, rather than vice versa. It may also prevent him taking on a replacement until the hearing is over.

Judging by the statistics for unfair dismissal claims (page 145) you have a reasonable chance of getting some form of conciliated settlement.

Use ACAS if you want to keep talking to your employer. But remember that the conciliation officer is not your representative. Many employers will settle even the most hopeless case against them for a 'nuisance value' figure of anything up to £100. It would cost your employer at least that for a day in a tribunal with a lawyer and witnesses, so this is something you can keep in the back of your mind when bargaining.

Settlement

If a settlement is reached with or without conciliation there are two procedures you can follow. You can simply withdraw the case. Technically, the case is dismissed by the tribunal, and you cannot come back if you do not get your money. On the other hand, if you settle the case between yourselves or through ACAS, the agreement can be reported to the tribunal which will record it as a binding decision. This means that it becomes an order of the tribunal and can be enforced through the county court. You do not need to extract an admission of liability from your employer, and very often it is a condition of the settlement that no liability is admitted, but if you have the tribunal record it, it is tantamount to showing you were unfairly dismissed. This might be useful if you are suspended from unemployment benefit, or in need of a clean sheet when you are looking for a new job. So it is always advisable to get your settlement recorded in writing by the tribunal.

If you use ACAS the usual procedure is that you and your employer sign a form, and once the conciliation officer has the cheque, (s)he will get the tribunal to record the settlement. Whether or not you use ACAS the form of words will depend on the type of agreement you have reached. You should be able to sign something like this:

I have received the sum of £___ in full and final settlement of all claims arising out of and in connection with my dismissal on (date).

It is important not to sign away '*all* claims against XYZ Ltd' (although this wording is often suggested) because this might preclude you claiming damages for something quite unrelated to the sacking, such as an industrial disease. So make sure you mention only the dismissal. The tribunal then makes a decision according to the wording you have agreed.

Dealing with employers

If ACAS is not successful, your representative might find it useful to talk direct to your employers or their representative a few days before the hearing to see if a settlement can be arranged. You are not in any way conceding if you make this approach, and the threat to your boss of wasting time and money in a hearing can be helpful.

'Without prejudice'

If an offer is made 'without prejudice', it means without prejudice to any subsequent action your employer might take. It can be withdrawn later. It really means that by making it your boss cannot be taken to admit liability, or to indicate a binding obligation to pay the amount offered. Similarly, in putting forward your figures for the loss you suffered, or stipulating the terms on which you will go back, you should say that this is without prejudice to any claim you may make at the tribunal if your terms are rejected. 'Without prejudice' documents will be respected by solicitors, and tribunals will refuse to admit them in evidence.

Adjournment

Hearings can be postponed usually by either party writing to the tribunal and giving a reason. You may need more time to prepare, or to conciliate, or your representative may not be free on the appointed day. Some tribunals are more flexible than others but generally they will allow one postponement by each party. Provided you give some notice you should not run the risk of having to pay the costs of the other side caused by the postponement. But the tribunal may order payment if you cause substantial last-minute inconvenience and the employer asks for costs.

Hearings that can't be finished on the appointed day will be reconvened on another. Unless you have told the tribunal you expect to go on for a second day, the chances are that you will have to wait – in some cases delays of seven or eight weeks have occurred. Always object if this happens.

The hearing

An interim hearing can be held in cases of dismissal for union activity – see page 228. If you want to prove a preliminary point, you could go to the tribunal to decide just this point, then adjourn.

This section gives guidance for **you**, or **your representative** if you have one, on tribunal procedure.

Administration

You or your representative will receive a letter telling you where and when the hearing will be held. It will usually start at 10 a.m. or at 2 p.m. The clerk will take your name and names of witnesses, and explain the procedure, so you should arrive a few minutes before the start. If you are unemployed the clerk will also ask you a number of questions about social security benefit you have received. This is to enable the DE to recoup this money from your employer if compensation is awarded. If you have a representative you will need to give him or her the up-to-date details about your job prospects, earnings, and social security payments.

Procedure

The chairman will usually start by outlining the procedure to be followed. 'Chairman' or 'Madam Chairman' is a proper and non-obsequious form of address. If you want to make any amendment, or to challenge a point of jurisdiction, for instance, that the employer failed to enter a defence in time, you should do it now. Likewise your boss will raise such issues as whether you have worked a sufficient number of hours and weeks to enable you to bring the particular claim, or whether you claimed too late. The party who has to prove the point goes first, and sums up last. If you are claiming unfair dismissal, and your boss admits you were sacked but claims it was fair; or if you are claiming victimisation and he admits you were treated in the way you describe but says it had nothing to do with your union activity, the batting order is:

1. employer makes an opening speech

2. calls first witness, who swears or affirms that (s)he will tell the truth, and answers questions.

3. you cross-examine

4. the tribunal asks questions

5. the employer re-examines

6. calls further witnesses

7. you make an opening speech, call first witness, and follow as **1–6** above

8. you sum up and address the tribunal

9. employer does the same

10. tribunal adjourns.

If your boss contests the fact that you were sacked, (saying you resigned) or if you are claiming equal pay, sex or race discrimination or other individual rights, then *your* side goes first and brings witnesses.

Opening statement

Your side need not make an opening speech but if you do your representative should briefly outline the nature of your claim and the kind of evidence your witnesses will be giving. This gives the tribunal an idea of how things will develop, and it is anyway a useful platform for your views.

Your witnesses

You should be clear about the facts that each of your witnesses will testify to. Strict rules of evidence and procedure are not followed but your case will be stronger, and you will be less interfered with by the chairman, if you do not 'lead' your witnesses. This means you should not put words in their mouth by asking questions that suggest the answer, or by asking them to confirm a long statement of your own.

For example, don't say: 'Is it correct that you saw the shift manager stagger drunkenly into the workshop and order Mr X to collect his cards when he refused to work on an unguarded machine?' Instead, ask the witness in separate questions to describe the manager's appearance and manner, what was said by each person, how close he was to them, and the condition of the machine.

After the other side and the tribunal have cross-examined your witnesses, you can then **re-examine** them. Here you can clarify statements made in the initial evidence in a way that is favourable to you, but you can't introduce new material at this stage.

Cross-examination

You **can** lead the other side's witnesses. You are aiming to extract statements that are beneficial to your case, and which show the witness is unreliable because of self-contradiction.

If your side's evidence is different, **you must give the other side a chance to comment on the events or conversations you say took place**. So if you are concentrating on what was said at the time of dismissal you must ask all the people who were there about it. Otherwise the employers will object when your witness raises the matter for the first time.

You should always object to hearsay (second-hand) evidence. Tribunals are not bound by the same rules as courts, which exclude most hearsay evidence. They often override objections to hearsay on the basis that it may be helpful and they will note that it is hearsay. But the damage is already done, particularly as the tribunal lay members may not be experienced in dealing with the relative value of evidence received. Hearsay statements cannot be admitted in a court to ascertain the **truth** of what is said in the satement.

> **Example:** The personnel manager (**P**) says he dismissed the worker (**W**) because the foreman (**F**) saw **W** clocking another man's card. Only **F** and **W** can tell the truth about what happened. **P** got it second-hand (hearsay) so he can't tell whether or not **W** actually did it. **P** can't therefore corroborate **F**'s evidence in the same way as a witness to the event could. So the evidence is a straight conflict between **F** and **W**.
> **But**
> **P** can say that as a result of a report he got from **F**, he dismissed **W**. He is not testifying to the truth of the report – he is simply saying what he did. You would
> 1. object to the evidence
> 2. cross-examine on whether **P** fully investigated the report
> 3. remind the tribunal in summing up that this evidence is hearsay.

Summing-up

This is your chance to talk directly to the tribunal. You (or your representative) will sum up your case and where there is a difference in the evidence you will say why your story should be preferred, and why the other side's is unreliable. You can also deal with the law and show how your boss's conduct was wrong, and you can mention any Acts, codes and cases that help you. You can also quote law textbooks, and DE Guides. Although the views expressed are not binding, they will often be very influential.

Finally, you should say what remedy you are looking for if you win – for example, reinstatement or compensation, equal pay, promotion etc. If you are claiming compensation for unfair dismissal, go for all the items set out on page 346. At least give the tribunal the basis on which they should assess compensation, such as the amount of weekly earnings.

The decision

The tribunal may give you your answer that day, in which case they will retire to discuss it and announce it on returning. Or they may 'reserve' their decision which means you will have to wait, sometimes for as long as 12 weeks. It can be a unanimous or two-to-one majority decision. Tribunals tend to reserve decisions too often. They usually do so if they cannot agree, or if there is a lot of conflicting evidence, or if the law is complicated. Sometimes you may get a decision on the day, with the reasons following in writing. In *all* cases you or your representative get a copy of the decision, and the written reasons for it, by post. It then is a public document. Printed at the end is the date on which the decision was entered in the register of decisions at Central Office and copies sent to the parties. This is the date from which the time limits for appeals and reviews run.

Enforcement

If your boss refuses to comply in full with a reinstatement order, you can apply to the tribunal for additional compensation. If he refuses to pay any compensation awarded, apply to the county court (or sheriff court in Scotland) for an order. You can get Legal Aid for this. The court will enforce the order and order your boss to pay costs.

Review

An application for review is a simple way of getting the case brought up again, and even of having an appeal of sorts.

It arises in a limited set of circumstances: the tribunal staff have made a mistake, new evidence has become available or a party did not know of the hearing. It can also arise when 'the interests of justice' (Regulation 10) require it, so you should phrase your application for review in these terms.

If granted, the tribunal will re-hear the whole or part of the case and the previous decision can be set aside or varied.

You must make your application within 14 days of the date the decision was sent to you. There is no special form but you must set out the grounds in full.

Appeals

An appeal from a tribunal decision can be made on a **point of law only** to the Employment Appeal Tribunal. You have to show that the tribunal made a legal mistake, or followed the wrong cases. This does not mean that matters of **fact** can never be raised, because if the tribunal based their decision on facts that did not exist, or evidence of facts which could not possibly be true, this can itself be a question of law – that no reasonable tribunal could have decided the issue in the way this one did. The EAT has power to refuse to hear any appeal that does not show a question of law.

The Appeal Tribunal sits permanently in London and Glasgow and can hold hearings anywhere. When hearing a case it consists of a High Court judge, and a present or former trade-union official and employers' representative. It has most of the powers of the High Court except that it deals only with **appeals**, and not cases heard for the first time. In this respect it differs from the National Industrial Relations Court, but otherwise it is what the NIRC was intended to be.

Your appeal must reach the EAT **within 42 days** of the date the tribunal decision was sent to you. Addresses on page 400.

Anyone can represent you at the EAT or you can do it yourself. You can get Legal Aid for legal representation. Despite the fact that lawyers do not have a monopoly, the proceedings and the correspondence are quite formal and geared to legal representation. Trade-union officials and individual workers do appear quite frequently. Unlike an industrial tribunal, expenses are not paid to the applicant and people attending. Only if a witness is **ordered** to be there will expenses be met. Costs can be ordered against a losing party, and this power is used more often than in industrial tribunals.

The EAT can order payment only if one party has acted unreasonably or the proceedings are improper or vexatious.

The EAT can dismiss your appeal, or can overturn the industrial tribunal decision. In this event it can itself make the decision you want, such as a calculation or the interpretation of an Act; or it can send the case back to the same or a differently constituted tribunal for a new hearing. It would do this if there were some facts, or a question of reasonableness, still to be decided.

Quite often the EAT says it would probably have decided the case differently to the tribunal. This doesn't entitle it to overturn the decision. Provided there was *some* evidence on which the tribunal could make a decision, the EAT can't interfere. This is in contrast to appeals against **wrongful dismissal**, where the appeal court can make a completely fresh decision on its own view of the facts.

Appeals from the EAT go to the Court of Appeal.

Summary

1. Most employment rights can be enforced in an industrial tribunal, but negotiation and direct action are more reliable methods.

2. You can get advice and representation from your union. State Legal Aid is not available for representation at a tribunal, but you can get advice and assistance from many solicitors on the £25 **green form** scheme.

3. There is in practice no chance that you will have to pay the other side's costs.

4. Time limits for making claims are strict, but tribunals have discretion in exceptional cases to extend the deadline.

5. At the hearing, you or your representative can bring witnesses, cross-examine and make opening and closing speeches.

6. You can get a tribunal to **review** its decision in some situations where the interests of justice require.

7. Appeals to the EAT must be on a point of law and be filed within 42 days of the written decision.

Forms Used for Claiming Your Rights

Form	Used for	See chapter
IT 1 – Originating application, pages 372–373	Written particulars of contract	3
	Time off	3, 13
	Itemised pay statement	3
	Medical suspension	4
	Guarantee pay	5
	Maternity	7
	Discrimination	8
	Equal pay	9
	Unfair dismissal	10
	Redundancy pay	11
	Victimisation	13
	Protective award	20
	Consultation over redundancy	20
IT 3 – Employer's reply, page 374	All the above	
EAT 1, page 375	Appeal from tribunal	22
SD 74(a)–SD 74(b), pages 376–378	Questionnaire on discrimination	8
IP 1, page 379	Insolvency – other debts	11
IP 2, page 380	Insolvency – notice	11
ACAS 34, page 381	Recognition	14
ACAS 72, pages 382–383	Going rate	17
ACAS 73, pages 384–385	Going rate – Wages Council industries	17
HR 1, pages 386–389	Consultation over redundancy	20

Form IT 1

ORIGINATING APPLICATION TO AN INDUSTRIAL TRIBUNAL

UNDER ONE OR MORE OF THE FOLLOWING ACTS: —

TRADE UNION AND LABOUR RELATIONS ACT 1974
REDUNDANCY PAYMENTS ACT 1965
CONTRACTS OF EMPLOYMENT ACT 1972
EQUAL PAY ACT 1970
SEX DISCRIMINATION ACT 1975
EMPLOYMENT PROTECTION ACT 1975
RACE RELATIONS ACT 1976

IMPORTANT: DO NOT FILL IN THIS FORM UNTIL YOU HAVE READ THE NOTES FOR
GUIDANCE. THEN COMPLETE ITEMS 1, 2, 4 AND 13 AND ALL OTHER
ITEMS RELEVANT TO YOUR CASE

To:—   The Secretary of the Tribunals
Central Office of the Industrial Tribunals (England and Wales)
93, Ebury Bridge Road, London SW1W 8RE   Telephone: 01—730—9161

1   I hereby apply for a decision of a tribunal on the following question (*State here
question to be decided by the Tribunal and explain the grounds overleaf*)

2   My name (*surname in block capitals first*) is Mr / Mrs / Miss ....

2(A)   OR our title (*if company or organisation*) is ....

2 and 2(A)   address ....

Telephone no. ....

3   If a representative has agreed to act for you in this case please give his name
and address below and note that further communications will be sent to him
and not to you   (*See Note 2*)

Name

Address and telephone no.

4   (a)   Name of respondent(s) (*in block capitals*) ie the employer, person or body
against whom a decision is sought (*See Note 3*)

Address(es) and telephone no.(s)

(b)   Respondent's relationship to you for the purpose of the application
(*eg employer, trade union, employment agency, employer recognising the
union making application, etc.*)

IT 1

Form IT 1 *continued*

5   Date of birth ....

6   Place of employment to which this application relates,
or place where act complained about took place.

7   Occupation or position held / applied for, or other relationship to
the respondent named above *(eg user of a service supplied by him)*

8   Employment began on .... and *(if appropriate)*

      ended on ....

9   Basic wages / salary ....

10   Other pay or remuneration ....

11   Normal basic weekly hours of work ....

12   (In an application under the Sex Discrimination Act or the Race Relations Act)
Date on which action complained of took place

      or first came to my knowledge ....

13   The grounds of this application are as follows: *(See Note 4)*

14   (If dismissed) If you wish to state what in your opinion was the reason for
your dismissal, please do so here.

15   If the Tribunal decides that you were unfairly dismissed, what remedy would
you prefer? (Before answering this question please consult the Notes for
Guidance for the remedies available and then write one only of the following
in answer to this question: reinstatement, re-engagement or compensation)

Signature .... Date ....

Form IT 3

Industrial Tribunals

NOTICE OF APPEARANCE BY RESPONDENT

To the Secretary of the Tribunals

Case Number ....

FOR OFFICIAL USE	
Date of receipt	Initials

1   I *do/do not intend to resist the claim made by

2   *My/Our name is *Mr/Mrs/Miss/title (if company or organisation)

    address

    telephone number

3   If you have arranged to have a representative to act for you, please give his name and address below and note that further communications will be sent to him and not to you

    name

    address

    telephone number

4   If the application relates to a dismissal

    a Was the applicant dismissed? *YES/NO

    b If YES, what was the reason for the dismissal?

    c Are the dates given by the applicant as to his period of employment correct? *YES/NO

    d If NO, give dates of commencement .... and termination ....

5   If the claim is resisted, please state the grounds on which you intend to resist:—

Signature .... Date ....

        *Delete inappropriate items

IT 3

Form EAT 1

FORM I

EMPLOYMENT PROTECTION ACT 1975
NOTICE OF APPEAL FROM DECISION OF INDUSTRIAL TRIBUNAL

1. The appellant is /name and address of appellant/:-

2. Any communication relating to this appeal may be sent to the appellant at
/appellant's address for service, including telephone number, if any/:-

3. The appellant appeals from
/here give particulars of the decision of the industrial tribunal from which the
appeal is brought/:-

on the following questions of law:-
/here set out the question of law on which the appeal is brought/.

4. The parties to the proceedings before the industrial tribunal, other than
the appellant, were /names and addresses of other parties - and of their representatives if applicable - to the proceedings resulting in decision appealed from/:-

5. The appellant's grounds of appeal are:-
/here state the grounds of appeal/.

6. A copy of the industrial tribunal's decision is attached to this notice.

Date: ....   Signed: ....

Form SD 74(a)

THE SEX DISCRIMINATION ACT 1975 SECTION 74 (1)(a)

QUESTIONNAIRE OF PERSON AGGRIEVED (THE COMPLAINANT)

Name of person to be questioned (the respondent)

To ....

Address

of ....

....

Name of complainant

1. I ....

Address

of ....

....

consider that you may have discriminated against me contrary to the Sex Discrimination Act 1975.

Give date, approximate time, place and factual description of the treatment received and of the circumstances leading up to the treatment (see paragraph 9 of the guidance)

2. On

Complete if you wish to give reasons, otherwise delete the word "because" (see paragraphs 10 and 11 of the guidance)

3. I consider that this treatment may have been unlawful because

This is the first of your questions to the respondent. You are advised not to alter it

4. Do you agree that the statement in paragraph 2 is an accurate description of what happened? If not in what respect do you disagree or what is your version of what happened?

This is the second of your questions to the respondent. You are advised not to alter it

5. Do you accept that your treatment of me was unlawful discrimination by you against me?
   If not

   a   why not?
   b   for what reason did I receive the treatment accorded to me?
   c   how far did my sex or marital status affect your treatment of me?

Enter here any other questions you wish to ask (see paragraphs 12—14 of the guidance)

6.

SD 74(a)

Form SD 74(a) *continued*

* Delete as appropriate If you delete the first alternative, insert the address to which you want the reply to be sent

7. My address for any reply you may wish to give to the questions raised above is * that set out in paragraph I above /the following address

See paragraph 15 of the guidance

Signature of complainant ....

Date ....

NB By virtue of section 74 of the Act, this questionnaire and any reply are (subject to the provisions of the section) admissible in proceedings under the Act and a court or tribunal may draw any such inference as is just and equitable from a failure without reasonable excuse to reply within a reasonable period, or from an evasive or equivocal reply, including an inference that the person questioned has discriminated unlawfully.

Form SD 74(b)

THE SEX DISCRIMINATION ACT 1975 SECTION 74 (1)(b)

REPLY BY RESPONDENT

Name of complainant

To ....

Address

of ....

....

Name of respondent

I. I ....

Address

of ....

....

Complete as appropriate

hereby acknowledge receipt of the questionnaire signed by you

and dated .... which was served on me on (date) ....

* Delete as appropriate

2. I *agree/disagree that the statement in paragraph 2 of the questionnaire is an accurate description of what happened.

If you agree that the statement in paragraph 2 of the questionnaire is accurate, delete this sentence. If you disagree complete this sentence (see paragraphs 21 and 22 of the guidance)

I disagree with the statement in paragraph 2 of the questionnaire in that

Form SD 74(b) *continued*

3. I *accept/dispute that my treatment of you was unlawful discrimination by me against you.

If you accept the complainant's assertion of unlawful discrimination in paragraph 3 of the questionnaire delete the sentences at a, b and c. Unless completed a sentence should be deleted (see paragraphs 23 and 24 of the guidance)

    a   My reasons for so disputing are

    b   The reason why you received the treatment accorded to you is

    c   Your sex or marital status affected my treatment of you to the following extent:—

Replies to questions in paragraph 6 of the questionnaire should be entered here

4.

Delete the whole of this sentence if you have answered all the questions in the questionnaire. If you have not answered all the questions, delete "unable" or "unwilling" as appropriate and give your reasons for not answering.

5. I have deleted (in whole or in part) the paragraph(s) numbered .... above, since I am unable/unwilling to reply to the relevant questions of the questionnaire for the following reasons:—

See paragraph 25 of the guidance

Signature of respondent ....

Date ....

SD 74(b)

Form IP 1

EMPLOYMENT PROTECTION ACT 1975

INSOLVENCY: APPLICATION FOR PAYMENT OF DEBTS DUE AT RELEVANT DATE

PLEASE READ NOTES 1 TO 5 OVERLEAF BEFORE COMPLETING THIS FORM

If payment in lieu of notice is due the supplementary application form should also be completed

I (full name) (state whether Mr/Ms) ....

of (full address) ....

National Insurance no. [ ][ ] - [ ][ ]   Income Tax reference no. ....

apply to .... (name of insolvent employer's representative)

of address ....

.... Tel. no. ....

or to the Secretary of State for Employment for any payments due to me under section 64 of the Employment Protection Act 1975

Name of employer ....

Business address ....

....

Place of employment if different from above ....

....

Date employment began .... Date employment ended ....

Occupation .... Works no. (If any) ....

Amount of week's gross pay £ .... (if not in receipt of regular payments, give details of any special arrangement eg piece work, bonuses etc)

....

....

If arrears of pay are due give period covered, number of days or weeks and total amount due ....

....

If holiday pay and/or accrued holiday pay is due give period covered, number of days or weeks and total

amount due ....

If any other payments are due give details ....

I have made no other application in respect of the payments detailed above and I understand that it may be necessary for you to refer to records prepared by the insolvent employer for the Inland Revenue and other Government Departments I hereby give my consent to the disclosure of such information as may be necessary for this purpose only.

(Warning: Legal proceedings may be taken against anyone making a false statement on this form)

Signature .... Date ....

IP1   381 411823 100M 3/76 H&W 752

Form IP 2

EMPLOYMENT PROTECTION ACT 1975

INSOLVENCY: SUPPLEMENTARY APPLICATION—FOR PAYMENT IN LIEU OF NOTICE DUE

<u>PLEASE READ NOTES 1 TO 4 OVERLEAF BEFORE COMPLETING THIS FORM</u>

1   (full name) (state whether Mr/Ms) ....

of (full address) ....

....

National Insurance no. ☐ ☐ ☐ ☐ ☐   Income Tax reference no. ....

apply to .... (name of employer's representative)

of address ....

....Tel. no. ....
or to the Secretary of State for Employment for any payment in lieu of notice due to me under Section 64 of the Employment Protection Act 1975.

Name of employer ....

Business address ....

....

Place of employment if different from above ....

Date employment began .... Date employment ended ....

Occupation .... Works no. (if any) ....

Date notice given .... Period of notice due ....

Payment in lieu of notice due:—

Daily or weekly rate of pay £............................... Total amount due £...........................

Nature of any new employment commenced during the period of notice:—

....

Date new employment began ....

Rate of pay (give daily or weekly rate) ....
If, during the period you are applying in lieu of notice, you claimed any Social Security benefits, please state:—

   1. Type(s) of benefit claimed ....

   2. Name(s) and address(es) from which payments received ....

....

If in receipt of remuneration under a protective award give period and amount of award ....

Details of any other remuneration received during the period of notice:—

Date   from .... to .... description .... £ ....

        from .... to .... description .... £ ....

        from .... to .... description .... £ ....

I have made no other application in respect of the payments detailed above and I understand that it may be necessary for you to refer to records prepared by the insolvent employer for the Inland Revenue and other Government Departments. I hereby give my consent to the disclosure of such information as may be necessary for this purpose only, and to the disclosure of information, relating to any Social Security benefits claimed, to the employer's representative.

(Warning: Legal proceedings may be taken against anyone making a false statement on this form)

Signature .... Date ....
IP 2   826 527381 50M 4/77 HGW 752

Form ACAS 34

ACAS 34

EMPLOYMENT PROTECTION ACT 1975

APPLICATION FOR THE REFERENCE OF A RECOGNITION ISSUE TO THE ADVISORY, CONCILIATION AND ARBITRATION SERVICE UNDER SECTION 11 OF THE ACT

Note: Only an independent trade union may make an application on this form (see definitions overleaf).

1. Name of the independent trade union making the application:

2. Address for correspondence about this application, and telephone number:

3. Name and address of the employer from whom recognition is sought: (If recognition is sought from two or more associated employers please give all their names and addresses).

4. The trade, industry, etc. in which the employer is engaged:

5. The description of the workers covered by the application (stating where appropriate the part of the undertaking in which they work):

6. Does the employer already recognise the trade union to any extent?

SIGNATURE: NAME IN BLOCK CAPITALS:

DATE: POSITION HELD IN TRADE UNION:

(This form may be signed only by an official of the trade union who is duly authorised to make such an application on behalf of the union.)

Form ACAS 72

ACAS 72

To: The Advisory, Conciliation and Arbitration Service:-

EMPLOYMENT PROTECTION ACT 1975: SCHEDULE 11, PART I
REPORT OF A CLAIM AS TO RECOGNISED TERMS AND CONDITIONS
OF EMPLOYMENT OR AS TO THE GENERAL LEVEL OF TERMS AND
CONDITIONS.

Write in
name of
organisation
reporting the
claim

1. Acting on behalf of _____
   _____

   I hereby report a claim to the Advisory, Conciliation
   and Arbitration Service that as respects

Name or
description
of worker(s)

_____

Name and
address of
employer

is observing terms and conditions of employment that
are less favourable than

Delete A or
B
if not
appropriate

A. the <u>recognised</u> terms and conditions

B. the <u>general</u> level of terms and conditions.

Para 2
should be
completed
only where
the claim
relates to
recognised
terms and
conditions

2. The following particulars relate to the claim as it
   concerns <u>recognised</u> terms and conditions of employment:
   (a) The recognised terms and conditions of
       employment apply in the following trade or
       industry or section of a trade or industry
       in which the employer in question is engaged:-

   (b) The recognised terms and conditions of employment
       were settled by the following agreement or award:-

   (c) The parties to the agreement or the award were:-

Form ACAS 72 *continued*

Para 3
should be
completed
only where
the claim
relates to
the general
level of
terms and
conditions

3. The following particulars relate to the claim as it
concerns the <u>general</u> level of terms and conditions:

(a) The trade, industry or section in which the
employer is engaged is:-

(b) The employers in the trade, industry or section
whose circumstances are similar to those of the
employer in question and who observe for
comparable workers the general level of terms
and conditions are as follows:-

Name and
addresses of
employers

SIGNATURE:

DATE:

NAME IN BLOCK CAPITALS:

POSITION HELD:

Address and Telephone Number:

Form ACAS 73

ACAS 73

To: The Advisory, Conciliation and Arbitration Service:-

EMPLOYMENT PROTECTION ACT 1975: SCHEDULE 11, PART II
REPORT OF A CLAIM AS TO COLLECTIVELY NEGOTIATED TERMS
AND CONDITIONS.

Write in
name of
independent
trade union

1. Acting on behalf of _____

   _____

   I hereby report a claim to the Advisory, Conciliation
   and Arbitration Service.

2. The claim relates to the following worker(s) who
   are members of the trade union:-

Names, jobs
or other
descriptions
of workers

3. These workers fall within the field of operation of:-

Name of wages
council,
statutory
joint
industrial
council,
Agricultural
Wages Board,
or Scottish
Agricultural
Wages Board.

4. The claim is as follows:

   (a) that the union is a party to one or more collective
        agreements and that those agreements cover a
     s   significant number of establishments within the
        field of operation of the *council/Board referred
        to in paragraph 3 *generally/in the district in
        which the worker is employed; and

* Delete in-
appropriate
alternatives

   (b) that in those establishments the circumstances of
        the employer are similar to those of the employer
        of the worker(s) referred to in paragraph 2 above; and

   (c) that the employer is paying him/them less than the
        lowest current rate of remuneration (disregarding
        any rate agreed to more than 12 months before the
        date on which the claim is reported) payable to
        workers of the same description under any of those
        agreements.

Form ACAS 73 *continued*

5. The following particulars relate to the claim:

    (a) The collective agreements referred to in the paragraph 4(a) above are:-

Name of the
agreements,
dates on which
they were made
and the
parties to
them

    (b) The employer of the worker(s) to whom this claim relates is:-

Name and
address of
employer to
whom the
claim
relates

SIGNATURE:

DATE:

NAME IN BLOCK CAPITALS:

POSITION HELD IN
TRADE UNION:

Address and Telephone No.

Form HR 1

EMPLOYMENT PROTECTION ACT 1975

EMPLOYER'S NOTIFICATION OF PROPOSED REDUNDANCIES UNDER SECTION 100

Please complete this form and return it to the nearest Regional Office of the Department of Employment.

QUESTIONS

1 Name, address and telephone number of employer.

....

....

....

2 Name of person to be contacted in connection with this form (include address and telephone number, if different from Q1).

....

....

....

3 Address of establishment at which employees are employed, (if different from Q1).

....

....

4 Please state the nature of the main business at the establishment named above.

....

HR 1

Form HR 1 *continued*

5 (a) What are the main reasons for the proposed redundancies at the above named establishment?

(Please tick the appropriate box(es))

Reduced demand for products or services	A
Completion of contract or part of contract	B
Transfer of activities to another establishment following a merger	C
Transfer of activities to another establishment for other reasons	D
Introduction of new plant or machinery	E
Changes in methods or organisation of work	F
Other reasons	G

(b) If you have ticked boxes D, F or G please give brief details

....

....

6 (a) What is the total number currently employed at the establishment?

....

(b) What is the total number you anticipate at present MAY be dismissed as redundant at the establishment?

....

(c) If available please give a breakdown of (a) and (b) by occupational groups.

	Employed	Redundant
Manual Skilled		
Semi-skilled		
Unskilled		
Clerical		
Managerial/Technical		

Form HR 1 *continued*

(d) Please state the number of apprentices and long
term trainees who may become redundant,
if known
....

(e) Please state the number of employees under 20
years old (including apprentices etc) who may
become redundant, (if known)
....

(f) Do you propose to close the establishment at which
these redundancies may occur?
....

7 On what dates will:
(a) the first proposed redundancy take effect?

Day	Month	Year

(b) the last proposed redundancy take effect?

Day	Month	Year

8 How do you propose to select employees who may be
dismissed as redundant? Please give brief details.

....

....

9 Give name(s) and address(es) of trade union(s)
recognised for categories of employees it is proposed
to dismiss as redundant.

....

....

....

....

Form HR 1 *continued*

10 (a) Give date when consultations began with union(s)

Day	Month	Year

 (b) Has full agreement been reached?
....

 (c) Is the redundancy being handled in accordance with a collective agreement on redundancies?
....

 If you answer YES please give brief details or send a copy of the agreement.

....

DECLARATION

I certify that the information given on this form is correct to the best of my knowledge.

Signature ....

Position held ....

Date ....

```
+---------------------------------------------------+
|            FOR DEPARTMENTAL USE                   |
|  +-------------+  +-------------+  +------------+  |
|  | 1           |  | 2           |  | 3          |  |
|  +-------------+  +-------------+  +------------+  |
|                                                   |
|  +-------------+  +-------------+  +------------+  |
|  | 4           |  | 5           |  | 6          |  |
|  +-------------+  +-------------+  +------------+  |
|                                                   |
|         +-------------+                           |
|         | 7           |                           |
|         +-------------+                           |
+---------------------------------------------------+
```

Glossary of Legal Terms

a week's pay: *see* week's pay.

Act: written law passed by both Houses of Parliament and signed by the Queen.

arbitration: system for settling disputes by reference to a person or persons who the parties to the dispute empower to make a decision.

associated employer: any two employers are associated if one is a *company* of which the other (directly or indirectly) has control, or if both are companies of which a third person (directly or indirectly) has control.

attachment-of-earnings: a court order requiring your employer to deduct a fixed sum each week from your wages to pay maintenance or a fine.

bankrupt: *see* insolvency.

certification officer: official responsible for giving certificates of independence to trade unions and checking union accounts.

check-off: system by which an employer, with your written authority, deducts union contributions from your wages and forwards them to your union.

code: document produced by official body, for example ACAS, to give guidance and which must be considered in any legal proceedings.

collective agreement: agreement or arrangement made by or on behalf of trade unions and employers or employers' associations relating to any of the list of subjects on page 241.

collective bargaining: negotiations relating to any of the list of subjects on page 241.

common law: used in this handbook to mean binding *judges' rulings.* Contrast statute law made by Parliament.

conciliation: method by which an independent person attempts to get a dispute settled by agreement of the parties. ACAS's main function, and a step available in all tribunal applications.

constructive dismissal: action taken by your boss which shows he has no intention of abiding by your contract and as a result of which you leave.

contract: legally binding agreement, made in writing or orally.

Court of Appeal: court which hears appeals on law from the High Court and County Courts and on law or fact from a Crown Court.

Court of Session: Scottish equivalent of English High Court (Outer House) and Court of Appeal (Inner House).

Crown Courts: locally-based courts staffed by judges and, in appeals from magistrates, lay magistrates. They try mainly criminal cases with a jury, but some civil work is done. The Old Bailey is the City of London Crown Court.

Crown employment: employment by a government department.

damages: compensation ordered by a court designed to put the innocent party in the same position he would be in if his contract had been carried out as agreed, or, in tort cases, as if the injury had never occurred.

dismissal: sacking, with or without notice, or constructive dismissal.

employers' association: organisation of employers (or a federation of such organisations) whose principal purposes include regulating relations between employers and workers.

fixed-term contract: contract of employment which ends on a specific date and which cannot be ended by either side giving notice before that date.

frustration of contract: automatic termination of a contract of employment due to some unforeseen event which makes it impossible to carry out the contract.

guarantee payment: daily payment employers must make to workers laid off.

High Court: court for hearing *civil* claims for more than £2000; commercial, tax and many matrimonial cases; and appeals from magistrates.

indemnity: promise to make good any direct losses arising when a person assumes a legal obligation.

independent contractor: worker, often self-employed, who is employed on a contract to render services, as opposed to an employee who works on a contract of service.

independent trade union: *see* trade union.

industrial tribunal: comprises a legally-qualified chairman or woman, with two lay members chosen from a panel nominated by employers and the TUC. Hears complaints under most of the legislation dealing with individual industrial rights, and appeals under the Health and Safety at Work Act. Does not have the powers of a court, for instance, to fine, or enforce orders.

injunction: temporary or permanent civil court order requiring a person to do or refrain from doing something which adversely affects someone's rights.

insolvency: inability to pay one's debts. Insolvent individuals and partnerships are bankrupt. Insolvent companies are put into the control of a liquidator or receiver and *wound up*.

interdict: Scottish injunction.

liquidation: winding up of a company – *see* insolvency.

mitigation: after a breach of contract or an injury you must take all reasonable steps to reduce (mitigate) the losses you suffer.

negligence: failure to do something that a reasonable person would do, or doing something a reasonable person would not do. It must result in a damage or injury to someone who you should expect to be affected by what you do or do not do. Negligence is a tort.

originating application: written complaint to an industrial tribunal giving details of your complaint. Usually use Form IT1 (see page 357) but not compulsory.

patent: government licence giving you the exclusive right to make or sell a new invention.

protective award: sum of money which a tribunal can order your boss to pay to you if he has made you redundant without properly consulting your union.

receiver: *see* insolvency.

redundancy: lessening or cessation of an employer's need for employees to do work of a particular kind.

repudiation of contract: action or words showing a refusal to abide by a contrast – *see also* constructive dismissal.

restraint of trade: illegal restrictive practice preventing an employee or former employee carrying on his or her trade or occupation.

social security benefit: (in this handbook) benefit payable as of right to people who suffer a specified hardship.

statute: *see* Act.

statutory instrument: law passed by a minister who has been given authority by an Act of Parliament.

stipendiary: salaried full-time legally qualified magistrate.

summary dismissal: sacking without proper notice or wages in lieu.

tort: civil wrong giving rise to civil proceedings between two parties, for which the courts order damages to be paid by one party to the other. The same wrong can be both civil and criminal.

trade union: organisation of workers (and a federation of such organisations, for example the TUC) whose principal purposes include the regulation of relations between workers and employers; includes organisations of workers such as shop stewards' committees. TU on the Certification Officer's *list* gets tax relief. A *listed* trade union can apply to become an *independent* trade union if it is not under the domination or control of any employer and not liable to interference from any employer.

trade union official: lay or full-time officer of a union, branch or section, who is elected or appointed according to the union's rules to represent members, for example, a shop steward.

Truck Act: statute forbidding payment in kind (truck) to manual and other workers.

union membership agreement: agreement between an employer and one or more independent trade unions which makes union membership a requirement for all employees, that is, a closed shop.

vicarious liability: rule of law by which someone is responsible for the wrongful acts of another, for example, an employer is liable for torts committed by employees in the course of employment.

a week's pay: the minimum payment you are entitled to under your contract. Used as the basis for calculating pay for most statutory rights – such as redundancy, unfair dismissal, maternity pay, guarantee pay.

worker: person who works, normally works, or is seeking work under a contract of employment, or for a government department or as a self-employed person. In this handbook worker usually means employee and Crown employee.

Further Reading

General

B. Hepple and P. O'Higgins, *Employment Law*, London, Sweet & Maxwell, 1976 and *Encyclopedia of Labour Relations Law* (3 vols, loose-leaf, updated)

K. W. Wedderburn, *The Worker and the Law*, 2nd ed., Penguin, 1971 and *Cases and Materials on Labour Law*, Cambridge 1967

B. Bercusson, *The Employment Protection Act Annotated*, London, Sweet & Maxwell, 1976

D. N. Pritt, *Law Class and Society, Book 1, Employers Workers and Trade Unions*, Lawrence & Wishart, 1970

C. D. Drake, *Labour Law*, Sweet & Maxwell, 1973

O. Kahn-Freund, *Labour and the Law*, 2nd ed., Sweet & Maxwell, 1977

R. W. Rideout, *Principles of Labour Law*, Sweet & Maxwell, 1976

Royal Commission on Trade Unions and Employers' Associations, *Report* (Donovan) HMSO, 1968

Local Authorities Conditions of Service Advisory Board, *Employee Relations Handbook*, 1977

NCCL, *Your Rights at Work* (short guide) 1978.

The Department of Employment and the Home Office publish *Guides* on the legislation. All excellent and all free.

Chapter 1

B. Weekes, *Industrial Relations and the Limits of Law*, Blackwell, 1975

Chapter 2

The Legal Systems of Britain, HMSO, 1976

J. A. G. Griffith, *The Politics of the Judiciary*, Fontana, 1977

Chapter 3

M. R. Freedland, *The Contract of Employment*, Oxford 1976

DE guides: *Contracts of Employment Act*; *Truck Acts*; *Itemised Pay Statements*; *Time off for Public Duties*
Incomes Data Services, *Employment Contracts*, 1976

Chapter 4

DE guide, *Medical Suspension*
P. Kinnersly, *The Hazards of Work*, 1st ed. London, Pluto, 1973

Chapter 5

DE guide, *Guarantee Pay*
Incomes Data Services, *Lay-Offs and Short-Time*, 1976

Chapters 7–9

T. Gill and A. Coote, *Women's Rights*, Penguin, 1977
P. Hewitt, *Rights for Women*, NCCL, 1975
J. Coussins, *Maternity Rights for Working Women*, NCCL, 1976
TUC guides, *Maternity*, 1977; *Race Relations Act 1976*
Home Office guides, *Sex Discrimination; Racial Discrimination*
DE guides, *New Rights for Expectant Mothers; Equal Pay Act*
EOC, *Guides to Aspects of the Sex Discrimination Act*
J. Powell, *Work Study*, Arrow, 1976
Incomes Data Services, *The New Race Law & Employment*, 1977

Chapter 10

J. McGlyne, *Unfair Dismissal Cases*, Butterworths, 1976
Incomes Data Services, *Unfair Dismissal*, 1976
DE guide, *Dismissal – Employees' Rights*

Chapter 11

C. Grunfeld, *The Law of Redundancy*, Sweet & Maxwell, 1971
DE guides, *Redundancy Payments Act; Facing Redundancy; Time Off; Employees' Rights on Insolvency*

Chapter 12

H. Calvert, *Social Security Law*, Sweet & Maxwell, 2nd ed., 1978
Supplementary Benefits Handbook, HMSO
T. Lynes, *Penguin Guide to Supplementary Benefits*, Penguin, 1974
Child Poverty Action Group, *National Welfare Benefits Handbook* (annual)

Chapter 13

TUC guide, *Paid Release for Union Training*
TUC *Disputes, Principles and Procedures*
DE guide, *Trade Union Membership*

Chapter 15

W. McCarthy, *The Closed Shop in Britain*, Blackwell, 1964
DE guide, *Trade Union and Labour Relations Acts*

Chapter 16

C. Hird, *Your Employer's Profits*, London, Pluto, 1975

Chapter 17

B. Bercusson, *Fair Wages*, Mansell, 1978
DE guide, *Minimum Wages*

Chapter 18

O. Kahn-Freund, *Laws Against Strikes*, Fabian Society 1973

Chapter 19

Labour Research Dept, *Picketing, a Trade Unionist's guide*, LRD, 1975

Chapter 20

DE guide, *Handling Redundancies*

Chapter 21

DE guide, *Continuous Employment and a Week's Pay*

Chapter 22

DE guide, *Industrial Tribunals Procedure*
Goodman, *Industrial Tribunal's Procedure*

Useful Addresses

Advisory, Conciliation and Arbitration Service

Northern Region
Westgate House, Westgate Road
Newcastle upon Tyne NE1 1TJ

Yorkshire and Humberside Region
City House, Leeds LS1 4JH

South East Region
Clifton House, 83–117 Euston Road,
London NW1 2RB

South West Region
16 Park Place, Clifton, Bristol BS8 1JP

Midlands Region
Alpha Tower, Suffolk Street,
Queensway, Birmingham B1 1TZ

North Western Region
Sunley Buildings, Piccadilly Plaza,
Manchester M60 7JS

Scotland
109 Waterloo Street, Glasgow G2 7BY

Wales
Phase I, Ty Glas Road
Llanishen, Cardiff CF4 5PH

N. Ireland
Labour Relations Agency
Windsor House, 9–15 Bedford Street
Belfast BT2 7MU

Central Arbitration Committee

1 The Abbey Garden
Great College Street
London SW1

Central Office of the Industrial Tribunals

England & Wales
93 Ebury Bridge Road, London SW1

Scotland
St Andrew House
141 West Nile Street, Glasgow G1 2RU

N. Ireland
2nd Floor, Bedford House
Bedford Street, Belfast BT2 7NR

Certification Officer

Vincent House Annexe
Hide Place, London SW1

Companies House

England & Wales
55 City Road, London EC1

Scotland
102 George Street, Edinburgh 2

N. Ireland
43–47 Chichester Street, Belfast 1

Commission for Racial Equality

Elliot House
10–12 Allington Street, London SW1E 5EH

Employment Appeal Tribunal (England & Wales)

4 St James's Square, London SW1

Employment Appeal Tribunal (Scotland)

249 West George Street, Glasgow G2 4QE

Equal Opportunities Commission

Overseas House
Quay Street, Manchester M3 3HN

Health and Safety Commission

Baynards House
2 Chepstow Place, London W2

Independent Review Committee

Congress House
Great Russell Street, London WC1B 3LS

Legal Aid

England & Wales
PO Box 9, Nottingham NG1 6DS

Scotland
Legal Aid Central Committee
PO Box 123, Edinburgh EH3 7YR

National Council for Civil Liberties

186 King's Cross Road, London WC1X 9DE

Trades Union Congress

Congress House
Great Russell Street, London WC1B 3LS

Wages Councils

The address of the Secretary of all Wages Councils is
12 St James's Square, London SW1Y 4LL

List of Statutes, Regulations and Codes

Statutes

Characters of Servants Act 1792
Unlawful Combinations of Workmen Act 1800
Combination Laws Repeal Act 1824
Combinations of Workmen Act 1825
Truck Act 1831
Master and Servant Act 1867
Trade Union Act 1871
Criminal Law Amendment Act 1871
Conspiracy and Protection of Property Act 1875
Truck Act 1896
Trade Disputes Act 1906
Trade Union Act 1913
Emergency Powers Act 1920
Trade Disputes and Trade Union Act 1927
Public Order Act 1936
Disabled Persons (Employment) Act 1944
National Insurance Act 1946
Companies Act 1948
Agricultural Wages Act 1948
Mines and Quarries Act 1954
Copyright Act 1956
Terms and Conditions of Employment Act 1959
Wages Councils Act 1959
Payment of Wages Act 1960
Factories Act 1961
Offices, Shops and Railway Premises Act 1963
Contracts of Employment Act 1963
Industrial Training Act 1964
Trade Union (Amalgamations) Act 1964
Trade Disputes Act 1965
Redundancy Payments Act 1965
Prices and Incomes Act 1966

Race Relations Act 1968
Transport Act 1968
Employer's Liability (Defective Equipment) Act 1969
Employer's Liability (Compulsory Insurance) Act 1969
Merchant Shipping Act 1970
Equal Pay Act 1970
Industrial Relations Act 1971
Immigration Act 1971
Attachment of Earnings Act 1971
Contracts of Employment Act 1972
Counter Inflation Act 1973
Health and Safety at Work Act 1974
Trade Union and Labour Relations Act 1974
Rehabilitation of Offenders Act 1974
Social Security Act 1975
Remuneration, Charges and Grants Act 1975
Social Scurity Pensions Act 1975
Sex Discrimination Act 1975
Industry Act 1975
Employment Protection Act 1975
Trade Union and Labour Relations (Amendment) Act 1976
Supplementary Benefits Act 1976
Race Relations Act 1976
Patents Act 1977
Unfair Contract Terms Act 1977
Criminal Law Act 1977

Regulations

Employment Appeal Tribunal Rules SI 1976 No 322
Industrial Tribunals (Labour Relations) Regulations SI 1974 No 1386+
    SI 1976 No 661
Rehabilitation of Offenders Act 1974 (Exemption) Order SI 1975 No
    1023
Fair Wages Resolution of the House of Commons 1946
Immigration Rules (House of Commons Papers) 1973

Codes

Disciplinary Practice and Procedures in Employment – ACAS Code
    No 1
Disclosure of Information to Trade Unions – ACAS Code No 2
Industrial Relations – DE Code under the Industrial Relations Act
Time off for Trade Union Duties and Activities – ACAS Code No 3

Index of Cases

Industrial law cases are reported in at least six different series of law reports. Most main libraries have Weekly Law Reports or All England Law Reports. It may be more difficult to find a library with the three main series of industrial cases reports. Universities, polytechnics, and major city libraries should have these.

Main page references are given in bold after each case.

Abbreviations

AER: All England Law Reports
KB: King's Bench Reports
ICR: Industrial Court/Cases Reports
IRLR: Industrial Relations Law Reports
ITR: Industrial Tribunal Reports
WLR: Weekly Law Reports

AER, KB and WLR have more than one volume for each year. All cases are cited by name, year, volume, law report, page.

For example:
North Riding Garages Ltd v Butterwick is reported in volume 2 of the Weekly Law Reports for 1967 at page 571.

■ Page in text

Index

Also in this series of Workers' Handbooks:

Christopher Hird

Your Employers' Profits

All you need to know to interpret company accounts, with information on:

Profits of Public Companies/Subsidiary Companies/ Private Companies/Nationalised Industries/ Disclosure/Directors' Reports/Profit and Loss Accounts/Balance Sheets/Limited Liability/ Concealment/Investment Grants